CHRISTIAN ETHICS AND MODERN PROBLEMS

CHRISTIAN ETHICS
AND
MODERN PROBLEMS

By

W. R. INGE, K.C.V.O., D.D.
<small>DEAN OF ST. PAUL'S</small>

GREENWOOD PRESS, PUBLISHERS
WESTPORT, CONNECTICUT

Originally published in 1930
by G.P. Putnam's Sons, New York

First Greenwood Reprinting 1970

Library of Congress Catalogue Card Number 72-104283

SBN 8371-3960-0

Printed in the United States of America

PREFACE

THIS book does not really need a Preface, since the Introductory Chapter explains what I have tried to do in it. But as this is probably the last considerable work that I shall have time to write, I will take the liberty of looking back for a few moments upon what I have attempted in the service of Christian truth as I have seen it.

From the time when I was ordained priest at the age of thirty-two, I have been convinced that the centre of gravity in theology was moving from authority to religious experience, and it was this conviction which led me to the study of Christian Mysticism, the subject of my Bampton Lectures in 1899. My professional work, until 1904, was that of a Classical Tutor at Oxford, and it was therefore natural that I was specially interested in the philosophy of Mysticism, which has always been closely associated with the school of Plato. I worked mainly on this subject during the years when I was Lady Margaret Professor at Cambridge. In 1917 and 1918, a tragic and anxious time for this country and for Europe generally, I gave the Gifford Lectures, at St. Andrews, on Plotinus, the greatest name in the roll of philosopher-mystics. These two volumes, the result of many years' labour, embody the best that I have been able to offer as a contribution to the philosophy of religion.

Since 1911, my life in London has brought me into closer contact with the intellectual, social, and moral problems of our own day. As a result of the Great

War, we have passed through a veritable, though happily peaceful revolution, which has shaken the foundations of our whole social and political structure. It was inevitable that after such a terrible experience all conventions, all traditions, all the convictions of the past, should be called in question. The deep discredit which that catastrophe was thought to have cast upon the old diplomacy was widely held to involve also the old religion. Not only was "the failure of Christianity," as proved by its inability to prevent the Christian nations from forming themseves into a mutual suicide club, proclaimed at every street-corner, but Christian Ethics, which had been almost taken for granted by the independent thinkers, philosophical as well as scientific, of the nineteenth century, were subjected to destructive and impatient criticism. In part this revolt only rendered more vocal and unabashed murmurs which had long found a subdued and half-reluctant expression. But in part there has been a real emancipation from traditions which no longer corresponded with the new scientific knowledge, and with the new aspirations of a revolutionary epoch. For better or worse, nothing is now taken for granted or accepted on authority. The morality of the New Testament must stand its trial before the conscience of our generation, to be accepted or rejected on its merits as a guide for the men and women of to-day.

To very many Christians, who find peace and confidence in the belief that their faith speaks to them with an infallible and absolute authority, this claim of the world to judge the Church, instead of the Church the world, seems arrogant and intolerable. My own belief in the Incarnation and in the abiding presence of the Spirit of Christ in the world makes me share this feeling. I have no confidence that the spirit of this age is wiser than the spirit of past ages. With all our unparalleled progress in natural philosophy and the applied sciences, there has, I think, been no intrinsic advance in human intelligence and wisdom. The lamentable condition of the arts may make us diffident about our power of penetration into the things of the spirit. And yet I have no doubt that in the unquestionable progress which the human mind has made in certain directions we have a true revelation characteristic of the age through which we are passing, and that this revelation must affect some of our ethical as well as of our philosophical traditions. A great task awaits us in this century. To borrow St. Paul's metaphor, the fire has come which must try the work of all the old builders, of what sort it is. The temple of God has been patched with much wood, hay, and stubble, the contributions of dishonest, ambitious, impatient builders. This must be consumed, that "the things which are not shaken may remain."

I have therefore been impelled, almost against my will, to leave the *templa serena* of divine philosophy, in order to take part in the turmoil of the street and the market-place. The storm-centre of religious controversy in post-war Europe and America is, it seems to me, the relation of the Gospel of Christ to problems of conduct. If the authority of Christ were rejected in this field, what would be left of Christianity would not be worth quarrelling over. For the Christian revelation is of a standard of values resting on an unveiling of the character of God and of our relation to Him; on this alone depends the whole scheme of Christian Ethics, which in their turn postulate the truth of the revelation in Christ.

The application of traditional morals to modern needs must be the work of many individuals, each bringing his honest and independent contribution to the task. I speak for no one except myself, and I am well aware

vii

what reception I may expect for parts of what I have written. But I have spoken throughout in perfect sincerity, and I hope that my book may do something to clarify the issues which more immediately concern us in this period of upheaval and agitation.

W. R. INGE.

CONTENTS

ix

CHRISTIAN ETHICS AND MODERN PROBLEMS

CHRISTIAN ETHICS AND MODERN PROBLEMS

CHAPTER I

INTRODUCTION

THE object of this book is to consider the relation of
Christian Ethics, the norm of which, for reasons to be
stated presently, I shall take to be the books of the New
Testament, to the civilisation of our own time, in so far
as our Western culture is moulded by conscious ideals.
To what extent are these ideals or principles in harmony with the Christianity of the New Testament as
a rule of life? Can the enlightened conscience of the
twentieth century still look back to the Gospel of the
first century for authoritative guidance, or must we admit that there has been a revolt against certain aspects
of New Testament morality, as there has undoubtedly
been a revolt against much of the morality of the Old
Testament? It is my wish to deal with these questions
in a temper of strict candour. I am writing neither an
apologia for Christianity nor an indictment of modern
civilisation. I shall endeavour to appreciate and do
justice to the characteristic convictions of the present
generation, many of which I share, though there may
be others which I regret and distrust. We are in the
middle of a revolutionary period, in which nothing has
taken a stable, much less a final, form. As might be
expected at such a time, many writers emphasise the
relativity and provisional character of all ethical prin-

ciples. This line of thought tends to minimise the authority and value of what Christians regard as an ethical revelation made nearly two thousand years ago. It was, we are reminded, historically conditioned; and the environment of Palestine in the first century was very unlike that of Europe and North America in the twentieth. This is a truth which I have no desire to deny or to extenuate. But there must be an absolute background against which all relative truths have to be set, if even the word relativity is to have any meaning. Every philosophy asserts and depends upon some permanent reality behind the flux of phenomena; and an ethical religion must demand a similar absoluteness for its fundamental principles. In Ethics, as in philosophy, only the superhistorical can hold the historical together.

The idea of moral obligation is a constant, and the ultimate values on which the Christian revelation rests belong to the eternal world. But that revelation is bound up with a definite doctrine of the relation of man to God, of the purpose of our probation here, and of the constituents of a good life. If we universalise Christian Ethics too much, we may be left without any definite guidance in particular problems. It is essential that we should admit that just as Christianity, as an intellectual system, is not consonant or compatible with any and every philosophy, so Christian Ethics are based on principles which are not accepted by all moralists. This will become clear in the course of our inquiry. The Ethics of Christianity are religious Ethics; they have their centre in God. This gives them a character of their own, which makes them generically different from secularist or materialistic Ethics. We shall therefore, in the latter part of this book, come upon genuine antagonisms between Christian ethical principles and other principles which are held, with equal sincerity, by some who are not Christians. It will be a difficult but necessary part of our undertaking to disengage what is essential and distinctive in the Christian view of life, entangled as this has been with a mass of traditional morality which has at best only a local and temporary validity.

The history of moral philosophy, from the Greeks to the nineteenth-century Utilitarians, does not fall within the scope of this book. Nor will it be necessary to examine in detail different types of ethical theory, as has been done by Martineau, Sidgwick, Green, and many others. My plan is to take the Ethics of the New Testament as embodying, on this side, the Christian revelation, and to bring these into comparison with the principles which seem to underlie the theory and practice of the white races in our own day. In this book I am concerned only with Western civilisation; I have neither the knowledge nor the space for a consideration of Asiatic peoples.

"That which is now called the Christian religion existed among the ancients, and has never failed from the beginning of the human race, until Christ came in the flesh, whence the true religion, which was already in existence, began to be called Christian." So wrote Augustine,[1] who had discovered, before his conversion, the close affinity between "the books of the Platonists" and the theology of the Fourth Gospel. The City of God, in his view, mingled with the earthly State from the creation of man, and will mingle with it to the end. Christianity has in all ages had its confessors who, it was charitably supposed, have received salvation; for the Logos was in the world under varied forms before the Incarnation. This thought, that "Christianity is as old as creation," is affirmed in the Prologue of the Fourth Gospel and in the first verses of the First Epis-

[1] Retract. 1. 13.

tle of St. John; it is common in the early Fathers, who had come under Platonic influence; in Augustine it is not held very consistently. It belongs obviously to an evolutionary, not to a catastrophic, view of the world's history, and for this reason it took no firm root during the long period when the dominant philosophy was supernaturalistic dualism. We moderns may be glad to find that it has a recognised, though insecure, place in early Christian thought. For we cannot be content to regard even a divine revelation as a bolt from the blue. The profoundest and most original of prophets still stands on the shoulders of those who went before him.

Christianity began with Christ in the same sense in which Platonism began with Plato, or, as Plato would have loyally protested, with Socrates. "The religion which is now called Christian" has been called Christian for nearly two thousand years, and has played a great part in history. It began as a reform movement, on the old prophetic lines, within Judaism; but it quickly decayed in its original home, and embarked on the conquest of the Hellenistic world, leaving the East to fall a prey to a typically Semitic religion, that of Mohammed. After a successful trial of strength with the imperial power, the great Church became itself a theocratic empire, and in the West followed the same course of evolution as the ancient Roman State, passing gradually from a modified democracy into a centralised despotism.

In spite of all attempts to preserve political unity, it has split up into innumerable sects, and at different times Christians have found their ideal in, or paid high honours to, such discrepant types as Simeon Stylites, Augustine, St. Louis of France, Francis of Assisi, George Fox the Quaker, General Gordon, and Howard the philanthropist. In the face of these violent and almost ludicrous contrasts, is it possible to speak of Christian Ethics at all? Is it one and the same religion which finds its ideal types now in a hermit tormenting himself like an Indian fakir, now in a learned scholar, now in a travelling missionary, now in a mystical visionary, now in a fighting man, now in a social reformer? Has not Christian morality a nose of wax, as Alan of Lille said of "authority"? Can it not be bent in any direction by the prevailing tendencies of successive historical epochs? Would it not be better to say at once that Christianity is the generic name for any religion professed by a man or woman with a white skin?

To these objections I shall try to answer that "Christian Ethics" is a name which has a meaning. I shall try to find, not a system, but a fountain of life which has never ceased to flow from its source in the life and teaching of the Founder. The river of Christianity (as Clement of Alexandria said) has received many affluents; the tree of Christianity has many branches, bearing diverse fruits of its own as well as many that are *non sua poma;* but beneath all diversities of type we can recognise, I think, manifestations of one and the self-same Spirit, dividing to every man severally as He will.

And yet I shall not maintain that the evolution of Christianity has been consistently (to use a biological term) orthogenetic. I shall not maintain that the Church has ever been infallible, supernaturally protected from error. On the contrary, the history of Christianity, like that of Buddhism, has been very largely a history of decline and perversion. Although in no age has the Spirit of Christ wholly deserted the society which bears His name, in no age has the Church escaped from the powerful reactions emanating from secular conditions. The persecutions, while in a sense they kept it pure, hardened its temper and stiffened its organisation. Constantly threatened with internal disruption, it was driven to progressive centralisation and repressive legislation. Its victory over the Empire was soon followed by several centuries of almost unredeemed barbarism, the most protracted and dismal retrogression which the human race has suffered within the historical period. The rediscovery of fragments of the ancient culture might seem to promise a fruitful alliance between religion and humanism; but the Renaissance quickened into activity the dormant memories of a glorious past, and made "Gothic barbarism" odious to the Latin races. This revival of classicism in Italy and elsewhere was one of the causes of the German Reformation, and of the wars of religion which followed it. The North had but little sentiment about the traditions of the Latin Empire. Thus Christendom in the West was disrupted; humanism was thrown back, and on both sides religion was narrowed, coarsened, and embittered. The Counter-Reformation remedied many abuses; but from that time onward the Roman Church has been merely Latin, not Catholic, and the Protestant Churches have suffered from the weaknesses of sectarianism. No branch of Christendom was ready to face the problems of the age of industrialism and of rapidly advancing science.

It is therefore quite impossible for me to follow those apologists who find in the institutional Catholic Church, speaking and acting through its political representatives or rulers, a real continuance of the Incarnation. The only true apostolic succession is in the lives of the saints. In trying to disengage the essence of Christian Ethics from what is accidental, I shall not be precluded by any reverence for tradition and ecclesiastical authority from finding in Church history aberrations on the largest scale, which still remain as stumbling-blocks, offending the conscience of the present age and distorting the ideal which the Gospel, when it was fresh from the mint, held up to mankind. These perversions, just because they were in accordance with the spirit of the age which generated them, have become especially obnoxious to a later time. In the difficult task of removing these morbid growths without endangering the life of the patient, the safest course for the modern Church is to return to the Christianity of the New Testament, and (changing our metaphor to one which St. Paul uses) to build afresh upon that foundation. The superstructure must be partially new, but the old foundation will suffice, when the incongruous erections which have been built upon it have been taken away.

I shall speak in detail of two distortions of the Christian religion which have had a very long and unfortunate history. The first is one-sided exaggeration of a genuine element in Christianity, the world-renouncing and self-denying aspect of our religion. I should be the last to deny that Christianity is an ascetic creed, that is to say, that it requires us to discipline ourselves, as athletes train for a race. Nevertheless in practice the ascetic ideal led to a manner of living and thinking which has many parallels in the history of Eastern religions, but which is completely alien to the sane and genial temper of the Founder, as portrayed in the Gospels. It is plain that the entire detachment from all earthly interests, which it was the object of these austerities to achieve, was possible only when a complete indifference prevailed about the welfare of secular society and the prospects of social improvement. The Ethics of the New Testament, it must be confessed, are open to distortion on this side. A social Gospel can be justifiably built upon the precepts of Christ and His apostles, but the attempt to reform secular society, the world which "lieth in the

Wicked One," was long neglected, for reasons which must be considered in the proper place. The early Church was ill protected against the encroachments of an extreme asceticism which logically belongs to a doctrine of the impurity of matter and the sinfulness of sensuous experience, ideas which are not part of the Christian religion. Traditional ecclesiastical Ethics, especially in the unreformed Churches, retain numerous survivals of this false ideal, which come into conflict with the enlightened conscience of our time. The subject will require careful handling, because the revolt against asceticism proceeds largely from mere utilitarianism, love of pleasure, and secularism. It is, in truth, much easier to fall below asceticism than to rise above it.

The second aberration has been far more disastrous, and its evil consequences do not seem to be diminishing. I shall try to trace to its natural causes the monstrous growth of a theocratic Empire in Europe, and to show how the Ethics of the Gospel have been at every point poisoned and distorted by the insatiable claims of this terrible organisation. Even the heroic self-devotion of the gallant soldier of the Church, even the gentle piety of the cloistered nun, have been almost turned into *splendida vitia* by the arrogance, bigotry, cruelty, and fanaticism which follow inevitably from a false notion of the Church and of its proper place in the world. The Western Catholic Church presents a magnificent spectacle, but in the light of the Gospel we must refuse to recognise in the priestly Cæsar of the Vatican a true representative of the Galilean prophet. The Roman Church furnishes a very melancholy illustration of the truth that the survival-value of an institution has no necessary relation to its fidelity to its original principles.

The Latin Church on its institutional side is the last chapter in the history of the Roman Empire; its connexion with the little flock which gathered round Christ is kept up only by the spiritual beauty of the characters which it still knows how to train. For the rest, almost all that offends the lay conscience in ecclesiastical morality—its fierce intolerance, its tortuous diplomacy, its indifference to truth, its trafficking in spiritual gifts, its refusal to recognise any moral obligations not sanctioned by its traditions and stamped by its own mint—all in a word which sets institutional Catholicism in permanent antagonism to modern civilisation—proceeds from the supposed duty of supporting through thick and thin the power, prestige, and wealth of a corporation. As against the unquestionable advantages which this fanatical institutionalism confers upon the Church as an organisation—the power of bargaining with governments and the enthusiastic support of wealthy bigots—must be set the hatred which in all Catholic lands is excited against the Church, and against the religion which it is supposed to represent. There is nothing resembling this hatred in Protestant countries, and in consequence we find in those countries a deep reverence for the character of Christ which has some influence on the conduct of many who never attend a place of worship. To take our own country as an example, Christianity as a leaven has a great though indefinable influence upon the character and moral ideas of the English people. In Catholic countries the people are, in common speech, either "devout" or "free-thinkers," and the free-thinker is usually untouched by any moral influences proceeding from Christianity. It seems to me that the political power of a highly organised Church is too dearly purchased at this price, and that our Lord's parables indicate that He meant His message to mould society in a very different manner. Only when it is recognised that the Church has no interests except the moral and spiritual welfare of the whole society in which it is placed; only when the Church is content to be the conscience of the nation, holding up, as a shining light, the standard of values which Christ came to earth to reveal, can the Church discharge the duty which it ought to perform. It is not enough that the individual should be willing to sacrifice himself for the institution; the institution also ought to be willing to sacrifice its tangible interests for the society which, in the name of its Master, it exists to elevate and redeem.

It is plain from what has been said that by the Ethics of Christianity, understood as I understand them, I mean the Ethics of the New Testament, and especially of the Gospels. After this date I have no confidence that the Church remained true to its marching orders. The policy of the Church must be justified or condemned by reference to the moral teaching of Christ, St. Paul and St. John. But is it possible to be sure that no contamination entered the little society even in the first century? Is it not possible that Christianity is like some chemical substances which are never found pure? If in every subsequent age we have to make allowances for distortions caused by the environment, is it likely that there are no traces of similar disturbance in the Ethics of the Gospels? We must not follow the example too often set in the nineteenth century by Liberal Protestant theologians, of taking the Gospels, and especially the character of Christ, out of their historical setting, and in the hope of presenting Him in His universal significance, dressing Him up, in defiance of every principle of sound criticism, as a model to be closely imitated by a German or English citizen in the industrial period. Only by placing Jesus and His disciples back in their historical surroundings, and giving due value to all that He inherited or accepted of the mental habits and beliefs of His people, can we hope to isolate what is universally true and precious in His life and teaching. The same applies to the other books of the New Testament, of which the most important are the Epistles of St. Paul. This will be the subject of my next chapter.

The task is notoriously difficult in the case of the Synoptic Gospels. We shall never know for certain how far the narratives have been retouched by the faith and love of the infant Church. The space occupied in all these documents by miraculous stories is disconcerting. There are signs of what the Germans call *Tendenz* in both St. Matthew and St. Luke; a proto-Catholicism in the First Gospel, and a leaning to Christian Socialism in the Third. Many critics find traces of "Paulinism" in St. Mark. On the other hand, Professor B. W. Bacon thinks that the Synoptic Gospels as they stand represent a reaction against the Pauline gospel of grace in the direction of the neo-legalism of the Christianised synagogue. The Fourth Gospel presents still more difficult problems. Not only is it our solitary specimen of a *genre* of literature quite unfamiliar to us, but it seems to presuppose a great spiritual movement in Asia Minor of which we know scarcely anything, a type of Christianity poles apart from Judaism, and yet different in some respects from the mind of St. Paul, though it might well be said that the thought of St. Paul was moving in this direction. If we had the writings of Marcion, who was not condemned till 144, we might find a startling resemblance between his teaching and that of the "Spiritual Gospel." In any case, the Johannine Christ must be regarded as speaking through the Spirit to the third generation of Christians.

It is well known that some very competent critics carry their scepticism about the historical value of the Synoptic Gospels so far as to leave very little of permanent and universal authority to the recorded utterances of Jesus Christ. Not to speak of the extravagant theory that we are not dealing with a historical character at all—a view which any sound critic must surely reject as absurd—there is a school which represents Jesus as a dreamer obsessed with apocalyptic notions about the approaching end of the world, and therefore without any thought of providing for a permanent society to carry on His work and transmit His teaching. These writers hardly disguise their conviction that the ethical teaching contained in the discourses of Christ must in these circumstances be regarded as of very subordinate importance. Some of them accept the phrase of Schweitzer, the most prominent advocate of this view, that the morality of the Gospels is an *Interimsethik*, a provisional rule of conduct during the very brief interlude between the proclamation of the supernatural cataclysm and its actual arrival.

It is necessary to come to some conclusion on this question before considering to what extent we are justified in treating the ethical teaching of the Gospels as having a permanent and universal value. For as the supernatural "end of the age" never came, if this expectation was really the fundamental presupposition of the whole of our Lord's teaching, we must surely set it aside as based on a delusion. And yet a full discussion of the controversy would be impossible in this book. The so-called eschatological theory—that the mission of Christ was essentially a proclamation of an approaching miraculous deliverance, which was to usher in a "kingdom of God," a theocratic *régime* in Palestine, with Jesus Himself, who had appeared on earth first as His own forerunner, as sovereign—no doubt arose as a reaction against the Liberal Protestant presentation of Him as the supreme pattern of all the civic virtues. It was pointed out quite truly that apocalyptism has left traces in almost all the books of the New Testament, and that we have no right to disregard this element because it is unwelcome to ourselves. The historical Christ cannot be modernised in the interests of edification.

If I had space to develop the arguments which to my own mind are decisive against the theory of Schweitzer and his friends, I should emphasise the profound sanity of Jesus, displayed in all His recorded words and actions. This sanity is not incompatible with a hope that God would soon intervene with power and establish a reign of righteousness on earth. But it is wholly incompatible with a delusion that He had been commissioned to predict a stupendous miracle, and to warn His contemporaries to prepare passively for it. The real question is whether a pure delusion generated the mission, or whether in the glow of their enthusiasm the disciples, and possibly the Master Himself, threw their ideals into the near future, and foreshortened the vision of their fulfilment, as idealists are always prone to do. The theory of Schweitzer makes Christ a psychological monster, and His character an insoluble enigma. And yet His character in the Synoptic Gospels comes out clearly, not only His profoundly religious and spiritual nature, but His deep wisdom, balance, and breadth of mind, even His irony and humour. These are not the characteristics of a half-crazy visionary.

I should further emphasise that Jesus placed Himself deliberately in the prophetic succession, living, preaching, and dying as a prophet. Now the prophets combined their earnest ethical exhortations with denunciatory predictions about a coming "day of the Lord." This combination of hortatory appeals with prophecy (in the narrower sense of the word) was the characteristic form of this type of preaching. But their moral exhortations were not determined by their expectation of any miraculous catastrophe. Neither, I maintain, were those of Christ. The definitely apocalyptic passages in the Synoptic Gospels are not numerous, and to my mind they stand somewhat apart from His other discourses. If we had to choose between rejecting these passages as later additions and explaining away the numerous sayings which are inconsistent with apocalyptism, I should have no hesitation, on purely critical grounds, in treating "the short apocalypse" and similar sayings as unauthentic. For the inwardness and spirituality of the Gospel teaching are manifest; "eternal life" is most closely connected with righteousness; the words "the Kingdom of God is not here or there, but within (or among) you" cannot be twisted into meaning merely, "the Kingdom is, or soon will be, upon you." Apocalyptism is essentially catastrophic; the salvation offered by Christ is, in striking parables, compared to the growth of a seed. The active benevolence which was the centre of His doctrine of obedience to God does not naturally agree with the inert quietism of those who have merely to sit still and watch for a miracle to which they themselves make no contribution.

The one-sidedness and exaggerations of the "eschatological" school seem now to be generally admitted. Erich Haupt says, "The solution of the problem seems to me to be attained only when our inquiry begins at the opposite point from that now usually occupied, with those passages in which the Kingdom of God is described as present. These passages form the interior climax of the message of Jesus." Toy, in his "Judaism and Christianity," says (perhaps rather too positively), "That the eschatological discourses were not delivered by Jesus in the form in which we now have them may probably be inferred from the fact that the disciples for some time after His death show no knowledge of their contents. The power of the Founder of Christianity was in His moral personality and in His conception of a thoroughly spiritual society." Harnack also says decisively, "We cannot derive the ethical ideal of Jesus from the eschatological." Or, to quote Peabody ("The Christian Life in the Modern World"), "To drag the background of the Gospels into the foreground, and to find in Jesus a Hebrew enthusiast announcing a Utopian dream, is to distort the perspective of His teaching and to rob it of unity and insight. Nothing is more unlike the teaching of Jesus than the apprehensive, excited, or nervous sense of an approaching catastrophe. The habitual attitude of Jesus in presence of the great problems of experience has a serenity, assurance, and sympathy far removed from the excited anticipations of abrupt and final change; and it becomes quite as probable that the vein of eschatological allusion which runs through the Gospels betrays the preconceptions of the evangelist as that it reveals the teacher's mind." A well-balanced discussion of the question may be found in Feine's "Theologie des Neuen Testaments."

Lastly, the way in which apocalyptism faded out of Christianity—the place of the Kingdom relegated to "heaven," and the time to the unknown and distant future, indicate that nothing essential was being surrendered when this Palestinian dream died a natural death.

In what category did the men of His own generation place their Master before He became the divine object of a religious cult? He was, of course, recognised as a religious teacher, a Rabbi. But it was admitted both by His disciples and by the multitude that He was quite unlike the other religious teachers with whom they were familiar. "The people were astonished

17

at his doctrine, for he taught them as one having authority, and not as the scribes." "A new doctrine!" they exclaimed on one occasion.

There is no doubt about the answer, which I have already given. It seemed to many that one of the old prophets, perhaps Elijah or Jeremiah, had been reincarnated in His person. Others even thought that John the Baptist, who had just been beheaded, had risen from the dead. He was habitually spoken of as "the prophet of Nazareth in Galilee." Nor did He repudiate this designation of Himself. Like other prophets, he was not honoured in His own country, or by His own relatives. He would not flee from Herod, because "it cannot be that a prophet should perish out of Jerusalem." If we compare the life and teaching of Jesus with what we know of the prophets, we cannot but be struck by the extraordinary similarity between them. The resemblance is not confined to one or two points; it is observable in the mode of life, in the method of teaching, in the essential character of the teaching, in the response which that teaching evoked, and in the manner of its preservation.[1] It is a common error to suppose that the line of prophets had entirely ceased for centuries before John the Baptist. There had been prophets early in the second century before Christ, if the late date of Zechariah be accepted. Apocalyptism had only partially taken the place of the old prophecy.

The prophets wandered from place to place, like the begging friars of the middle ages, subsisting on the offerings of the faithful. They preached wherever they could find an audience—in the Temple precincts, in open spaces, in synagogues, and in private houses. The method of teaching by parables or proverbs was

---

[1] See the admirable article by Professor Kennett, "Jesus the Prophet," in *Hibbert Journal*, Oct. 1906.

the common form of prophetism. In the Old Testament the parables are sometimes disguised as visions, sometimes acted dramatically. These devices were unsuited to the audiences addressed by Christ, who were less unsophisticated. But the Old Testament prophecies are often suggested by the same homely and familiar objects and scenes of daily life as the parables of the New. And we must remember the essentially *poetic* character of prophetic teaching. When we read the dialogues in the parable of the sheep and the goats, the description of Dives and Lazarus in the place of departed spirits, or the cursing of the barren fig-tree (which recalls the dramatic warnings of the old prophets) we must avoid prosaic literalism. A comparison of the "eschatological" passage in Matt. xxiv. 29 with Isaiah xiii. 9–13 will prove how completely our Lord, if He uttered these words, was adopting a method of speech with which all His auditors were quite familiar. As Professor Kennett says, He *understood* the prophets, as none else in His generation;— He understood the prophecy of Malachi about Elijah; He understood Daniel's apocalypse, and the allegory of Jonah. "If His words were found in Hebrew, they would at once be recognised as belonging to the volume of the prophets."

In my next chapter I shall take it as proved that Jesus Christ stood before His contemporaries as a teacher of righteousness, that His method was that of the earlier Jewish prophets, and that in the Synoptic Gospels we have a trustworthy account of the substance of His ethical teaching. But we must not regard Him who said, "Who made me a divider over you?" as a legislator, a second Moses. Such was not at all His object. The true interpretation of the Gospel Ethics will consist in eliciting the presuppositions on which they depend, the principles which animate them, the illustrations of them furnished by the character and actions of Jesus, and the application of them to very different circumstances. There may be legitimate differences of opinion here and there as to the inferences to be drawn from these principles, but I maintain with ever-increasing conviction that we have in the Gospels a true and clear picture of a revelation through a character which, as far as fallible men can judge, was perfect and consistent.

"The Christian doctrine of morals," says Schleiermacher, "should be the presentation of communion with God which is conditioned by communion with Christ the Redeemer, so far as it is the motive of all acts of the Christian—that manner of action which proceeds from the supremacy of the Christian religious self-consciousness." This puts the matter rightly. The active life of Christ Himself was throughout determined by His sense of communion with God the Father, whom it was His mission to make known to mankind. As the consciousness of Christ was the life of God in the soul of a human being, so the inspiration of the Christian is the mind of Christ, now operating as the Holy Spirit, in his soul. This divine presence in the human soul is a principle of life, of sanctification, and of enlightenment. Strictly, we do not take as our model merely the human Jesus. *Conversio fit ad Dominum ut Spiritum,* as Bengel says. This was the history of St. Paul's conversion, and in the Fourth Gospel the doctrine of the Spirit of Christ as the Guide and Teacher of the Society, and of individual Christians, is the leading motive of the whole treatise. "This Johannine principle," says B. W. Bacon, "is the Church's charter of intellectual freedom."

In this way we can escape from a purely static conception of the Christian revelation. The tendency to a slavish following of the letter, or to an unreflecting obedience to a fixed tradition, is dangerous, and such subservience to authority is not required of us. We have a right, in virtue of our knowledge of the mind of Christ and belief in His continued spiritual presence, to condemn and repudiate immoral doctrines and irrational taboos, even when they come to us supported by ecclesiastical tradition. The obligation to do this, and to speak the truth as we see it, is too much ignored in religious circles. No censure is passed upon those who defend and propagate the silliest and most unworthy superstitions. There is no excuse for refusing to apply the principles of the Gospel to circumstances very unlike those which came within the purview of the human Christ, or for denying the competence of the Spirit of truth to teach humanity many truths which believers in the first century were "unable to bear." Christ did not burden His Church with a code, or confine posterity to the crude beliefs of an unscientific age. He was, we may repeat, a prophet, not a legislator.

There are some who disparage morality—"mere morality," as they like to call it—as religion at a very low temperature. The ethical maxims of Confucius, the worldly prudence and good sense of Proverbs and Ecclesiasticus, the cool rational exhortations of the eighteenth-century deists, may occur to us as examples of this kind of religion. William James quotes an amusing estimate of this type of character. "Dr. Channing was excluded from the highest form of religious life by the extraordinary rectitude of his character." We may recall our Lord's smiling reference to the ninety-nine sheep who went not astray, and we may think how admirably this satire pricks the prosaic unmystical respectability exhibited by many model citizens whom we have known. But the example of our Lord Himself, whom William James seems unable to fit into his "varieties of religious experience," should make us hesitate before accepting such a paradox as the words about Channing. Those who disparage morality in the name of religion are usually the adherents of some non-ethical religion. To suppose that any religion is better than "mere morality" is a grievous mistake. For, as Professor Whitehead has lately told us, "religion is not always a good thing; it is often a very bad thing." The enemies of the true religion are they of its own household; not atheism, impiety, and scepticism, from all of which recovery is possible, but the false religions which Christianity may have scotched, but has certainly not killed. These unethical religions sprang up again under the protection of the Churches. There are unethical types both of Catholicism and Protestantism, which show their nature by despising rectitude of conduct. Dilettantism in art and emotionalism in feeling both predispose to a kind of religiosity, but not to the religion of Christ. The worshippers who sing "Doing ends in death" are usually worthy and innocent people with very limited intelligence. But there is an antinomian Protestantism, as there is an accommodating Catholicism. Such churchmen need to be reminded that the "weightier matters of the law" are "justice, mercy, and truth," not any traditions of the elders, and not any delusion that we may "continue in sin that grace may abound."

The religion of Christ is through and through an ethical religion. When Harnack quotes Mark XII. 28–34, the passage which says that love to God and our neighbours is the sum total of the Law, as a grand declaration of moral and spiritual religion, he is well aware that such love can in neither case be an idle emotion, but must show itself "in deed and in truth." The God whom Christ revealed is a moral Being, and the service which He claims from us lies wholly within the sphere of conduct, which nevertheless is so extended as to cover the whole man, with all his actions, words and thoughts. It is an ethical religion, but it was from the first, and still remains, a *religion,* not an ethical system. The centre of Christianity is God, not nature or man or an ideal society some day to be realised. Its values are eternal values, which therefore do not depend for their validity on temporal happenings in the past or in the future. Ethics and religion are brought together in the religion of Christ, which does not regard the divine law as an alien power, enforcing its will by rewards and punishments. The rewards are neither arbitrary nor external—in part they are already enjoyed; the punishments are the natural fruit of sin, which, "when it is perfected," is the death of the soul. Christian Ethics are therefore free and autonomous, though revealed. The revelation is "the perfect law, the law of liberty." For without law there can be no liberty. The inner harmony without which there can be no personal self-determination is a harmony of unified purposes, not of satisfied desires. "Repression," so frivolously condemned by amateur psycho-analysts, is necessary to reduce to discipline the disorderly mob which rages within us. But the only external, authoritative rule is given in the life and teaching of Christ as recorded in the New Testament. And this is hardly external, for it is accepted and interpreted by the *testimonium Spiritus Sancti* declaring itself in the Christian society and in the individual conscience.

Although our Lord declared that His yoke is easy and His burden light, the moral requirements of Christianity are exceedingly searching and exacting. In a sense, love makes all sacrifices easy, and the "rest of the soul" which the Master promises is an inexpressible relief after the inner turmoil of a divided allegiance; but the way of the Cross is no flowery path. There is profound spiritual insight (where we should not have expected to find it) in the lines of Hesiod about what Christ calls the way of the narrow gate. "The sweat and toil of virtue the immortal gods have set in front. Long and steep is the road that leads to it, and rugged at first; but when one reaches the top, then it is easy, though still difficult." But men are always prone to slip out of the stern requirements of a creed which demands a consecration of words and thoughts as well as of actions. There is another religion ready to hand, which appeals to the natural man. This kind of religion makes only two demands upon us—to practise the virtues of a combatant on the side of an institution, and to perform ritual observances. This simplification of requirements was one secret of the success of Islam. We shall see in the sequel how far this natural tendency has depraved the morality of the Christian Church.

The seat of authority in morals may be a law regarded as divine, or the conscience, the inner light, regarded as inspired. Religious Ethics always rest upon these two, or on one of them supporting the other. Those who reject these sanctions have to fall back upon some calculus, such as the greatest pleasure for themselves, or the greatest happiness of the greatest number, or progress towards some ideal state of society pictured by the imagination and accepted by the will. This may be the pursuit of the highest good for society and its members, which we regard as attainable, or partially attainable, on earth, or to be achieved only in a higher state of existence. I shall have to show in a later chapter that the greatest confusion prevails in our current judgments of right and wrong. Modern civilisation has, consciously or unconsciously, rejected earlier standards without establishing any others in their place. The strongest appeal now seems to be to a kind of emotional utilitarianism with a calculus of pleasure and pain.

The rational basis of Christian Ethics is mainly intuitional—obedience to the will of God as revealed to the human heart by the indwelling Spirit of Christ. The records of the earthly life of Jesus are regulative; they supply a criterion for "the discernment of Spirits." But this intuitional basis receives a closer determination by the doctrine of the individual soul as eternally precious in God's sight, and by the law of love, which as a philosophical principle means that we are members one of another, so that the welfare of all is the good of each. This definitely rules out egoism; and the injunction to strive after moral perfection ("even as your Father which is in heaven is perfect"), which can be achieved only by the sacrifice of the good for the better, and of the better for the best, rules out all hedonism, altruistic as well as selfish. Whether aspirations for the future perfecting of human society on earth can be included in the Christian ethical scheme must be considered later. I shall maintain that they can, but only on condition that merely secularist ideals of social progress be abandoned. This follows from the presuppositions of Christianity as to the purpose for which immortal spirits are placed on their probation in this world of space and time.

The desire for reward and the dread of punishment are not repudiated as motives in the Gospel. That the Judge of all the earth will do right was the fundamental conviction of Hebrew religion, and remains in Christianity, though the external and almost materialistic conception of divine favour and displeasure which made theodicy a standing enigma to the Hebrews, is in principle rejected under the new dispensation. Sometimes, as in the parable of Dives and Lazarus, a rather crude doctrine of compensation seems to be indicated. But even in the Gospels concessions are made to current modes of thinking. The twelve apostles were men of their time, and (while they walked with Christ in Galilee) not even saints or mystics. They were chosen as typical of the best qualities of the common people—courage, loyalty, and willingness to give up all for their Master. And the parable of Dives and Lazarus is only a parable; that is to say, it illustrates a particular lesson, in this case the duty of the unselfish use of wealth. The basis of morals in love is far more strongly insisted on. Too much has been made by some writers on Ethics of the selfish calculation which they believe to be at the root of Christian morality. A cool head and a cold heart never yet brought anyone to the foot of the Cross. What was said about the alleged apocalyptic foundation of Christianity may be repeated here. Eschatological belief is the projection of faith. To the irreligious mind these beliefs are usually too vague and shadowy to influence conduct.

That "the Universe is friendly" is the belief of Christians, with the proviso that the ultimate laws of the universe are spiritual. There have been a few who have been willing to face the possibility that the nature of things is unfriendly to man. Huxley's Romanes Lecture is a classical example of this mood, though such thoughts really lead not so much to pessimism as to Manicheism. "The world is very evil"; but, as Huxley suggests, we can show our loyalty to a higher principle which "resists the cosmic process." Where there is no confidence in a power of effective resistance we have only a Promethean defiance of the supreme Power, a theatrical gesture which even the poetical genius of Victor Hugo or the eloquent prose of Mr. Bertrand Russell can hardly save from toppling over into absurdity. Some saints have wished that heaven and hell were blotted out, so that they might serve God from love alone. This wish is entirely intelligible, in view of the coarseness and crudity of popular eschatology; but these saints have not regarded the God whom they wished to serve for love as withdrawn from control of the real world. "We may spiritualise our God over-much," is the bold warning of Professor W. Wallace.

The Christian worships and trusts in God as the *Valor valorum*,[1] the supreme reality in whom all the ultimate values are eternally and perfectly realised. Homage to the ultimate values is the worship of God. Therefore, when we remember the wide extension of τὸ καλόν in Greek thought, we may say with Aristotle that we act "for the sake of the Beautiful, which is that which is common to all the virtues"; and we may think that the Pythagorean maxim, ἀληθεύειν καὶ εὐεργετεῖν, "be true and do good," anticipates very worthily St. Paul's "Be true men in love."

[1] Nicholas of Cusa.

CHAPTER II

EVEN when we are dealing with a divine revelation in its simplest and purest form, like unworn and untarnished coins fresh from the mint, we have to remember that it takes two to tell the truth, one to speak and one to hear. None can receive a revelation which is unrelated to his education, his habits of thought, and his experience of life. The Ethics of the New Testament must not be taken out of their historical setting. Ideas must be given through something, and the something is a very imperfect human nature and social environment.

The environment in which the Gospel of Jesus Christ was first proclaimed was not the cosmopolitan Hellenistic civilisation, as it might have been found in Asia Minor, Egypt, or Rome, but the most isolated and stubbornly resistant portion of Rome's Eastern conquests. Not till we come to St. Paul will it be necessary to consider the impact of the new teaching upon Hellenism, and the influence of Hellenism upon it. But in estimating the condition of Jewish religion in the time of our Lord we must forget neither the infiltration of Babylonian and Persian ideas into Hebraism, nor the difference in religious atmosphere between Jerusalem and northern Palestine. We must also, since our documents in their present form are later than the destruction of the Temple, be careful not to antedate changes of thought and belief caused by that event.

The foundation of what we know as Judaism (not of the older religion of the Hebrews, which was monolatrous rather than strictly montheistic) was the doctrine of one God, and the denial of the gods many and lords many of Paganism. The God of the Jews was not only the Creator of the world but its Ruler, to whom were ascribed the attributes of omnipotence, omniscience, justice, and mercy.[1] He had no body or shape, and might not be represented under any human or animal form. The earlier notion of a jealous and vengeful Being, who resented the honours paid to any other, had not been outgrown; but these conceptions had been to a large extent moralised. The errors which most excited the wrath of Jehovah were— so the prophets taught with increasing emphasis—not neglect of the ceremonial honours due to the Deity, but injustice and immorality.

And yet the irrational prejudice against "idolatry," which the Jews quite erroneously supposed to be mere fetish-worship, remained. The Jewish creed also remained rigorously nationalistic. The Jewish State or Church, for we can hardly separate them, was a theocracy. The one and only God whom a strict monotheism could acknowledge was the God of the Jews. No tolerant syncretism was permitted. A Greek might say that Zeus was the Greek name of Jehovah, and Jehovah the Hebrew name of Zeus; but to a Jew such an identification was blasphemy. Jehovah was the true God; Zeus, if he existed, was a devil.

In the time of Christ the nation was divided into religious parties which became also political parties. The two extreme factions, the Sadducees and the

---

[1] Mr. Christopher Dawson shows how under Islam the East, rejecting Hellenic influences, swung back into the conceptions which were congenial to it. The divine omnipotence, he says in a very fine phrase, once more blazed in solitary splendour, like the sun over the desert.

Zealots, were numerically small. The Sadducees, sceptical and worldly, were the party of the nobles and priests; the Zealots were fanatical revolutionaries. Between these extremes came the bulk of the population, who were guided, especially at Jerusalem, by the Scribes and Pharisees.

It is important to realise that since sacrifice could be offered only at Jerusalem, the priesthood of the capital did not play a large part in the religious life of the country people. Very many Jews never even visited Jerusalem. The priests did not claim the power of absolution, and there were no sacraments. The link between God and man was the Law or Torah. Modern Jewish writers protest against the notion that the Law was felt by the ordinary practising Jew to be a heavy and irksome burden. They point to the 119th Psalm as a typical utterance expressing the love, delight, and reverence which the contemplation of it evoked in the pious Jew. Even Jehovah was supposed to find pleasure in studying the Law. When such ardent affection as this exists, commands are multiplied in order to increase the happiness and blessedness of those who obey them.

The Law, therefore, and not the priesthood or the Temple, was the main object of reverence. The social and religious centre was the synagogue, where the officials were not priests, but expounders of the Law. The destruction of Jerusalem did not even endanger the permanence of this religion, because the whole sacerdotal and sacrificial system was in fact superfluous. There is no sign that a restored Jewish State in Palestine is likely to revive the old sacrifices.

The sacredness and infallibility ascribed to the Law were a bar to progress, since the early books of the Old Testament are full of cruelties and crudities which civilisation had long outgrown at the Christian era.

But the casuistry of faith, which shrinks from making any acknowledgment of error, can render these survivals far less morally noxious than a strict interpretation would lead us to expect. Allegorism and other devices can always be employed, and always are employed when the infallibility of tradition is erected into a dogma. The real evil is not so much in the sanction which might be found in ancient codes or documents for barbarous or immoral actions, though many horrible crimes have been so justified, as the failure to discriminate between ritual and ethical ordinances, which are placed on the same level and enforced by the same authority. The effect of this is inevitably to blunt the keen edge of conscience, and to open the door to evasions of the plainest duties.

Nevertheless it may be asserted that the moral standard of Judaism was in some respects much higher than that of the surrounding nations, and that the most characteristic features of Christian Ethics were by no means so strange to Jews who accepted the Gospel as is sometimes supposed. This has been lately brought out by several learned Jews, such as Mr. Montefiore, whose admiration for the teaching of Christ has not led them to forsake their national faith. For instance, though the teaching of some Rabbis about divorce was very lax, they condemned all sexual gratification outside marriage. The later Judaism had entirely purified public worship from Oriental obscenities; there were no longer any "holy men" or "holy women" attached to the service of Jehovah. Pederasty was sternly forbidden, and also infanticide. Justice, pity, and kindliness were emphasised; the precept "thou shalt love thy neighbour as thyself" was not invented by Christ. Almsgiving was classified with prayer and fasting as an imperative duty. Nor was Jewish morality altogether external. The Rabbis laid great stress on the necessity of overcoming "the evil disposition" which resembled the "original sin" of Christian theologians.

It was part of the Oriental and Jewish idea of religion to make free use of divine threats and promises as a powerful incentive to virtue, and "to hate with a perfect hatred" the enemies of Jehovah. These became by an easy process identified with the surrounding nations, who retaliated by accusing the Jews of hatred of the human race, and of churlish refusal even to show the way to a Gentile traveller.

But we must distinguish, more carefully than most writers have done, between the Judaism of Jerusalem and that of Galilee. Northern Palestine was the home of a fairly prosperous and well educated peasantry of mixed race, who were in close contact with Gentile residents and traders.[1] The apocalyptism which has been so much exaggerated by New Testament critics in our day was never very acceptable to the learned Judaism of the capital; it was a popular movement of thought, which took various forms, so various that it is impossible to make a consistent creed out of it. But, in one form or another, the hope of a miraculous intervention in human affairs seems to have sunk deep into the minds of the pious country folk in Galilee.

The commonest form of the belief seems to have been that a national deliverer would reign at Jerusalem, and that then would occur the last judgment. Some exalted the expected deliverer into a superhuman Being, who was waiting, as it were, in heaven till his hour was come. The hope was widely held that the days of the Messiah were very near at hand. The idea of a kingdom of God, or reign of righteousness, on earth was very prominent; and the notion was not

---

[1] Socially, there may not have been much fraternising. Bishop Gore points out that Christ is not recorded to have visited either of the Greek towns on the Lake, Bethsaida (see, however, Matt. ii. 21) and Tiberias.

strange to the Jews that in a sense we may enter into the Kingdom here and now by holiness of life.

Even at Jerusalem legal righteousness as practised by the ordinary God-fearing Jew was not so odious a thing as we often believe. The popular opinion of the iniquity of "the Jews" is mainly derived from the Fourth Gospel, which reflects the bitterness of the time when the evangelist wrote. We may be sure that Jesus never denounced "the Jews." The religion of the Law was not an odious thing; but it was an almost fatal obstacle to the reception of a higher revelation, by reason of its fierce and narrow nationalism, its failure to distinguish between moral and ceremonial obligation, its preoccupation with rewards and punishments, its propensity to regard suffering as a penalty for sin, and (in the hierarchy at least) its aristocratic disdain of the multitude who had neither the leisure nor the learning to study the Law and the mass of oral tradition to which an almost equal authority was ascribed. By its obstinate opposition to and rejection of Christ it put itself entirely in the wrong. And yet in the events which culminated in the crucifixion we can discern a genuine tragedy, a conflict of ideals. The Jewish hierarchy represented the Catholic idea of the Church; Jesus was a layman, who preached a layman's religion. In the light of history we can see more clearly than was possible to the first generation of Christians that the Gospel was much more than a prophetic revival within Judaism. The movement initiated by Christ was certain either to cool down and disappear, like other pietistic revivals within a great Church, or to disrupt the ecclesiastical structure to which it opposed itself. The situation was more clearly defined when St. Paul began to preach to the Gentiles. That apostle loved his nation and their traditions; but his Jewish opponents saw more clearly than he did that his teaching struck a mortal blow at the Jewish Catholic Church which had its seat at Jerusalem.

The Judaism of the Diaspora was very different. The Jewish colonies scattered throughout the Hellenistic world were not much more interested in Palestine than the modern Jewish communities in Europe and America. Their racial loyalty was unimpaired; but they were not, like the Judæans, almost cut off from the secular culture of their age. They knew too much to expect a resuscitation of the Maccabean monarchy. They had some tincture of Greek philosophy, especially Stoicism and the Platonic doctrine of the immortality of the soul. They retained their reverence for the religious books of their creed only by the use of fantastic allegorism. The isolated figure of Philo shows how little we know of a type of belief which must have had wide ramifications. It is very significant that in "the persecution which arose about Stephen" the apostles were unmolested; Stephen was judicially murdered as a Liberal or Modernist.

In this chapter, however, we have to deal in the first instance with Palestine at the time of the Galilean ministry, and to remember that our subject is the ethical side of the new revelation. The environment of the original Gospel is much stranger to us than the contemporary civilisation of Rome or Greece. It was a society in which laws of nature were hardly recognised. All was miracle, if we may speak of miracle when there are no natural laws to be "suspended." The significant events of history are catastrophic, interventions of an arbitrary divine power. In psychology, the human soul is inhabited by good and evil spirits. The breath of Jehovah inspires the prophets; physical as well as moral disease is caused by Satan and his satellites. There is more demonology even in St. Paul than we like to admit; under a somewhat different form the belief in intermediate spiritual powers was as common in Judaism as in Paganism. Hence arises a real difficulty for us moderns. A very superficial Liberalism in theology quietly sets aside the whole doctrine of evil spirits, while retaining and making the most of all that is said in the New Testament about the Holy Spirit. This is a shallow and almost disingenuous eclecticism. Christ Himself believed in evil spirits, and in their power of establishing themselves as inmates of the human soul. Just as belief in heaven is never very seriously held when its dread counterpart is rejected, so belief in the indwelling of the Holy Spirit is not much more than confidence in the guidance of our own best thoughts, unless we believe also in malignant influences proceeding from active powers "in the heavenly places." For the early Christians the moral struggle was dramatised as a conflict between the Spirit of holiness and "the world-rulers of this darkness," fought out in the arena of human personality. The language of the New Testament is dramatic and symbolic; but the essential fact is that the moral conflict is based on antinomies which are superhuman and, to our limited apprehensions, absolute. Christianity lifts psychology out of mere subjectivism, and morality out of mere relativism. This is a fact which, whether it be welcome or not, must be stated with the utmost clearness at the outset of an inquiry like the present. The Christian point of view gives to conduct an absolute value, and makes the individual soul a combatant in a Miltonic war. When we come to the consideration of modern ethical problems, we shall find ourselves unable, as Christians, to adopt the secularist standard of right and wrong, though on the other side we shall not be willing to leave traditional morality unscrutinised. This is indeed the fundamental problem towards the solution of which I have applied myself to make a humble contribution in this book.

To those who heard the discourses of Christ, and to the early converts to Christianity, the Gospel seemed "a new doctrine" (Mark i. 27). "If any man be in Christ, he is a new creation," says St. Paul (2 Cor. v. 17). I hope to discuss in this chapter the originality of Christian Ethics. But in religion, as in everything else, we must not forget the tart apophthegm of Sir Fitzjames Stephen, that "originality consists in thinking for ourselves, not in thinking differently from other people." Nor did the Christian Church ever commit the folly of the revolutionary, who believes that it is possible to make a clean sweep of the past. The early Christians were willing to acknowledge continuity with the Jewish dispensation, and, after the struggle with Marcionism, to canonise the Old Testament as an integral part of its sacred literature. As time went on, a similar continuity was quite illegitimately asserted between the Jewish priesthood and the Christian ministry. On the other side, the second century Apologists and the Christian Platonists not only acknowledged their obligations to Pagan philosophy, but admitted divine inspiration in Heracleitus, Socrates, and Plato. If St. Paul identified the life-giving rock which accompanied the Israelites in the desert with the indwelling Spirit of Christ, Clement of Alexandria counted Greek philosophy among the affluents of the great river of the church. Augustine finds in Neoplatonism almost the whole of Christianity except the Incarnation, and mentions a priest of Cybele who said, "*Et ipse pileatus* (Attis) *Christianus est!*"

If this continuity both with Judaism and with Paganism was felt to exist in the Christian religion generally, it is obviously true of Christian Ethics.

THE ETHICS OF THE NEW TESTAMENT

Writers like Clemen[1] have collected a remarkable series of parallels to our Lord's most striking sayings, from Seneca, Epictetus, Plutarch, and others. But even closer parallels to the primitive Christian temper might be found in the sacred books of the East, where no borrowing is possible on either side. From Lao Tze is quoted: "He that humbles himself shall be preserved entire. He that bends shall be made straight. He that is empty shall be filled. He that is worn out shall be renewed. He that has little shall succeed; he that has much shall go astray."[2] In the third century before Christ Asoka the Buddhist ruler of India had the following list of virtues inscribed in stone in various parts of his empire: "Compassion, liberality, truth, purity, gentleness, peace, joyousness, saintliness, self-control."[3] This closely resembles one of St. Paul's catalogues. We are quite justified in finding in these parallels with Oriental thought evidence that Christianity, which is now the least Asiatic of all the great religions, had originally a character which might have commended it to Indian and Chinese piety. But such resemblances do not discount the originality of Christian Ethics. For the character of an ethical revelation depends largely on the proportional value given to various duties, and above all on the dynamic energy to carry them out. The Rabbis may have taught nearly all that Christ taught; but St. Paul found no power in their precepts to overcome the resistance of our lower nature, and if parallels can be discovered in their writings for most of the Sayings in the Sermon on the Mount, how much they taught that fortunately is not to be found there! What heavy burdens, grievous to

---

[1] Carl Clemen, "Religionsgeschichtliche Erklärung des Neuen Testaments," 1909.
[2] B. Russell, "Sceptical Essays," p. 102.
[3] Babbitt, "Democracy and Leadership," p. 159.

be borne, they laid on men's shoulders, burdens from which those who accepted the light burden and easy yoke of Christ were forthwith entirely free. As for Indian thought, the strong personalism of the Gospel makes a generic difference; and Platonism had a precious gift to bestow on Christian philosophy, which it could never have learned from India—the rich and living "spiritual world" (κόσμος νοητός) interposed between the shoreless ocean of Nirvana and the unreal phantasmagoria of the visible world.

The Ethics of the New Testament are closely bound up with the character of Christ. Irenæus answered the question of the Marcionites, "What new thing did Jesus bring?" by saying, *"Omnem novitatem attulit semetipsum afferens."* Although it is true, as Dr. Glover has lately insisted, that His mission was to reveal the character and nature of God the Father, and not His own, His consciousness of a unique relationship with the Father led Him to offer His own example as the pattern to which His disciples should conform. It is certain that He inspired in them an intense reverence and loyalty which determined their whole future lives. Our Gospels are not merely the record of oral teaching—they are portraits of a living man. So strong was the conviction that the revelation consisted not in word but in act and power, that the first believers made no attempt to draw up a manual of conduct from His reported sayings; and the Synoptic Gospels give us a standard of values and an example—these and little more. To this restraint we owe it that so little in the Gospels is of merely local and temporary importance, and also that a constant reference may be made to "the mind of Christ" as shown in action. It has often been said, and truly, that the possession of a historical Founder gave Christianity a decisive advantage over the cults of Isis and

Mithra. But Mohammedanism shows that a religion may have a historical founder whose personal character cannot serve as an ideal for his followers.

Doubts have sometimes been expressed whether the "Imitation of Christ" is a practicable rule for Christians. "The imitation of Jesus," says Harnack, "in the strict sense of the word, did not play any noteworthy rôle either in the Apostolic or in the old Catholic period."[1] St. Paul, though he understood the mind of Christ as very few have done since, did not care to study the details of His ministry. His faith rested on a personal experience of the Spirit-Christ, and on the sacramental or universal significance of the voluntary humiliation and sufferings of a Celestial Being. Those who have found in the Pauline Christ the "divinised hero of a cult" are not wholly wrong, though they have pushed this idea to an extreme which would make the theology of St. Paul, a convert from orthodox Judaism, quite inexplicable. My point here is that he did not study the details of Christ's human life with a view to imitating His manner of living. The type of mysticism founded by St. Bernard arrived at the imitation of Christ in a peculiar manner. The "poverty" of Christ must be embraced by the soul which desires to be formed in His image. Thus the self-emptying of Christ was the model for the "purification" which was the first stage in the mystical ladder of perfection. But this is not much like the modern tendency to find in the human Christ a pattern to be followed in our daily conduct. The compilation of Lives of Christ, arranged with this object, is a modern development.

Most of these lives are very unsatisfactory, being put together from quite inadequate materials. Some

---

[1] Harnack, "History of Dogma," Vol. I. p. 67. In my opinion this statement is too sweeping. The Apologists and Irenæus speak of the human Jesus as a model for our imitation, and Cyprian says, "In Christ there is given to us an exemplar of life."

of them are descriptions of a perfect character, as the writer imagines a perfect character to be; others are sentimental romances; others rely much on local colour, or on a study of the manners and customs of Palestine. We cannot be surprised that many scholars have condemned all such attempts as a mistake, in spite of the pathetic eagerness of the public to read any book which presents a clear picture of that wonderful life. After nearly two thousand years, a Life of Christ is the most lucrative to its author of all biographies.

No real biography of Jesus Christ can ever be written, and much that we should like to know remains uncertain. But the figure of the Saviour is not shadowy; His character lives; the Gospels give us a genuine portrait. The obvious *naïveté* and uncritical simplicity of the Evangelists forbid us to imagine that they could have created such a picture. If their object had been merely the apotheosis of the founder of a cult, the human traits which we find in the Gospels would have been suppressed or overlaid with honorific legend. I do not say that there is no tendency of this kind in the Synoptics; they contain a few things which we feel to be quite incongruous; but these are not numerous, and do not blur the clear impression of a real likeness. I will venture, though with much diffidence, to enumerate the features which seem to me to stand out most plainly.

The traditional portraits of Jesus Christ, in illustrated books and pictures, express only a serene and gentle dignity, sometimes even with a slightly effeminate look. The Gospels do not give this impression of Him. He is described as deeply moved by compassion, by anger, perhaps even by fear. But His was a commanding personality; no one ever dared to take liberties with Him.

Nor was gentleness the chief attribute of His teaching. He spoke of God as our Father; but was fatherhood associated with good-natured forbearance at this time? I think not. He did not shrink from making the severest demands on His followers—sometimes to "leave all," home, work, and possessions. Even when no such external renunciation is required, Christianity is the sternest of all creeds, because it claims the whole man, his words and thoughts as well as his actions. The weakness and ineffectiveness of modern preaching may result partly from the failure of the preacher to claim from us all that he should claim. Christianity, faithfully presented, is a creed for heroes.

The immediate effect of His teaching was an impression of power, of authority and mastery, the commanding dominance of a leader of men. Again and again the word "power" is used in connexion with His personality. Those who, like Paulsen, have found that His character is marked by renunciation of life; those who, like Renan, have spoken only of "infinite sweetness, vague poetry, universal charm"; and those who, like Hase, say that "never did a religious hero shun so little the joys of life," give impressions so one-sided as to be misleading. He appeals mainly to the will, and not in emotional language. He calls for a moral decision. This appeal is made with a royal independence of traditional authority, as is proved by His language about the Sabbath, about the wine-skins, in the story of the adulteress which has found its way into manuscripts of St. John, and in the treatment of the Ten Commandments in the Sermon on the Mount.

He was not a fanatic, an anarchist, a socialist, a dreamer, or an Essene ascetic. His discourses display, not only perfect sanity and balance, but (if one may say so without presumption) great intellectual power. We have to remember that His reporters were not intellectually gifted men; they were inadequate to their task, and probably missed many examples of His irony, that weapon of the misunderstood, and the playfulness with which He half expressed truths which they could not grasp. His prescience is shown by His sorrowful vision of Jerusalem in ruins, and the even sadder prediction that He was "not come to bring peace, but a sword." Although He discouraged "vain repetitions" (like the recitation of a prescribed number of Paternosters or Ave Marias), He spent much time—even "the whole night"—in prayer and meditation. We also infer that at all times He lived in close mental communion with God, whom He loved to address as "Father." A Jew with His education would know by heart a great many of the Psalms, and even on the Cross His prayers took this form.

When we turn from the character of Christ to His precepts (though we must in part interpret the first by the second and the second by the first), we find no system of Ethics, no code of rules for conduct, but an outlook, a manner of thinking and acting, a standard of values, which necessarily penetrate every corner of the personality. At the root of Christian Ethics lies what Harnack has called a transvaluation of all values in the light of our divine sonship and heavenly citizenship. To the man who boasts of his possessions He says, "Thou fool." He can even say, "He that hateth his life in this world shall keep it unto life eternal." (The difference between the two lives in such utterances is clearly qualitative, not durational.) In proclaiming the reality of this higher realm of values, He raises immeasurably the status of the human soul, which can breathe in this region.

The *inwardness* of Christ's Ethics has been rightly emphasised by Matthew Arnold and many others. From within, out of the heart of man, proceeds all that can exalt and all that can defile him. The Commandments are broken in thought before the sinner proceeds to overt acts, and the sin remains, even if no open offence is committed. This is a method which links our Lord's methods of treatment with those of modern physicians. He always attacks the disease, not its symptoms. He rebukes acquisitiveness rather than wealth, lust rather than adultery, hatred rather than war or violence. Being poles asunder from the ecclesiastical mind, He sweeps away all labels with sovereign contempt, and levels all barriers by ignoring them. No human being was by Him cast out beyond the pale for being a sinner, a foreigner, or a heretic.

It has been said that the problem of human conduct is to find a sufficient motive. That this is true in social and economic problems needs no demonstration, though it is often forgotten; it is no less the problem of the moralist. Some have made their appeal to pride; some to *esprit de corps;* some to the hope of reward and the fear of punishment. Christ's appeal is summed up in the "new commandment" of *love.* So much unreal sentiment hangs about this word, that a few words about its real meaning seem to be necessary. "Love to God" is talked about more often than felt. It comprises the consciousness of deep dependence, the sentiment of devout gratitude, and the conviction that the love and the presence of God surround us like an atmosphere. There was in the early Church an enthusiasm which gradually cooled later. Mystical literature contains abundant testimony as to what the love of God may mean and has meant to many.

The best expression of Christian love to our neighbours is the well-known saying, "When thou seest thy brother, thou seest thy Lord," which only repeats our Saviour's own words, "Inasmuch as ye have done it unto one of the least of these my brethren, ye have done it unto me." Christian love is the recognition of a fact—the brotherhood of humanity in Christ, involving a claim—that in all things we should seek the highest good of our neighbour, as if his good were our own. There are some Christians who think that they are fulfilling the command of love by showing themselves merely soft-hearted and compassionate in relieving the wants of others, while aiming at a very different standard for themselves. I dare not say that this is unchristian, for the relief of bodily suffering is very prominent among moral duties in the Gospels; but it becomes dangerous when the bestower of charity thinks more of himself than of the recipient of his bounty. This type of religion is always much more interested in cure than in prevention, in the relief of suffering than in fortifying the sufferer. In such cases, and they are very numerous, there is a confusion in the standard of values, which greatly diminishes the redemptive effect of true Christian love. For Christ, the soul alone is of primary importance, though works of mercy and charity are given a high place in the list of moral duties. We must not assume that in a less simple state of society He would have preferred direct relief to other methods of helping those in trouble.

In our generation, and especially in our own country, there has been much thoughtless and superficial denunciation of "individualism." This is usually only a part of an attempt to revive the spirit of institutionalism, and the combative energy which this temper always generates. But there is also a tendency to disparage that type of religion which aims at individual perfection, and to praise those who would find in Christianity only a social and communal creed.

I shall have to speak presently of the real blindness of early Christianity to the future welfare of humanity in this world. But here we are concerned with our Lord's own teaching. This was individual and universal; very little stress is laid on any forms of association which come between the personal life and the whole of mankind as God's children. Professor Whitehead has lately argued that "within the millennium before the birth of Christ, the communal religions were ceasing to be engines of progress. On the whole they had served humanity well. But their work was done."[1] "They were not straining forward to make the common life the City of God that it should be. They were religions of the average, and the average is at war with the ideal." In their different ways, both Roman Paganism and Judaism were communal religions; Christ shattered them both, though it was not long before the spirit which He had exorcised returned in Catholicism. The difference is that communal religion always defines itself against those whom it excludes and hates; the Gospel excludes none but those who exclude themselves.

Christian Ethics are a morality of simplification. The sin of hypocrisy is merely the supposed necessity of acting a part, where no pretence or concealment should be necessary.

"My peace I give unto you; not as the world giveth, give I unto you." The words of Ozanam on this subject are as true as they are eloquent. "There are two doctrines of progress: the first, nourished in the schools of sensualism, rehabilitates the passions, and promising the nations an earthly paradise at the end of a flowery path, gives them only a premature hell at the end of a way of blood; whilst the second, born from and inspired by Christianity, points to progress in the victory of the spirit over the flesh, promises nothing but as prize of warfare, and pronounces the creed which carries war into the individual soul to be the only way of peace for the nations."[2]

---

[1] Whitehead, "Religion in the Making," p. 38.
[2] Ozanam, "History of Civilisation in the Fifth Century," Vol. I. p. 3.

That nothing happens without God's will was a firm conviction of Christ. It is a hard lesson, which some of the saints have learnt. It follows that all things work together for good to those who love God. This is the optimistic side of the Gospel: it does not exonerate those through whom offences come; but it does contradict the semi-Manichean hypothesis of a limited struggling God, which is frequently revived, especially in times of national trouble.

The Gospel affirms a fundamental optimism; but it faces the extremity of temporal evil as no other creed has done. Without attempting to make man invulnerable—that last infirmity of all Greek philosophy—it accepts the Cross. The idea that the character "is made perfect through suffering" was not strange to Plato, and appears in the later books of the Old Testament. It is only in quite modern times that the very notion of chastisement has become unwelcome, and that the hopeless attempt has been made to present Christianity without the Cross. The doctrine of the Atonement perhaps hardly belongs to a book on Christian Ethics; but it may be worth while to distinguish between vicarious punishment, which is immoral, and vicarious suffering, which love is willing to endure. It is most important to realise that the Christian keeps no *meum* and *tuum* account with his Maker. He makes no claim to individual justice, remembering what treatment his Master received. We shall receive justice at God's hands, no doubt, but not what the unregenerate and unloving would call justice. Only those who are willing to lose their soul ($\psi v \chi \acute{\eta}$) for Christ's sake shall find it unto life eternal.

Humility has been misunderstood or misrepresented by critics of Christianity in all ages. It means pure receptivity. "What hast thou that thou didst not receive? But if thou didst receive it, why dost thou glory as if thou hadst not received it?" It means "thinking soberly, according as God hath dealt to every man the measure of faith." It does not mean wilful self-disparagement and refusal to accept responsibilities for which we are fitted. Still less does it encourage an old Jewish saying, "Ever be more and more lowly in spirit, for the prospect of man is to become the food of worms." [1] This is the monkish perversion of humility, not the humility of the New Testament, which honours "the body of our humiliation" as "the temple of God."

The attitude of Christ towards sin raises difficult questions, because the sense of guilt seems to us to be more tragic in some of the greatest disciples of Christ than the Master Himself would have approved. In the Gospels, sin is seldom mentioned except in connexion with forgiveness, and (as in Jewish theology generally) "repent" means, not "grieve," but "turn." St. Paul had had a personal experience, quite foreign to Christ Himself, of the struggle between the higher and the lower nature; he was intensely conscious of sin as a positive malignant power. We must also bear in mind that as the faith and love of the Church progressively recognised in Jesus, first the apocalyptic Messiah, then the unique Son of God, and finally the divine Logos incarnate, the mystery of the Passion deepened, and instead of the suffering servant of Jehovah described in Deutero-Isaiah, a symbolic figure representing the nation and bruised for its salvation, the tremendous doctrine of a suffering God entered into the heart of Christianity. An infinite sacrifice, it was said, was needed to atone for an infinite transgression. So for Christianity sin, instead of being a disease or a defect of goodness, is invested with the positive attributes of a malignant "prince of this world." It is not doubtful that Christ Himself be-

[1] Gore, "The Sermon on the Mount," p. 26.

lieved in powers of evil; and there is nothing inconsistent with His sayings in St. Paul's picture of a cosmic duel, in which human souls are the battlefield and the prize of victory. He unquestionably taught that unclean spirits, no less than the Holy Spirit, may make their abode within us.

This belief in the positive malignancy of sin is ethically important. In Platonism, the process of purification consists in "scouring" the figure which represents ourselves, cleaning away the mud, perhaps cutting and planing here and there, but just restoring to its original beauty a work of God which had fallen into neglect. No evil can defile the higher part of our nature, which belongs to the spiritual world. So in the Bhagavad-Gita the sage, "yielding to body's needs nothing save body, dwells sinless amid all sin, nowise bound by bond of deeds." When therefore St. Paul speaks of "cleansing us from all defilement of the flesh *and spirit,*" he is departing decisively from Greek and Oriental philosophy. To the Greeks evil was environmental; to Christianity, it belongs to the world of spirit.

Christianity maintains a moral, not a metaphysical dualism. The powers of evil are not rivals of the Deity whose "seat is in heaven"; but for beings on their probation the struggle is real, and the issue not predetermined. Morality lives in the internecine conflict of right and wrong; in the sphere where the victory has been won, and the enemy subdued, morality as we know it no longer exists; it has passed into something higher. And so in the sphere of morals Christianity is sterner, more tragic, less optimistic, than Platonism. For the latter, a man may perhaps lose his soul, but not the soul that would have been his if he had not been a bad man. Christianity has a more definite conception of personality, and the person, the Ego, the soul ($\psi v \chi \acute{\eta}$) may be finally lost. The death unto sin and the new birth unto righteousness is a transformation through which every redeemed soul has to pass; and the death which is spoken of is no mere metaphor.

The problem of evil is never discussed in the Gospels. The nearest approach to it, when our Lord says, "It must needs be that offences come, but woe to that man by whom the offence cometh," does not remove our familiar difficulties. The religion of Christ rejects on the one side the cosmic optimism of the Platonists, on the other side the metaphysical dualism of the Manicheans. This combination of ethical dualism with religious monism is true to experience; it works; but the failure to solve the problem leaves a gap in the line of defence. It is the most signal instance of the truth that Christianity is not a philosophy generating a religion, but a religion in search of a philosophy.

It has often been observed that Christ was more tolerant of sins of passion than the Catholic Church, which while under the influence of asceticism tended to regard the lust of the flesh as the cardinal moral evil, and that He was decidedly more tolerant of what was merely disreputable than typical Protestantism. Both tolerances are part of the inwardness of His ethics, and of His indifference to the secular ordering of social life. He and His disciples lived on an exalted plane, where the temptations of the senses are scarcely felt. It may well be that, even outside the circle of those who had been called to preach the Kingdom of God, the sexual morality of Palestine at this time was really superior, not only, as I have said, to that of contemporary Paganism, but to that of modern Europe. In any case, very little is said about sex in the Gospels. The hard Puritanism of the Pharisees and Scribes, as shown, for example, in the story of the adulteress whom Christ refused to condemn, was doubtless repugnant to Him. He reclaimed the fallen by compassion, and by the indulgence which only the absolutely pure can be trusted to show.

From the very first, the Christians needed new words, or words used in a new sense, to express the ethical ideas which they had learned from Christ. Such words are love, joy, peace, humility, faith, and hope. One of the most remarkable of these is *joy,* as an element in the good life. Negatively, it means freedom from anxiety, release from the cares of life, those "troubles that never come" which spoil so much of human happiness. Positively, it is the state of mind natural to those who have heard the good news, who live surrounded by affection and good-will given and received, and above all who live in the consciousness that the love and care of their heavenly Father continually watch over them. The word "joy" may or may not have been as frequently on the lips of the earthly Jesus as the Fourth Gospel reports; but as an interpretation of His attitude to life the Johannine discourses are unquestionably true. St. Paul, who was probably not a light-hearted man by nature, emphasises again and again the "joy and peace in believing" which his acceptance of the Gospel had brought him, and which he wishes to see in the lives of his converts. It became a tradition of the Christian character. Hermas reprobates the sin of *tristitia,* as Spinoza does; and this characteristic of the Christian temper survived, slightly tarnished perhaps, till the time of Augustine, who was attracted by it in what he saw among his Christian friends before his conversion. He speaks of the *sancta dignitas continentiæ, serena et non dissolute hilaris,* as a pleasant feature of Christian social life. St. Francis of Assisi revived this old tradition; he insisted that the bridegrooms of "my lady Poverty" must never appear to be unhappy.

The sins which chiefly aroused the indignation of Christ were hypocrisy, hard-heartedness, and worldliness. The three are more closely connected than might appear at first sight. Hypocrisy, to which the Gospels have given such a bad name, merely means *acting*. The hypocrite need not be a Tartuffe or a Pecksniff; he is only one whose outward demeanour is not an index of his inward state. Browning has said that we all have two sides to our souls, one to face the world with, the other to show to a woman whom we love. It is impossible, doubtless, always to bear our heart upon our sleeve; even the Sermon on the Mount recommends reserve in some circumstances; we are not to give what is holy to the dogs, nor to cast pearls before swine. Wise men have recommended a certain solemnity in the company of fools. But the true Christian is more transparent than other men. He has nothing to hide; and what he shows unconsciously is the best part of him. The purity of heart which admits to the vision of God is mainly single-heartedness, complete sincerity. Hypocrisy came before the eyes of Christ chiefly in the form of religious Pharisaism; and in truth it is difficult to exaggerate the mischief done by men who profess the highest motives which seem to their neighbours not to be necessary in order to account for their actions. Such men make the name of Christian stink in the nostrils of those who deal with them. The more successful the imposture is, the more evil are its ultimate effects. There is such a thing as protective mimicry in human society as well as in the animal kingdom; the successful and popular ecclesiastic may occasionally furnish a distressing example of it. And the underlying motives of this kind of hypocrisy are likely to be the other two faults which moved the displeasure of Christ—absence of real love for our fellow-men, and calculating ambition.

Want of sympathy for the troubles and weaknesses of others is a besetting temptation of all intellectualists. It appears in the proud, self-contained character which in antiquity was called Stoicism, and in the Christian form of it, which is Calvinism. That religion can be intensely cruel has been proved many times, and never more horribly than by Christian fanatics. Christ taught that benevolence and beneficence are not enough; there must be genuine sympathy or fellow-feeling. Nor must our hearts be open only to our fellow-countrymen or fellow-churchmen or those of our own class; we owe what the New Testament calls love to men and women as such. There is no doubt that this part of Christ's teaching commended the Gospel strongly to the oppressed classes; but the lesson has not been easily learned. Among religious people, over-severity in judging some kinds of delinquents, whose sins we have perhaps been able to avoid without difficulty, is a very common fault. Even a murderer is not summed up by calling him a murderer. We cannot execute him (as perhaps we are obliged to do for the protection of society) without hanging with the same rope several other men who probably do not deserve to be hanged. God's mercy is justice; man's justice should often be mercy.

The world, in the religious sense, has been defined by Bishop Gore as "human society as it organises itself apart from God." It is an association for co-operative injustice with limited liability. When we consider the different contributions made by Pilate, the chief priests, Judas and the mob to the condemnation and crucifixion of Christ, we can understand how the guilt of an appalling crime may be distributed among several persons, none of whom would have been morally capable of carrying it through alone. It is this possibility of distributive iniquity which makes religious or moral associations necessary, both for collective protest and for the mutual protection of those who aim at a higher standard. Even without thinking of the terrible acts of injustice of which nations and societies are sometimes guilty, "the world," as Wordsworth says, "is too much with us." The essence of worldliness is to mistake means for ends. The worldling is devoted to some of the instruments of a good and happy life, as if they were ends in themselves. Christ found the most salient instance of this error in the love of accumulation, which He called the service of Mammon. What He had in His mind was mere hoarding, not profitable trade, of which He speaks without censure in His parables; but we must not eviscerate His warnings of their plain meaning. Worldliness, and the covetousness which is a common form of it, indicate a radically wrong estimate of values, an irrational worship of mere instruments, without thought either of their intrinsic worth, or of the injustice of appropriating selfishly what has really been created by the whole society in which we live. Such a radical error can hardly coexist with the service of God.

Christ, as I have said, was not a legislator. He held up standards; He laid down principles; but He left nothing at all like a code behind Him. Are there any exceptions to this? Some have maintained that in the matter of the marriage law He did intend to legislate. This problem will be more conveniently dealt with in a later chapter.

We must now consider the criticisms and objections that have been made against the Ethics of the Gospels. Although most of these can be shown to rest upon misunderstandings, there remain some quite intelligent objections, put forward in good faith. To consider these fairly will help us to understand, from a different angle, some characteristic features of the Gospel teaching.

Some have complained that the Gospel does not recognise the ethical value either of art or of natural beauty, and have compared it unfavourably with the graceful products of Hellenic worship. The attitude of the Church to "idolatry" is an important subject, but this is not the right place to discuss it. There was no painting or sculpture among the Jews, and (in our Lord's time) very little poetry. But Eucken does not shrink from saying that "Christ effected an artistic transformation of human existence." His feeling for nature seems to have resembled Wordsworth's. Wordsworth had no doubt at all that a field of lilies is more beautiful than Solomon in all his glory; but two thousand years ago there were not many who saw with his eyes. And Christ seems to have loved the mountains just as Wordsworth did. He climbed them when He wished to be alone with God; He chose them as the scene of impressive events in His ministry; they seem to have been His favourite resort when He could spare time from the work of His mission. Fine works of art hardly came within His purview, but we must not make Him responsible for the iconoclasm of some of His followers. It was He who first saw the beauty of childhood, and by His purity and sincerity He cleared away some of the worst obstacles to noble art.

In China and Japan the people are said to be shocked by Christ's disparagement of family ties. A few texts in the Gospels, such as "he that loveth father or mother more than me is not worthy of me," grate upon their ideas of piety, which are deeply rooted in devotion to parents. Now we must admit that Christ sometimes used hyperbolical language in His popular teaching, trusting to remove misapprehensions on another occasion. The words about "hating" father and mother, which rationalists of the baser sort are fond of quoting against Him, would be shocking if they were not so manifestly contrary to the whole tenor of His teaching. In this case we may perhaps, for once, allow something to the apocalyptists, with their *Interimsethik*. As even St. Paul thought, "The time is short: let those who have wives be as though they had none." But was there not some reason for denouncing the corporate selfishness of the family group? The assumed solidarity of the family has often been made the pretext for various kinds of cruelty and injustice. We have only to think of the family massacres which were considered so natural in antiquity, even in the early books of the Old Testament; of the vicarious executions—father for child, or child for father—which do not scandalise barbarians; or of the widely held belief in the family curse, wreaking "justice" to the third or fourth generation. Even in modern times, is not ambition for the family often responsible for much unscrupulousness, for much greed, for deliberate unfairness in making appointments? Quite apart from the higher call which Christ addressed to His apostles, some loosening of a bond which had been drawn too tight was desirable, and perhaps still is so.

I have no wish to deny that a strange blindness about the future pervades all the Ethics of the New Testament, including the Gospels. The prayer in the Didache, "Let Grace come, and let the world pass away. Come, O Lord (Maranatha). Amen," breathes a very different spirit from our popular hymn, "Thy Kingdom come, O God." All through this book we shall have to confess that in many of our social problems we cannot find the help in the Gospels which we should have welcomed, because the early Christians never thought about an earthly future for the human race. This is a real omission, I will not say a defect, in the canonical books. But it is not true to say that it throws the moral teaching of the New Testament as a whole out of focus. The idea of a future life—a scene of reward and punishment—has sometimes drained the present life of its interests; but this cannot be said of the Gospels; and in St. Paul the Spirit-Christ was a present possession, so that the "spiritual man" could not feel himself altogether an exile from heaven while on his probation here. All that we can justly say is that our duty to posterity did not interest the early Christians any more than it did Marcus Aurelius or the Neoplatonists.

"Christianity is slave-morality." So Nietzsche proclaimed, by way of condemnation. So also our modern socialists and anarchists have proclaimed, meaning to distinguish sharply between Jesus, the proletarian preacher, and His disciples. Of course nothing can be much further from the modern proletarian revolutionary than Jesus, whether we regard either His social position and education or His methods and aims. But the charge of Nietzsche, whether we take it as blame or praise, requires a little more consideration.

Like many other neurotic men of letters—our own Thomas Carlyle is an example—Nietzsche had a sentimental admiration for the rough-handed man of action. He himself was condemned to ply his generation with words; he would have preferred to deal out blows. There is, he thought, a master-morality, acted upon by the few who are naturally fitted to rule, and there is a slave-morality, evolved for self-protection by the multitude who are fitted only for servitude. The "great blond beast" is a law to himself; he knows that the strong ought to control the weak. The weak may combine, and crush the strong by the weight of numbers; but this is the way to degeneration. Christianity was a revolt of this kind; and Christianity has won its great success by imposing on society generally a code of conduct which was devised in the interest of inferior types. The success of this propaganda moves him to great indignation. The triumph of Christian Ethics has handed over the world to "cows, women, sheep, Christians, dogs, Englishmen, and other democrats." In proportion as it is complete, this creed means the sacrifice of the strong and noble to the weak and base. It would put a stop for ever to all hopes of racial progress; and this is the worst service that any religion could do for humanity. For what is great in man is that he is a bridge and not a goal; he is the rope between the animal and the superhuman. Other Germans, like Seeck, have taken up the same cry. Christianity exalts all the servile and feminine virtues—patience, forgiveness, meekness, obedience, kindness to those in trouble; and systematically disparages the manly virtues of courage, patriotism, self-reliance, disinterested love of truth, and veracity.

I do not forget that Nietzsche distinguishes between the Founder of Christianity and the religion which bears His name. He is the author of the epigram, "There has been only one Christian, and he died upon the cross." His diatribes against an emasculated morality have some justification, and modern scientific Ethics can only be grateful to him for insisting on the improvement of the human race as a large part of any sound ethical ideal. But his wild blows against the encouragement of mercy and pity strike the Founder no less than His disciples; and the charge of "slave-morality" has undoubtedly been brought against the Gospel itself. This is therefore the right place to deal with it.

It would be easy to prove that Nietzsche's masterminds and Carlyle's heroes were not at all the kind of men that Nietzsche and Carlyle represent them to have been—that Cromwell, for example, was an opportunist, with no taste for violence. The romantic "hero," who hacks his way through all obstacles, is a figment of armchair historians. But the quarrel between Nietzsche and Christianity goes deeper than this. It is possible to organise society on the basis of a ruling class exercising complete control over a submissive multitude. States of this type usually begin by conquest; the descendants of the conquerors illustrate "master-morality," the descendants of the conquered illustrate "slave-morality." Christianity can tolerate a social order of this kind, but assuredly its tendency is to claim inalienable "natural rights" for every human being as such. Its deep-rooted individualism revolts against the sacrifice of whole classes in the interest of State-efficiency. And so the Gospel undoubtedly gave new hope and self-respect to the unprivileged classes in the Roman Empire. Ancient civilisation had too narrow a basis. It confined women to home duties (though this was much more true of Greece than of Rome); it despised manual labour, except in agriculture, and acquiesced in slavery. These depressed or injured classes had too little interest in the old culture to ensure its survival after the master-class had disappeared by war, massacre, and racial suicide. This seems to be the normal fate of a civilisation which is content to refine the upper crust without leavening the whole lump. A civilisation which tries to include the whole nation is inevitably vulgarised and partially debased in the process, but its gains are more likely to be permanent. There is, besides, the feeling of justice. If the achievements of civilisation are valuable, they ought as far as possible to be shared by all. Christianity has nothing to do with democracy as a form of government or as a form of State; but as a form of society it is unquestionably democratic. And in this it has the support of public opinion in our time; Nietzsche's aristocratic bias has the air of an anachronism.

The relation of the Gospel to modern democratic and socialistic ideas has naturally been much discussed in our time. Both sides are anxious to claim the immense authority of Jesus Christ, whether on the side of social revolution or of continuity in the existing social order. The plan of this book makes it almost necessary to divide this discussion, for the application of Christian principles to modern problems belongs to a later chapter. Here I must try to present a picture of the general attitude of Christ to economic questions, so far as these came within His purview.

The fundamental antagonism between Christianity and Marxian Socialism is loudly proclaimed by the Socialists themselves. Peabody [1] quotes the following utterances as typical. "The first word of religion," wrote Engels, "is a lie." "The idea of God," said Marx, "must be destroyed; it is the keystone of a perverted civilisation." "It is useless," says Belfort Bax, "blinking the fact that the Christian doctrine is more revolting to the higher moral sense of to-day than the Saturnalia or the cult of Proserpina could have been to the conscience of the early Christians"; and in another place: "Socialism utterly despises 'the other world,' with all its stage properties." "It is only natural that the Socialists should resent with some indignation the continual reference of ideal perfection to a semi-mythical Syrian of the first century, when he sees higher types." Many other examples of the same kind might be quoted. Quite consistently, the disciples of this creed in Russia have during the last twelve years martyred more Christian priests than all the Roman emperors from Nero to Diocletian.

---

[1] Peabody, "Jesus Christ and the Social Question," p. 16. I have found much help from various books by this excellent writer.

There are, however, some Socialists who claim Christ as one of themselves. "Poverty," says Nitti in his "Catholic Socialism," "was an indispensable condition for entering the Kingdom of Heaven." "The Sermon on the Mount," says an American, "is a treatise on political economy." "The worst charge that can be made against a Christian," says another, "is that he attempts to justify the existing social order. Revolution is the Christian's business." These are mild specimens of the language sometimes used; Christ is represented as a Socialist agitator.

These extravagances would not survive a sober study of the Gospels. But here we have to admit some difference of emphasis in the three Synoptic Gospels on the subject of wealth and poverty. It is in Luke that the Christian socialist finds all his favourite texts. Keim even accuses this evangelist of "gross, naked Ebionitism." The Lucan form of the Beatitudes, pronouncing blessings and curses on external conditions as such, so that the rich are rejected because they are rich, and the poor accepted because they are poor, is only one example out of several. It is in this Gospel that we have the parables of the rich man and Lazarus, of the rich fool, and of the good Samaritan. But it is not true that even Luke preaches Ebionitism. No disciple of Christ could suppose that in the Kingdom of Heaven men are to be rewarded in proportion to the scantiness of their possessions in this life. And the very significant refusal of Christ to adjudicate on a case of disputed ownership, a refusal clinched by the warning to beware of covetousness, is recorded by Luke.

It is not really doubtful how our Lord regarded these questions. He had His own standard of values, and among these values He ranked wealth very low indeed. He complained, not that wealth was badly distributed, but that it was grossly over-valued. His attitude was one of gentle detachment touched with irony. He consorted mainly with the common people, that is to say, with the self-respecting and fairly well educated peasantry who belonged to His own class! but He neither avoided the society of the rich nor showed any repugnance to their way of living, except when their wealth was dishonestly come by or selfishly spent. In this tolerance He differed from some of the Old Testament prophets, who denounced the rich as such, and still more from the Jewish writers of His time, who cultivated "a genius for hatred" of the rich. "To pass through their literature," says a German writer, Rogge, "is like passing through Dante's Inferno, except that there nowhere appears any trace of that divine pity which the great Italian permits." There is a touch of this fierce class-feeling in the Epistle of James, but nowhere else in the New Testament. The Ghetto, as we have observed in Russia produces not only usurers but communists. But Christ thinks so little of money that He feels only an amused contempt for the avaricious, and honestly thinks that the "poor," who in Northern Palestine were not very poor, have the best of it. Nevertheless, He does not spiritualise life so far as to preach indifference to temporal misfortunes. Sickness for Him is sickness, and want is want. He would have had no patience with those who on the plea of being above such sordid interests do nothing to relieve those who are in distress. This combination of indifference to comfort and luxury with a readiness to help physical misery is very characteristic of Christianity, where it has been faithfully accepted. Sometimes, as I have said, Christians have shown a degree of mental confusion by excessive pity for troubles which they could bear easily themselves; but even this is better than Stoic apathy.

Peabody summarises the evidence very well. "Such

seem to be the principles of the teaching of Jesus—the view from above, the approach from within, and the movement towards a spiritual end; wisdom, personality, idealism; a social horizon, a social power, a social aim. The supreme truth that this is God's world gave to Jesus His spirit of social optimism; the assurance that man is God's instrument gave to Him His method of social opportunism; the faith that in God's world God's people are to establish God's Kingdom gave Him His social idealism."[1] Troeltsch also states the truth about the social teaching of the Gospel very clearly and justly. "Neither the teaching of Jesus nor the growth of the early Church is the product of social agitation or the consequence or corollary of a class-conflict. The great redemptive hope of the Kingdom of God on which the teaching is based and which inspires the whole Church is not the hope of a perfected social condition but the moral and religious ideal of a world under the unobstructed rule of God, where all true values of the spiritual life will have their justification and recognition. Here is the fundamental truth from which our study must proceed."[2]

There can be no doubt that He would have condemned the externalism both of modern civilisation and of the political remedies advocated as a cure for its evils. The remedies of the Socialists are purely and aggressively environmental; they run counter to one of the profoundest maxims in the Gospel, that which bids us clean first the *inside* of the cup. Christ would have agreed with Herbert Spencer's epigram, "There is no political alchemy by which you can get golden conduct out of leaden instincts." So strong is His emphasis on the worthlessness of any improvement which is mere-

[1] Peabody, "Jesus Christ and the Social Question," p. 104.
[2] Troeltsch, "Soziallehren," p. 17. In a long footnote he discusses the views of several German writers on the whole question, especially commending Harnack.

ly external and not intrinsic, that the eugenists have, not without reason, claimed Him as in full agreement with their principles.

"To speak of the economics of the New Testament," says Holtzmann, "is as impossible as to speak of its dietetics, its astronomy, or its meteorology." This is, I think, over-stated. Christ refused pointedly to decide disputed questions of ownership or distribution; but the New Testament has a great deal to say about the Ethics of consumption, and the two cannot be entirely dissociated. And if it is true, as it possibly is, that the energetic service of Mammon requires the whole man, His unmistakable verdict is "Thou fool," on a man who so misspends his life. We are right to remind ourselves that He rebuked hoarding, not investing, and that the apocalyptic expectations of His disciples must be taken into account; but when all is said and done, the life which He considered safest and most desirable was very different from that of a successful man of business.

I think that if such questions had been brought before Him, He would have emphasised the law of *service*. "Whosoever will be chief among you, let him be your servant, even as the Son of Man came not to be ministered unto but to minister." Now what the world calls success consists almost invariably in extracting from society, in one form or another, a much larger recompense than is due, whether we consider the time and trouble expended, or the reasonable wants of the recipient. Where the main object of business is not to give people what they want, but to strip them of what they have, it falls under the censure of Christ. But when, in Bishop Westcott's words, "the honourable purchaser and the honourable seller meet in business for the work of citizens," there is no suspicion of blame attaching to trade. We may also remind ourselves that industrial civilisation would be impossible if the large majority of those engaged in business were not passably honest and industrious. But how many fortunes are made by men who are not honest, but who profit by the integrity and industry of their subordinates? It was actually a shock to many Victorian employers when their "hands" began to show the same acquisitiveness which they themselves had long practised. Many employers have unconsciously counted on the loyalty, honesty, and industry of their employees as something which they had a right to demand and expect without making any return.

There are some (Harnack and Herrmann in their joint volume, "The Social Gospel," seem to be among them) who go further, and think that the possession of capital is inconsistent with Christianity. They call attention to the emphasis with which Christ forbids anxiety and worry, such as the ownership of capital entails. But has not the man *without* capital much more temptation to be anxious? I think that these distinguished writers overshoot the mark in their desire to be quite honest, and that they do not sufficiently consider the vast difference between modern and ancient societies. The problems of capital and labour certainly cannot be solved by the mere citation of verses from the Gospels.

We come to another objection. "Christian morality," says John Stuart Mill, "has all the character of a reaction. It is in great part a protest against Paganism. Its ideal is negative rather than positive, passive rather than active; innocence rather than nobleness; abstinence from evil rather than active pursuit of good; in its precepts, 'thou shalt not' predominates unduly over 'thou shalt.'" Cotter Morison brings the same charge with more animus and an obvious bias; Lecky inclines to the same opinion. He contrasts the dirty monk, a fanatical savage driven half mad by senseless mortifications, with the civilised and honourable citizen of Pagan Athens or Rome. This charge has indeed been continually repeated. It is alleged that the Christian ideal denies the value of the interests which the healthy-minded man regards as valuable, the good things of this life, and lumps them together with obvious vices under the name of the world and the flesh. It teaches us to run away from, or to be afraid of, the normal human life.

Now this criticism is directed far more against what the Christian Church afterwards became than against the original Gospel. It is obvious that the teaching of Christ was not "a reaction against Paganism." Asceticism is the subject of my next chapter, and need not be discussed here. As an attack upon the Ethics of the Gospel this criticism is unjustified. Christ Himself was not an ascetic, though He endured great privations in the work of His mission. His teaching was not negative. The frequent "thou shalt not" of the old dispensation is not to be found in His discourses. The Beatitudes have often been compared with the Decalogue to show how positive Christian morality is as compared with Jewish. However, the most distinctive thing about the Ethics of the Gospel is not the positiveness of its precepts, but the inwardness of them. The typical form of Christ's exhortation is not "Do this and abstain from that," but "Be a person of such a character."

From a rather different side comes the criticism that the Ethics of the Gospel, though beautiful and elevated, are quite impracticable. Some of the precepts are couched in such extravagant language that hardly anyone has tried to apply them literally. And, even if we allow that Christ employed the method of hyperbole, and that common sense is enough to show what His meaning was, His whole outlook, it is said, was based on idealism which overlooks the defects of human nature. For example, is "resist not the evil man" a practicable precept? If we accept it, must we not conclude, as even Professor Percy Gardner has done, that the Christian must be content to own no property which "the evil man" might covet? What would become of a nation which resolved that in no circumstances would it resist aggression? Again, is Christian morality compatible with life in an industrial community? Is there such a thing as honest trade? Is not small business a form of gambling and big business a form of war?

This is a really difficult problem. How difficult it is is proved by the fact that very early in the history of the Church a double standard of practice was recognised. Some, it was said, were called to take upon themselves the whole yoke of the Lord; others might save their souls by accepting a secondary standard which admittedly fell short of perfection, and was practically a compromise with secular practice. What Troeltsch calls the sect-type of Christianity revolted vigorously against the double standard; but the Roman Church, which takes human nature as it is, accepts the fact that many Christians do not feel called to be "perfect." This may be held to be a confession that the Ethics of the Gospel, which (with the doubtful exceptions of the words to the rich young man, "If thou wilt be perfect, sell all thou hast," and the enigmatical "he that is able to receive it, let him receive it") do not seem to recognise a double standard, are strung too high for ordinary human nature. I think we must admit that they are so. The standard in the Gospels is heroic and perfectionist; it is not, as we cannot remind ourselves too often, a code of permissible conduct for a large community.

As for the statement that a consistent Christian who went into business would infallibly be ruined, I think it is exaggerated. There are many "entirely honest merchants," as Ruskin said of his father. The Quakers, as a body, have the reputation of being scrupulously honest and usually successful. But no doubt there are businesses where crookedness is so habitual that a high-minded man had better keep out of them. More might be done to purge Christian commerce of its doubtful elements if the society of believers were more compact and more able to protect one another. But Christ would not have thrown the blame, as so many now do, on industrialism itself. Professor Peabody says well: "The fundamental evils of industrialism are not mechanical but ethical; not primarily of the social order, but of the unsocialised soul. No rearrangement of production and distribution can of itself abolish the commercial instincts of ambition and competition, nor even the baser desires of theft, covetousness and deceit. A new order could not survive a year unless administered by unselfish minds and co-operative wills."

Lastly, some have objected that Christ does not teach that virtue is its own reward and vice its own punishment. He urges His disciples to do right by telling them that "great is your reward in heaven," and terrifies them by the warning, "Fear him who after he hath killed hath power to cast into hell; yea, I say unto you, fear him." We may frankly admit that Christian preaching has often laid so much stress on future reward and punishment that the purity of the Christian motives has been somewhat impaired. I do not think that this alleged selfishness has had so much effect as is often supposed; for these promises and threats are seldom believed in by irreligious persons so strongly as to induce them to forgo the more certain and tangible advantages which the world, the flesh, and the devil offer. In superstitious times this may not be altogether true; and I should be the last to deny that the Church has lost heavily, from the highest point of view, by trying to cajole and frighten the irreligious into behaving as if the truths of religion were real to them. But in our own time at any rate I do not think that self-regarding motives, based on a calculation of future happiness or misery, have much influence. On the other hand, it does not seem to me that the desire to "save our souls" is an unworthy one, nor that it can be sharply distinguished from what we should admit to be the highest motive, the love of God and of goodness. Our souls, we are taught, are of value in God's sight, and they are committed to our keeping. They represent the plot of garden which we are bidden to tend, the bit of the line which we are commissioned to defend. As Bishop Gore says, "We cannot separate love for God from a desire to find our own happiness in God. We must crave for ultimate satisfaction, recognition, and approval. There is a true self-love; and a true self-love seeks satisfaction in the fellowship of God in the eternal world. He that said, 'What is a man profited if he shall gain the whole world and lose his own soul?' said also, 'He that saveth his soul shall lose it.' " [1] Therefore, in spite of sayings like "great is your reward in heaven," it would be quite wrong to say that Christ recommended the life of virtue as a good speculation. There has been too much of this in later Christian teaching and we are reaping the fruits of it. The doctrine of eternal life has been vulgarised, and by being vulgarised it has become incredible. I could almost make my own the words of Mr. Urwick ("The Message of Plato," p. 214), in an interesting discussion of the light thrown upon Plato's "Republic" by Indian thought. "The true teacher brushes aside curious questions and brings us back to the sole essential matter—the possibility of the manifestation of the grace

[1] Gore, "The Sermon on the Mount," p. 106.

of God. The great fact is rebirth—that is, birth into spiritual life. Heaven and hell and purgatory are all facts, but they are little facts. The wise man knows these facts, and neither fears nor cares; for beyond them all is the big fact of rebirth into the incorruptible and eternal life." The appropriate punishment of an evil life is not to be baked in an oven; it is to become incapable of seeing God, here or hereafter.

"Not even now," wrote John Stuart Mill in words which have often been quoted, "would it be easy even for an unbeliever to find a better translation of the rule of virtue from the abstract into the concrete than to endeavour so to live that Jesus Christ would approve our life." "If men would set this before themselves there would be fewer unbelievers," was Pusey's comment. The Sermon on the Mount is the description of a *character;* it does not profess to lay down in advance how such a character would show itself in all possible circumstances. "Christianity," as one of the Cambridge Platonists says, "is a divine life, not a divine science." Christ describes to us the conditions of "blessedness," which is the kind of happiness that we should desire, and obtain, if we were indifferent to our own selfish interests. There is no real contradiction here with what was said in the preceding paragraph.

"The life of Jesus," says Du Bose, "would not be a gospel to us if it were not a revelation and a promise of human blessedness. We see in Him the meaning, the value, the worth, which not only justifies to us and reconciles us to our life and its conditions as they are, but enables us to find in it the highest satisfaction of which our natures are capable and the highest enjoyment to which our spirits and personalities can attain. . . . We can be or do perfectly only that which we supremely love, and which therefore it is our supreme pleasure, happiness, or blessedness, to be or to do.

Blessedness therefore is at once the measure and the condition of the perfect life." [1] Both the conditions and the rewards of blessedness are spoken of by our Lord as to be found, imperfectly, no doubt, but actually, even in this present life. Those *are* blessed who are what He described. The Kingdom of God is within us; it is not our environment but our own reaction upon it which makes us blessed or unblest. And yet our present state is very incomplete. The promise is that we may become something higher than ourselves, something of what God is. Christ does not condemn us for this insufficiency, but only for not being aware of it. In the words of Du Bose, "He finds fault that we have not enough of the Spirit to know that we violate it, nor apprehension enough of the law to know that we transgress it; that we have not enough of holiness to want it, or of righteousness to hunger and thirst after it."

The Ethics of the Gospel set up a most exacting ideal of conduct. They appeal to those who are children in malice but full-grown in understanding. *"Ego sum cibus grandium,"* as St. Augustine heard the Lord saying to him; "be a man, and thou shalt feed upon me."

In passing from the Gospels to St. Paul's Epistles we come into a clearer light; for whereas some uncertainty must rest upon the records of our Lord's life and teaching, trustworthy as we believe them to be in their broad outlines, we know more about St. Paul than about any other character in antiquity, with the possible exception of Marcus Tullius Cicero. It is true that until lately Paul has been half buried under Paulinism. Commentators have quite forgotten the simple folk to whom he spoke and wrote his letters.

[1] Du Bose, "The Gospel in the Gospels," pp. 86, 87.

We cannot doubt that a few pages of such a book as Pfleiderer's "Paulinism," excellent as it is in its own way, would have reduced the Thessalonians or even the Corinthians to the condition of Eutychus of Troas. But the materials for a historically sane estimate of the man and his writings are present, and they have now been utilised in a series of admirable books, German and English. We can understand St. Paul now better than he has been understood at any previous time. For even of the second century Harnack can say that no one understood Paul except Marcion—and he misunderstood him!

The limited scope of this chapter prevents me from discussing such disputed questions as the authenticity of Ephesians, 2 Thessalonians, and the Pastoral Epistles. We may form an estimate of Pauline Ethics without using these documents, though for my own part I do not think there is a word of Ephesians which St. Paul would have disowned, whether the style is his or not. Nor will it be necessary to say much about the development in his theology which may be traced between his earliest and latest Epistles. It is certain that he seems to change rather rapidly (for only about a decade separates his earliest extant writings from the latest) from Jewish apocalyptism to a Christ-mysticism and a Logos-philosophy not unlike that of the Fourth Gospel. But we must not regard these two types as mutually exclusive. Belief in the indwelling Spirit of Christ was the centre of his personal religion from the first; and on the other hand there is no sign that he ever outgrew his expectation that "the time is short," an illusion which may have affected his moral counsels at certain points.

But since we are not dealing with a professor of philosophy, or a systematic theologian, but with a saint and missionary whose whole mind was absorbed by religion, we cannot separate his ethical teaching from his character. The change which his conversion brought with it was not primarily a moral change. There is no reason whatever to suppose, with Lagarde and others, that he had ever been a careless or loose liver. He had always, we may guess, served God with zealous devotion; his alleged intolerance, which never quenched a tender affection for the human beings among whom he worked, is unhappily so often the accompaniment of religious zeal, that we can hardly regard it as a blot on his character. As a Christian, he remained a zealot; but we can hardly accuse him of ever forgetting Christian charity in his dealings with bitter and unscrupulous enemies. It is probable, though not certain, that the brutal judicial murder of Stephen, of which he was an eye-witness, and the last words of the heroic martyr, made a deep impression upon him, though it was not till some time had passed that it brought him to abandon his hostility to the new faith. But his own account is that he had become dissatisfied with the Pharisaic law, which had no dynamic force to help men to obey it. The vision on the road to Damascus revealed to him not only the glorified Jesus, but his own state of mind. With characteristic energy he made a complete severance from his former ties, and proclaimed himself an active disciple of the Crucified. No sooner had he taken this decision, than a new source of joy and strength overflowed, irradiating his whole being. There was a new feeling of triumphant life. Henceforth he is conscious of being in real contact with a living and personal spiritual power in which without hesitation he recognised the Spirit of Christ. This intimate relationship with the Spirit-Christ is unquestionably the core of his religion. All the rabbinical subtleties, all the arguments about nature and grace, justification and sanctification, which fill so much space in post-Reformation theology, are quite secondary.

He was a visionary, a mystic. But in writing to the Corinthians he has to go back fourteen years for his last experience of a trance such as Porphyry tells us was occasionally enjoyed by Plotinus. Special leadings and inhibitions, like those which Socrates received from his "dæmon," he knew well; and prayer was for him a real communion. But we can easily believe that he was too active, too seldom alone, for the frequent trances of the cloistered saint.

His absorption in purely religious interests left him no time for worldly pleasures and æsthetic appreciations. There is something a little grim in his attitude towards marriage. It may be that we should have found him a trifle unbending and ungenial in common life. But he was certainly not morose or unhappy; his frequent references to joy as one of the chief Christian graces are quite sincere.

If we ask how he thought of the Christ of experience, the answer must be that he thought of Him as *Pneuma,* Spirit. The gift of the Spirit comes purely from God, but it is offered to all, and spurned only by the "reprobate." We are to prepare for it, and to give all diligence never to "grieve" or "quench" the divine guest. The critic of St. Paul must give full weight to the constantly repeated words *"in* Christ." The mystical Christ could do what the idea of a Messiah could never have done. This conception, developed in the Fourth Gospel, has been the life-blood of Christianity ever since. Luther's words, "Seek thyself only in Christ and not in thyself; so thou shalt find thyself in Him for all eternity," are quite Pauline, and profoundly Christian.

My subject is Christian Ethics, and I cannot pass over without comment the attempt made by some modern scholars, not all of them Catholic, to fasten upon St. Paul an unethical, almost magical, doctrine of the sacraments. With every wish to be impartial, I cannot find anything of the kind in his Epistles. Baptism, for him, does not bring about our fellowship with Christ; it was not the decisive moment in his own conversion; it merely sets the seal on the gift of God. When St. Paul, protesting against antinomianism, says, "Shall we continue in sin that grace may abound?" grace certainly means not the baptismal gift, but forgiveness through faith in Christ. It is inexplicable to me that writers like Professor Lake, who are not concerned to justify a magical view of the sacraments, can find it in St. Paul. The references to baptism in the Epistles are few and not enthusiastic. He thanks God that he baptized hardly any of the Corinthians. "Christ sent me not to baptize but to preach the Gospel." [1] In the entire Epistle to the Romans, that document in which he sets forth and defends his own conception of Christianity, baptism only enters his mind once, and the Lord's Supper not at all. The "unmediated and naked sacramental conception," which Schweitzer finds in St. Paul, is entirely absent from his mind and from his writings. When we turn to the Lord's Supper, we find Dieterich asserting as a certain fact, that according to St. Paul's view, "Christ is eaten and drunk by the faithful and is thereby in them. The process is actual." [2] Is it possible that St. Paul, a Jew, should have dallied with the idea of *eating* a divine Being? When he speaks, in one of the crucial passages, about "partaking of the table of demons," does he mean the table on which the flesh of demons was eaten, or the table at which a demon was the spiritual

---

[1] H. A. A. Kennedy, "St. Paul and the Mystery Religions," p. 234. This whole chapter should be studied.
[2] Weinel.

host? The latter, of course. In both the idol feast and the Christian Supper, solidarity with the divine Being is confessed and confirmed by partaking of a common meal. Just as in every individual the "whole process of Christ" has to be re-enacted, so that the Incarnation generally might be and was spoken of as a sacrament or mystery, so the Church was able to quicken the faith and kindle the imagination of the believer by the acted parables which were called sacraments. It is of course true that when once the sacramental idea has been allowed to enter, unethical views of sacramental grace are likely to follow. Possibly the "baptism for the dead," which St. Paul mentions as a custom at Corinth, without praise or blame, may indicate that a magical view of the effects of baptism had already crept in. But that any weakening of the purely ethical demands of Christ was countenanced by St. Paul himself, I see no reason whatever to believe. Still less can I believe that he in any way sanctioned an analogy with the purely savage belief that we can acquire the merits of a slain animal or human being by eating his flesh. Porphyry at the end of the third century was disgusted with the language used about the Eucharist by Christians in his day, and refused to accept the excuse that it was only used figuratively. This stumbling-block still exists. It is unfortunate that we cannot do without symbolical language, which the ingrained materialism of the vulgar accepts as prosaic fact. But the opponents of sacramentalism are often themselves not free from materialistic literalism, and condemn as fetish-worship what deserves a more sympathetic name. The natural language of devotion is poetry, not science.

"The apostolic age was the age of the Spirit." [1] What was manifest in the lives of the believers was a holy enthusiasm, a buoyant consciousness of personal

[1] Bartlet and Carlyle, "Christianity in History," p. 41.

inspiration, to which parallels may be found in the early Franciscans and Quakers. As Deissmann points out, [1] this mental state is expressed by St. Paul not only by the preposition "in" (*"in* Christ"—where the emphasis in on the preposition) but by what he calls the mystical genitive—"the faith of Christ, the hope of Christ, the peace of Christ, the patience of Christ, the obedience of Christ, the sufferings of Christ, the afflictions of Christ." In each case it is presumed that the particular experience or assurance of soul in the Christian takes place in the mystical and spiritual fellowship with Christ. The experience described is simple; the language used about it is varied. Too much ingenuity has been expended in distinguishing, for example, between justification and sanctification; these so-called concepts run like rays from the central point, the felt presence of the Spirit-Christ. To anyone who has studied the Epistles of St. Paul with this clue, it seems strange that he should ever have been so expounded as to appear arid and scholastic.

"Justification"—if we must define it—is the judicial sentence of acquittal. It is not precisely either the impartation or the imputation of righteousness; but we are to assume that a divine pronouncement is in accordance with truth. The thought of the apostle is intelligible only through appeal to the "mystical genitive." Another cycle of metaphors, in which God is spoken of as an enemy to whom we are now reconciled, has had unfortunate consequences, for which St. Paul is not to blame. We should think of "enmity" as that which is terminated by "peace," and consider how much the apostle is able to make of "Christ our peace."

"Redemption" was an idea readily intelligible in an age of slavery as a social institution. As justification is the acquittal of the accused, so redemption is the

[1] Diessmann, "St. Paul," p. 141.

liberation of the slave by purchase. Here again we find a suggestive thought in Deissmann.[1] "Among the various legal forms by which in the time of St. Paul the manumission of a slave could take place we find the solemn rite of purchase of a slave by a deity. The owner comes with the slave to the temple, sells him there to the god, and receives from the temple treasury the purchase money, which the slave has previously deposited there out of his savings. The slave thus becomes the property of the god, but as aganist all the world he is a free man." St. Paul uses formulas which occur regularly in inscriptions relating to manumissions. The metaphor of "adoption" was also more familiar to readers in antiquity than it is to us.

These metaphors are not intended to represent different things; "they sound together in harmony like the notes of a single full chord." In one place[2] wisdom, righteousness, sanctification, and redemption are set together as the result of being "in Christ Jesus."

St. Paul was also able to identify his sufferings with "the afflictions of Christ," and to believe that his own afflictions played their part in the great work of redemption to achieve which Christ suffered. This thought, which was revived effectively in the last century by James Hinton in his "Mystery of Pain," is not to be taken into the field of dogmatic controversy. It has brought comfort to many sufferers, from St. Paul's day to our own.

The Apostle's own experience included a very drastic breach with old ties. It was natural to him to think of ethical progress, not as a continuous upward movement, but as a crucial choice between the old and the new. "If any man be in Christ, he is a new creation." So the lower nature is "the old man," who

[1] *Ibid.*, p. 150.
[2] I Cor. i, 30.

is to be utterly disowned and cast out. The Johannine Christ insists with equal emphasis on the necessity of being "born again"; and Christ Himself spoke of the necessity of being "converted." But conversion, for a Jew, meant only a decisive turn of the will in the right direction; there is nothing in the Synoptic Gospels so uncompromising as St. Paul's language about the crucifixion of the old man. It is permissible to think that both St. Paul and St. Augustine, drawing on their personal experience, depicted the moral conflict as a more tragic thing than many good people have found it. Nevertheless, we have to remember that it is the saints who see the moral world in silhouette, and the sinners who recognise only various shades of grey.

The Platonising side of St. Paul's thought is very apparent in such sayings as "The things that are seen are temporal, but the things that are not seen are eternal," and "We all with unveiled face reflecting like mirrors the glory of the Lord are transformed into the same image from glory to glory." The influence of Plato upon Christianity became stronger afterwards, especially in the Greek-speaking part of the Catholic Church, and it is one of the strands in the mind of that complex genius Augustine. It is indeed quite impossible to tear Platonism out of Christianity, and those philosophies, whether materialistic or pragmatist, which have revolted against Plato find it very difficult to accommodate themselves to Christian thought. That being so, it is all the more important to call attention to certain differences between St. Paul and Plato, differences which belong not only to speculative philosophy, but to moral practice.

The chief of these is the relation of the higher to the lower part of human nature. The Platonists, though they had no wish to consent to any disruption of the personality, taught that the real man belongs to the eternal world, and is therefore impeccable and indestructible, while the bodily life is bound up with the unreal and continually changing realm of "matter," from which the soul has to ascend, leaving behind it the clogging or polluting accretions which it contracted by "coming down" into the lower world. They found it difficult to answer the question whether the soul sinned by "coming down," and whether it would not have been better for it to remain always "yonder." St. Paul's Jewish training helped to preserve him from this disparagement of "things here," which, it should be said, has been very much exaggerated by critics of the later Platonists. Although "Spirit" in his Epistles occupies much the same position as the Platonic *Nous,* as a sphere of existence strictly superindividual and only to be reached by a transformation of the empirical self; and although for him also the soul is the bridge between the divine life and unredeemed existence, he does not identify "the body'" with "the flesh." The "flesh" is a moral category; it means the lower instincts erected into a principle of life and action. "The body" is not excluded from redemption, nor from eternal life. It is true that in his belief "flesh and blood cannot inherit the Kingdom of God, neither can corruption inherit incorruption." There speaks the Platonist. But the redeemed and beatified Spirit is not to be wholly disembodied. A "spiritual body" is prepared for it. It is idle to inquire whether St. Paul really conceived of Spirit as a highly rarefied, quasi-gaseous form of matter. Such views were held by some of the Stoics, and they appear in the Christian Stoic Tertullian. It is not till Plotinus that the words "God is Spirit" are wholly purged from this sublimated materialism. But St. Paul was not a professor of philosophy; the interest of his conception of a spiritual body, which in strict philosophy has not much value, is purely religious.

When he thought of the redemption of the body, it was a part of his faith that the whole personality—spirit, soul, and body—must be preserved blameless against the day of Christ. The spiritual body, which is being prepared for us, is already in part ours. As the outward man decays, the inward man is renewed day by day. Our bodies are already temples of the Holy Spirit. As we rise on stepping-stones of our dead selves to higher things, we discard nothing that belongs to our true nature; our bodies are part of that true nature when they are fully controlled by spirit. This belief in the sanctity of the body is obviously connected with the doctrine of the real Incarnation of Christ. Those Christians who accepted the Platonic disparagement of the outer life in space and time were logically driven to "docetism"—the theory that the human nature of Christ was only an appearance, a kind of acted parable.

The ethical consequences of this belief in the redemption of the body are to be seen in the deeper guilt attached to sins which defile the body, especially sexual offences. St. Paul dwells on these more than Christ ever did, but there is no reason to think that Christ would not have approved of all that he says. The main difference, perhaps, is that Christ thinks more of impurity as a state of thoughts, while St. Paul, who is obliged to take account of the moral dangers to which his converts were exposed in such cities as Corinth, explains why fornication, in particular, is not permissible to a Christian.

It is often said that St. Paul's view of marriage is already vitiated by the ideals of asceticism which played so important a part in the history of the Catholic Church. This aberration will be the subject of my next chapter. St. Paul had been consulted by the Corinthians on this subject. The Church at Corinth was perplexed and divided. There were some who objected to marriage altogether, on ascetic grounds; others thought it possible, and desirable, for husband and wife to live together without physical union. It is probable, though not quite certain, that this practice is referred to in the difficult passage in 1 Cor. vii. 36, which is otherwise interpreted in our English versions. There is no other evidence that virgin marriages were recognised in the Church at this early date; but the language of this Epistle proves sufficiently that ideas about the impurity of sexual relations, even within marriage, were current in the Corinthian Church. The contemporary Essenes, it may be remembered, were celibates on principle.

St. Paul does not wholly reject these ideas. The regulations which he lays down show much sympathy with the ascetic ideal, but they are tempered by common sense. Husband and wife are not to live apart, except for a time by mutual consent, and marriage, though not the highest choice for those who are expecting the day of the Lord, is a holy estate, into which men and women may enter without any moral scruples whatever. In many cases, he thinks, the alternative is between marriage and the torments of repression; such persons are wise if they marry.

Feminists have taken offence at his language about the inferior status of women. It is not a subject on which he could be expected to anticipate the modern movement for sex-emancipation; his task was merely to issue recommendations for the little society which looked to him for advice. His regulation that women must cover their heads at public worship was no doubt based on a strange superstition; we cannot cut demonology out of St. Paul's Epistles.

His advice about divorce also arose from specific questions which had been put to him. Some thought that as marriage in itself is immoral, a Christian husband and wife ought to separate. St. Paul answers in the negative. Secondly, if husband or wife had been converted to Christianity, ought this to end the marriage? St. Paul says No, unless the Pagan partner wishes for a divorce. It does not seem that the question of remarriage had been raised, nor the question whether a person already a Christian should be allowed to marry a Pagan.

Before leaving the Pauline Ethics, it is necessary to refer to a passage which is difficult because it is isolated, but which at first sight seems so prophetic of the doctrine of progress, as held in the nineteenth century, that it has become a favourite with modern expositors. The passage in question is Romans viii. 19–23, "For the earnest expectation of the creation waiteth for the revealing of the sons of God. For the creation was subjected to vanity, not of its own will, but by reason of him who subjected it, in hope that the creation itself also shall be delivered from the bondage of corruption into the liberty of the glory of the children of God. For we know that the whole creation groaneth and travaileth in pain together until now. And not only so, but ourselves also, which have the first fruits of the Spirit, even we ourselves groan within ourselves, waiting for our adoption, the redemption of our body." The sympathy with nature which seems to breathe in these words, and which is really present in them, appeals strongly to modern thought. Some have found in them a hope that the lower animals may in some sense be sharers in the redemption brought by Christ; others that the whole order of nature may some day be released from the cruelty which now pervades it. On such a passage might be based a discourse on our duties to the brute creation, and to the natural beauties which modern civilisation destroys. But we must be cautious in introducing into St. Paul's Epistles ideas so foreign to his customary thought. The passage really rests on the apocalyptic vision of "a new heaven and a new earth," predicted in Isaiah LXV. 17, and expanded with fanciful detail in the Book of Enoch. The notion of a new earth, endowed with preternatural fertility was a common form in apocalyptic literature. I fear, then, that this remarkable passage has no very deep meaning; the superiority of St. Paul's vision is only that the "redemption of the creation" is to be universal, and not merely for the benefit of the chosen people.

It is not necessary to say much about the ethical teaching of the other books of the New Testament. The special object of the Epistle to the Hebrews, the work of an unknown writer, probably in the reign of Domitian, was to comfort a group of Christians who were in some danger of relapsing into Liberal Judaism, or as we should say Unitarianism, under the double stress of a threatened persecution, and of the disappointed hopes of a return of Christ to earth in glory. The emphasis of the moral teaching is on faith, hope, patience, and courage. Life is a long-distance race, in which the heroes who have won their crowns sit as witnesses of our endurance, and Christ awaits us at the goal. At the end of the Epistle there is a string of moral precepts, in which we may notice warnings against ascetic teachings about marriage, and possibly against materialistic views of the Eucharist.

The Epistle attributed to James stands rather by itself in the New Testament. Here we undoubtedly find a trace of the Jewish hatred towards the rich, who, it is interesting to observe, are now represented within the Church. Next to oppression of the poor, the author lashes with his censure the sins of the tongue, and emphasises the duty of practical benevolence. The

Epistle is unlike St. Paul, but may well be typical of Christian exhortation at the end of the first century.

In the Johannine books the ethical standpoint is mystical and Pauline. The command of love is very strongly emphasised, but there are perhaps signs that it is "the brotherhood," that is to say, the society of believers, rather than mankind as men and women, who are now regarded as the proper objects of affection and sympathy. The moral dualism is very strongly marked; the evangelist seems to see the world in black and white. This, however, is part of his method; he is not thinking of problems of conduct, but is depicting the Incarnation as a cosmic drama, in which the principles of good and evil stand face to face. The most epoch-making feature of the book is the spiritualising and universalising of Messianic Christianity, and the clear intention to substitute an evolutionary for a catastrophic conception of the work in the world of the Paraclete, who is Christ Himself under another form. God is revealed in Christ as Light, Life, Love, and Spirit.

Finally, although in this book no attempt can be made to trace the historical evolution of Christian Ethics from age to age, it may be worth while to sketch in outline the moral life of the primitive Church, from such evidence as is available.

In the Apology of Aristides (in the reign of Antoninus Pius) we have an idealised picture of the life of the Christian community. Such descriptions are not to be accepted without qualification; but they at least show what were the qualities which the Church most esteemed, and wished to exhibit in the eyes of the Pagan world. The Christians, we are told, live in the hope and expectation of the world to come. They do not commit adultery nor fornication; they do not bear false witness; they are honest in business. Their women are pure; they call their slaves, whom they have persuaded to accept the faith, brethren without discrimination. They love one another, and are charitable to all who are in need. But they try to conceal their good deeds from the public eye. When we compare this picture with the warnings issued by St. Paul (*e.g.* in Colossians, III and IV) against immorality, covetousness, anger, malice and lying, we seem to find a higher standard in the second century than in the first. This I believe to be the fact. St. Paul's converts were still in contact with the Pagan vices to which they had been exposed before their conversion. In the second century a Christian society had not only been established, but was kept pure by the danger of persecution. In the Shepherd of Hermas, as in the Epistle to the Romans, the Christian *temper,* with its note of joyousness and total freedom from vindictiveness, is emphasised.

There is an interesting piece of testimony in Lucian, the Voltaire of antiquity. He says of the Christians: "Their original law-giver had taught them that they were all brethren one of another. They become incredibly alert when anything happens which affects their common interests; on such occasions no expense is grudged." Cæcilius also says, in Minucius Felix, "They recognise each other by means of secret marks and signs, and love one another almost before they are acquainted." Tertullian gives details about the administration of charity in his time. The Church, though reasonable care was taken to keep out impostors, must have resembled a large benefit society with very liberal management. The authorities exerted themselves to find work for those who were able to work, and gave doles to the unemployed. On this side, it has been compared to a labour-union.

The beautiful picture of Christian life in the second century, in Pater's "Marius the Epicurean," may be taken as substantially true.

CHAPTER III

WHEN we look at the birth and early growth of Christianity as a historical event, a movement within the Roman Empire in the first and second centuries of our era, we can see that it was not isolated, but was part of a widespread religious revival. Like other spiritual upheavals, it bears the stamp of the age in which it appeared. The age in which it appeared was a time of moral and spiritual advance, but of political and social stagnation. In common with the contemporary Pagan writings, down to and including Plotinus and Porphyry, Christian literature reflects a society without earthly hopes or ambitions. Men were content to live in the present. There were no "causes" in antiquity. It is true that Palestinian Christianity had a strong apocalyptic element, and in that sense looked towards the future. But apocalyptism was essentially catastrophic, not evolutionary. It looked forward not to the progressive amelioration of the existing social order under the guidance of the Church, but to its destruction by divine intervention. The effect was to deprive existing organisations of all interest and importance. Even the Church was a brief stop-gap till the Kingdom of God should come.

Messianism had no proper function within Hellenistic Christianity, and would have disappeared even more speedily than it did if there had been any other vision of a terrestrial future to take its place. But, as we can see from contemporary Pagan writings, there was none. Greek philosophy, which with the Ionians who founded it had been occupied with bold cosmological and physical speculations, in almost complete detachment from mythology and cultus, had become anthropocentric with Plato, Aristotle, Zeno, and Epicurus, and was now preparing to enter its latest phase as a guide to the saintly or mystical life. Religion was becoming exclusively a spiritual discipline, apart from all worldly interests. Plato's Republic had taken wings, and abandoned this earth altogether.

This recognition that early Christianity, like its rivals, was blind on one side, because the society in which it lived had no vision of the future,[1] lays upon us the task of estimating the loss which this limitation inflicted upon Christian Ethics. We shall be driven to admit that as a religion of faith, hope, and love it could not fully develop itself under these conditions. Still less could the leaven permeate the whole lump during the welter of brutal savagery which followed the break-up of the Western Empire. The Greek element in European civilisation, for a long period almost extinguished and forgotten in the West, awoke into new consciousness at the Renaissance, and in modern times has created an emancipated science and a secularised vision of human progress. How far Christianity can maintain or recover its position as a permanent factor in civilisation, by accepting and identifying itself with ideas which were foreign to it at the time of its origin and earlier growth, will be the subject of later chapters. In this chapter

---

[1] A few passages may be found to support the contention that this statement is too sweeping. Thus Irenæus says: "God arranged everything from the first with a view to the perfection of man, so that goodness may be manifest, justice made perfect, and the Church fashioned after the image of His Son. Thus man may at last reach maturity, and, ripened by such privileges, may see and comprehend God." ("Adv. Hær." V. 36.)

I shall argue that the world-renouncing ideal of conduct which occupies the foreground of Church history in the early centuries is by no means the full and natural expression of the spirit of Christianity, but is rather the mould into which it flowed while it was still liquid, and in which it congealed during a long period of decadence and barbarism.

Nevertheless, I am not in entire agreement with those who in our day are fond of speaking of "the mistake of asceticism." They are glad to remind us that Jesus Christ Himself "came eating and drinking," and was so far from satisfying the expectations of those who thought that a prophet ought to live like Elijah or John the Baptist, that they accused him of being "a gluttonous man and a wine-bibber." And yet the danger of "conformity to this world" is at present so much more serious than the opposite error of extreme other-worldliness and renunciation, that I am very far from wishing to brush aside the great ascetic movement as if it were merely a perversion, from which we have nothing to learn. It may be possible in discussing it to distinguish the wholesome from the morbid, the genuinely Christian from alien influences.

It is an obvious truth that asceticism is more prominent in St. Paul's Epistles than in the Gospels, and in the second and third centuries than in the first. This tendency may be regarded either as a growth or as a retrogression. It has been maintained by some writers that the history of a great religion is always the history of a decline. Renan is one of those who have taken this view. Ideals, he thinks, necessarily become degraded when they are brought into touch with realities. The saint and prophet see visions only when they turn their backs upon the world of experience. When they try to carry out the injunction, "See that thou make all things according to the pattern shewed thee on the mount," their great ideas enter into combination with alien facts; they become coarsened and vulgarised. The ideas evaporate or congeal, and either process is fatal to them. Or they are strangled by the institution which was formed to protect them, and after awhile their purifying power is exhausted. Then the forces against which the new revelation ranged itself resume the upper hand; and though in name the new faith may survive and flourish, it has had very little permanent influence upon the course of events or the characters of men. Examples are ready to hand in the degradations of Buddhism and of Christianity itself.

This is the view which not only agnostics, but those Protestant historians who are opposed to Catholicism, mysticism, and asceticism tend to take. They derive their whole inspiration from the records of the Gospel when it was fresh. After the Apostolic age they can find little to praise. In the transition to Catholicism, they think, the Church was not only Hellenised but Paganised. The pure milk of the word was corrupted by Greek philosophy; and the free democratic constitution of the primitive Church was transformed into a rigid hierarchic system, which, following the example of its prototype the Roman Empire, became more and more despotic. I shall not dispute the justice of this censure, as regards the government of the Church. But I am not prepared to condemn asceticism as simply the disease of a moribund civilisation. Nor do I think that history justifies the theory that a new religion is nothing more than a transient eruption of spiritual energy. A great religion like Christianity has the means of reforming itself from within; there is in it a never-failing fountain of living water, which Christians attribute to the indwelling Spirit of Christ, or of God. Those who take a pessimistic view of Christianity sometimes forget the very great difficulties with which the

Church had to contend, and the achievements which may fairly be ascribed to its influence.

I see no traces of continuous decline or senile decay in Church history. There have been periods of retrogression. A religion, as lived, cannot be much ahead of its adherents. A decadent people will have a decadent religion; and perhaps we may think that while the religion of a healthy man is the best part of him, the religion of a degenerate is the worst part of him. Religion may be, and often has been, a very bad thing. Organised political religion has generally been a bad thing. But though the Church in the dark ages and the middle ages may seem to have been divided between an idle flight from the world and a most unspiritual worldly ambition, it was partly by means of these opposite perversions that it held its own against barbarism and even kept alive some pitiful fragments of the ancient culture.

Asceticism, or rather *ascesis,* means simply a course of training, as men train for a race. For example, Aristotle says that the Spartans had an admirable military training, which procured for them success in war; but after their victories they always failed, "because they had never practised any other kind of *ascesis,* more important than military science." All who seriously desire to succeed in any walk of life must concentrate themselves upon it. They must reject what is superfluous; they must endure hardness; they must renounce much in order to win what for them is the pearl of great price. Plato anticipated St. Paul in drawing a parallel between athletic training and the discipline which is demanded from all who would enter for the great race—the career of virtue and holiness. In modern usage the ascetic is one who makes these renunciations for the sake of moral and spiritual excellence. The service of Mammon may demand equally great sacrifices; but we do not think of the keen business man as an ascetic, nor speak compassionately of the "mistake" which he has made in subjecting himself to so much self-denial.

The ascetic, as we use the word, is the athlete of religion. He "strives for the mastery" in a field where most people are content if they can pass muster. Sometimes, but illegitimately, the word asceticism is supposed to imply deliberate maltreatment of the body by means of fasting, abstinence from sleep, scourging, and similar methods of mortifying the flesh. These have often been adopted as part of the ascetic life, but many have lived in strict training without resorting to any of them.

There is hardly any religion, or any country, in which ascetic discipline has not been practised; but it is in Asia, and especially in India, that it has been pushed to its furthest limits. Buddha tried in vain to mitigate its excesses. Among Asiatic religions it is least prominent in Judaism, where vows of temporary consecration to Jehovah, and rules of ceremonial "cleanness," are hardly to be set on the same footing as maltreatment of the body as the enemy of the soul. The fasts of the Pharisees, however, undoubtedly were the model for the Christian fasts on Wednesday and Friday; and the small sect of the Essenes was ascetic in the sense usually given to the word. Dr. Oesterley would give fasting rather more importance; "it had been a rite in use among the Jews long before the time of Christianity."[1]

In Egypt the priests of Isis were celibates and vegetarians. In Greece the Orphic brotherhoods, ever since the sixth century before Christ, were distinguished by their prohibition of animal food; they also practised fasting. Rohde says, "The things and conditions from

[1] "Commentary on the Bible," Vol. II. p. 15. (S. P. C. K.)

which the Orphics abstained were those which represented in the symbolism of religion, rather than involved in actual practice, dependence upon the world of death." Rohde in my opinion underestimates the moral element in Orphism, which I believe, with Gomperz, to have been very great. The reasons given for vegetarianism were superstitious, but the object of fasting was self-discipline. The Pythagoreans, who were closely connected with the Orphics, preached a severely simple life, vegetarianism, disciplinary periods of silence, and sexual continence. The priestesses of Delphi and Achæan Hera, and the Roman Vestals, were bound to strict virginity.

The case of Plato is difficult, because he was a many-sided man. I agree with Eucken that "in his relinquishment of the world we have the real Plato and the consistent Plato, but by no means the complete Plato." The asceticism of the true Platonist has always been sane and moderate; the hallmark of Platonism is a combination of self-restraint and simplicity with humanism. This is, I think, true not only of the Platonists and Neoplatonists of antiquity, but of the philosophical mystics of Christianity, who carried on the Platonic tradition. It was probably a consequence of their comparatively mild self-discipline and of their healthy mental activity that they were seldom troubled by those agonising nervous reactions which in the cloister were called the Dark Night of the Soul.

The ascetics of classical antiquity were not the Platonists but the Cynics. Arising in the outskirts of Greek culture (few of the early Cynics were pure Hellenes), the sect flourished for a time, and was then absorbed into Stoicism, only to have a revival of popularity under the Roman Empire. The Cynics were extreme individualists, who therefore called themselves "citizens of the world"; they aimed at complete inde-

pendence by reducing their needs to the barest minimum. The virtuous man must above all things be
self-sufficing. These begging friars of the ancient
world were sometimes saints, sometimes coarse and
vituperative vagabonds, unpleasant in their habits.
Speaking generally, the motive of their asceticism was
independence of externals rather than self-mastery
or training for the beatific vision. To be without wants
has always been one of the inducements of the ascetic
life, but it is not the highest motive. The Cynical
tradition led direct to the savage monks and hermits
of the desert, who intimidated towns and villages with
the clubs which they called "Israelites"; the higher
kind of Christian asceticism has no affinity with Cynicism as it was usually known.

The centre of Christian Ethics, as taught in the
New Testament, is the love of God and man; ascetic
practices, especially in the Gospels, have a very subordinate place. Christ "came eating and drinking";
that is to say, He went about among His countrymen,
and lived as they did. He had nothing to do with the
Essenes, and it was objected against Him that "thy
disciples fast not." It is very significant that allu-
sions to fasting have been interpolated in several places
in later manuscripts of the New Testament (Matthew
xvii, 21; Mark ix. 29; Acts x. 30; 1 Cor. vii. 5). Such
unscrupulousness is disquieting, since we cannot tell
whether this tampering with the sacred text in the interest of later ethical ideas began before the date of
our earliest manuscripts. There is no doubt that moral
maxims which seemed to the Church to be of a questionable tendency were in danger of being extruded from
the Canon. Examples are the story of the man found
working on the Sabbath, found in the Cambridge manuscript of St. Luke, and that of the woman taken in

adultery, which hovered half in and half out of the received texts.

But though there is no asceticism of the familiar kind in the Gospels, Christ emphasised the necessity of real detachment from earthly cares and bodily delights. He occasionally used very strong expressions, such as the duty of cutting off the right hand if it causes us to offend. Things that are innocent in themselves may be inexpedient for us; and this principle may involve very severe acts of renunciation.[1] We must neither whittle down such sayings too much, nor forget that Christ sometimes even spoke humorously, as in the well-known saying about the camel and the needle's eye. I doubt whether the expectation of the "day of the Lord," even if Christ Himself shared it, had much influence on His ethical precepts. Quite apart from this expectation, He recommended a very simple and natural mode of living, mainly on the ground that the pursuit of luxury and comfort is likely to occupy too much of our attention. It is quite clear that He never suggested that Peter and His own brothers should leave their wives; and they did not leave them.

The ascetic element in St. Paul requires more attention. The Apostle was confronted not only by the licentiousness of Pagan society, but by doctrines which condemned even marriage as unclean. As Dobschütz says,[2] to understand this line of thought we must realise that the ancient world saw something demoniacal in the act of generation. Sometimes, as in the cults of Astarte and Aphrodite, it was deified; sometimes

---

[1] Some modern critics have thought, as Origen did, that in extreme cases self-mutilation may be indicated as a safeguard against the sins of the flesh. But I am convinced that the words about those who "have made themselves eunuchs for the kingdom of heaven's sake" are not meant to be a precept for Christians.

[2] Dobschütz, "Christian Life in the Primitive Church," p. 40.

it was held to be a pollution. The rule that copulation involves one day of ceremonial defilement was widespread, and is acknowledged in the Mosiac Law. But the Christian, it was argued, must be clean always. St. Paul separates himself strongly from this view. He was a celibate himself, and it must be admitted that his scales were weighted on the side of celibacy, but he knows that he cannot appeal to any word of the Lord in disparagement of marriage. And so he ordains that if a married pair agree to a suspension of the marital relation, it must be only for a short time, and for the purpose of more intense devotion. As regards extra-marital indulgence, he is absolutely strict. In this he was only maintaining the view which had come to prevail among the Jews, though among the Gentiles it was seldom advocated, and very seldom observed. Musonius Rufus the Stoic condemns all indulgence outside marriage; Dion Chrysostom inveighs with righteous indignation against prostitution; Epictetus recommends complete chastity to those who are able to practise it. But St. Paul's demands must have sounded severe to his Gentile converts.

There are signs that some Christians were already aspiring to heroic feats of self-conquest. The enigmatic passage in 1 Cor. VII. 36 is best explained (as I said in the last chapter) as the earliest reference to a practice which afterwards became common, and which seems to be presupposed in a passage of the Didache. There were spiritual betrothals between an unmarried man and a maiden, who would sometimes share the same bed. St. Paul, without forbidding the practice, is aware that an honourable marriage is likely to be the most innocent end of such an experiment.

There had been a case of incest at Corinth, and St. Paul tried to deal with it by placing the offender under a ban, which, he seems to have expected, would be followed by his death, as in the case of Ananias and Sapphira recorded in Acts. This, however, did not occur.

But the most important aspect of St. Paul's injunctions about sexual morality is not the particular decisions which he made in circumstances of great difficulty, but the ground on which he bases the obligation to purity. Every Christian is, or should be, "a temple of the Holy Spirit." The Spirit of God dwells in us, unless we are reprobates. "The temple of God is holy, which temple ye are." The Holy Spirit, as Christ Himself had taught, cannot dwell in an impure soul; the shrine must be kept immaculate for His presence. No defilement whatever attaches to the normal relations of married people; but to be "joined to a harlot" does convey pollution; and so with all other irregularities. It cannot be emphasised too strongly that this is the source and sanction of the law of purity among Christians. The other motives which are frequently adduced as grounds of moral conduct are at best subsidiary. The decisive argument is that sexual transgressions defile the soul, and drive the Holy Spirit out of it. The question whether all extra-marital intercourse is necessarily contaminating is, as we all know, hotly debated in our day. There have always been very many who in practice have disregarded this part of Christian Ethics, and there are some now who openly repudiate it. This will have to be dealt with in a later chapter. Here it is only necessary to insist that in the New Testament the motive for continence is neither the wrong done to the other partner in the act, nor the ascetic motive of crushing the lower appetites, but the obligation to keep not only the soul but the bodily members pure from sin. "Shall I take the members of Christ, and make them the members of an harlot?" is St. Paul's most characteristic appeal.

In the matter of eating and drinking, the attitude of the apostle is surprisingly broad, liberal, and tolerant. "All things are lawful to me, but all things are not expedient. All things are lawful to me, but all things edify not." The question was raised in an acute form by the practical difficulty of being sure that butcher's meat had not been part of a Pagan sacrifice. The extreme scrupulosity of the Jews in these matters, down to the present day, and of Orientals generally, is well known. At the bottom of it was the superstition that "demons" might find an entrance into the body of him who consumed meat that had been offered to them. St. Paul reminds his consultants that "an idol is nothing in the world," though he does not quite follow this to its logical conclusion. To eat meat which the eater *knows* has been offered to "demons" is uncharitable, because it hurts the conscience of "the weak"; but otherwise it does no harm. The same liberty is claimed in the observance or non-observance of feast-days and fast-days. "One man esteemeth one day above another; another man esteemeth every day alike. Let every man be fully persuaded in his own mind. He that regardeth the day, regardeth it unto the Lord; and he that regardeth not the day, to the Lord he doth not regard it. He that eateth, eateth unto the Lord, for he giveth God thanks; and he that eateth not, to the Lord he eateth not, and giveth God thanks." We are sometimes irritated by St. Paul's controversies with Judaism, which we think no longer concern us. A comparison of this passage with the current Catholic and Anglo-Catholic teaching about the sinfulness (for example) of non-fasting communion should convince us that "traditions of the elders" are a permanent danger in religion, and that the exhortation to "Stand fast then in the liberty wherewith Christ hath made us free" is by no means unnecessary or out of date.

In one of his latest letters, that to the Colossians, we find St. Paul face to face with an ascetic movement of a somewhat different kind. In Galatia the enemy was Jewish legalism; at Corinth contamination with Paganism was chiefly feared. At Colossæ also there was a Judaising element, and attempts were made to enforce Old Testament rules about food; but the chief danger seems to have come from Oriental dualism. The Colossians were attracted not by obedience to cermonial ordinances, but by an arbitrary mortification of the flesh, which, the Apostle says severely, pretends to a harsh discipline of the body, but in reality leads to pride, and perhaps (the text in Col. ii. 23 is obscure and may be corrupt) even stimulates the desires which it wishes to destroy. He has come to see the danger of the wave of extreme asceticism which was sweeping over the East. It is not quite easy to reconcile this attitude with his earlier avowal that "I buffet my body and make it my slave"; but whereas this latter implies severe self-discipline to make him more worthy to be a preacher to others, the Colossian heresy was dualistic, and pointed to what was later called Gnosticism and Manicheism.

In the Apocalypse (xiv. 4) it is considered the highest state to have abstained altogether from the commerce of the sexes. This passage cannot be explained away; it proves that the cult of virginity was already established before the end of the first century.

Our knowledge of the wide movement called Gnosticism is very imperfect, and there has been a tendency to condemn it with too little discrimination. It was not the name of a single sect or heresy, but a very prevalent tendency in the thought and religious practice of the time. In speculation, it was a barbarised

Platonism, with a strong trend to metaphysical dualism. Its exaggerated asceticism, especially in matters of sex, may have been partly a reaction against the licentiousness of the age, which was stimulated by the institution of slavery. But the notion that the body and all its functions are impure does not really belong to European thought; it is an Oriental fancy. Redemption to the Gnostic meant the separation of what had been unnaturally conjoined; to the Christian it means the re-union of what had been unnaturally separated. The object being to win freedom from the solicitations of the senses, the majority looked to asceticism for deliverance; but there were some who, like a modern school of psychology, taught that "repression" is a mistake, and that the bodily cravings should be indulged, so that they may not be troublesome. Some Gnostic sects, especially the Carpocratians, were accused of carrying this method into practice in a very scandalous manner. Even in I Timothy IV. 3 (this Epistle is probably rather later than St. Paul) we hear of false teachers who "forbid to marry." The apocryphal writings of the second century are full of denunciations of marriage, and in them we find the beginnings of those inverted romances in honour of virginity which were evidently the favourite reading of many Christians.

The gospel of renunciation did not spare private property. The Carpocratians anticipated nineteenth-century Socialists in proclaiming that "*La propriété c'est le vol.*" Complete abandonment of all possessions was demanded. With this went a campaign for vegetarianism and abstinence from alcoholic drinks. Like some modern Americans, who alter "wine" into "raisin-cake" whenever it occurs in the Bible, the Gnostics, offended by the statement that John the Baptist ate locusts, altered one letter of the Greek word and made him eat "oil-cake." Christ could not have "desired to eat the Passover," so a negative was coolly inserted into Luke XXII. 15.

Abstinence from marriage, from wine and flesh, and renunciation of all private possessions, were the three main precepts of the "encratite" life, which was described as "bearing the whole yoke of the Lord." These were Gnostic tenets; but there was no fixed boundary between Christian and half Christian Gnosticism. The main distinction came to be that while the Catholic Church admitted the call of strict asceticism, but denied that it was obligatory upon all, or in any way necessary to salvation, the "sect-type" (as Troeltsch calls it) attempted to prove that these demands were made upon all Christians, and bore themselves arrogantly towards those who lived in the world. On the one side we have the double standard of morality—the easier standard which is "sufficient," and the heroic standard for those who wish to be "perfect." On the other side we have the desire to impose an impossibly heavy yoke on all who would be saved. The Catholic solution was the only possible one in the prevailing state of opinion. The ascetics were the popular heroes; it was much if the Church could declare that it was not the duty of ordinary people to imitate them.

As time went on, Christian Cynicism was practically confined to the hermitages and monasteries; but the cult of virginity rose higher and higher. Methodius, who was a pioneer in the East as Tertullian was in the West, represents virginity as the goal of the Incarnation. "Virginity is exceedingly great and wonderful and glorious, and to speak plainly, following the Holy Scripture, this most noble and fair practice is alone the ripe fruit, the flower and first-fruits of incorruption. And therefore the Lord promises to admit those who have preserved their virginity into the Kingdom of Heaven. For we must consider that virginity walks on earth, but reaches the heavens."

As Harnack says, it is difficult for us to form a conception of the hold which this form of asceticism possessed over the mind in the fourth and fifth centuries, or of the manner in which it influenced imagination, thought, and the whole of life. "Virginity was the specifically Christian virtue, and the essence of all virtues." Augustine does not really differ much from Jerome. We shall not understand the famous Confessions unless we realise that the mental struggle which convulsed him was not the choice between loose living on the one hand and the Christian rule on the other, but between normal sexual relationships, whether within or without marriage, on the one hand, and "virginity"—the life of a monk—on the other. In his time strict celibacy was already expected of Pagan philosophers; the apologies of Porphyry for his marriage are very instructive for the hold which asceticism had by this time gained even on Pagan society. Ambrose ignores this when he claims that virginity is that which is really original and most precious in Christian morality. "This virtue," he says, "is our exclusive possession. The heathens had it not; it is not practised by the barbarians who are not yet civilised; it is not found among any of the animals. We breathe the same air, we share in all the conditions of an earthly life, we are not distinguished from them in birth; we escape from the miseries of a nature similar to theirs only by our virgin chastity." The notion that the soul is the bride of Christ, to be kept spotless from any other love, was emphasised by Ambrose, and from him spread over the whole Church. It became the favourite dream of countless virgins of the cloister, whose meditations have been often quoted by modern psychologists as examples of transferred or sublimated eroticism.

Lecky has spoken, not too severely, of the repulsive language which the saints and Fathers of the Church habitually used about marriage. It is very rare, as Milman also points out, that the social and political aspects of marriage as an institution are alluded to. The attitude which they take up is purely individualistic. The only thing to be said for marriage, according to Jerome, is that it produces virgins for the next generation; otherwise, "virginity is the axe to cut down the wood of marriage." The physical details of copulation are dwelt upon in order to arouse disgust. "It was expressly enjoined" (as Lecky writes) "that no married persons should participate in any of the great Church festivals if the night before they had lain together, and St. Gregory the Great tells of a young wife who was possessed by a demon because she had taken part in a procession of St. Sebastian without fulfilling this condition. In the vision of Alberic, in the twelfth century, a special place of torture, consisting of a lake of mingled lead, pitch, and resin, is represented as existing in hell for the punishment of married people who had lain together on Church festivals or fast days." Since Lecky wrote, Ramsay and Hogarth have found Pagan inscriptions in Asia Minor which show that at heathen temples ritual pollution was incurred in the same manner.

It is plain that we have here something different from mere asceticism—namely, taboo-superstition. Anthropologists like Sir James Frazer have collected examples from all parts of the world of similar rules of temporary continence, not only before taking part in religious ceremonies, but also before engaging in the two most serious duties of the savage life, hunting and fighting. It would be wearisome to give details, since the rules vary only in degrees of severity. In some Red Indian tribes a youth who has taken his first scalp has to remain continent for six months. Abstinence before hunting or fishing is the rule in Uganda, the Upper Congo, New Guinea, East Africa, Mexico, British Columbia, Burma, the Marquesas Islands, among the Esquimaux, and in other places. Ceremonial impurity of this kind may sometimes be got rid of by auricular confession, which is regarded as a sort of spiritual purge or emetic. It is no small part of the strength of Catholicism that it appeals, under clever disguises, to some of the most barbarous and primitive racial thought-habits, which still operate subconsciously in the minds of many civilised persons. The feeling that there is something mysterious and uncanny about birth and death is easy to understand, and sympathetic magic extended the sentiment of awe which surrounds the beginning and end of life to the acts which determine such events, to procreation at one end and the taking of life at the other. Every thing or person offered to a deity must be ceremonially pure; the obligation is lifelong in the case of persons who are wholly in the service of a divine Being.

All the evidence shows that the movement towards asceticism was growing in the Hellenistic world independently of Christianity, and that so far from being a genuine Christian innovation, it invaded and captured Christianity as soon as the latter became a Hellenistic religion. It entered in through Gnosticism; the Great Church was compelled to compromise, though it did not encourage its most extravagant forms, but rather tried to check them. The ideal remained unchanged after the great barbarian invasions; but the era from the break-up of the Western Empire to the Reformation and Counter-Reformation seems to have been a time of almost unbridled sexual licence, in which the priests, monks, and nuns were not much better than the laity. Lea's "History of Clerical Celibacy" is considered by more recent historical students to give a fairly accurate picture of morality during the so-called ages of faith. A few saintly mystics lived in severe mortification; and after the Reformation there was a real improvement in the morals of the Roman clergy, which has lasted till the present day. It is now possible to insist on genuine celibacy for the priests, instead of providing each of them with a *focaria,* or "priestess," for the protection of his parishioners.

All students of human nature must be interested in the problem why practices so contrary to the ordinary pursuit of pleasure and happiness should fill so large a space in the history of mankind. It might be thought that the inevitable troubles of life are sufficient for us, without exercising our ingenuity to punish and torment ourselves gratuitously. This is the opinion of almost everybody in this comfort-loving age; but it most certainly has not been the opinion of everybody in former times. It is therefore important for the purpose of this book that we should consider the chief causes which have led men and women to leave the world, or, while living in it, to embrace a life of renunciation and onerous self-discipline.

In all religions a very important part must be assigned to the desire to *escape.* That man must be very well contented with himself and his surroundings who has not often longed, with the Psalmist, that he had the wings of a dove, that he might fly away and be at rest—at rest from the provoking of all men and the strife of tongues, from the competitive *mêlée* of claims and counterclaims, the ambitions, intrigues and anxieties of social life, even from the too insistent demands of friends and relations, and, last but not least, from himself. "Let us fly hence to our dear country," as the disciples of Plato have repeated one after another. There are a few people who are so well adjusted to their environment that they do not feel, or rarely feel, this nostalgia for the infinite. These are the naturally unmystical. They may be strict moralists; they may "live ever in their great Taskmaster's eye"; but the longings and aspirations, the blessed communions and the painful derelictions of the mystic are not for them. The majority, however, are not contented, and seek an escape in one way or another. Routine labour is a distraction for some; busy devotion to a cause satisfies others; many find relief in the insidious habit of day-dreaming; others turn to God when the world around them seems hostile, and find in prayer and meditation a sanctuary where they can be at peace.

But civilisation has sometimes passed through phases in which there were no "causes" to work for, and in which society has seemed to have no reason for its existence. We have seen that the decay of the ancient civilisation was such a time. Sir Samuel Dill[1] draws a vivid picture of the wretched conditions in the West of Europe after the barbarian invasions. The security of social life had been shattered. There was a portentous increase of poverty; and just as in the Cynic movement of the second century, broken man, without any real call to the religious life, sought a refuge in the monastery or hermitage from the hardships of a precarious existence. We must remember, as Sir Samuel Dill emphasises, the condition of society from which the recluse wished to escape. If of noble blood, he knew the ghastly secrets of great houses. If of meaner lot, he had felt the weight of despotism. Perhaps he had had his simple cottage burnt in a military raid; he had had his humble suit rejected by an

[1] Dill, "Roman Society in Gaul," p. 358.

unjust judge; he saw no way of escape except one. But higher motives were at work—a sense of disgust and futility even among youths and maidens to whom life offered the normal satisfactions; a nobler ideal than that of a pleasant life in the world opened before them; and very many broke away from their families to join some community of world-renouncing ascetics. Those who have visited such establishments as the group of monasteries on Mount Athos testify that these inducements to leave the world and live in pious seclusion are as strongly felt now, in some parts of the world, as they ever were. It does not seem to be true that the life of the cloister is usually unhappy, though beyond question the repression of natural instincts often produces morbid conditions of various kinds. Many are able to adapt themselves to the rigid routine of the "religious" life; their other tastes soon atrophy from disuse; and the inmates of the monastery or nunnery, who have become totally unfit for any other mode of existence, pass their time in inert contentment. A few derive a much more positive happiness from this strange manner of life. Hermas speaks of the joy which was a feature of many Christian ascetics in his time. And much later, the English mystic, Richard Rolle of Hampole, writes: "Men suppose that we are in torture and in penance great; but we have more joy and more very delight in one day than they have in the world all their life. They see our body, but they see not our heart, where our solace is. If they saw that, many of them would forsake all they have to follow us." The merry mood of the early Franciscans, who were called God's jesters—*ioculatores Dei*—is well known. To have made an irrevocable decision sometimes brings great lightness of heart.

Our moral judgments on this way of gaining peace must depend on our view of what is called mysticism.

If what the mystic calls communion with God is only a kind of delicious day-dreaming; if the state of mind into which he aspires to enter, and the experiences which come to him when he is in it, are purely subjective, we shall probably regard the life of renunciation and devotion with some impatience and contempt. We may grant that it brings peace and joy to those who pursue this course; but is it the kind of peace and joy which we should be justified in choosing for ourselves? Innumerable tasks remain to be fulfilled in the world outside. Should we not, as soldiers of Christ, select one or more of these, and try to leave some corner of the world better for our having lived in it? We may admit that this is good advice for the majority, and yet we may insist that the interior life is at least as important as the exterior; that "to pray is to labour"; that the exploration of the high places of the spiritual adventure is a quest of high value not only to the explorer but to the world generally; and above all, that the mystical experience may justly claim to be in fact what those who have enjoyed it always declare it to be, a genuine vision of those higher modes of existence which are out of our reach while we live here, but which are not entirely beyond the apprehension of "reason in her most exalted mood." It is only a very crude and materialistic calculation that will deny the debt of the world to the saints, who at the price of their heart's blood have augmented incalculably our possession of those higher values in which one man's gain is not another man's loss, and which the world can neither give nor take away.

The life of the cloister is regularly austere, but it does not necessarily involve deliberate self-punishment. This is usually added as a penance for sins already committed, or as a prophylactic against expected temptations. The notion that pain is an expiation of moral guilt is almost universal; it underlies the custom of offering sacrifices, and affects, sometimes unconsciously, our theories of punishment. It is a very natural thought that we may mitigate the just punishments which the Deity will inflict upon us in a future state of existence, by subjecting ourselves to voluntary suffering here on earth. But this is not all. There is a remarkable passage in St. Paul's Epistles in which the apostle says that he rejoices in his sufferings for the sake of his flock, and "fills up that which was lacking in the afflictions of Christ for his body's sake, the Church." The doctrine of the efficacy of vicarious suffering, based on this text, has played a large and noble part in Christian asceticism. Baron von Hügel gives one or two touching examples of it from his own experience. For example, a nun reclaimed a girl who was living in sin with a man, by flagellating herself every day until the girl could stand it no longer, and terminated the unlawful connexion. It is easy to object that a good God cannot be supposed to enjoy inflicting torture on those who disobey His will, and that a just God cannot be supposed to accept the suffering of one person as the expiation of the sins of another. But the logic of the heart is less uncompromising, and refuses to condemn the desire to suffer for the sins of the world.

It is less easy to answer the objection that the ascetic life presupposes a theory of the duty of man which is neither that of the New Testament nor that of modern ethical thought. To put it shortly, it presupposes the theory that our duty is before all things to avoid sin, mortal sin at all costs, and venial sin so far as possible. The plan of the ascetic life is to cut off all occasions of sin. Many Catholic divines have expatiated on the dreadful nature of sin in such a way that the whole of morality assumes a negative aspect, and manly virtue is mutilated or impoverished. Cardinal Newman, who had a curious love of presenting the paradoxes of Catholicism, the points in which Catholic Ethics conflict most violently with the moral ideas of secular society, in the most glaring and repellent form, wrote the following monstrous and absurd sentence. "The Church holds that it were better for sun and moon to drop from heaven, for the earth to fail, and for all the many millions who are upon it to die of starvation in extremest agony, so far as temporal affliction goes, than that one soul, I will not say should be lost, but should commit one single venial sin, should tell one wilful untruth, though it harmed no one, or steal one poor farthing without excuse." [1] This passage is a *reductio ad absurdum,* not of the belief that the dictates of conscience are absolute, but that the enlightened conscience takes no account of the tendency of our actions to promote or injure the temporal welfare of mankind. We shall find that this error has had a far-reaching effect on Catholic Ethics, and has helped to make them, on the whole, an impediment to civilisation and progress.

Although we may fairly answer the charge that the life of the saint is useless to the world by replying that in point of fact it is far from useless, it is not so easy to answer the charge that many of the saints did not care whether it was useless or not. We do not think that we were sent into the world to avoid venial sins. The talents committed to us are not to be wrapped up in a napkin, but to be put out to interest for the benefit of our fellows. We should ask not whether a man is good, but what he is good for.

> "Ci gît Louis, ce pauvre roi,
> On dit qu'il fût bon ; mais à quoi?"

[1] Newman, "Anglican Difficulties," p. 120.

There is indeed a profound difference between the type of character which Newman as a Catholic priest holds up for our admiration and that which he describes unsympathetically, but in language of wonderful truth and beauty, as the ideal of secular society, especially in England. [1] The character of a gentleman, as he describes it, needs much deepening and purifying to make it really Christian; but it is an insult to our ethical sense no less than to our ideas of good citizenship, to prefer, as he does, the dishonest and untrustful Irish beggar-woman "who is chaste and goes to Mass" above the honourable and actively useful man of the world. And when he adds that the main object of a gentleman is to present a decorous and graceful front to the world, he seems to misunderstand radically the mainspring of what is best in the English national character.

I have spoken of the desire to escape from our surroundings, and to avoid sin, as two of the chief motives of the ascetic life; and the craving for self-punishment as another. We must distinguish from these, as partially different, the desire for complete subjugation of the flesh, resting on the dualistic notion that the spiritual world is that state of existence which is wholly detached from the contamination of matter and the life of the senses. This is the side of asceticism which can be studied best in India; but it was prevalent in Egypt, the chief home of early eremitism. Pillar saints, like St. Simeon Stylites, were not a Christian innovation; Lucian mentions this curious custom. [2] But in the Christian Church, as Lecky says, "for about two centuries the hideous maceration of the body was regarded as the highest proof of excellence. A sordid and emaciated maniac, without knowledge, without patriotism, without natural affection, passing his life in a long

---

[1] Newman, "The Scope and Nature of the University Education."
[2] Lucian, "Syrian Goddess," p. 28.

routine of useless and atrocious self-torture, and quailing before the ghastly phantoms of his delirious brain, had become the ideal of the nations which had known the writings of Plato and Cicero and the lives of Socrates and Cato." That there was a thoroughly morbid side to these extravagances cannot be doubted. Modern psychology has invented the word masochism for that perversion of the sex-instinct which takes the form of self-torture. It does not seem to have been efficacious in rooting out the concupiscence which it specially aimed at destroying. The extremely unpleasant stories of how the monks and hermits dreaded the mere sight and approach of a woman, even of their own mothers and sisters, are almost the most revolting part of the mass of stories about these much-venerated men —stories some of which we may hope are untrue, but which, whether true or false, give a faithful picture of the kind of conduct which at that time was thought to indicate heroic virtue. A modern physician of the soul, prescribing for erotic obsessions, would recommend anything rather than a *régime* of solitude, idleness, and violent mortification. And yet even in these outrages upon human nature the spirit of emulation spurred on the ascetics, collected in their thousands in the desert, to surpass the austerity of their neighbours. If one man lived on the top of a low pillar, his neighbour must mount a higher one; if one dragged about a weight of eighty pounds, a rival would tie himself to a hundred and fifty pounds. One would become famous by living at the bottom of a well, another by wallowing in a marsh infested by mosquitoes. Some rolled in thorn-bushes, a sovereign remedy, it was thought, for the lust of the flesh; others went about on all fours, and tried to eat grass, like cattle. The force of collective mania, we may think, could no further go. It is certainly one of the strangest chapters in the history of mankind.

But there is one other motive which must not be overlooked, namely, the desire to induce the mystic trance. Plotinus, whose mysticism is based on a foundation of rationalism, regarded this ineffable experience as the very rare culmination of a long and intense spiritual and intellectual discipline. Much as he valued the few visions of the Absolute which had been granted him, for the sake of the wonderful feeling of blessedness and final achievement which they brought, the supreme vision was even more treasured as the experimental proof of his philosophy, which led up to the "One beyond existence." The Christian mystics were for the most part less patient. They came to expect these divine favours even at an early stage of their spiritual ascent. And it was soon found empirically that fasting, long prayer, and meditation, and especially mental concentration on a fixed point, were very conducive to these unusual states of consciousness. The joy of entering for a time into the immediate presence of God, as they believed, was so acute that they were very willing to submit to severe self-discipline in order to attain to it. It can hardly be doubted that here again grave psychological errors were committed. Attempts to force on artificially these very abnormal mental states inevitably lead to severe nervous reactions, in which the depression, wretchedness, and fear of being abandoned by God are quite as violent as the joys of the mystical state.

These seem to be the chief motives for adopting an ascetic discipline. The methods vary greatly. Enough has perhaps been said about the attempt to crush all sexual desires, which has had a profound influence upon Christian Ethics from the first. The obligation of continence, except in marriage, does not indeed rest, for Christians, on any ascetic discipline; it depends, as I have said, on the conviction that all indulgence outside marriage is in itself contaminating. But the ascetic motive has generally been present, especially in the very widespread doctrine, which is still held in the Roman Catholic Church, that celibacy or virginity is a higher state than marriage, so that a special reward in heaven is kept for those who have preserved their bodies throughout life free from this indignity. Almost the last traces of this belief, outside the Roman Church, seem to have disappeared in our own generation. The attitude of mind which was common in the early centuries is now almost unintelligible to us, and if we read the Fathers of the Church in bulk, and not in selections, we feel ourselves in an utterly strange atmosphere. The romances, once so popular, about brides who refused to live with their husbands, and husbands who enthusiastically agreed to "Platonic" marriages, prove to us how far we have travelled since those days. The question sometimes forces itself upon us, whether what we now call Christianity is the same religion as that which once went by the name. We could hardly claim that it is, if we had not the New Testament.

Silence was another method of mortification. It was known among the Greeks at least from the fourth century before Christ, and probably began with the familiar ritual silence, enjoined in the fear of ill-omened words. The monks and hermits vied with each other in counting the number of years since they last uttered a word. There is, as perhaps we might expect, not much evidence of this form of mortification among female devotees; but in certain male foundations it became an important part of the discipline, and this, I believe, is still true, especially in the houses of the Trappists and kindred establishments.

Abstention from food, or from some kinds of food and drink, is, of course, a very familiar and almost universal form of asceticism. Primitive peoples are generally very gluttonous when food is within reach, though they are capable of long fasts when they can get none. The Greeks were on the whole very abstemious; but the richer Romans were monstrous eaters, like the upper classes in England in the eighteenth century. Savages have so many superstitions about food that more than one origin may be found for the notion that fasting is meritorious or pleasing to the higher powers. The belief that it is a means to acquire supernatural faculties, and to learn secrets known only to divine beings, is very common. Westermarck mentions it as found among the Esquimaux, North American Indians, Zulus, Tunguses, and the Hebrews (Ex. xxxiv. 28; Deut. ix. 9; Dan. ix. 3). This belief is not mere superstition. It has been proved empirically that, as Chrysostom says, "Fasting makes the soul brighter, and gives it wings to soar on high." The fact is that most people who can procure food whenever they wish for it tend to eat too much. Many in our day who have tried the experiment of giving up flesh food have recorded that a lighter diet has added to their efficiency, and especially to their mental activity. Prolonged abstinence is no doubt an error in the opposite direction, but Shelley's words are true: "To this principle of the mind overshooting the mark at which it aims we owe all that is eminently base and excellent in human nature." Here and elsewhere we have to allow for the sub-conscious survival of very crude notions. In eating and drinking, barbarians believe, we take into ourselves the qualities of the creatures which we consume. The cannibal hopes to acquire the bravery of the enemy whom he has slain and eaten. The Coreans sometimes eat the flesh of the tiger, to make them more formidable to their foes. In other places hares are not eaten, for fear of acquiring their cowardice. The British parent encourages his boy to eat beef till he is blue in the face, to make him strong, like an ox. In some religions, communion with a god is to be achieved by eating his flesh, a notion which in a refined and symbolical form survives even among civilised peoples. So it is feared that ritual pollution may be involuntarily incurred by the food which is still in the stomach when the worshipper takes part in a religious or magical ceremony. Fasting on the day before an important rite is almost universal; when food has been taken, purges are sometimes prescribed in order to get rid of it. This primitive notion lies behind the rule of fasting communion, to which Catholics attach an otherwise unintelligible importance. The same persons who are shocked at the idea of communicating except on an empty stomach will be heard to remind the faithful that after the reception of the consecrated elements Christ is their guest in a literal sense, "for a time," the time being that occupied in the natural process of digestion. Where animals are sacrificed, these also have to be ritually "clean." Fasting after a death is mentioned in 2 Sam. 1. 12, and is an almost universal custom. Various explanations have been given, such as the fear of swallowing the spiritual contagion diffused by the near presence of death. But a strong motive is undoubtedly the wish to grieve with the dead, and to show sympathy by abstaining for a time from bodily pleasure. The initiation-fasts of savages, such as the aboriginal Americans and Australians, are often exceedingly severe. Fasting before and after a birth is also very common; and as the husband has usually to fast as well as the wife, it is not easy to find an explanation. It is akin to the strange superstition of the *couvade*. It is equally difficult to explain the apparently arbitrary prohibitions of certain kinds of food to certain persons, *e.g.* women and young boys, either at all times or at some periods. In all such cases we may perhaps say that it is futile to hunt for explanations of practices for which those who obey them are quite unable to give any reason, except, "such is our custom." The tyranny of fashion is a sociological fact of the utmost importance. Horror of innovations may have a great survival-value in primitive societies, and this conservative instinct may give the true explanation of many customs, absurd and mischievous in themselves, which are preserved by it, sometimes for thousands of years.

When we turn to the historical evolution of fasting in the Christian Church, we find that Christ left no regulations about fasting, except that when practised it should be secret and unostentatious. He is recorded to have fasted for "forty days"—*i.e.* for a considerable time, before the beginning of His ministry, and we may assume that He observed the one obligatory fast in the Jewish Calendar, on the day of Atonement. It is almost certain that He did not "fast twice in the week," like the Pharisees; for it was objected against Him that "the children of the Pharisees fast, but thy disciples fast not." For a long time after the foundation of the Christian Church fasting was quite unregulated, and St. Paul, as we have seen, lays down the rule that every individual must be allowed to obey his own conscience in the matter. Barnabas, Justin Martyr, Hermas, and Clement of Alexandria give warnings against making it an external practice. The true fasting is to serve the Lord with a pure heart.

The duty of abstaining from flesh and wine was much discussed at this time. The Peripatetics, Stoics, and Epicureans allowed the eating of flesh; the Pythagoreans and most of the Platonists forbade it. Plutarch and Porphyry were convinced vegetarians. The Philonic Therapeutæ and most of the Egyptian Christians took the same view, as did the Gnostics generally. St. Paul says that the Christian is free, but must "walk charitably." The First Epistle to Timothy recommends Timothy to "take a little wine" for the sake of his health.

The custom of fasting before a religious festival is ancient, and is not always due to the superstition mentioned above. Hooker doubtless explains the custom rightly. The fasts were set as "ushers of festival days, to temper the mind, lest contrary affections should make it too profuse and dissolute." The accentuation of fasting, and the enactment of precise rules about it, were principally due to the Montanists; it is a remarkable instance of the partial victory gained by heretical and schismatical movements over the Great Church, which was on the whole on the side of sanity and moderation. The Montanists attached special importance to "xerophagy," which means abstinence from anything juicy or liquid, except water.

The long Lenten fast took root slowly, after much diversity of practice. It was at first short and mild; the period of forty days was, of course, chosen in imitation of the fast of Christ before the Temptations. The practice of the Church became stricter after the end of the persecutions, in the fourth and fifth centuries. It was then that the observance of Friday, and also of Wednesday, as fasts became the rule of the Church. Saturday too was often kept as a fast in the West; the observance of the Rogation and Ember Days is peculiar to the West. In the sixth century, the season of Advent began to be observed, but seldom as a regular fast, except in the rule of some monastic orders. Bede mentions that some devout persons fasted for forty days before Christmas. The Wednesday fast was gradually discontinued.

In the Eastern Church the rules about fasting are now more severe, and apparently more strictly observed. The Wednesday and Advent fasts are still obligatory, but Advent is much less rigorously observed than Lent. Travellers in Eastern Europe have observed that in common estimation fasting is of more importance than the weightier matters of the law, such as honesty, truthfulness and chastity.

These rules do not seem to have had much effect in checking the gluttony and drunkenness of the barbarians who overran the Western Roman Empire. The "Penitentials" give an extremely unfavourable impression of the manners of the clergy as well as of the laity in the Dark Ages. Westermarck gives references for the following tariff of punishments. A bishop who has been so drunk as to vomit while celebrating the Eucharist is to do ninety days' penance, a presbyter seventy days, a monk or a deacon while assisting at the same service sixty days, a clerk forty days. To impose any kind of dietary discipline upon such savages must have been useful; there is not much evidence whether the rules were strictly kept by the laity.

Modern fasting, at least in the West, is almost always more symbolical than real. Even the substitution of fish for flesh, which Queen Elizabeth sought to enforce on the ingenious ground that we must encourage the fisheries, is so managed as to be no hardship at all. In fact, anyone who does not allow for the principle of substitution in religion, which has enabled human sacrifices and other morally revolting customs to be abrogated without shocking the intense conservatism of the devout mind, will be tempted to think contemptuously of the "fasting" Catholic, who sometimes performs his or her austerities with the help of a French cook. Such sham fasts are morally worthless, and do none of the good which we have admitted in genuine acts of abstinence. We can only say on the other side that it is useful to assure ourselves that there is something, no matter what, which we are willing to do or not to do out of loyalty to the institution to which we belong. In the absence of such tests, it may become difficult to point to any single action which we perform simply because we are Churchmen. The Roman Church fully understands the value, for an institution, of these small but frequent tests of obedience.

A repulsive but not unimportant branch of asceticism is the deliberate cult of dirt. Our disgust at the filthiness of the ancient saint may be somewhat modified if we remember how recent is our extreme care for cleanliness. In countries where water is scarce, the cleanliness which we owe to the Western bath-room is impossible. Even the ancient Greeks were probably much less particular than we now are. Until quite modern times body-vermin were rather a joke than an object of horror. Not to speak of the condition of Thomas à Becket's shirt, and of the cassock of St. Francis of Assisi, we may remember that Samuel Pepys and his wife were "very merry" one morning when they found that they had been sleeping in a lousy bed. Medieval soldiers would not have suffered so acutely from the lice in the trenches as the Western armies did in the Great War, though Æschylus mentions this as one of the hardships of the campaign before Troy. [1] Gibbon is amused by Julian's boast that "his beard was populous," but I am inclined to think that the emperor was jesting. The Pagans did not make a cult of filth as such. Even Epictetus, who was more Neo-Cynic than Stoic, exhorts his disciples to be clean and sweet in person. Christian monasticism made no such sacrifice to decency. Augustine, who was a gentleman and a cultivated man, advises some nuns not to wash frequently, but at the usual intervals, that is to say, once a month. This would certainly have seemed quite sufficient to fine ladies at the time of the Renaissance and later. Queen

---

[1] Æschylus, "Agamemnon," 562. I have no doubt this is the meaning of ἔνθηρον.

Elizabeth is said to have neglected to clean the inside of the cup which she decked with such elaborate splendour; and one of the mistresses of Louis XIV was constrained to remonstrate with her royal lover for the extreme pungency of his close proximity. Dr. Samuel Johnson confessed that he "did not love immersion." But Jerome went much further. While living as a hermit in Syria, he tells us, "my skin was covered with such a coating of dirt that I looked like a negro." Lecky gives more evidence to the same effect.

Tortures like those of the Indian fakirs were not only common in the East; they spread to the far West. An Arvernian anchorite walled himself up for years, so as never to be seen. Another loaded himself with chains in a prison, festering with sores and crawling with vermin; another carried a large stone on his shoulders day and night. A pillar-saint boasted of his exploits of endurance to Gregory of Tours. [1] To expatiate on these tortures would be unpleasant and unnecessary; a terrible example may be found in the life of the mystic Suso. But other medieval mystics were more sane. There is a sensible passage on the subject in Hylton's "Scale of Perfection."

Self-flagellation seems to have been introduced first in religious houses in Central Italy. It is not enjoined by Benedict, but became more and more common from the eleventh and twelfth centuries. "It was reduced to a fine art at Fonte Avellana by Dominicus, surnamed Loricatus, about 1050."[2] Zöckler enumerates the prescribed number of strokes; the most complete course went up to three million. We may hope that the skin of the devotee became leathery enough not to feel very much[3]. Processions of Flagellants in the fourteenth

---

[1] Dill, "Roman Society in Gaul," p. 356.
[2] Hastings, "Dict. of Religion and Ethics," *s.v.* "Asceticism."
[3] Zöckler, "Askese," p. 529 *n.*

and fifteenth centuries poured over the country; but there had been an earlier outbreak about 1259, of which Salimbene writes: "The Flagellants went through the whole world. All men, small and great, noble knights and men of the people, scourged themselves naked in procession through the streets, with the bishops and men of religion at their head; peace was made in many places, and men restored what they had unlawfully taken away; and they confessed their sins so earnestly that the priests had scarcely leisure to eat. In their mouths sounded words of God and not of man, and their voice was as the voice of a multitude." The outbreak in the fourteenth century, which spread westwards from Hungary, seems to have been occasioned partly by the approach of the terrible plague called the Black Death. The bands of Flagellants marched to the music of hymns, some of which became popular. The epidemic subsided gradually, and was actively discouraged by the hierarchy. But as a means of self-discipline, either in penitence for sin or as a prophylactic, it is by no means extinct in Roman Catholic countries. There has even been a curious recrudescence of collective self-flagellation in Spanish America, among the Hermanos Penitentes of New Mexico and Colorado (1850-1890). The Russian Klysty are also Flagellants.

It is doubtful whether any experienced director would now recommend flogging as a remedy for the temptations of sex. The normal result of it, whether practised on self or on another, is to stimulate this appetite in a violent manner. Some schools have abolished corporal punishment for this very reason. Mr. Graham Wallas says that when the pain-nerves have been for a long time unstimulated, a man or boy may find the sensation of pain actually pleasant. "I can myself remember," he says, "being one of a group of boys who one evening varied the intolerable monotony of boarding-school prep. by running needles through the lobes of our ears in order to enjoy the sensation. Most people can understand how the monks and nuns came to long for the smart of the scourge."

What was called poverty, and was really renunciation of all private possessions whatever, may be reckoned as one kind of asceticism. It would be true to say that the only experiments in communism which have ever had any success have been in the monasteries, where the two conditions of a religious basis and of celibacy make the system much easier to work than in ordinary society.

It is not surprising that all this denudation of life should sometimes have produced an actual longing for death. But it would, I think, be more scientific to attribute the *tædium vitæ* and the desire to escape from life in the world, which were at one time common, to the same cause or causes, whatever these may have been. For it was not confined to the Christians, and it appeared before asceticism was systematised. Seneca speaks of *libido moriendi,* and several instances are recorded of suicide for trivial reasons. Clement of Alexandria blames those who "rush on death"; and readers of Gibbon will remember the passage in Tertullian: "When Arrius Antoninus was driving things hard in Asia, the whole Christians of the province in one united band presented themselves before his judgment-seat —on which, ordering a few to be led to execution, he said to the rest, O miserable men, if you wish to die, you have precipices or halters. . . ." Epidemics of suicide —and this was nothing else—are by no means uncommon.

The Cynic Peregrinus caused himself to be burnt alive before a wondering crowd at the Olympic festival. His end is described, with no sympathy, by Lucian, who looked upon his sacrifice as a telling finale to a career of self-advertisement and charlatanism. But it seems not to have been an isolated instance, for St. Paul, in 1 Cor. XIII., says, "Though I give my body to be burned, and have not charity, I am nothing." St. Paul, as a Roman citizen, was never in any danger of being burned alive; the reference is probably to theatrical self-immolation, like that of Peregrinus.

Unhappily, the passion for mortification was not confined to the body. The sacrifice of the intellect to authority was also commended as a gift acceptable to God. Hence in part came that horrible blasphemy against the divine endowment of reason, which makes it so fatally easy for a priesthood to nip in the bud any revolt against the absurdities which the disciple is required to accept. "What must be the face-to-face antagonist," asks Cardinal Newman, "by which to withstand and baffle the all-corroding, all-dissolving energy of the intellect? . . . What is intellect but a fruit of the Fall, not found in paradise or Heaven, more than in little children, and at the utmost but tolerated by the Church, and only not incompatible with the regenerate mind." [1] It seems almost incredible that this obscurantism should have been echoed by a secular philosopher, Henri Bergson, who writes, *"L'intelligence est caractérisée par une incompréhension naturelle de la vie."* [2]

Nevertheless, I do not believe that the early Christians were the chief obscurantists of their time, and I think that great injustice has been done them in this particular. There was a movement of anti-intellectualism among the Pagans of the first century. When Seneca exclaims, with reference to philosophical problems, *"Quid mihi ista lusoria componis? Ad miseros*

---

[1] Newman, "Parochial and Plain Sermons," Vol. 5.
[2] Bergson, "Evolution Créatrice," p. 179.

advocatus es," we might be listening to a twentieth century popular divine. Plutarch, or rather his revered father, thinks that "the ancient faith is enough; if you begin to criticise, there is no knowing where you will stop." The Christian Platonists of Alexandria, and the Cappadocians, not to speak of Augustine, were anything rather than obscurantists. The "sacrifice of the intellect" came later, and belongs, not to asceticism, but to the subject of my next chapter.

An important change in Christian aceticism followed its capture by the hierarchy. From the time of the martyrs the saint had been very independent of the Church. Mysticism, with the discipline which it involved, had been almost an alternative road to heaven, a rival of Church and Sacrament. To a large extent this has always been and always must be so. Mysticism is independent of time, place, nationality, and creed. In reading extracts from great mystics we might often be in doubt whether the writer was a Neoplatonist, a Sufi, a Buddhist, a Catholic, or a Quaker. Mysticism is pure religion. For this reason the great Churches have never been able to do without it, and yet have never been able to control it entirely or subordinate it to their aims. It has been throughout a rival to every monopolist claim, a potential enemy to all priestcraft. But the medieval Church was on the whole successful in harnessing this unruly force. We need only think of the scholastic mystics, Bonaventura, Albertus Magnus, and the Victorines, and of Thomas à Kempis. Still more successfully was monastic asceticism ecclesiasticised. The monasteries became for a time more active, more charitable, more learned, and less austere. At the same time discipline was from an early date employed very vigorously against those who had broken Church rules. Mr. O. D. Watkins, in his "History of Penance," writes: "A remarkable accompaniment of penitential discipline in the West was the imposition upon penitents, even when reconciled, of grave disabilities extending over the whole term of life. These are first prominently mentioned in the letter of Siricius, Bishop of Rome, (A.D. 384–398). No person who has been a penitent may marry, and if already married he may not resume cohabitation. No such person may undertake military service, or engage in trade, or attend the games of the circus." It is, however, hardly credible that these rules were enforced.

The capture of asceticism by the institutional Church has worked in the direction of mildness. A developed legalism always operates against real asceticism, though it revels in light penances which are effective and not too difficult tests of obedience. Stricter rules are recognised for the few who wish to follow them, but compromises with the lay world are freely admitted. Hence the great development of which is called symbolic asceticism, in which the element of bodily deprivation and suffering is reduced to a minimum. Among the Jesuits, asceticism has a different motive. Its object being the conquest of the world, not flight from the world, the exercises are disciplinary, intended to make those who practise them more efficient and more completely submissive to their superiors.

The attitude of the Reformers, and of the Reformed Churches, towards asceticism has recently been much discussed. Troeltsch and other German scholars have drawn a necessary distinction between the teaching of Luther and that of Calvin, and they have shown that it was no accident if the Calvinist countries have shown far greater readiness to adapt themselves to the conditions of modern industrial society than either the Catholics or the Lutherans. It has even been said that the successful business man, if he is not a son of the Ghetto, is usually a grandson of John Calvin.

Luther, who had known the monastic life from inside, reacted strongly against it. He allows very little value to self-chosen austerities. It is better to sweep a room carefully than to fast and flog oneself in a cloister. He is not opposed to self-denial, but he insists that the demands of Christianity in this as in other ways apply to all Christians. Like theologians of the "sect-type" (to which in other ways he does not belong), he rejects the double standard of morality. There is, however, one important branch of Christian Ethics in which his language is coarse, shocking, and quite unchristian —namely, that of sex. He denied the possibility of continence. *"Wer seiner Mist oder Harn halten müsste, so er's doch nicht kann; was soll aus dem werden?"* His remedy is universal marriage; he wished to stone adulterers. But if the wife is not "bonere and buxom," as our First Prayer Book has it, the husband is excused. *"Wollt nicht deine Frau? So kommt das Magd!"*

Troeltsch rightly insists that in the Protestantism of the sixteenth century the implications of the ascetic idea have not disappeared, but only changed their form. In many ways the Reformers belonged to the middle ages, not to the modern world. Lutheranism did away with the two planes of Christian morality, mainly because Luther saw in separation from the world an illegitimate simplification of duty. But he never accepted the world as moderns tend to do. On the contrary, he preached self-denial and submission, a transference of all hope to the future life, and a glad acceptance of persecution. And yet the principle on which this attitude rested was so undefined that Lutheranism has, on the whole, been found consistent with a hearty acceptance of the good things of the present life.

In the writings of Calvin, a strong and steady self-control, reaching to every department of life, is advocated. All the elect are bound to strive after perfection. Self-denial in itself is not meritorious; but he who wishes to promote the Kingdom of Christ will be temperate in all things. The Christian will not abstain from what is necessary or useful; but he will be very sparing in any pleasures which go beyond these limits. In the typical Calvinist, as I have said elsewhere, we find a vigorous political interest, but not for the sake of the State; a steady diligence in labour, but not for the sake of riches; a careful, often intrusive social organisation, but not for the sake of increasing human happiness; a zeal for productivity without any great interest in the objects of production. This gives a peculiar character to all societies based on Calvinism. On the one side, almost for the first time the dignity of work as work is upheld, and on the other, since the value of work is not measured with reference to any ulterior motive, there is sometimes a strange blindness to the maladjustments of industrial society.

The weakness of the system is not so much that it makes life gloomy, as that it does not rationalise production. Productive activity in business is regarded as the typically godly life, and it is assumed rather too hastily that what is good discipline for the individual is good for society. Hence civilisation under Calvinism is characterised by an intense but rather unintelligent activity; there is great confusion as to the objects of communal life and its true values.

I have said that the Reformers rejected the double standard of moral excellence which was accepted by Catholicism. This double standard rests ultimately on the words of Christ to the rich young man, "If thou wilt be perfect, sell all thou hast and give to the poor"; and perhaps also on another saying in connexion with ascetic practices: "He that is able to receive it, let him receive it." It was indeed the expedient by which the

Great Church was able to make concessions to Gnosticism and similar movements without being entirely captured by them. That some are called to a higher degree of saintliness, a more heroic standard of virtue, than others seems obviously true. It could be denied only by minimising the merit of ascetic virtue on the one hand, and by raising the standard of what will pass muster on the other. The Reformers wished to do both. But it may be worth while to quote a typical explanation of what the two lives meant in the early Church. The following paragraph is from the "Apodeixis" of Eusebius, in the fourth century, probably about 315 A.D.

"The disciples, accommodating their teaching to the minds of the people, as the Master commanded, delivered to those who were able to receive it the teaching given by the perfect Master to those who rise above human nature; the other side of the teaching was meant for persons still in the world and in need of treatment. So they made allowances for the weakness of the majority, and told them, either in writing or orally, what rules they ought to keep. Two ways of life were thus given by the law of Christ to His Church. The one is above nature and common human living. It admits not marriage, child-bearing, property, nor the possession of wealth, but wholly and permanently separate from the customary life of men, devotes itself to the service of God alone, in its wealth of heavenly love. They who enter upon this course seem to die to the life of mortals, to bear with them nothing earthly but their body, and in mind and spirit to have passed to heaven. Like superior beings they gaze on human life, and discharge the office of priests to God for the whole race. . . . The other life, more humble and more human, permits men to unite in pure marriage and to have children, to undertake office, to command soldiers who are fighting in a good cause; it allows them to attend to farming, trade, and other secular interests. . . . A kind of secondary piety is attributed to them, giving such help as their lives require." A very significant passage follows, illustrating the indifference of the Christians to the future of humanity in this world. "The men famous for goodness before Moses lived when human life was first beginning and organising itself. We live when it is near its end. They therefore were anxious for the increase of their descendants, and that the race might grow and flourish. But these things are of very little interest to us, who believe the world to be perishing and running down and nearing its last end . . ., while a new creation and the birth of another age is foretold at no distant time."

But it must not be supposed that there was no asceticism of a more traditional kind among Protestants. We read that John Fletcher of Madeley (1729–1785), a typical Evangelical of the eighteenth century, sat up two nights every week for reading, meditation and prayer, and lived wholly upon vegetable food. William Wilberforce also led a very austere life, and it would be easy to find many other instances in that century and in the early part of the nineteenth. The founders of the Oxford Movement also led extremely simple lives, and some of them, like Pusey, even returned, as a remedy against special temptations, to rough medieval methods of buffeting the body. Within the last fifty years, it would be safe to say, real austerities have almost vanished from all sections of the Anglican Church, and no doubt also from the Free Churches.

We cannot leave this subject without noticing the queer, almost arbitrary rules and prohibitions which have taken the place of the older asceticism in the Protestant countries. Such prohibitions were common among the Gnostics, and they have been revived wherever the "sect-type" has appeared in Church history. But they are a strange phenomenon in the highly civilised and very self-indulgent societies of our own day. The history of the Puritan Sunday, often called the Sabbath, might fill a volume. Sabbatarianism still lingers, as a strongly felt conscientious scruple, among many simple folk; but the tradition has broken down almost completely in English society as a whole, and even in Scotland the days seem far distant when Bismarck complained that he was rebuked in London for whistling on Sunday. The indignant statesman, by an unfortunate inspiration, took the next train for Edinburgh! There is, of course, not the slightest reason to think that because the Jews were forbidden to work on the seventh day of the week Christians are forbidden to play on the first day. But the reservation of set days for religious observance and abstention from week-day occupations has been found so helpful that it is foolish to ridicule the Protestant Sabbath. In spite of the absurdities often connected with it, many elderly people remember with gratitude the weekly interruption of tasks and recreations which was imposed upon them in their youth, and doubt gravely whether the adoption of what used to be called the Continental Sunday has been an advantage. Meanwhile, the whole of the workers now claim a weekly day of rest for other than religious reasons; and practically no one is found to advocate a seven-day working week. The Sunday is therefore secure, whether God is remembered on that day or not.

Card-playing, theatre-going, and attending race-meetings were all tabooed by the Evangelicals, but reasons might, no doubt, be found in each case. There was, however, a real distrust of pleasure as pleasure. I think I have read that when Sir Walter Scott, as a child, said that he liked the soup, half a pint of cold water was poured into it. Children were kept away from the fire in cold weather, and if flagellation had gone out of fashion in the monasteries, it was religiously practised in schools and in the home. Light literature was forbidden, apparently on the ground that it was "not true."

But nothing is more characteristic of militant Protestantism than the embittered campaigns against alcohol and tobacco. We may grant that excess in alcoholic drinks is very common, and that many lives have been ruined by it. But a moderate consumption of alcohol could not be called sinful by any reasonable man. Nevertheless, it is treated as if it were a deadly sin by the fanatics of "temperance," who have even induced one great nation to attempt to abolish it altogether. The same set of fanatics are now trying to forbid cigarette-smoking, and perhaps all use of tobacco. It is very significant that these "fads," and the attempt to enforce them on everybody, are hardly known in Catholic countries. They are chiefly Anglo-Saxon, and specially characteristic of those who in England are called nonconformists. We have already found that it is a mark of the sect-type to allow no secondary Christian morality—no pass-examination for the weaker brethren. What is right for some is right for all. This view does not make for liberty and toleration. It cannot be doubted that, for some occult reason, far more indignation is aroused by the transgression of an artificial rule, some tradition of the elders, than by laxity in keeping the weightier matters of the law. The most harmless action may acquire by association a symbolical guilt, which makes the performance of it distressing to the beholder. The anti-tobacconist, whose favourite text is "Worship the Lord with clean lips," may feel actually sick at the smell of a cigar, just as some of the monks and hermits experienced physical disgust at the sight of a woman.

We may now take a general look over the strange field in which we have been wandering. Two things are certain: one that in Christianity, as lived and practised, asceticism has held a very prominent place; and the other that the majority of Christians in the twentieth century neither practise it nor feel any qualms at having discontinued it. The first of these two statements has been abundantly proved even by the cursory survey which is all that I could find room for in this book. For centuries asceticism, and especially the cult of virginity, seemed both to the Christians themselves and to their Pagan neighbours the most original and distinctive feature of their religion. For many more centuries, even down to our own day, abstinence from marriage has been, in the greatest of Christian Churches, indispensable to the highest reputation for sanctity. Objection may be taken to my second statement, that asceticism has now been generally abandoned. But I cannot allow that either the petty dietary rules of the Catholics, or the various little taboos of the sectarian Protestants, deserve to be called ascetic practices. Nor, in spite of the derivation of the name, which merely means training, can we justly use the word of that care for physical and mental fitness which induces many people to diet themselves strictly and practice systematic muscular exercises. The motive is different. The last fragment of real asceticism in the average Englishman's life (I am speaking especially of the large middle class) was the cold bath in winter. The hot-water tap in the modern bath-room has killed even this survival.

This is one of the rather sudden breaks with tradition which make it plausible to say that we are no longer Christians. It is my object in this book in no way to extenuate the almost revolutionary changes which separate the new Christian Ethics from the old, but to show, what is at least my own strong conviction, that traditional Christian Ethics had wandered a long way from the original Gospel, and that in paying respect to the enlightened conscience of our own time we may often find ourselves coming back nearer to the religion of Christ and His Apostles. There is not the slightest reason to think that Christ would have commended Simeon Stylites, or Henry Suso, or the Flagellants. He would probably have laughed heartily at the American prohibitionists, when they begged Him to reverse His miracle at Cana in Galilee.

There are a few pages near the beginning of H. G. Wells' "Mankind in the Making" which express so admirably our deep alienation from the old asceticism on its most important side—its horror of procreation—that I shall take the liberty of transcribing his argument in an abbreviated form. It is, he says, one of the chief discoveries, or rather rediscoveries, of our age that we are only the transitory custodians of an undying life, which it is our privilege and duty to hand on. In some of the noblest books of antiquity, such as the Meditations of Marcus Aurelius, we are repelled when he exhorts himself to blot from the page, as non-significant, "unborn to-morrow and dead yesterday." "The whole literature of the world," says Mr. Wells, "until the nineteenth century had well progressed, is lacking in any definite sense of the cardinal importance of births, and of the training and preparation for future births." Schopenhauer realised it, and being an intensely egotistical man, he was made miserable by it. But we may avail ourselves of his vision without submitting to his pessimism. This is obviously a telling illustration of what I have said already, that the ancient world was blind on one side, seeing no future for mankind. It is only a long view of history that is likely to be comforting, and the ancients had no long views. The modern man cannot with a clear conscience try to lead the life of a disembodied spirit, repudiating his obligations as the temporary custodian of a precious deposit. The old mystic's epigram, "He to whom time is as eternity, and eternity as time, is delivered from all stress," ignores the fact that the time-process is real and significant for those who are sent to live in it, and that its significance extends far beyond the span of single lives.

Nevertheless, when all is said that can or ought to be said against the strangest aberration in all human history, there are profound truths in the ascetic ideal, which modern civilisation is neglecting at its great peril. In the first place, a cheap Gospel is doomed to ineffectiveness; religion demands real sacrifices of pleasure and comfort. And it is good that there should be specialists in this as in every other pursuit. There is such a thing as a vocation to the saintly life. The renunciations which we sometimes suppose to have been made from a perverse love of being miserable were mostly made in order to concentrate the mind and will on the supreme quest. The parable about the pearl of great price was often quoted. We do not think this degree of concentration on some great worldly gain unintelligible or foolish, though we may not be willing to go into such severe training ourselves. The pursuit of holiness is surely at least as worthy an object as any vulgar success. As a matter of fact, it does not lead to disillusionment, but to peace and happiness.

We have heard a great deal lately about the unwisdom of "repression." We are told that when one tendency or part of experience has been driven into the subconscious, and held under by voluntary effort, it is always striving to come to the surface again. The result is not peace of mind and good health, but various neuroses and psychoses which can be relieved only by liberating the imprisoned tendency. Most psychologists think that this theory has actually thrown light on some obscure disorders of the personality, and that it has indicated a hopeful line of treatment in many cases. But it is obviously very liable to abuse, if it falls into the hands of persons who want an excuse for indulging their appetites.

Against these we must insist that our nature is not harmonious to start with, and that no harmony can be achieved by giving the rein to every instinct, impulse, and desire. The disorderly mob of desires must be controlled by the central authority of what the Stoics called the ruling principle—the dedicated conscience. This subjection involves real repression, which is not less real if some substitute for the repressed instinct is found by what is called sublimation.[1] The thwarted instinct may find an outlet on a morally higher level; but to begin with, it has often to be treated as an enemy or a rebel. Nor does victory over the animal nature always exempt us from further and perhaps harder struggles. Cassian says: "The athlete of Christ, as long as he is in the body, is never in want of a victory to be gained in contests; but in proportion as he grows by triumphant success, so does a severer kind of struggle await him." In the spiritual warfare there is no exemption for those over fifty.

One reason why this troublesome conflict is thrust upon us seems to be biological. We have changed our habits more quickly than our natures. Just as our bodies are not fully adjusted to our modern practice of walking on our hind legs instead of on all fours, so there are disharmonies in our mental constitution. We need both the self-regarding and the other-regarding instincts, but no one can say that they are harmonised in our experience. The herd-instinct, which makes us gregarious, discourages individual freedom, checks experiment, and

[1] Compare the passage quoted from Mr. Urwick's "Social Good," in Chapter VI.

encourages pugnacity against other groups. These difficulties call for rigid self-control and self-discipline.

The idea of getting and spending at high pressure, which in America is sometimes called "consumptionism," is barbarous and unchristian. The simple life, with the leisure for thought and communion with God which is its reward, is the life that Christians ought to live. Many have thought that voluntary poverty, accepted by a few high-minded persons as the most desirable state, would be a valuable protest against the crude mammon-worship and vulgar luxury of our time. The simple life is not the ascetic life in the severer sense; it only means the renunciation of what is superfluous and not helpful towards the higher ends of life. It conforms more nearly to the Puritan than to the Catholic form of asceticism.

Does not the problem really resolve itself into two questions: (1) What are the proper limits of specialisation? and (2) How far are what we call the lower experiences a help, and how far are they a hindrance, to the higher life?

We are familiar with the criticism of our civilisation, that it divides not only labour but the labourer. In striving after the maximum of mass-production, we often forget that the personality of the worker is cramped, starved, and mutilated. Very few are allowed to develop their whole faculties harmoniously. Success in almost any field requires this disastrous renunciation in all directions except one. Are we not in danger of falling into that condition in which "wealth accumulates, but men decay"? And does not the same objection apply to the exclusive pursuit of "a fugitive and cloistered virtue"? Does it not produce stunted and warped specimens of humanity? To this two answers may be given, which do not pretend to justify the excesses of asceticism, on which a plain verdict has been given in this chapter. A certain mental impoverishment must be accepted as the necessary price of specialisation. We all have to learn some particular trade, and to lose something by not knowing something of all other trades. This is the tax which we have to pay for living in society, with the advantage of profiting by the skill of all the other specialists whom we employ. But the evil of specialising may easily be exaggerated. Almost any work that is well done takes on a universal quality; it educates us more widely than its restricted scope might lead us to expect. A broad mind is not much cramped by a narrow sphere. I do not defend the life of a recluse of whom it might be said, in the words of Parnell's "Hermit," "Prayer all his business, all his pleasure praise"; for such prayers and praises must surely be very empty; but the true saint is generally a man of warm sympathies and a shrewd judge of human nature. The same is usually true of great scholars and scientific workers; though I'm afraid I cannot include the mere commentator, who lives in his library, and sees men as books walking. I have not solved the problem of specialisation. It is a matter of degree; and we may find room for the man who has no hobby but a genial and intelligent interest in life generally. There are many sincere and excellent Christians who are neither saints nor ascetics.

In answering the second question, I shall make use of William Wallace's Gifford Lectures.[1] For Plato, nature is the eternal law of righteousness, the law that works through reason unto good. And yet in this life the soul is a charioteer who has to drive two horses, one gallant and spirited, the other sluggish and cowardly. There are therefore two views which wrestle in Plato's mind, of which one sees nature as the starting-point of spirit, a germ which by discipline and the stimulus of society may become more adequate as the vehicle of the

[1] Wallace, "Lectures and Essays," p. 136.

higher life. Virtue is not unnatural, but the very path of nature. But on the other side a less cheerful view of self-development is to be found in his writings, and especially in those which are held to belong to the later years of his life. He was never a "dualist"; but his outlook tends to become more ascetic and other-worldly. We may have sympathy with both ways of looking at the world. There is a death to be died, as well as a life to be lived; the spiritual life is not in so simple a line of ascent as pre-Christian philosophy believed. At the same time, there is a real continuity in experience; we cannot, with the Catholics, admit a dualism of natural and supernatural. The natural is itself also supernatural, and can be taken up with us into the Kingdom of the Ideas. The world, as Plato dared to say, is not only God's creation, but His only-begotten child, the image of Himself. This is not contrary to the teaching of St. Paul, who does not identify the "body" with the "flesh." Asceticism which rests on dualism is always harsh and unsympathetic; it sometimes falls into the very materialism which it seems to repudiate, since to invest matter with a positive malignity is to give it more substance than the orthodox view, which makes it only an instrument for the actualising of spiritual values.

But practically, each person must decide for himself or herself how much indulgence in pleasure, amusement, and relaxation can be permitted without detriment to the spiritual life. Even persons with moderate incomes now live far more softly than was possible to anyone before the days of cheap mass-production. Those who are in earnest in their wish to follow the footsteps of our Master will be well advised to "take their share of hardship as good soldiers of Jesus Christ." William James advises everyone to do something, no matter what, every day for no other reason than that he would rather not do it. Such a practice of self-mastery in trivial things must not be despised. Until we have tried to do it, we do not realise the humiliating fact that we cannot trust our wills to control our actions. The acquisition of this self-control by steady discipline will greatly increase our happiness and self-respect, and will be of great value to us in resisting moral temptations.

The need of such discipline is doubtless less for those who work hard and are debarred from many luxuries. Edward Thring, the famous headmaster of Uppingham, was accustomed to say, "I cannot see the use of fasting. To a man who tries to do his duty life is a perpetual fast." But if "fasting" means voluntary self-denial of any kind, the experience of the saints is against him. I believe that some form of voluntary discipline is necessary for everybody. And therefore I must conclude this chapter on Asceticism with the words, "*Abusus non tollit usum.*"

CHAPTER IV

"La multitude qui ne se réduit pas à l'unité est confusion; l'unité qui n'est pas multitude est tyrannie."—PASCAL.

"Since the triumph of the Church, the ecclesiastical organisation has everywhere gone astray. The Roman Church is the most complete expression of Erastianism, for it is not a Church at all, but a State, in its organisation, and the worst form of a State—an autocracy."—BISHOP CREIGHTON.

IN my last chapter I considered the consequences, as illustrated by history, of turning Christianity into a purely world-renouncing rule of life. The errors thus committed are partly due to metaphysical dualism, a plausible but, as almost all are agreed, a false philosophy, of which the classic example is the religion of ancient Persia, a religion which had a long life in the near East and even in the West, in the forms of Gnosticism and Manicheism. But in the main, Christian asceticism rested, not on any philosophical belief consciously held, but on the desire to escape from a social environment at once corrupt and miserable, and to take refuge in prayer and meditation, undisturbed by the claims, the anxieties, and the temptations of life in the world. Since this withdrawal into the inner citadel is an important part of all higher religion, and especially is essential to those mystical experiences which are the crown of the devout life, I was unable to treat asceticism as anything worse than a one-sided exaggeration of a genuine element in Christianity. The morals of asceticism are too self-centred; but the self to whom so much seems to be sacrificed is not the self of our surface consciousness, but the hidden man of the heart, who in his intense preoccupation with the presence of God, and communion with Him, has reached something of the universality of the sublime object of his quest. It is not to be desired that the "religious" vocation, in the narrower sense of the word, should cease to be recognised as legitimate and honoured as worthy.

In this chapter I have to deal with a perversion which in my opinion is wholly alien from the spirit of the Gospel and the intentions of the Founder. The development of the Church into a great political corporation may be explained by historical causes which made it, in a sense, inevitable. Writers like Loisy have argued that since the Church was compelled either to transform itself in this manner or to perish, and since we must assume that its Founder did not wish it to perish, no further justification is needed for the political methods which were thrust upon it in the struggle for existence. The conditions were not made by the Church, but had to be accepted by it. Thus, although the changes through which the Church has passed are not to be denied, we may assert its continuity and identity with the Church of the Apostles—the continuity and identity of a living organism, which has to adapt itself to its environment. "If you want to prove the identity of a grown man with the infant of thirty years ago," says Loisy, "you do not try to squeeze him again into his cradle."

This argument seems to beg the question at issue. Are we justified in assuming, as the Catholic Church has usually assumed, that the Spirit of Christ has permanently incarnated Himself in an institution, inspiring the institution with infallible wisdom, and dispensing the grace of God through the medium of its officers, who enjoy a monopoly of this privilege? Is this privileged position indefectible, whatever abuses may arise in the administration? Is the possibility that a Church, like an individual, may gain the whole world and lose its own soul, excluded? Are we not permitted to apply to an ecclesiastical corporation the one test which the Sermon on the Mount seems to sanction as of universal validity? "A good tree cannot bring forth evil fruit, neither can a corrupt tree bring forth good fruit. Therefore by their fruits ye shall know them." Necessity, "the tyrant's plea," may, though not without protest, be adduced to justify the statecraft of a Machiavelli, a Cavour, or a Bismarck. But it is a fatal concession to accept it as a plea for the crimes of a society which claims to be divine, and which can justify its tremendous claims in the eyes of the world only by showing that the mind and character of Christ are apparent in its public actions as well as in its private devotions. "If any man have not the Spirit of Christ, he is none of his," says St. Paul. "Religion," says Landor, "is too pure for corporations. It is best meditated on in our privacy and best acted on in our ordinary intercourse with mankind." "By plausible and dangerous paths," wrote Lord Acton, "men are drawn to the doctrine of the justice of history, of judgment by results, the nursling of the nineteenth century, from which a sharp decline leads to *The Prince*" (of Machiavelli).

History seems to show that the powers of evil have won their greatest triumphs by capturing the organisations which were formed to defeat them, and that when the devil has thus changed the contents of the bottles, he never alters the labels. The fort may have been captured by the enemy, but it still flies the flag of its defenders. It is one of the tragedies of history to see the worst men sometimes fighting in a good cause, and the best men in a bad cause. Catholics have been very slow to see the moral pointed by the action of that typical ecclesiastical statesman, Archbishop Caiaphas. We may be pretty sure that half the great bishops whose names are honoured in Church history and are inscribed on the roll of saints and doctors would have behaved as he did.

The whole of this chapter will, I am afraid, be offensive not only to any Roman Catholics into whose hands the book may fall, but to many in my own Church. Those who think with Professor Josiah Royce that Christianity is essentially "loyalty to the beloved community," and who, unlike the American philosopher, think that the beloved community is to be identified with the institution to which they themselves belong, will feel that an attempt has been made to weaken the mainspring of their religious life. Their loyalty is bound up with a symbol of some kind, a name or a rite or a formula, and it is partly nourished by the hatred which some other name or rite or formula inspires in their minds. I cannot help hurting their feelings. The ramifications of the disastrous theory of the Church which I have called theocratic imperialism are so wide, and its effects upon religion and ethics so poisonous, that many have thought, not without reason, that fanatical Churchmanship has been the worst foe of Christianity, the devil's master-stroke against the revelation of Christ. "I could worship the Crucified," said Algernon Swinburne, "if he came to me without his leprous bride the Church."

And yet I do not wish this chapter to be taken as a bitter attack upon the great Catholic Church of the West as a form of Christianity. It is true, unfortunately, that the worst manifestations of the spirit which I am to describe are to be found in the history of Roman Catholicism. But I shall try to find examples of the same perversion from other Churches; and even if little can be found to praise and much to censure in the bloodstained annals of the Roman Church, I shall be dealing, not with the gentle and truly Christian piety which has sheltered itself so loyally and gratefully under that banner, but with the last chapter of the history of the Roman Empire, which perpetuated itself in a marvellous fashion in the institution which it first tried vainly to destroy, and then tried only too successfully to capture. Roman imperialism still survives, the most imposing of all political anachronisms, in the palace of the pontifex maximus on the Vatican. There was a time, under the later Renaissance, when the paganising and dechristianising of the Church seemed to be almost complete. The revolt of the northern nations was largely caused by the return of Italy to the classical traditions which the Renaissance rescued from long oblivion. The Italians quite consciously tried to shake off the accretions of northern barbarism, and the northern barbarians were not slow to realise that a Church so purged provided no religion for them. Whether, but for Luther and Calvin, the Olympians would have come back into their own it is impossible to say. It was no doubt only a literary fashion when the humanist poets called the Christian God *"Jupiter,"* *"superum pater omnipotens,"* and *"regnator Olympi"*; but we may at least say that the return to Greece and Rome had ousted almost all that the early Church had taken over from the Hebrews, except indeed the spirit of passionate intolerance, which, but for the Reformation, might have gradually died down, since it is quite unhellenic.

It is absolutely clear that the idea of a politically ordered Church was totally foreign to the mind of Christ Himself. While He was on earth He never contemplated a new Church or a new religion. His earthly mission was that of a prophet and reformer within the Jewish State. The political and sacerdotal parties at Jerusalem soon came into conflict with Him, as they had done with "the prophets that were before" Him; and He made no effort to conciliate them. He disappointed the Zealots by proclaiming that His Kingdom was not of this world, and by discouraging political agitation. He was even more antipathetic to the stiff churchmanship of the Scribes and Pharisees. It is a matter of dispute how far He sanctioned, and some would say even shared, the apocalyptic hopes which were undoubtedly cherished by many of His disciples. But in any case, the contemporary Messianism which has left traces in the Synoptic Gospels was a quietistic creed. The deliverance was to be supernatural, the preparation for it purely personal. Nothing could be further removed from ecclesiastical theocratism than the original Gospel. Caiaphas and his friends knew their enemy at once; such men are seldom mistaken when the interests of their Church are threatened.

Christ came among His countrymen as a layman, preaching a lay religion. In the inner circle of His followers there was not a single priest. He was also singularly tolerant, except indeed when He was confronted with ecclesiastical bigotry and unethical formalism. The Gospel of Mark cIX. 38–40) describes how John complained of "one casting out devils in thy name; and we forbade him because he followeth not us," and the answer of Christ, "Forbid him not; for there is no man which shall do a miracle in my name, that can lightly speak evil of me. For he that is not against us is on our part." This passage must be authentic, and is very significant.

And yet the spirit of partisanship and intolerance, with the hatred and injustice which it evokes, found its way even into the presence of the Master. James and John wished to call down fire from heaven upon a Samaritan village; and an early legend makes St. John rush out of a public bath when he saw the heretic Cerinthus enter the building. The unfortunate saying, "Tell it unto the Church, and if he neglect to hear the Church, let him be to thee as a heathen man or a "publican," which is put into the mouth of Jesus, is an audacious anachronism, as the contemptuous reference to "publicans" might lead us to infer, apart from the absurdity of making Christ speak of the Church, when as yet there was no Church; but the words show what ideas were already held by Christians even before the end of the first century. The Gospel of Matthew is the most important evidence of this change. The writer was a Jew, who could read the Old Testament in Hebrew; he is also one of those who appropriate the Greek word *ecclesia.* In his Gospel is found the fateful and certainly apocryphal passage in which Christ seems to institute Peter as His vicar on earth. In his view the "Kingdom of God," no longer understood in an apocalyptic sense, has been taken away from the Jews and transferred to "another nation," which can only mean the Christian community.

St. Paul, especially in his later Epistles, dwells on the idea of a "glorious Church," of which the type is laid up in heaven, but which is the archetypal pattern of an earthly Church, the body of Christ, one in spirit if not in organisation. The Christians are for him, a converted Jew, the ancient people of God, the heirs of the promises. How completely he accepted the continuity is shown by the curious passage in which he says that the rock which followed the Israelites in the wilderness "was Christ." Thus the Jewish idea of the Church very soon took root within Christianity. In the (spurious) First Epistle of Peter the writer addresses his Gentile flock as "a chosen race, a royal priesthood, a holy nation, a peculiar people." In the Apocalypse we read that "Christ made us a kingdom and priests to

God." The same ideas are prominent in the Epistle to the Hebrews. (It is needless to say that in this early literature no order of priests is thought of; the believers, collectively and individually, are the "royal priesthood.") In the Johannine books (apart from the Apocalypse) the word "Church" does not occur, an omission which is certainly significant; but "John" retaliates on the Jews all the hatred with which these latter regarded the Christians, as apostates from their Church. In no book of the New Testament is the Church said to *act* as a legal or legislative body. Any such centralisation was obviously impossible in the first century.

In Hermas and 2 Clement, the mystical idea of the Church as a kind of Gnostic *æon* is already present. The Didache seems to adopt Jewish prayers for the unity and deliverance of the chosen race. The wistful prayers of the homeless Jews for reunion in their own land pass into aspirations for the institutional unity of the Christian Churches. The spurious conclusion to the Gospel of Mark puts into the mouth of Christ an uncompromising declaration, such as He could never have made, that *extra ecclesiam nulla salus*.

The infiltration of Jewish ideas into the Christian Church, at the very time when the breach between Christianity and Judaism had become definitive and irreparable, is a remarkable phenomenon. The hatred of the Jews against the Christians is intelligible, since they could not be expected to understand the truth, that Christianity had only completed the process of inwardly transforming Judaism into a universal religion. They only saw that the Church had robbed them of their sacred books, even teaching that it had never belonged to the Jews, who were always an accursed race, but to the Christians, who had existed in a sort of suspended animation from the first. Absurd and unjust as this was, it was a necessity for the Church, which must heartily disown the Jews without surrendering their book or their traditions. For a religion can never proclaim itself *new*. Marcion, who wished to discard the Old Testament and begin with Christ, interpreted by St. Paul, was much more logical; but the Church could not afford to give up the support of an ancient dispensation. Therewith came in the fatal error of claiming a continuity between the Jewish priesthood and the Christian ministry. Historically the claim is ridiculous. St. Paul knows of no Christian priests; but Ignatius uses the analogy of the Old Testament priesthood to buttress the growing pretensions of a Christian hierarchy. Tertullian and Cyprian use sacerdotalist language without scruple; and in some versions of the Didache, though not the oldest, "prophet" is actually changed into "priest." The word "sacrifice," at first consciously metaphorical, is soon used literally of the Christian liturgy. From the Jewish tradition also came the practice of fasting on Wednesday and Friday, of observing one day in the week as holy, and the use of penance as a sign of or substitute for repentance. Catholicism, which on one side is a paganising of Christianity, is on another side a Judaising of it. St. Paul had been keenly alive to the danger; but his early training prevented him from seeing that some of his own teaching pointed in that direction.

While the idea of the Gospel, as a prophetic and ethical message for lay folk, was thus being changed into the idea of a theocratic Church, the attitude of the Church towards the secular State was submissive and almost obsequious. This policy is very apparent in several books of the New Testament. Some have detected even in the narratives of the Passion a desire to exonerate the Roman governor, and to fix the whole guilt on the Jews. In the Acts the provincial govern-

ment of the Roman Empire appears, though not uniformly, in a favourable light. The Epistle of St. Paul
to the Romans, and the First Epistle of St. Peter, contain strong exhortations to loyalty and obedience to
the laws. The same wish to give no offence to the government is apparent in the Pastoral Epistles, and in
the Apologies of the second century. At the same time,
the most bitter hatred against Rome is apparent, under
a thin disguise, in the Apocalypse, which is believed to
incorporate a Jewish document.

During the whole period of the persecutions, there
is no evidence that the Christians were ever politically
dangerous. I can recall no example of a rebellion, even
on a small scale, organised by the Church, in spite of the
most extreme provocation. And yet the imperial authorities seem quite early to have regarded the Church
as a peculiarly dangerous institution. When we consider the large tolerance which was the settled policy of
the Roman government towards alien religions, and
the special exemptions accorded to the Jews, who were
really politically dangerous to the utmost of their ability, the suspicion and dislike aroused by the Christians
seem difficult to account for. Why were the Christians
put to death for refusing to sacrifice, though no such re-
quirement was made of the Jews? Why did the best
and most patriotic of the Emperors distinguish themselves by persecuting this innocent sect? Was it the
crass stupidity of the Roman Tsars, who by organising
pogroms against harmless people hammered them into
a militant corporation, or did the government dimly
discern behind this *latebrosa et lucifugax natio*[1] the
growth of a power which would bring emperors to
Canossa and lay its scourge on the backs of kings?

The question is not easy to answer, because the
Pagan writers even as late as the second century were

[1] Minucius Felix, "Octavius," 8.

very ill-informed about both Jews and Christians, and apparently regarded "the third race," as they called the Christians, as almost beneath their notice. In Pliny's famous letter to Trajan, and in the Emperor's reply, there is no trace of any suspicion that the Church might be dangerous. The Emperor had forbidden trade unions and other associations, on the general ground, familiar to all autocracies, that political disaffection may shelter itself under seemingly innocent social or religious societies. Pliny thought that this principle was bearing hardly on the Christians, whose meetings, as he had discovered after careful inquiry, were quite innocuous. His letter, read between the lines, is clearly a suggestion that the Christian worship should not be interfered with. Trajan will not alter his rule, but instructs Pliny how to prevent it from being abused. It is not likely that there were many more executions, or tortures of deaconesses, in Bithynia-Pontus. The early persecutions were sporadic and half-hearted. The total number of martyrs before the third century was very small compared with the victims of religious persecution in the middle ages and at the beginning of the modern period. Not much concealment was necessary in the time and place of public worship, and we never hear of a congregation being netted in a church. But towards the end of the second century Celsus, writing as a patriotic Roman official, is alarmed by the indifference shown by the Christians to the safety and welfare of the Empire. He appeals to the Church not to cease from revolutionary propaganda, for of this it had never been guilty, but to take its part in saving civilisation from being destroyed by the barbarians.

As the third century went on, the attitude of the Roman government changed. The Emperors and their officials felt that they were in the presence of a really dangerous *imperium in imperio,* which was potentially, if not actually, a menace to the State. In much the same way, some modern statesmen feel that when trade unionism is strong enough to paralyse the economic life of the country and blockade the community by a general strike, Parliament is no longer master in its own house. The later persecutions, and especially the great persecution under Diocletian, were deliberate attempts to crush the corporate power of the Church, at a time when it was really too strong to be attacked. The complete failure of the attack led to a concordat, and to the first experiment in Cæsaropapism.

But long before this, the language of churchmen had been confident, and occasionally defiant or arrogant. Melito, in his "Apology" to Marcus Aurelius, claims that "this *philosophy* of ours has brought rich blessings to your empire. Ever since it appeared in the reign of Augustus, the power of Rome has increased, and will continue to prosper under you and your son if you will protect the philosophy which arose with the empire; since when, the empire has suffered no mishaps." Celsus, writing at the same time, took a very different view of the Church as a pillar of the State; it is interesting to compare the two appeals. Hippolytus, also before the end of the second century, boldly contends that the "new people" are the true world-empire, of which the Roman is an evil copy! Tertullian boasts of (and seemingly exaggerates greatly) the numbers of the Christians, and proclaims their entire indifference to the secular State. It is plain that the Church spoke with two voices on this point.

The persecutions, so far as they were more than "pogroms," were mainly the work of the "old Romans," who could not understand why anyone should object to sacrifice to the State gods; it seemed to them as perverse and disloyal as the conduct of a Communist who sits down for the national anthem. But their view, like that of all the conservative reformers, from Brutus and Cassius to Celsus, was out of date. Although the very tradition of civil and public liberty was lost, there was now one field, that of religion, in which the State could no longer dictate. At the end of the great persecution the State had to give way. Constantine gave the Christians their charter, and at once secured their loyalty. He gave the Church certain rights, and gained in return the passive obedience which was not contrary to Christian teaching. Thus began the alliance known as Cæsaropapism, which has proved itself to be one of the most stable forms of despotism. The Church was not slow to assume the airs of a victor. Even in the reign of Constantine, Hilary of Poitiers resents the interference of the State in religious affairs as vehemently as a medieval pontiff. Athanasius resists Constantine himself, and Ambrose actually humbles Theodosius, and informs Valentinian III that "in matters of faith bishops are wont to judge emperors, not emperors bishops." This, it should be noticed, is a state of things absolutely unknown in classical antiquity. But the alliance stood firm, at least in the Eastern provinces; it gave the monarchy a spiritual basis. The spirit of revolt had to appeal, not to the Church, but to the Old Testament or to the Pagan republicans.

Nevertheless, the beginnings of a State Church were "Erastian" enough. "The bishops," as Professor Hearnshaw says, "were compelled to accept Constantine as a patron, not as a penitent; as a master, and not as a disciple. He did not even receive Christian baptism till, twenty-four years after his conversion, he came to his deathbed. He remained all his life pontifex maximus; and he assumed, as by imperial right, the headship of the Christian Church in his dominions. Though still unbaptised, he talked and presided at the opening of the great Œcumenical Council of Nicæa, held in his summer palace, and he was hailed as bishop of bishops."

These claims by the secular government alarmed many of the faithful. The heresies called Arianism, Donatism, Nestorianism, and Eutychianism were in part political protests against Erastianism, and were dealt with by the civil government accordingly.

Yet the victory remained with ecclesiasticism. The subjects of the Empire believed in the Church, though not in liberty or nationality. Theology had conquered philosophy; Tertullian's views had prevailed. Christians must not apply to doctrine the promise "Seek and ye shall find." "What (he asks) has Athens to do with Jerusalem, or the Academy with the Church? . . . Away with all who wish to introduce a piebald Christianity of Stoicism and Platonism and dialectic! Now that Jesus Christ has come, we need no longer curiously inquire, since the Gospel is preached. . . . There is nothing further that we have to believe beyond our belief. To be ignorant of everything outside the rule of faith is to possess all knowledge." This would have been blasphemy to Clement, Origen, and the Cappadocians; but "Fundamentalism" has numbers on its side. We can sympathise with the patriotic Pagans who could not understand the new world. They saw that their cause was lost, and looked with distaste at those who cared nothing for liberty or country or freedom to think, and who were willing to be the grovelling slaves of a despot, on condition of being tyrants within their own domain.

To a large extent this was a victory of Asia over Europe. All these ideas were old and familiar in the East. This is how Mr. Whittaker sees it.[1] "The political history of classical antiquity may be described

[1] "The Neoplatonists," pp. 1–4.

as the slow passage from the condition of self-governing communities with a subordinate priesthood to the condition of a theocratic despotism. This was a reduction of the West to the polity of the civilised East. . . . Christian Ethics from the first accepted absolutism as a political datum. Christianity consecrated for the time an ideal in accordance with the actual movement of the world." This is an illuminating sketch; but it would be the greatest blunder to suppose that the Christianity which conquered the Empire was an Asiatic creed. The Catholic Church was the last creative achievement of the Hellenistic Age, and was European in all essentials, even if we admit that the restored Persian Empire, from which the Byzantines borrowed their elaborate Court etiquette, had some slight influence also upon thought. Nor is there in the Orient anything corresponding to the Papacy. Mr. Whittaker was thinking of the survival of the Byzantine polity in the Russian empire, now destroyed.

The religion and ethics of Porphyry, the disciple of Plotinus in the latter part of the third century, are so much like those of his Christian contemporaries that we may wonder at the bitter hostility between Christianity and Paganism. The sarcasms of Celsus on the credulity and low intellectual standard of the Christians were already ceasing to be fair when he wrote, and within the next fifty years the brilliant Christian School of Alexandria entirely removed this reproach from the Church. There was indeed quite as much ignorant superstition, and more obstinate conservatism, among the Pagans. The Church was now becoming a mystery-religion with which the spiritual Platonism of the age had much in common. Both for the old religion and the new, these devout philosophers solved the problem of providing a religion which should satisfy the educated and the uneducated alike. On the lower intellectual level is a mythological religion, accompanied by sacraments, the efficacy of which might be conceived by the vulgar as purely magical. The middle part of the ascent is occupied by a strict moral discipline and a rationalistic theory of the universe. At the top is that mystical vision of God which is substantially the same in all creeds, lands, and times.

Augustine was well aware how little there was which separated him from Porphyry, that declared enemy of the Church, except indeed their different attitudes towards the old culture. That hostility was too strong to be overcome, and it ended in the destruction of the ancient civilisation. This misfortune may seem to us unnecessary, when we consider how much of the polytheism and idolatry was soon smuggled into the Church. But the Jewish prejudice against a plurality of divine objects of worship, and against graven images, was still intensely strong. Tertullian, with his accustomed intemperance of language, calls idolatry "the chief crime of the human race, the supreme guilt of the age, the entire reason of judgment." In the third century no paintings except of animals and plants seem to have been allowed in the churches, and the Synod of Elvira enacts that "what is worshipped must not be pictured on the walls." No one who has appreciated the spiritual value of sacred art, for instance in many Catholic churches, can find anything but barbarous materialism in the notion that "idolaters" actually worship stocks and stones. But in the fourth century, as later in the Protestant Reformation, men felt that they were engaged in a life-and-death struggle, and the visible symbols of the rival religion offered too tempting a target to the pious vandals. What the Pagans thought of such sacrilege may be gathered from the beautiful and dignified protest of Maximus of Tyre. "God is the Father and Creator of the things that are, older than the sun, older than the heaven, master of time and eternity and of all changing nature. Law cannot name Him, voice cannot describe Him, nor eye behold Him. It is because we are not able to apprehend Him as He is that we fall back upon words and names and the forms of living creatures, and representations in gold, silver, and ivory, and plants and rivers and mountains and groves. In our desire for knowledge of Him we call earthly things good and beautiful, from His nature. So lovers take delight in representations of their beloved, and have pleasure also in anything that belonged to the object of their affections, which can aid the memory." This subject belongs to our present inquiry only as showing the uncompromising attitude of the Church to its defeated rival. But the Christians at this time raged chiefly against the inanimate symbols of Paganism; it would not be easy to name any Pagan martyrs.

Sacramentalism, which, though foreign to the mind of Christ, invaded the Church so early that attempts to represent Catholicism as a corruption of primitive Quakerism have failed, naturally increased the power of the priesthood, and corrupted the severity of moral teaching. Barnabas could still say that "right fasting is righteousness and brotherly love," and James that true religion (or *cultus*) is to visit the afflicted and to keep oneself unspotted from the world. But it had not been left to the Christians to discover what havoc these magically conceived rites may make of morality. Diogenes the Cynic asked whether the robber Patæcion was better off in the next world than the hero Epaminondas, because the former had been initiated, and the latter had not. And Ovid, tracing the *ex opere operato* theory to a Greek source, exclaims—

"Græcia principium moris dedit; illa nocentes
    Impia lustratos ponere facta putat.
A! nimium faciles, qui tristia crimina cædis
    Fluminea tolli posse putatis aqua!"

But here, as throughout this chapter, we shall be forced
to admit that a lower religion has always an immense
advantage over a higher, because the appeal of religion to the vulgar usually succeeds in proportion to the
positiveness of its assertions and the crudity of its symbols.   There is happily no reason to think that the
world lost anything of value by accepting the Christianity of Augustine instead of the galvanised Paganism
of Julian; but it is impossible to deny that the Christianity which conquered the Empire was vastly inferior
to the Gospel of Christ and St. Paul.   The persecutions
hardened and stiffened the Church against the better
side of the old culture; and a corresponding hardening
and stiffening resulted from the severe inner conflicts
against Judaisers, Gnostics, Montanists, Marcionites,
and other heretics.   Even in the later books of the New
Testament we can find traces of great bitterness against
the Jews.   There are few victories that leave no scars
on the victors.

Before attempting a sketch of the process by which
the Western Church became a theocratic despotism,
it is necessary to distinguish sharply between the relations of Church and State in the East and in the West.
In the East there was no abrupt break between the
ancient culture and that of the middle ages.   The
Church lived in the surroundings amid which it had
been born.   It had not to instruct the civilised Byzantines in law or letters or art.   But this East-European
civilisation did not penetrate very far westward.   In
the fourth century Rome, where Marcus Aurelius had
written his Meditations in Greek, and Plotinus, who

died in 269 or 270, had lectured in Greek, was once more a purely Latin city. And when the barbarians swarmed over the West, it was left to the Roman Church to teach them the rudiments of civilised government. It is ungrateful to minimise the debt which civilisation thus owes to the Church of Rome, though the priests and monks allowed very much to perish, and acquiesced in the disastrous severance of the Latin world from the still-living and in many ways far superior culture of New Rome. My object here is to emphasise the very different authority wielded by the Roman Church, as the heir of the dead Western Empire, from that which belonged to the Patriarchs of the Greek-speaking provinces. The Roman Church was quite conscious of being the representative of the Empire, which had now been Christian long enough to win the loyalty of Christians. The gradual separation from the East was made reluctantly; but the pride and loyalty of the Western Church centred in the Eternal City, Old Rome.

A few words must be said about the growth of the Catholic hierarchy. There was a strong tendency under the Empire to form associations, and it was natural that the Christian Churches should organise themselves in the same way. What mainly distinguished the Christian societies was the charitable element, which, where the majority were very poor, was important. The bishops (ἐπίσκοποι) seem to have been at first the dispensers of the alms of the congregation. They were assisted in this work by the deacons. The presbyters were a committee of senior members, who bore the same title as the Jewish elders. Theirs was "the ministry of the word and sacraments," and the exercise of discipline. Before long, a single bishop became president in each community; the convenience of such a rule, and the general usage of the time, made this arrangement quite natural. It became customary to speak of the bishop as the successor of the "apostle" who had founded the church, and lists of these presidents, authentic or otherwise, were early compiled. But it was not conceded that he could act without his college of presbyters, who formed what in Roman constitutional usage was termed a *"consilium."* Nor, it appears, was any rigid rule made in early times that laymen might not exercise what were afterwards regarded as priestly functions. The Montanists tried unsuccessfully to perpetuate the claim that all Christians have the same privileges; and it does not seem that their opponents declared at first that special spiritual powers were conferred by ordination. The attempt to affiliate the Christian ministry to the Jewish priesthood naturally assisted claims which would in any case have been made, owing to the tendency of the age to centralise power. The complete separation of the clergy from the laity followed from the recognition of Christianity by the State under Constantine. The fiscal exemptions which were then granted amounted to a real endowment of the Church, and made the clergy independent, to a large extent, of the offerings of the faithful. At the same time, the separate churches met in councils, and formed confederations; this again was a necessary and salutary process. But the State soon intervened to put down dissentient minorities, and forbade new associations to be formed. This was really an unwritten article in the Concordat; it was to the advantage of the Church to be united as a single society, and it was easier for the State to deal with one acknowledged spiritual authority. Thus everything tended to encourage the idea that the one great Church on earth was a visible copy of the one glorious Church which had been the ideal of Christian hope since the first century. But the type which the unified Church followed was not that of a federation of democracies, but of a centralised monarchy, like the State itself.

The parallel between the Church and the Empire was drawn by Christians themselves, and is not repudiated by Catholics even to-day. Bellarmine says: "The Church is an organised social body, as visible and palpable as the Roman people." Mr. Belloc accepts without qualification the statement that the Church is the heir of the Empire, so that the Reformation may be regarded as a rebellion of barbarians against their lawful sovereign. The Church, from the Catholic point of view, is a metaphysical entity descended from heaven. The Incarnation is continued in the collective holiness of the Church, and in the divine graces which are entrusted to its administration through its officers, and to no other persons or bodies of men. St. Paul had helped to establish this mystical idea of the Church in his Epistle to the Colossians, and in the Epistle to the Ephesians, if this is his work; but he never identifies his ideal Church with the scattered communities over which he presided. Nor had the later hierarchy begun in his time to exist, even in germ. The head of the Church at Jerusalem was not an apostle, but James, the Lord's brother. It appeared for a few years as if a sort of Christian Khalifate might establish itself in the family of the Founder.

The capital of the Empire was the inevitable seat of the central government of the Church, when the necessity of such centralisation was recognised. The need of unity and the need of obedience were impressed upon the Church by the Gnostic and Montanist controversies; and Rome could, in conformity with its traditional genius for rule, supply and enforce both. Gnosticism was overcome mainly by the much more rational and scholarly Platonism of the Alexandrians and the Cappadocian Fathers. Several articles in the

Apostles' Creed are directed against Gnosticism. It passed its zenith in the second century, and is attacked by Plotinus as well as by the Catholics. But the struggle with Montanism was prolonged, and ended in a victory of the priest over the prophet, which exalted the power of the episcopate. There was a steady tendency to identify the Church with the Kingdom of God. When we come to Cyprian, we find the often-quoted declaration that the Church is like Noah's Ark, outside of which no soul can be saved.

From the Jews the Catholic Church borrowed the useful idea of a sacred and infallible "tradition." This was early embodied in a "rule of faith, absolutely unalterable and irreformable," as Tertullian declares. Tertullian also says that the appeal to the tradition of the Apostles is much more effective in dealing with heretics than the appeal to Scripture, which may be quoted on either side, so that *"aut nulla aut incerta victoria est."* The Roman Church, especially, disliked argument; its function was to give sentence, not to plead.[1] But the appeal to apostolic authority necessitated an audacious rewriting of history, to the effect that the twelve Apostles drew up a rule of faith, to which nothing had since been added, and that the bishops were the successors of the Apostles. In point of fact, there was no regular episcopate at Rome before the reign of Hadrian, and the legend that St. Peter presided over the Roman Church may or may not have a historical basis. But apart from the Petrine legend the Church of Rome claimed to have preserved the apostolic tradition with such singular purity that that

---

[1] The famous dictum, "Roma locuta est; causa finita est," is a misrepresentation. Augustine's words (Serm. 132) are: *"iam de hac causa duo concilia* (=decisions of councils) *missa sunt ad sedem apostolicam: inde etiam rescripta venerunt. Causa finita est: utinam aliquando finiatur error."* He does not say that the case is necessarily finished because Rome has spoken.

Church ought to be recognised as the final court of appeal in all disputed questions about doctrine.

Some modern, or Modernist, Catholic writers have given a new turn to the doctrine of tradition by treating it as the spirit of the institution, the genius of Catholicism, which may even be regarded as the divine Spirit dwelling in the Church. In this way it may be said to be infallible; but the old claim that nothing has ever been changed is quietly dropped. The Church, on this theory, not only guards tradition, but creates it. This is really to surrender the idea of tradition. For why should the universal knowledge which the Roman pontiff must be deemed to have *"in scrinio pectoris sui"* be called tradition? There is no appeal to antiquity against a papal pronouncement. As Pius IX is reported to have said, *"La tradizione, sono Io."*

The notion of a college of twelve Apostles, with supreme authority, is unhistorical. St. Paul applies the name of apostle not only to himself and Silas, but to Barnabas, Apollos, and the obscure Andronicus and Junias (Rom. xvi. 7.) The first link in the chain which connects the twelve with the episcopate is wanting; none of the twelve Apostles was ever a bishop, or thought of founding an order of bishops. The gap is very poorly filled by the equally unhistorical assertion of the Council of Trent, that the *vetus sacerdotium* of the old Law was *translatum* into the Christian priesthood. I have spoken earlier in this chapter of the primitive functions of the *episcopus,* who was certainly no *sacerdos.* The change was inevitable when the Eucharist came to be called a "sacrifice," and this happened early. In Cyprian the bishop is said to offer to God the same sacrifice which Christ, the *summus sacerdos,* offered, namely Himself.

We are so much accustomed to the idea of an evolution from autocracy to democracy that we forget that in certain circumstances the natural and inevitable process is in the reverse direction. The Roman republic gave way to the dictatorship of the *princeps,* the "first citizen," a camouflaged monarchy. Then, after the disorders of the third century, the mask was wholly dropped, and the Emperor, who had long been frankly called "the King" by his Greek-speaking subjects, though the word *rex* was abhorred by the Romans, became a regular Sultan. The development of the Catholic Church followed the same course. The little democracies of the first century placed themselves, not uniformly but in most places, under a single officer, the bishop. But the process of centralisation went on; and the temper of the times required that at the head of the œcumenical Church there should be, not a mere senate of bishops, but a single supreme ruler, a "bishop of bishops." There was resistance, long and strenuous, on the part of local Churches and their bishops or patriarchs; but the logic of the system prevailed in Western Europe. One bishop, who must necessarily be the Bishop of Rome, was raised above the rest and placed in the dazzling position of vicar of Christ on earth, and *de iure* spiritual ruler of the whole Christian world.

It was necessary, of course, to prove a divine origin for this usurpation, and the alleged words of Christ to St. Peter—"On this rock I will build my Church," were most convenient. Was such a promise ever made to any other of the Apostles? If not, the occupant of the chair of Peter was the divinely appointed head of the Church on earth. Perhaps the first assertion of this authority was in 194, when the Pope Victor imperiously declared that all who did not follow the Roman custom as to the time of keeping Easter were heretics, thus excommunicating the Churches of Asia. Protests were naturally raised, and Tertullian speaks indignantly of the new titles which the Bishop of Rome has taken—*pontifex maximus* and *episcopus episcoporum*. But these protests were quietly ignored, and fifty years later the Emperor Decius declared that he would rather have a rival emperor at Rome than the Pope. It was about this time that Cyprian of Carthage, a masterful personality, roundly withstood Stephen of Rome to the face. "You think to expel others from the Church; in doing so you excommunicate yourself." Brave words, but the trend towards a centralised monarchy was too strong for him. Origen might deny that the promise to Peter was exclusive: "Every disciple of Christ is a rock, and on every such rock is built the polity of the Church." Right or wrong, this interpretation did not suit the need of the times.

After the Concordat under Constantine, the See of Rome soon became the prize of violent ambitions. Pope Damasus, nicknamed *matronarum auriscalpius,* gained it by a furious faction-fight with his rival Ursicinus, after which 137 corpses were counted in the basilica of Sicininus. A cynical Pagan, according to Jerome, remarked, "Make me Bishop of Rome, and I will be a Christian." Nevertheless, the councils of the fourth century gave the Bishop of Constantinople the same rank as to the Bishop of Rome, and the East has always maintained this claim. When there were two emperors, there must obviously be two ecclesiastical jurisdictions, parallel to each other.

It has been customary to attach great importance to the forgeries by which the claims of the Roman See were supported, especially to the False Decretals. Beyond doubt, these counterfeit title-deeds were extremely useful to the Popes; but it does not appear that the Decretals were deliberately forged at Rome. The best authorities are now agreed that they were produced by the Frankish Church in the early part of the ninth century, and that their object was not to increase the power of the Popes, but to exalt the position of the clergy as a whole, as against the secular authorities. But they also aimed at curtailing the pretensions of the metropolitans in the interest of the diocesan bishops; and for this reason stress is laid on the supreme authority of the Bishop of Rome, and the right of appeal to him. This seems to have been only a recognition of existing conditions. It is not true to say that the national Churches were in any sense independent of Rome in the dark ages.

The coronation of Charles the Great by Pope Leo was a landmark in the history of the Papacy, because it not only put the Roman Church in a new relation to Western civilisation, but it terminated the shadowy supremacy of the Greek emperors as the lawful successors of the Cæsars, a position which had been sometimes galling to the Bishops of Rome. Charles himself is said to have been much displeased at the way in which the ceremony was performed.

When the Carolingian Empire broke up, a welter of pure savagery again almost submerged Western Europe, and the Papacy suffered cruel degradations in what was called the Pornocracy. From this the Church was partially rescued by the vigorous Hildebrand (Gregory VII) in the latter half of the eleventh century. Hildebrand determined to stop the buying and selling of offices, and to assert the spiritual independence of the Church. The result was a violent quarrel with the Emperor Henry IV, in which the two potentates proclaimed each other deposed. Hildebrand put forward the claim, never, I think, so plainly asserted before, "that the priests of Christ are the fathers and masters (*magistri*) of all kings and princes. The climax of Papal power was in the reign of Innocent III, near the beginning of the thirteenth century.

It was he who compelled an English king to admit that he held England as a fief of the Papacy. In all the quarrels between Pope and Emperor, it is possible to represent the Popes as contending for the freedom of the spiritual power from secular interference. The Popes sometimes repudiated any desire to interfere with the political authority of the secular power; even Innocent III did so. But when the Church is itself constituted as a political society, such a delimitation is impossible. This has been the fatal dilemma of Catholicism. A kingdom not of the world may preserve its spiritual independence; a political Church cannot; it must either serve or rule.

The fullest expression of Papal claims is in Innocent IV's Commentary on the Decretals (1243–1254), and in the famous Bull *Unam sanctam* published by Boniface VIII in 1302. On the eve of the Reformation, Alexander VI made over the New World to Isabella of Castile and Ferdinand of Aragon by the Bull *Inter cetera divinæ,* 1493. The terms of this deed of gift are amusing to Americans. "Acting on our own initiative, from pure generosity and certain knowledge, and with the plenitude of our apostolic power, we make over all the islands and continental lands which have been discovered or may hereafter be discovered, towards the West and South, by drawing a line from the North Pole to the South Pole, whether these continental lands already discovered and hereafter to be discovered are towards India or towards any other part of the world; this line is to be drawn a hundred leagues west and south of the Azores and Cape de Verde Islands, provided that the said lands were not in the actual possession of any other Christian king or prince on Christmas Day of last year, by the authority of Almighty God, granted to us in the person of St. Peter, and as vicar of Jesus Christ, which authority we exercise on earth, to be held by you, your heirs and successors for ever, with all and every right of sovereignty thereto pertaining, in accordance with these presents." I have slightly abridged the verbosity of the original; but it is plain that an infallible authority has placed all North and South Americans for ever under the absolute rule of the Kings of Spain and Portugal.

The right claimed by the Popes to depose temporal sovereigns and release their subjects from their allegiance was occasionally exercised. The King of Bohemia was deposed as a heretic in 1464, and his kingdom offered to the King of Hungary. A sanguinary war was the natural consequence. Julius II invited "any neighbouring king" to seize the dominions of the King of Navarre, a suggestion readily acted upon by Ferdinand of Aragon.

The spiritual claims were more ubiquitous and intensive. The Pope was absolute over all spiritual persons and things everywhere; and men were spiritual if they had taken orders or vows; fields, houses, barns were spiritual if the land belonged to the Church. This Papal kingdom lay scattered over Europe, including a slice of every parish. The clergy owed no allegiance to the secular power; they were not under the laws of the land, and paid no taxes to the State. But there was a constant drain of wealth to Rome. Under the system of "Reservations," the Pope could declare certain benefices vacant, and appropriate the emoluments. Finally all benefices were put under the Holy See, and the Roman Chancery compiled a tariff of prices for which each might be bought. It would take too long to enumerate the other exactions of the same kind— the Tithes, Annates, Procurations, Subsidies, and the notorious Dispensations. Luther describes the Roman Curia as a place "where vows are annulled, where the monk gets leave to quit his Order, where priests can enter the married life for money, where bastards become legitimate, and dishonour and shame may arrive at high honours. There is a buying and selling, bargaining, cheating, and lying, robbery and stealing, debauchery and villainy and all kinds of contempt of God, so that Antichrist could not reign worse." The Papal Court was almost as extravagant as that of the French Kings. Leo X appointed 60 chamberlains and 140 squires, selling these offices for 90,000 and 112,000 ducats respectively. Places thus bought were personal property, transferable by sale.

Let us pause for a few moments in this summary of the strange and perhaps inevitable transformation of the "little flock" who gathered round Christ in Galilee into the world-wide domain of a priestly autocrat. The idea of history as the tale of Two Cities—the City of God and the City of Antichrist—was drawn out by Augustine in his most ambitious but not his greatest work. In the East, after the State ceased its hostility, the Church became on the one hand the right arm of the monarchy, on the other an organ of spiritual teaching through a system of ritual. In the West, where the Church was the one strong society in the midst of a civilisation dying in chaos and disorder, it was called upon to save what could be saved out of the wreck. Nor was the Church deaf to this summons. The monasteries, from being merely schools of asceticism, became disciplined organisations in the service of the Church. The Saxon monks, for example, converted Germany from heathenism. It has been said truly[1] that in the dark ages the only citizenship that remained to a man was his membership of the Church. The Church was a world in itself, with its own traditions and its own laws. While secular society was falling back into a barbarous feudal aristocracy of

[1] Chr. Dawson, "Progress and Religion," p. 166.

168

freebooters, the Church was conscious of being the heir of a higher culture. The success of the Papacy was after all the victory of an idea over brute force—the idea of a single religious commonwealth. In an age of horrible brutality, the character of which may be studied in such books as Luchaire's History of Social France in the reign of Philippe Auguste, not only religion but education, art, and the care of the sick and destitute were parts of the work of the Church. To a very limited extent, the Papacy exercised some control over international disputes, and sometimes used it on the side of justice. Nor will any competent scholar speak disparagingly of the scholastic philosophy, which in the first dawn of what was afterwards called the Renaissance brought Christian theology into line with the best thought of the time. In accordance with the doctrines of the Neoplatonists, the Schoolmen taught that human reason is a copy or adumbration of the divine mind: *"ratio nihil est nisi natura intellectualis adumbrata."* Until the great awakening which emancipated the European mind from ecclesiastical tutelage, the Catholic Church of the West played in many ways a beneficent part in history. Without it, the relapse of Western Europe into barbarism might have been so complete that all continuity with the older civilisation might have been lost.

In the sphere of morals, our present subject, the Penitentials of the early middle ages give a most repulsive picture of the habits of the people. But there is reason to think that the Church at this time made strenuous efforts to enforce decency; and that when the influence of ecclesiastics declined in the fourteenth and fifteenth centuries, licentiousness became more open and unashamed.

The end of the Hohenstauffen Empire seemed to mark a complete victory for the Popes. But they witnessed the fall of the German Empire only to find themselves confronted with the rising national consciousness of England and France. Boniface VIII made magnificent gestures, and proclaimed, in the famous Bull *Unam Sanctam, "subesse Romano pontifici omnes humanas creaturas declaramus, definimus, et pronuntiamus omnino esse de necessitate salutis."* But before he died the Papacy was under the control of the French kings. The "captivity" of the Popes at Avignon, which began in 1309, was a heavy blow to the prestige of the Curia. The Papacy seemed to have become the creature of a civil power, which was not even an Italian government. And when at last the Popes returned to Rome, the great Schism shattered for a time their moral authority. Marsilius of Padua openly attacked the theory of the Papal supremacy, and thus paved the way for the Reformation. The Great Schism was only terminated by General Councils, which pointed to a reversion from autocracy to constitutionalism; but the time was not ripe for this, and the Conciliar movement, which was to have made great reforms in the Church, came to an end without having done anything important. It gave an opportunity, however, for the disaffection of Northern Europe to find a voice. Complaints against the avarice, greed, and corruption of the hierarchy resound through the fifteenth century.

One of the worst evils of elaborate institutionalism is that it requires a costly administration. The central establishment of the Catholic Church was on a magnificent scale, and was a continual drain on the resources of the faithful. A priesthood cannot levy taxes by force, and in consequence is driven to every sort of disreputable expedient in order to raise money. This is a side of Church history which closely concerns us in this inquiry. No impartial historian can deny that the fiscal requirements of the Catholic Church have obliged it to resort to barefaced threats and promises, to shameless frauds and pretended miracles, to corrupt intrigues with secular powers, to the cruelties of the Inquisition, which, as we shall see, was even more anxious to confiscate property than to burn heretics, to the sale of indulgences, and to other methods of deceit and extortion. A Frenchman will often be heard to say even now that religion in France is *une commerce;* and so it is in most parts of Catholic Christendom. Fiscal considerations, indeed, are at the root of many of the scandals of Catholicism.

The Church had a fixed income derived from the ten per cent. tax on all incomes, which every Christian was supposed to pay, and which, as regards landed property, was a legal obligation. There were also large donations and legacies in land, but almost always to some particular parish diocese, or conventual house. There was no provision for the central government. Our ancestors in the middle ages did not like to be taxed; they grudged even the taxes which they had to pay to their own kings. "The King should live of his own," they said. Hence the weakness of the medieval monarchies. The King might live of his own, if he was very economical, and kept out of foreign wars; otherwise, his subjects might squeeze him, as they did Charles I, or compel him to accept foreign subsidies, like Charles II. The complaint against Papal exactions was therefore not always reasonable, if we grant the right of an international corporation to raise money for its own purposes. It was this right that was challenged as the consciousness of nationality grew stronger, and jealousy of an alien jurisdiction more bitter. At length in Protestant countries the alien jurisdiction was discarded altogether; in Catholic countries some kind of treaties had to be made between the national and the international governments.

Eucken says very truly that under medieval Catholicism a religion of pure inwardness—the religion of the mystic—had existed side by side with a hierarchical system. The two had never worked together without friction, as may be seen from the numerous sects of heretical mystics which tried to claim the right to exist before the Reformation. But the mystic is seldom a rebel; he usually shelters himself under an ecclesiastical authority which in reality means little to him. At the beginning of the modern period, however, individual spiritual religion was increasing in force under the influence of a genuine revival among the laity. Mystical devotion was by no means confined to the cloister. The question as to the seat of authority became acute, and a sharp conflict was inevitable. The reformed Churches, without knowing or intending it, inaugurated a new type of Christianity. But it is right to recognise that the religious revival had already begun in the parts of Europe which retained their allegiance to the Papacy, and that the numerous religious reforms in the south of Europe were not entirely the work of the Counter-Reformation.

It was the Renaissance, and not the Reformation, which brought to an end the tutelage in which the Catholic Church had held the semi-barbarous peoples of Western Europe. Henceforward, the dominating position which the Church had assumed, and had exercised on the whole with the consent and to the advantage of the populations subject to its authority, required justification. It was the product of an unique and very anomalous state of affairs. At the beginning of the dark ages, an ancient and effete civilisation, which could no longer maintain itself in arms, still lingered on in the midst of warlike barbarians, who admired and reverenced the knowledge, the art, and the traditions which they were unable to preserve without the help of an institution embodying them. This was the office of the

Western Church. But an international Church, with claims to universal sovereignty, even if only in "spiritual things," is not a natural form of polity when nationalism is strong. There may be a spiritual and independent commonwealth of religion, as there is a commonwealth of scholarship and science. In all these fields, national prejudices and jealousies can be and ought to be laid aside. But an international political organisation, levying contributions, making laws, controlling secular education, and demanding obedience even at the polling-booth, is an anachronism and a nuisance. Having no adequate justification for its existence as a political institution, and inspiring no loyalty except among those who are devoted to its interests, such a body inevitably comes more and more to live solely for its own preservation and aggrandisement. It may show a great survival-value, long after its services to civilisation have been changed into serious disservices. This is, on the whole, what I believe to have happened to the Roman Catholic Church. Its usefulness as an institution belongs to the time when it was educating the barbarians. From the time of the Renaissance downwards it has been an obstacle to civilisation and progress. After the Reformation, it struck an alliance with the continental type of despotism, and in France procured the Revocation of the Edict of Nantes. Since the rise of the democratic movement it has made desperate efforts to control primary education, and to maintain Catholic schools for children, and colleges for the adolescent. It is hoped, unhappily not without reason, that a twist given to the immature mind may determine its shape for life. Another expedient is to espouse the cause of disaffected provinces, encouraging them in rebellion and resistance to authority, and giving very ready absolution for political crimes, even for cowardly murders. In Poland at one end of Europe, and in Ireland at the other, this policy has been very successful; though the shrewder members of the heirarchy have realised that if the causes of discontent were removed, the Church would suffer severely.

The theoretical basis of the Papal autocracy has been strengthened by the decree of infallibility in 1870, though this decree contradicted a great body of Catholic opinion, which regarded General Councils as alone infallible. Modern Catholic apologists still accept the infallibility of General Councils, but assert that no Council is General unless the Pope presides at it and approves of its decisions. In defiance of history, Leo XIII declared in an encyclical that in the decree of 1870 "no new opinion is introduced, but the ancient and constant faith of all ages is asserted." The submission of the vast majority of the bishops is very significant. It resembles the abject retractations of prominent Russian Communists when threatened with excommunication by Stalin.

And yet the fundamental falsehood, the $\pi o\hat{\omega}\tau o\nu\ \psi\epsilon\hat{\upsilon}\delta o\varsigma$ of Catholicism, began long before the Renaissance. The monopolist claim of the Western Church which adds so much to its survival-value, implies a monstrous conception of the character of God. It points straight back to the tribal deities of the old Semites, and to those parts of the Old Testament which are most alien to the spirit of the Gospel. We read in Exodus how Moses commanded the sons of Levi to go to and fro in the camp, slaying all who, as worshippers of the Golden Calf, had not been "on the side of Jehovah," and in Numbers how the chiefs, who had gone after Baal-Peor, are "hung up unto Jehovah before the sun." In Deuteronomy we read: "If thine own brother, son, daughter, wife or bosom friend entice thee secretly saying Let us go and serve other gods, thine own hand shall be first upon him to put him to death." This external classification of the elect and the reprobate is above all else abhorrent to the spirit of Christ. It is absolutely unethical, and revoltingly unjust. One of the Cambridge Platonists said truly, "Such as men themselves are, such will God appear to them to be"; but the converse is equally true, that those who worship an unjust, fanatical, and hideously cruel God are likely to develop the same qualities in themselves. When salvation is supposed to depend, not on the possession of "the mind of Christ," but on membership of a body and participation in sacramental rites, religion is almost completely de-ethicised, and the standard of right and wrong is likely to be much lower than among high-minded persons who care little for religion, but act according to their instinctive notions of what is just, decent, and honourable. The inevitable result has been a passionate revulsion against clericalism, and the cry *"Écrasez l'infâme,"* which until the rise of Marxian Communism was never directed against the Founder Himself, but only against those who profess to speak in His name.

The traditional Christian eschatology points to a sharp division of mankind into the saved and the damned, the former class to be rewarded with bliss unspeakable in the presence of God and His angels, the latter doomed to suffer atrocious and unending torments. This idea of divine justice is flatly contrary to our most rudimentary ideas of equity and mercy; it corresponds to nothing that experience reveals to us about ourselves or our fellow men. The old proverb that some are over-bad for blessing and over-good for banning, is not nearly strong enough. We have never met anybody who deserves to be tortured through all eternity. The Roman Church has mitigated the monstrosity of the doctrine by intercalating purgatory between heaven and hell; but Protestants often forget that purgatory is not a second examination for those who are near the borderline, but a painful discipline intended to fit those whose lives have been accepted for a blessed state for which they are still partially unprepared. The doctrine that all will be saved at the last is quite different, and has very little Church authority. The Liberal of Protestants at the present day have turned hell into a purgatory, and future retribution into future probation. This belief seems to many to be the only one which is consistent with the goodness of God, and I am far from saying that this is not a strong argument for it; but marks a wide departure from Christian tradition.

Traditional eschatology has on the whole been prejudicial to morality, especially in giving it a negative bias. The threats of hell-fire are intensely horrible to everyone who believes them, while the descriptions of the bliss of heaven are not always attractive. Accordingly, fear has been more potent than hope among the majority of Christians. Moreover, if the Last Judgment is a pass examination in which some "get through" and the rest are "ploughed," there must be some single test question which decides the result; otherwise it would be almost impossible to draw a line anywhere without manifest injustice. In the parable of the sheep and the goats, which does not profess to be more than a parable, we are told that such a question will be asked. Those who have loved and befriended their brethren will be saved, those who have not done so will be lost. But as there are infinite degrees of compassion or charity and of the negation of those virtues, this parable does not help us in this particular difficulty. The test of Church membership, though wholly unethical, does supply a dual classification. It is possible to answer "Yes" or "No" to the question whether any person belongs to the institutional Church or not. Catholics have never maintained that all who die in communion with their Church will be saved, but they have often asserted that all who die outside this communion will be damned. I am well aware that many Catholic authorities have made earnest attempts to repudiate this horrible doctrine, and that probably few Catholics to-day sincerely believe it. Much play is made with the doctrine that "invincible ignorance" is a plea which may be accepted at the Last Judgment, and charitable hopes are placed in the "uncovenanted mercies of God." But the whole Catholic system rests on the uncompromising judgment quoted from Cyprian, that he who has not the Church for his Mother cannot have God for his Father, and that the Church is Noah's ark, outside which no lives can be saved.

The monopoly claim of Catholicism is thus made infinitely more unjust and more horrible by the pictures of hell which few before our own day have wished or dared to call in question. To investigate the sources of this hideous nightmare would take up too much of my space, and all the contributory causes taken together seem to me inadequate as an explanation. It has always been considered part of the business of religion to terrorise the irreligious; and a disposition to disbelieve or disregard the menaces of a Church may sometimes be countered by making them more appalling, just as the criminal law sometimes enacts specially severe penalties for offences which are difficult to detect. We may also remember that disproportionate rewards and punishments did not offend the moral sense of a simpler age; that the criminal law was then excessively cruel; and that there was enough superstition to make the threats of ecclesiastics a real check upon the lawless oppression of the weak by the strong. Here it is necessary only to point out that the current ideas about the future state put a terrible weapon into the hands of the hierarchy, which became indeed the chief instrument of their power. The English reformers complained of "purgatory pickpurse"; but these financial extortions were only a small part of the tyranny which the Church was able to exercise, while it was believed that the Deity has committed to the Catholic hierarchy the keys of heaven and hell.

The logical results of this tremendous, and as we must think wholly unfounded, claim have been very far-reaching. The first that we must consider, and the most dreadful, is religious persecution. There had been very little of this in antiquity. Cleanthes, according to Plutarch, thought that the Greeks ought to prosecute Aristarchus for impiety, because he "moved the centre of the universe." Aristarchus in fact anticipated the discoveries of Copernicus and Galileo; but it does not seem that he was in any way molested. Socrates was charged with not recognising the gods which the City recognises, and introducing strange gods of his own; but there is not much doubt that his real offence was that certain young oligarchs had sat at his feet. Plato, however, cannot be acquitted of wishing to establish a kind of holy inquisition in his ideal commonwealth, which in more ways than one foreshadowed the institutions of the Catholic Church. The Romans could act very severely against any foreign cult which they considered immoral, and they showed disapproval of rites which the State had not sanctioned. The persecutions of the Christians have been briefly discussed in this chapter. The Persians, who had shown themselves capable of intolerance, both in Egypt and when they destroyed the temples of the Greek gods,[1] were

[1] Herodotus thought that Cambyses must have been "very mad" to persecute the Egyptian religion, and accused Xerxes of wanton impiety

almost friendly to the Jewish religion. The fierce intolerance of the Hebrews is notorious. The Catholic Church therefore succeeded to the persecuting traditions both of the Jews and of the Roman Empire. During the persecutions the Christians appealed to the rights of conscience, as persecuted sects always do. Even after the Edict of Milan, for some time it did not abuse its privileges as much as might have been expected. Professor Gwatkin says that in the age which followed Constantine there was a good deal of toleration, which "died out with Theodoric the Ostrogoth, and reappeared with William the Silent."

And yet a settled policy of repression began with Constantine. An edict of 325, the year of the Council of Nicæa, made possession of the books of Arius a capital offence, and in 380 heretics are threatened not only with divine but with imperial "vengeance." The Government was afraid (not without reason) of religious rioting.

It is only fair to the Church to observe that in early times the impetus towards persecution did not come from the ecclesiastics, but from the common people. Either from superstitious fears or from sheer love of cruelty, the masses in the earlier period welcomed the maltreatment and execution of suspected heretics; in the later middle ages it was quite otherwise. When Priscillian and six of his followers were put to death at Trier in 385, Ambrose and Martin of Tours protested against the crime. Chrysostom denounced the execution of heretics as a monstrous sin. Augustine was in favour of liberty of conscience while the Donatists held the ascendancy in Africa, but when the Cath-

---

for burning the Greek temples. Cicero ("de Republica" 3–9, 14) understood Eastern intolerance better. *"Eam unam ob causam Xerxes inflammari Atheniensium fana iussisse dicitur, quod deos, quorum domus esset omnis hic mundus, inclusos parietibus contineri nefas esse duceret."*

olics got the upper hand, he frankly changed his mind. *"Hæc opinio mea (neminem ad unitatem Christi esse cogendum) non contradicentium verbis sed demonstrantium superabatur exemplis."* (Ep. 93). Henceforward his view was precisely that surmmarised by Macaulay in his Essay on Mackintosh. "I am in the right, you are in the wrong. When you are the stronger, you ought to tolerate me, for it is your duty to tolerate truth: but when I am the stronger, I shall persecute you, for it is my duty to persecute error." This has always and everywhere been the attitude of the Roman Catholic Church, which has never listened to Cromwell's quaint remonstrance, "In the bowels of Christ think it possible that you may be mistaken."

Theodosius II and Valentinian III punished the slightest deviation from orthodoxy as a *crimen publicum*.[1] Justinian codified all the existing laws against heretics, and a number of Manicheans were stoned at Ravenna in 556.[2] But whole centuries followed when heresy was not felt to be dangerous, and, at least in the East, there was very little persecution. Pope Nicholas I (858–867) condemned the use of torture.

In the eleventh century the treatment of heresy became more savage, but at first the kings and the mob were more cruel than the churchmen. In 1022 thirteen Cathari were burnt at Orleans by order of the King of France, and in 1076 the populace took the law into their own hands and burnt one of the same sect. In 1144 the Bishop of Liége rescued a number of Cathari whom the mob wished to burn. In 1163 and later the fanatical populace of Cologne burnt a large number.

The policy of the ecclesiastics changed for the worse when milder measures failed to extirpate Puritan re-

[1] Article "Persecution" in Hastings, "Dict. of Religion and Ethics."
[2] In the paragraphs which follow I have made free use of Dr. Cadoux's admirable and learned book, "Catholicism and Christianity."

form. The worst criminal was Pope Innocent III (1198–1216), who ordered a crusade to exterminate the harmless Albigenses in the South of France. In 1209 the Abbot Arnold Amaury, Papal legate, wrote jubilantly that at the capture of Béziers 20,000 persons were massacred, men and women, and children together. When some of the soldiers asked how they should distinguish orthodox from heretics, the legate gave the order, "Kill them all; the Lord knows who are His." The Archbishop of Toulouse was said to have destroyed half a million lives.

In 1216, the year of his death, Innocent held an Œcumenical Council in the Lateran. The Council decreed that all secular rulers were to be made to swear to "exterminate" heretics, on pain of excommunication and the release of their subjects from their allegiance. It is idle to pretend that "exterminate" means only banishment; it was not so understood at the time, nor was it meant to be so understood.

By the middle of the thirteenth century, the Dominicans, a new Order, had taken the Inquisition into their own hands. There was no appeal except to Rome. Burning alive was made the regular mode of execution in 1231.[1] The trials were an utter travesty of every principle of justice; and Lea is probably right when he says that among all the curses introduced by this horrible tribunal none has caused greater misery than the adoption of some of its methods by the secular criminal Courts. Except in England barbarous and unjust procedure in trying prisoners prevailed everywhere till the close of the eighteenth century.

It is unnecessary to expatiate on the horrors of the Inquisition. Those who wish to study the most ghastly chapter of human history may find details in Lea, Lecky, and more recent books. The imagination is

[1] Coulton, "The Inquisition," p. 54.

most keenly stimulated by reading the *précis* of a trial by torture, drawn up at the time for the benefit of the Inquisitors, who were usually not present. Lea transcribes a detailed narrative of the torture of a Spanish lady who was accused of wearing clean linen on Saturday, and of not eating pork. Her plea that she liked clean linen and did not like pork was rejected as summarily as her request not to be stripped quite naked. What follows will not be copied out here. The use of torture was expressly ordered by Papal Bulls of 1252 and 1259. By an exquisite hypocrisy, the Church "handed over to the secular arm" (*"ecclesia abhorret a sanguine"*) those who were to be burnt; princes who refuse to burn the victims were to be excommunicated.

Those who were not tortured but only imprisoned hardly fared better. The Consuls of Carcassonne, in their official protest of 1286, described the prisons of the Inquisition there[1]: "Some are so dark and airless that the inmates cannot tell night from day, and thus they are in perpetual lack of air and in complete darkness. In others are poor wretches in manacles of iron or wood, unable to move, sitting in their own filth, and unable to lie except upon their backs on the cold earth; and they are kept for a long time in these torments day and night. In other dungeons there is lack not only of light and air but also of food, except the bread and water of affliction, which is given most scantily."

Even the Bolsheviks have not quite equalled the reign of terror which lay heavily over Western Europe for centuries, cowing all except the most heroic, and effectually preventing intellectual progress, which cannot exist without freedom of thought and speech. It was a cruel age, and it was almost universally believed that God is more cruel than the most fercious earthly

---

[1] Coulton, "The Inquisition," p. 54.

tyrant. Of course this belief is itself a proof that cruelty at that time aroused very little moral reprobation; but it gave an effective answer to any who were shocked by the torture and judicial murder of inoffensive citizens, whose lives, as even their persecutors were constrained to admit, contrasted very favourably with those of the most orthodox. Coulton says: "About 1233 a suspect, brought before the tribunal, protested as follows in order to clear himself from all suspicion of heresy: 'Hear me, my lords! I am no heretic. I have a wife, and cohabit with her, and have children; and I eat flesh and lie and swear and am a faithful Christian.'" No wonder that the last words have been omitted by two Catholic historians of the Inquisition! For the ghastly torments of hell, it was supposed, were decreed by God against all heretics. And so, as Thomas Aquinas argues, "If false coiners and other felons are justly condemned to death without delay by worldly princes, much more may heretics, as soon as they are convicted, be justly not only excommunicated but slain out of hand."

It is often contended by modern writers that the number of persons actually burnt was less than was formerly supposed. Torquemada is credited with 2000 burnt, and 40,000 otherwise punished, a proportion which has been adduced to show that even the prince of inquisitors did not love shedding blood for its own sake. Between 1498 and 1809 the Spanish Inquisition is said to have burnt over 23,000, and otherwise punished over 200,000. These numbers cannot be given with any confidence. But the large number whose lives were spared shows that another motive was at work besides the extirpation of heresy. This motive was spoliation. Alvarus Pelagius, a Franciscan of the fourteenth century, complains that whereas the worldly goods of the heretic ought to be divided into three parts, one for the civil government, one for the officials of the Holy Office, and one for the necessary expenses, his brother-friars appropriate it all. "They are also fond of punishing heretics only by confiscating their money." It is not to be wondered at that in 1375 the Inquisitor Eymeric complains: "In our days there are no more rich heretics, so that princes, not seeing much money in prospect, will not put themselves to any expense; it is a pity that so salutary an institution as ours should be so uncertain of its future."[1]

This terrible weapon could be made an engine of secular tyranny. It was only necessary for a prince to declare his rival a heretic, and the machinery of the Holy Office could be used against him. In 1409 the Council of Pisa deposed two Popes on the ground that their rivalries were tantamount to a denial of belief in the one Catholic Church. A hundred years earlier the Venetians were declared heretics because they opposed the annexation of Ferrara by Clement V. In this and other instances the Pope condemned the inhabitants of a contumacious city to *slavery*. But the strangest story is of how Philip the Fair used the Inquisition to destroy the Pope's own Janissaries, the Templars. The motive in this case was almost entirely fiscal; but on no other occasion did the Holy Office act with more hideous cruelty and contempt for justice.

The Reformation naturally added new fury to the persecuting spirit. The Catholic Paul Sarpi estimates that 50,000 persons were put to death for their religion in the Netherlands between 1522 and 1556. In 1524 an inscription was put up at Seville stating that since 1492 nearly 1000 persons had been burnt and 20,000 otherwise punished. Under Philip II the roll of Dutch martyrs was increased by 25,000. In 1565 Pius IV issued a "creed" which became a normal pledge to be

[1] Coulton, "The Inquisition," p. 47.

taken by converts to Rome. It demands absolute obedience to all declarations of the Church, and "anathematisation, damnation, and rejection of all heresies." On August 24, 1572, began the famous massacres in France, in which about 70,000 Protestants were slain. On hearing the joyful news, Gregory XIV celebrated a special High Mass of thanksgiving, and struck a medal with the inscription "Ugon ottorum Strages, 1572." Vasari was commissioned to depict the massacre in a series of frescoes in the Papal palace. In England, in the happily short reign of "bloody" Mary, only a few hundred perished; but the Pope was undoubtedly privy to the numerous plots to assassinate Elizabeth. William the Silent was actually murdered in 1584; his assassin was encouraged by the Jesuits, and in 1610 the tolerant Henri IV of France met the same fate. In the same period appeared the great work on "Criminal Theory and Practice," by Farinocci, procurator-general of Paul V. It contains a learned and exhaustive account of methods of torture, extending to 250 pages. The children of heretics ought "so to sink in misery and want, that life will be a punishment to them and death a comfort." [1]

After the beginning of the eighteenth century persecution became less sanguinary, though in Spain, where a strong vein of cruelty has always co-existed with many admirable qualities, over a thousand persons were burnt in the first half of the century. Cadoux shows that there was no relaxation in Catholic theory; the most ruthless persecutors were canonised, and the massacre of St. Bartholomew was extolled in authorised books. But Voltaire lifted up his voice against the judicial murder of Jean Calas, and public opinion could no longer be disregarded, at least in France. Down to the outbreak of the Revolution the Catholic clergy

[1] Cadoux, "Catholicism and Christianity," p. 572.

agitated and protested against toleration; but their teeth were now to be drawn, we may hope for ever.

Napoleon abolished the Spanish Inquisition in 1808; the French soldiers had penetrated into some of the dungeons, and were revolted by what they found there. But there is very little evidence of any change of heart even in the nineteenth century. When the power of Napoleon fell, the Inquisition was restored in Spain and in the Papal States, and Pius VII protested against religious liberty in France. He also denounced the Bavarian Constitution for granting liberty to Protestants. In 1832 Gregory XVI issued an encyclical which by the violence of its language shows the fury of the Vatican at being deprived of its favourite weapon. "From this most foul fountain of indifferentism flows that absurd and erroneous opinion, or rather *deliramentum,* that liberty of conscience is to be assented to and vindicated for everybody." In 1851 Pius IX made a concordat with Isabella of Spain, in which the terms were that all cults except Catholicism were to be excluded from Spain, and that all education was to be Catholic. In 1856 the same Pope protested against religious liberty in Mexico. In 1862 a concordat was made with Ecuador on the same terms as that with Spain. In 1877 the *Dublin Review* published a vigorous defence of religious persecution. In 1885 Leo XIII condemned toleration, in the encyclical *Immortale Dei.* In 1888 another encyclical declares that the State ought to tolerate no religion except Catholicism, and adds that "although in the extraordinary condition of these times the Church usually acquiesces in certain modern liberties, because she judges it expedient to permit them, she would in happier times exercise her own liberty." In 1906 the Roman Catholic Archbishop of Malta expressed deep dissatisfaction at the establishment of religious liberty in that island; and in the present year (1930) the hierarchy of Malta is conducting a bitter agitation against the British Government for favouring religious equality. In the "Catholic Encyclopædia" (1908–1912) the statement is several times repeated that the Church has never relinquished the right to resort to the old methods of extinguishing heresy. Even in 1927 a Protestant widow at Segovia was sent to prison for two years for saying that the Virgin Mary had children by Joseph, born after the birth of Jesus. The fact that this is clearly stated in the Gospels does not prevent it from being heretical for all Catholics.

These examples are selected from a vast number which might be cited. Even now there is very little sign of any change of heart. In Spain, the only European country where such things are possible, the Church shed innocent blood only twenty-two years ago. "Francisco Ferrer had devoted himself to the founding of modern schools in the province of Catalonia. He was a rationalist, and his schools, which had a marked success, were entirely secular. The ecclesiastical authorities execrated him, and in the summer of 1909 chance gave them the means of destroying him. A strike of workmen at Barcelona developed into a violent revolution. Ferrer happened to be in Barcelona for some days at the beginning of the movement, with which he had no connexion whatever, and his enemies seized the opportunity to make him responsible for it. False evidence, including forged documents, was manufactured. Evidence which would have helped his case was suppressed. The Catholic papers agitated against him, and the leading ecclesiastics at Barcelona urged the Government not to spare the man who founded the modern schools, the root of all the trouble. Ferrer was condemned by a military tribunal and shot on October 13." [1]   It is probably the last time that such a coup will be attempted.   A shout of indignation went up from every country in the civilised world, although the name of Ferrer was almost unknown outside Spain. Many streets were named after him.   Public opinion was quick to recognise that the priests had claimed another victim, and in the twentieth century.

Cadoux quotes numerous passages from modern Catholic writers in justification of persecution.   He also notes the outspoken denunciation of the whole system by a few noble-minded Catholics like Lord Acton.   "The principle of the Inquisition is murderous," Acton wrote; "and a man's opinion of the Papacy is determined by his opinion about religious assassination."   Cardinal Gibbons has lately asserted that the Roman Church has always been the friend of liberty of thought.   We need not stop to wonder at the sublime effrontery of such a statement.   In America even Roman ecclesiastics must pay some lip-service to public opinion.   We have rather to ask whether a man can be a consistent Catholic without advocating persecution, whenever circumstances allow it to be employed.

It is as certain as anything can be that if Christ had come back to earth at any time during the so-called ages of faith, He would have been promptly burnt alive as the most poisonous of heretics.   Dostoieffsky has pictured what His reception would have been even in a less barbarous age.   The maxim of Caiaphas, "It is expedient that one man should die for the people," has been often repeated by ecclesiastics in the form *"Melius est ut unus pereat quam unitas."*   How deeply this principle can corrupt the sense of justice in a Catholic country, even in our day, is illustrated not only by the fate of Ferrer in Spain, but by the treatment of Dreyfus in France.   Zola's "Rome," now almost forgotten

[1] Bury, "A History of the Freedom of Thought," p. 231.

in this country, is a perfectly fair picture of ecclesiastical justice when administered by Roman Catholics. If the Catholic Church had been stronger in France, Dreyfus would have died on the Devil's Island.

I said at the beginning of this chapter that my object is to show the fatal consequences of a false theory, not to denounce the particular Church which has given the most flagrant examples of these consequences. I have called this chapter "Theocratic Imperialism," and have shown that persecution is the natural and inevitable result of a certain theory of the Church. But, it may be asked, has not persecution stained the records of other Christian bodies, which have never aspired to, or claimed, universal empire? And if so, must we not modify the judgment which ascribes all these horrible cruelties to the assumption that Christianity must be a world-empire with a capital city, and that this capital city must for all time be situated on the banks of the Tiber?

The earlier Protestantism, in its chief forms, was certainly intolerant. Some of the minor sects pleaded for liberty of conscience, but minor sects always plead for liberty of conscience until they become major sects. On what principle were the Anabaptists, a body of Christian Socialists, persecuted by Lutherans and Calvinists? Why were the absolutely harmless Quakers maltreated both in Europe and in America, where four of them actually suffered death? Why did Calvin cause the Spaniard Servetus to be burnt alive? Why, above all, were many thousands of "witches" executed in Protestant countries?

I put aside the answer that the extent of Protestant persecution has been grossly exaggerated by Catholic apologists, and that many of the Catholic "martyrs" in Elizabeth's time had come to England in order to murder the Queen or to plot against the government of the country. [1]   Persecution is so alien to the spirit of Protestantism that examples of it must be judged much more severely than the atrocities of the Roman Church, which are an integral part of its political methods.

I have not space to discuss the horrible history of trials for witchcraft, which, as Lecky says, were terminated not by the Churches, whether Catholic or Protestant, but by the rise of rationalism.

> "Hunc igitur terrorem animi tenebrasque necesse est
> Non radii solis neque lucida tela diei
> Discutiant, sed naturae species ratioque."

But these trials illustrate a fact which must not be forgotten as a partial extenuation of persecution—the fear of divine vengeance descending upon a community which tolerates diabolical arts within its borders.   The fact of witchcraft was supposed to be guaranteed by the Bible.   Evidence for its potency was abundant, since superstition will always manufacture the food it feeds upon.   The prevalent callousness to human suffering did the rest.

But the real answer is that the great Reformers themselves belonged to the middle ages, and were far from realising all the implications of their teaching. Modern Protestantism has unequivocally abandoned persecution—not only one sect or one party among Protestants, but all Protestants together.   Therefore, although there is the gravest reason to expect that the Church of Rome would revive its persecuting edicts,

[1] In 1569 Pius V sent money to aid a rising against Elizabeth, with a letter in which he trusted that the kingdom would be delivered from "the basest servitude of a woman's lust," and recovered to "the primitive obedience to this Holy Roman See."   A little later he issued a Bull excommunicating the Queen and absolving her subjects from their allegiance.   "This woman having seized the crown and by a monstrous usurpation challenging the authority and jurisdiction of supreme head of the Church of England, has brought the kingdom to a lamentable condition."

which have never been disavowed, if ever circumstances made such a thing possible, everyone would laugh at the notion of the Church of England pressing Parliament to revive the statute *de haeretico comburendo.*

What has caused this great change? Why has religious persecution now no friends except among Roman Catholics, some of whom are obliged almost to suggest that infallibility may have erred in blessing the Inquisition and canonising some of the most ruthless persecutors? I cannot answer this question without discussing the problem whether, in fact persecution is always wrong, and if so, why. I am not writing a history, but a book on ethical questions; and this seems to be one of the points where modern ethical theory and practice have diverged most decisively from Christian tradition. We shall find that the question is by no means easy to answer; but the discussion ought to throw some light on the main subject of this chapter.

At first sight it seems impossible to find any excuse for such an abomination. Lecky, who rightly connects it with the doctrine that *extra ecclesiam nulla salus,* says with generous indignation: "Persuade men that when they are ascribing to the Deity justice and mercy they are speaking of qualities generically different from those which exist among mankind—qualities which we are altogether unable to conceive, and which may be compatible with acts that men would term grossly unjust and unmerciful; tell them that guilt may be entirely unconnected with a personal act, that millions of infants may be called into existence for a moment to be precipitated into a place of torment, that vast nations may live and die, and then be raised again to suffer a never-ending punishment, because they did not believe in a religion of which they had never heard, or because a crime was committed thousands of years before they were in existence: convince them that all this is part of a transcendently righteous and moral scheme, and there is no imaginable abyss to which such a doctrine will not lead. You will have blotted out those fundamental notions of right and wrong which the Creator has engraven upon every heart; you will have extinguished the light of conscience; you will have taught men to stifle the inner voice as a lying witness, and to esteem it virtuous to disobey it." [1]

Lecky's book has been a quarry for all subsequent writers on the subject. He is careful not to throw all the blame on the Roman Church. For example, the doctrine of exclusive salvation was dear to the first Reformers, and the language of men like Jonathan Edwards about the damnation of infants is quite as horrible as anything that could be found in Roman Catholic writers. It is also significant that Hobbes, the anti-Christian philosopher, was "perhaps the most unflinching of all the supporters of persecution." His position is that it is the province of the civil power to determine the religion of the nation, and to punish as rebels all who refuse to conform. It is only fair to Roman Catholics to note that the idea of coercion in matters of faith was, as late as the seventeenth century, not felt to be a monstrosity even by those who rejected Christianity. On the other side, toleration had stalwart friends in Harrington, Milton, Jeremy Taylor, and Chillingworth. Milton nobly declared that "opinion in good men is but knowledge in the making," and that "if a man believes things only because his pastor says so, or the assembly so determines, without knowing other reason, though his belief be true, yet the very truth he holds becomes his heresy."

A nineteenth-century Liberal, if asked why persecution is wrong, would probably have evaded the question by saying: Persecution is always ineffectual. But

[1] "History of Rationalism," Vol. I. p. 386.

no one defends ineffectuality. Therefore no one can defend any persecution. To which, unfortunately, a historian must reply, *Nego maiorem.* The major premiss is untrue. Persecution, if applied at the right time, and with sufficient ruthlessness, is often effective. Christianity was rooted out of Japan by persecution; Protestantism out of Spain and Italy; in France its growth was checked. The truth is that a religious movement follows the same law as an epidemic. For a time, not usually a very long time, it is acutely infective, and spreads like wildfire. This is the time when by taking very rigorous measures it can be prevented from extending its conquests. Afterwards it becomes endemic in the lands which it has successfully invaded, and occasionally overspreads its boundaries; but it is no longer a conquering creed. Christianity itself has won no more signal triumphs since the conversion of the Northern barbarians. It penetrated, in the early middle ages, to India and beyond, but was unable either to maintain these conquests or to prevent the victorious march of Islam, which itself after a time lost its power of assimilation, except among the African savages. Protestantism was dangerous to the Roman Church for a time; now it makes very few converts in Southern Europe and is stationary in France. It cannot be said, therefore, that persecution is always bad policy for the persecutor, if his only object is to prevent the spread of opinions which he considers wicked and mischievous.

The most elaborate discussion of the whole subject is in Leslie Stephen's "An Agnostic's Apology," part of which I will summarise and comment on.

Do we admit that it is morally right for a man to avow opinions which he sincerely believes, or do we contend that it is wicked to hold any opinions which differ from our own? Catholicism really asserts the latter, but it is increasingly difficult, in the modern world, to maintain it. And if it demands virtue to hold an unpopular opinion, the persecutor is punishing men for conduct which he himself admits to be virtuous. It is not a parallel case to say that we execute Thugs for murder, although they think murder right. We cannot tolerate murder, but we can hardly think that a man deserves to be burnt for being honest. This argument, however, can be turned by a.utilitarian, who may say that the balance of happiness, or the public good, requires the suppression of an honest advocate of poisonous opinions. Many who are opposed to religious persecution would approve of the silencing, by whatever means, of Bolshevik agitators.

But the utilitarian will hardly support persecution when he realises all that it involves. A religious opinion cannot be isolated from the whole body of a man's beliefs. We cannot tear it up by the roots, while leaving the soil in which it grew untouched. Practically, we have to choose between tolerating what we think error and suppressing all intellectual activity over a very broad area. The medieval Church did not interfere with the dialectical subtleties of the schoolmen; the Bolsheviks do not prohibit the study of natural science; but the former effectively crippled natural science, and the latter ostracise philosophy and religion. The price is enormously high; and those who wish to study the forbidden subjects inevitably come to hate the tyranny which prevents them from obeying what they feel to be a call. The Inquisition ruined Spain as a first-class Power, as Lenin has temporarily ruined Russia. For the tyranny which seeks to exterminate an opinion must be of the most searching kind. It must pursue not only the conscious heretic, but everyone whose thoughts may lead himself or others in the direction of heresy. This can hardly be done without strangling all original thought and making intellectual progress impossible.

No such results follow from suppressing immoralities committed in the name of religion. Moral toleration has its limits. The alleged command of a god ought not to shelter such institutions as human sacrifice, widow-burning, and religious prostitution. Those who wish to practise such atrocious acts cannot be allowed to take refuge behind an invisible accomplice. This consideration, which few will dispute, throws some light on the question which we are discussing. The suppression of religious practices is not always or necessarily wrong; but the appeal is to the moral sense of mankind. To imprison, torture, and burn men and women, whose moral conduct is admitted to be irreproachable, because they refuse to belong to a political corporation, or because they hold opinions which are not orthodox, is tyranny of the worst kind.

But, it may be said, are not men punished, at least in time of war, for refusing to perform the services which their country requires of them? And if so, is it not equally a culpable dereliction of duty to renounce allegiance to the universal Church, which was founded by Christ? This question will indeed bring us to the conclusion of our discussion.

There is not the smallest reason to think that Christ ever contemplated the evolution of His little flock into a theocratic empire. The universal Church and the universal Empire are parallel ideas, which belong to a state of society that has long passed away. There is no more reason why an Englishman should acknowledge fealty to the Pope than why he should pay taxes to the King of Italy. There is nothing essentially Christian about the Roman Church on its political side. But it has the strength as well as the weakness of an institution which refuses to compromise with the spirit of the age. It has gained in strength by refusing to bow the knee to the ideas of 1789 or to nineteenth-century

Liberalism. These ideas, which at one time seemed irrefragable, are now falling into partial discredit. Similarly, although it has never done more than tolerate modern Capitalism, it is well known that it absolutely refuses to make terms with Communism. Many, therefore, who dread the violence of revolutionary movements look to the Catholic Church as a possible rallying ground for all who do not wish the traditions of Western civilisation to be obliterated, and the legacy of the past—of Palestine, Greece, and Rome—to be squandered. The Church stands like a impregnable fortress amid the welter of half-civilised barbarism, like a rock surrounded by raging seas. It represents the conviction that revolutions are after all superficial, since human nature and the fundamental conditions of human life do not change. In comparison with other religious bodies, the Roman Church shows a great courage; it is not afraid to rebuke and condemn fashionable enthusiasms, and to appeal to an older and deeper wisdom. This stability gives it a wonderful dignity, and supports the immeasurable pride with which it confronts the modern world. Besides these advantages, its form of government, with an elected but irremovable sovereign, endowed, as is claimed, with infallibility when he chooses to speak *ex cathedrâ,* is one of the most ingenious and successful of all political experiments. In the nineteenth century, the age of doctrinaire democracy, the Papacy appeared an anachronism; in the twentieth, the age of dictatorships and repressions which make the friends of liberty shudder, and of democratic senates which are despised by those who elect them, it may even compel admiration as the best of all attempts to solve an insoluble problem—that of devising a form of government which shall not be a nuisance or a laughing-stock.

To despise such an organisation is a proof of want

of intelligence. The Roman Church is a most formidable corporation, and we can understand the arrogance of those who belong to it. But as an institution it represents a complete apostasy from the Gospel of Christ. In almost every particular it has restored that kind of religion to destroy which He suffered Himself to be nailed to the Cross. And in its insatiable ambition to wield political power, to make the world-wide Roman Empire once more a reality, with boundaries wider than Augustus or Trajan ever dreamed of, to embrace the whole of mankind in one vast spiritual dominion, it has plunged into that career of fraud, violence, repression, and cruelty which has made many public men besides Gambetta say *"Le cléricalisme, voilà l'ennemi."*

Nor does any recovery seem possible. The strength of the institution is so closely bound up with the policy of centralisation, of immobility, and of military obedience, that reformers within the Catholic body are really as dangerous to the Church as the Church thinks them to be. And yet, with all its astuteness, it cannot hope to realise its ambitions. For a time, its steady propagandism and clever intrigues seem to indicate the conquest of new territories, in England, for example, and in the United States. But then suddenly the people awakes to a sense of its danger, and an explosion of anger follows which shows that a free nation will never tolerate a church-directed government. The idea of world-conquest is a dream, and an absurd dream. Secular education, and the better education of women, will undermine what remains of the once tremendous power of the Church. It will live, and will very likely show less signs of weakness than the Protestant Churches. But whereas these are content to be factors in a changing civilisation, critics of new experiments, but not because they are new, and upholders of a morality which is based not on tradition but on the broad principles of the Gospel applied to modern problems, the Church of Rome cannot escape from the medievalism which holds it in bondage. There is very much in the modern view of life with which it cannot be reconciled; and it has constantly to deplore the defection of independent and forward-looking minds. The adhesion of a few accomplished men of letters has recently given it some additional prestige, and placed at its service the trained skill of eloquent advocates; but meanwhile Science, now wholly emancipated, goes on its own way, and gradually creates a mental atmosphere which excludes the whole world-view of Catholicism. The very stability which has long given it such unparalleled power of resistance will probably at last be its undoing.

However this may be, and it is no part of my plan to prophesy, we find in this imperialistic ambition the worst perversion that Christianity has ever undergone. "Violence," says the Epistle to Diognetus, "is not an attribute of God"; it is certainly no part of the Gospel of Christ. The idea of corporate reunion is (as the German militarist said of peace) "a dream, and not even a beautiful dream." The only apostolical succession is in the lives of the saints; the only union is "unity of the Spirit in the bond of peace"; the only holy Catholic Church is that of which the type is laid up in heaven. God does not necessarily pardon those whom a priest has absolved; He has given no monopoly of grace to any corporation; He does not send unbaptised infants to hell or to limbo. "Not he that saith unto me Lord, Lord, shall enter into the kingdom of heaven, but he that doeth the will of my Father who is in heaven." Ceremonial righteousness means no more to the genuine Christian than it did to Christ. "Not that which goeth into a man defileth a man, but that which cometh out of a man, that defileth him." "This He said, making all meats clean." We need no earthly mediator, no courtiers to introduce us to the throne of grace. Catholics are taught that where the interests of the Church are concerned, nothing else matters. With heretics, it is said explicitly, *"fides non est habenda."* [1] For the true Christian, on the other hand, the Church exists only to serve the highest welfare of the people; the Church of England, for example, ought to have no "interests" apart from those of the nation. The method of the Gospel is from the individual to society, from within outwards. The more it leavens society, the less, perhaps, will the power of the Church become, and the less need will be felt for a large Christian ministry. Is this a prospect which we ought to deplore? Not at all. The one object of a good educator is to make himself unnecessary.

If those who are bitterly opposed to Christianity will take the trouble to trace those things in it which arouse their indignation to their true sources, they will find, I think, that almost everything which offends them comes from ecclesiasticism, not from Christianity. Religious societies must exist, and it is not likely that a class of officials will ever be found who do not wish to increase their power. But as soon as we recognise that the history of the great Church is the history of a monstrous abuse, which has made the word of God of no effect by its traditions, we shall be more ready to go back to the fountain-head, and to judge

---

[1] The dishonesty of Roman Catholic controversy moves the indignation even of Bishop Gore ("Roman Catholic Claims," p. 112): "Perhaps there is nothing which gives to the minds of intelligent and truth-loving men so invincible a prejudice against the Ultramontane system and temper—nothing which so radically convinces them that it is not divine—as the certainty that Ultramontane writers will always be found manipulating facts and making out a case, will never behave as men who are loyally endeavouring to seek the light and present facts as they are." Dr. Coulton has done good service in exposing the habitual bad faith of Romanist scholars, which horrified even such loyal Catholics as Newman and Acton.

of modern problems by the broad principles of the New Testament, in entire detachment from ecclesiastical tradition, which has completely upset the moral standard of the Gospels, counting disobedience to the hierarchy a graver offence than sins against love, truthfulness, humility, or purity.

To these modern problems we must now turn. If it be said that in regarding nearly the whole of Church history as an aberration from the intentions of the Founder I am surrendering the citadel, I cannot agree. Two thousand years are a very short time in the history of humanity. Circumstances favoured the growth of a political Church; other circumstances may promote its decay. But the revelation of Christ is a permanent enrichment of the human race, which is very far from having yet exhausted all that the revelation potentially contains. A thousand years hence, when the idea of Rome as the world's capital will evoke only a smile, mankind will still be wrestling to draw out temporal meanings from the eternal Gospel, and they will still be sitting at the feet of Jesus Christ. Beyond Pheidias, said Rodin, art can never go. Beyond Jesus of Nazareth, we may add, the moral stature of humanity can never go.

CHAPTER V

THE AGE OF SCIENCE

THE development of Natural Science, which was the child of the Renaissance and not of the Reformation, followed the great revival of Humanism which itself followed the great intellectual awakening in the age of the Schoolmen. "Modern Science," says Mr. Christopher Dawson ("Progress and Religion," p. 184), "owes its birth to the union of the creative genius of the Renaissance with the mathematical idealism of Platonic metaphysics. This romantic marriage was the source not only of a new physical synthesis, but of the vast material and economic progress of the modern world." As Henri Poincaré has said, "We have only to open our eyes to see that the conquests of industry which have enriched so many practical men would never have seen the light if these practical men had been the only ones to exist, and if they had not been preceded by disinterested madmen who died poor, who never thought of the useful, but who were nevertheless guided by something more than their own caprice." This awakening divides the middle ages from the dark ages which preceded them. The dark ages, from the fall of the Western Empire till the eleventh or twelfth century, were really dark; the middle ages, though still barbarous in some aspects, have a place in the history of civilisation. It is interesting to observe that the course of Greek

philosophy, which began with the naturalistic speculations of the Ionians, and ended with the theocentric
philosophy of the Neoplatonists, was now repeated in
the reverse order. The call of Science was at first heard
only by a few; the new faith had its martyrs and confessors, such as Roger Bacon, Bruno, and Galileo. Its
victory is still incomplete, but it has deeply coloured
the minds of nearly all educated persons, and it is apparently destined to be the strongest force in Western
civilisation. Natural Science has its cradle in the
West, as the higher religions have had their cradle in
the East; but both are readily transplanted and ac-
climatised. Even in Asia the disintegrating effect of
the new knowledge upon consecrated tradition and custom is being felt.

The first article in the scientific creed is not causation, but uniformity of sequence. Science has nothing
to do with causation; we do not say that summer is the
cause of winter, nor day of night. Causation implies
a purposive will, a teleology, which produces real
change, and not merely a mechanical unpacking of what
was potentially present from the first. Whether Science
must admit the existence of purposive force, in order to
account for the phenomena of life and mind, is hotly
debated among scientific experts at the present time.
The majority of biologists are still adherents of the
mechanical theory, and condemn as "Neovitalists" those
philosophical thinkers who are convinced that the laws
which prevail in the inorganic world are insufficient to
account for the higher activities of conscious beings.
Their opponents argue that the evolution of instinct
and intelligence cannot be fortuitous.

It does not fall within the scope of my book to discuss this question, in spite of its great importance for
philosophy. But it is highly significant that at the very
time when materialism was in the ascendant among stu-

dents of nature, a belief was prevalent in a kind of inner teleology, operating throughout Nature, which in its unconscious working evolved higher and higher types, the chief criterion of improvement being greater complexity of structure and function. This was originally a conception of the Deists; it was very congenial to the optimism of the nineteenth century. It was pointed out that this was the process by which man was slowly developed out of the amœba, and it was hastily assumed, not only that a process which culminated in ourselves must be a matter for congratulation, but that the same evolution towards greater complexity must last for ever, and must hold good for all other parts of the universe. This belief, which constituted a great part of the secular religion of many persons in the last century, was a pure superstition, in part a residuum of half-religious optimism about the destiny of creation, and in part the product of the heavy enthusiasms of a revolutionary age.

The notion that evolution is an automatic machine for bringing on the millennium made the attractiveness of naturalism for the nineteenth century. We can only view with astonishment the support given to this dream by real men of science, such as Herbert Spencer and, to a modified extent, by Darwin himself. The real attitude of Science is neither an optimism nor a pessimism. There is evolution in some parts of the natural order, involution in other parts. There is no progress in the whole, nor can we assume that the more complex is always "higher" than the simpler, whatever meaning we may give to "higher" and "lower," words which have no place in natural science. The human race is still in its childhood. The earth has been in existence about two thousand million years, the human race, recognisable as human, probably about one million years. Civilisation is a very recent experiment, covering about one per cent. of the life of the species. We know of no reason why there should not be lineal descendants of ourselves and our friends on the earth a million years hence, but it does not follow that they will be men, still less civilised men. The analogy of insect civilisations, such as those of the termites, ants, and bees, suggests that sooner or later our species will come to rest in a condition of stable equilibrium, and that when this is established the gift of conscious reflexion, which is useful only in periods of transition, will probably be withdrawn. But since man does not possess the virtues of the busy bee, or of the ant which is a model to the sluggard, and since he has in fact reached his present position by an irrepressible desire to save himself trouble and to live beyond his income, it is perhaps more likely that social evolution will continue, possibly at an accelerated speed, for an indefinite period, in which case the man of the far future will be more different from us than we are from the apes. Science permits these speculations, but does not in any way guarantee their accomplishment. And the ultimate extinction of all life on our planet is as certain as anything can be.

The decay of this secular religion in the twentieth century has produced a widespread disillusionment. A successful religion (real Christianity has never been successful) is a superstition which has enslaved a philosophy, and the philosophy which was supposed to guarantee automatic progress, attractive as it is, labours under the disadvantage of being almost the only philosophy which can be definitely disproved. Its disappearance will be an advantage to the higher religion, because a hope which rests on a rotten foundation is an obstacle in the way of reasonable idealism. The thinkers of our day are more and more ready to recognise the existence of a kingdom of values, exalted above space and time, and independent of the problematical advances which may or may not be in store for the human race.

There has indeed been a significant return to the old doctrine of recurrent cycles, in Hartmann, Nietzsche, and many others. From another side, warnings have been uttered that civilisation itself may not be in the line of biological progress. Writers like Austin Freeman in England and Müller-Lyer in Germany hold that environmental progress has actually stopped biological progress. Tools may end by depriving us of the use of our hands, legs, and brains, a process which seems to be already beginning. Edward Carpenter wrote a book called "Civilisation, its Cause and Cure." Similar uneasiness is betrayed by Haldane (the younger), Bertrand Russell, Schiller, and the eugenists. In Thomas Hardy and many other representative writers there is an undernote of deep disillusionment.

But men no sooner learned that evolution is not necessarily beneficent than revolts against the fundamental postulate of Science began to break out. The belief in uniformity, or rather in continuity, as a universal law had taken the place of Fate in ancient mythology. The contemplation of the remorseless working of natural law has often a crushing effect on the imagination. Many would prefer to be under a more human dispensation, even if, like most human governments, it was sometimes arbitrary, capricious, and cruel. And so the fundamental postulate of the sciences has still to contend with the older theory of supernaturalistic dualism, of a catastrophic instead of an evolutionary order of nature. The advantage of this theory, for many minds, is that it resolves, in a rough and ready manner, the dualism of fact and value. It enables us to relate all experiences to each other on the same plane, the supernatural being regarded as an alternative system of world-government, interfering with the natural order in the interest of morality or of the glory of God. In this way faith is given a factual basis within the phenomenal world, and religion is intertwined with common life at many points. If miracles are of frequent occurrence, and are part of the dispensation under which we live, there is no escape from the direct operations of the Deity in the world, and our dependence on this double system must then be recognised even by those who have no religious instincts and no admiration for the Christian ethical ideal.

But the disadvantages of this reversion to antiquated types of thought are greater, and such as to condemn the whole hypothesis. In the first place, the natural order has all the appearance of a closed system. All the sciences work on this assumption, and find that the results justify the repudiation of supernaturalism. It would indeed be impossible for Science to continue its labours if unaccountable suspensions of natural law were liable to occur. Besides this, to dovetail acts of God among natural events is to degrade the spiritual as well as to confuse the natural. Belief in miracle as a fact of experience despiritualises religion.

This does not imply that there is anything necessarily unscientific in belief in a higher spiritual order, a kingdom of values, of which the natural order, as known to Science, is a partial and abstract representation. It is not contended by men of science, if they have any tincture of philosophy, that the natural sciences give a complete picture of reality. Their measurements are purely quantitative; they are valid for certain purposes; but the only value which they take into account is that of truth in the sense of inner coherence and verifiable correspondence with fact. They are not concerned to assert that the most comprehensive panorama of the natural order would be a complete explication of reality. Even the human spirit, which, as Macarius said, is "the throne of the Godhead," is unable to apprehend more than a small part of the counsels of God; why should we assume that He reveals Himself more perfectly in external and inanimate nature? We are indeed almost driven to a belief in an eternal kingdom of values, or, as Plato would say, of forms or ideas; for the doctrine of psychophysical parallelism is no solution of the problem of reality. If the philosophy based on naturalism is true, there is no room for the higher faculties of our nature—no room for art, morality, philosophy, religion, nor even for Science itself. If the world of values floats like a luminous haze over a real world of measurable and ponderable things, it is a mirage, for the existence of which it is impossible to account. Nor will neutral monism satisfy us, for if reality is neither material nor spiritual, we can know nothing about it, and our beliefs serve only to cancel each other in incurable self-stultification. The dogmatic agnosticism of the last century does not escape the dilemma which was fatal to the older scepticism. As Münsterberg says: "Every doubt of absolute values destroys itself. As thought it contradicts itself; as doubt it denies itself; as belief it despairs of itself." To deny every thought which is more than relative is to deprive every thought, even sceptical thought itself, of its own presuppositions.

We must then believe that the spiritual world, the realm of the absolute values, is the real world, and that the world of Science is a construction valid for certain purposes. This the most philosophical scientists are now, for the most part, ready to admit. In the words of Lotze, "Absolutely universal in its extent, completely subordinate in its significance, is the part which mechanism has to play in the structure of the world." Mechanism, as Lichtenberg suggested, may be the teleology of the inorganic world. Whitehead, however, complains that we have to admit the persistence of "the fixed scientific cosmology which presupposes the ultimate fact of an irreducible brute matter or material, spread throughout space in a flux of configurations. In itself such a material is senseless, valueless, purposeless. It does just what it does, following a fixed routine imposed by external relations which do not spring from the nature of its being. It is this assumption that I call scientific materialism. . . . The narrow efficiency of the scheme was the very cause of its supreme methodological success." But it may be suggested that the invincible reluctance of Science to admit any interference with the closed order which it postulates for its own purposes is not the result of materialism, but rather of fidelity to that one among the absolute values which Science is pledged to serve. Its objection is not to the recognition of other absolute values, but to the interference with scientific truth which results from transforming the spiritual into the supernatural, and so intercalating the "higher order" into the "lower" on the plane of the lower. It cannot be a matter of indifference to Science whether an alleged event "went through the form of taking place," or is a product of the creative imagination.

Miracle is the bastard child of faith and reason, which neither parent can afford to own. But the Christian philosopher is faced with very difficult problems, because, while all serious modern thought is evolutionary, the framework in which Christian theology is set is catastrophic. The abandonment of the catastrophic view will possibly demand a rather drastic reconstruction of dogma. But in this book I am concerned only with Ethics. If we give up the old notion of miracle, as a suspension of the ordinary sequence of events by supernatural agency, can we any longer maintain the moral miracle of conversion, the power of grace to do what unaided human nature cannot do, the forgiveness of sins, and the redemption of sinful man through the power and goodness of God? Are we not driven back to Huxley's dramatic picture of a man playing chess against an unseen opponent who never overlooks an error? Is not this moral determinism the very thing against which Christianity protests? What else is the good news of the Gospel but this, that we are saved "not of ourselves; it is the gift of God"?

My answer is that in the moral and spiritual world we are not dealing with ponderables. It is a matter of experience that the cold hand of determinism is not laid upon our souls. Explain it how we will—or rather I fear we cannot explain it—there is freedom in the kingdom of the Spirit. But even here, I believe that the scientific conscience has its protests to make against certain theological doctrines. Forgiveness without change of heart—grace imputed but not imparted—a change of status towards God effected by sacerdotal magic— these are theories of the relation between man and God which the conscience of our age, supported by the scientific hypothesis of unbroken continuity, rejects. And it will be seen that they are all unethical theories. Whatever power we may assign to grace, whatever indulgence we may hope for from a merciful Judge, it must remain true that "whatsoever a man soweth, that shall he reap."

What kind of Ethics might be expected to issue from the dominance of natural science which we have found to be one of the chief characteristics of our age? I think that Naturalism may develop, and has developed, in two widely different directions. One of these may be shortly designated as atheism, which means the denial of objective reality to the absolute values. The other is pantheism, an apotheosis of Nature, as the seat of a cosmic Soul. Pantheistic Ethics have a fairly well-defined character. They tend to a refined sort of nature-worship—a nature-mysticism such as we find at its best in

Wordsworth, but also in Goethe. The character so fostered is unworldly without holiness, abstinent without asceticism; it meets the world with what Clough calls a "Stoic-Epicurean acceptance"; is kindly without any profound pity, and tends to minimise the importance of separate individuality, and of personality, whether human or divine. Pantheism tends to be cold in face of the mystery and suffering of the world. Christianity has often combated this creed rather fiercely, just because something not unlike it is implied by much of its own teaching. But the Hebraic element in Christianity is stubbornly anti-pantheistic. Pantheism in practice soon leaves the domain of exact science, and borrows freely from simple animism, from poetry, and from mysticism. It is an attitude towards life rather than a philosophy.

On the other hand, Naturalism proper, which claims that the whole system of nature is calculable in terms of mathematics and mechanics, is either an abstract method, recognised as valid only for certain purposes, or, as happens more often, it is a very unsatisfactory philosophy. It is often blamed, and no doubt rightly, for neglecting the fact of consciousness. The naturalist may account for nature, but not for himself as an observer of nature. But a more comprehensive error is the rejection of all the "imponderables," of all the higher values which Naturalism, when it aspires to be a philosophy, turns into an entirely inexplicable and phantasmal cloud of subjective judgments, which have no influence on the world of reality. Just as Science resents the intrusion of the spiritual, caricatured as the supernatural, within its own domain, so, and with still better reason, do philosophy and religion resent this treatment of the realities with which they deal. I have pointed out elsewhere that the simplifying process by which Naturalism aims at reducing everything to the fundamental laws of movement in general ends finally in a statement of the nature of reality in mathematical symbols, which are valid whether there is anything corresponding to them in nature or not. "So (I have said) the philosophy which professes to be grounded on the solid rock of observed phenomena, severely rejecting all subjective human valuations, ends in pure mentalism, which is independent of the existence of any external world whatever."

But the floating mass of opinions in a society which has accepted Science among other factors of its working hypotheses is a jumble of pantheism and Naturalism, combined with other elements taken over from other traditions. The trend towards materialism is partly the result of the rather gross character of nineteenth-century industrialism, and partly of the accident that Science explained celestial phenomena, natural history, and physics before it made any deep study of mind. Hence a premature synthesis was attempted on materialistic lines. Our knowledge of mind is still very incomplete, but psychology is already in revolt against the old mechanism.

In England, however, the naturalists were really anxious not to allow their theories about nature to upset traditional morality. Our leading men of science were excellent Victorians, who generally left us with a very conventional morality, based largely on Christian tradition. But the younger men are much more independent. It is from them, rather than from the men of the nineteenth century, whether, like Herbert Spencer and Darwin, they surveyed the process of evolution with hope, or whether, like Huxley in his famous Romanes Lecture, they regarded it as an enemy of morality, that we may learn the real tendency of naturalistic ethics when emancipated from earlier traditions.

These men reject the hedonistic calculus of Bentham. The test and standard to which all traditional moral rules are brought, and by which they are accepted or condemned, is their tendency to promote or hinder the full healthy development of human nature. It is because, in their opinion, this criterion has never been really applied since the victory of the Christian Church that they are ready to set aside, as mere taboo-morality, much of what has passed for accepted truth in matters of right and wrong. Asceticism is rejected *in toto,* as based on an obsolete doctrine of the impurity of matter. The sexual morality inculcated by the Church, which has never been observed with any strictness by the average sensual man, is now openly repudiated, even by women, and the freedom which was often practised with a bad conscience is now claimed without any sense of guilt. In accordance with the ideal of full healthy development, morality as a whole has acquired a more positive character, and the avoidance of sin is no longer valued as the test of goodness. Virtue is to be autonomous, and to be pursued without hope of future reward or fear of future punishment. The welfare of the species, and the better organisation of society, take the place of other-worldly aspirations. Moral censure is almost confined to anti-social conduct. Those who are most thoroughly under the influence of the scientific spirit disapprove of the soft humanitarianism which governed public opinion during the hundred years' peace. They distrust sentimental philanthropy and democracy, and tend to be rather hard in the social surgery which they advocate. On this side Nietzsche is a representative of the scientific temper. Their contemptuous rejection of old-fashioned delicacy leads some of them to advocate such experiments as those of Voronoff, and to look forward to a time when sexual intercourse and procreation will be regarded as separate things.

These seem to be the chief characteristics of a morality inspired by natural science. But we may take a broader survey of modern life, and attempt to characterise our present secularist culture, whether it draws its principles directly from Science or not.

Professor Percy Gardner has said that "of the various enthusiasms of our day there is none save secularity which is not to be reconciled with Christianity." This judgment is, I believe, right, though it sounds harsh. It is not that the secularist ideal is wanting in power. As Eucken says, "The movement proceeds towards a powerful concentration of life upon immediate existence, upon a development of natural culture, which forbids all progress, interpretation, and elevation beyond the realm of ordinary life. The kernel of such a life is built up by the empirical investigation of nature, together with technics and the practical politics of human society. There originates then a newer and more secular type of life with such energy and self-consciousness as have never been hitherto witnessed. Such a type of life has verified itself through undreamed-of achievements; it has opened out a large field of new tasks which have drawn man ever more exclusively into their vortex, and which have busied him almost breathlessly. The more the spiritual activity binds itself to such a reality, the more shadowy and untenable becomes each and every religion." That this ideal can inspire fanatical enthusiasm, with a persecuting cruelty at least as ruthless as any religion, has been proved in more than one revolution; but disillusion soon follows. As Gardner says: "Christianity starts with paradoxical axioms, which lead to a life which has for eighteen centuries passed as noble and lofty. Secularity starts from axioms apparently obvious and full of common sense; yet it leads in practice to a quagmire which there is no passing, to practical failure out of which there is no escape."

Eucken complains that the present-day civilisation, in spite of all its great achievements, "has no inner solidarity of conviction, no thought-world which embraces the human soul, no dominating ideal of life. Accordingly it cannot ground morality in the core of our being, nor give it a form corresponding to the stage of world-historical development and work. . . . Whereas man was once held responsible before the bar of morality, now morality has to justify itself before man; the old-time judge now stands in the dock."

An individualistic philosophy resting on an universal law of nature recalls the Ethics of Stoicism, and Hatch's judgment that the Ethics of Christendom are, or were for a long time, Stoic rather than Palestinian. There is no doubt that Christian Ethics owe much to Stoicism, nor that both Calvinism and modern science are ethically Stoical. But the extent to which Stoicism has been changed in being Christianised may be gauged by one sentence from the "De Natura Deorum" of Cicero: "Men confess that they have received prosperity from the gods; no one ever alleges that he has received a virtue from God."

Nevertheless it would be unjust to attribute modern secularism of the vulgar type to the influence of Science, which is an ennobling study. The philosophy based on Science may have something to answer for; but the causes of practical materialism, which is what the writers just quoted have in mind, are not to be found in any intellectual system, but in "original sin, the corruption of man's heart." There has never been a time when moralists have not been justified in exclaiming "*O tempora! O mores!*" The prevalent ideas of the time do no more than determine the direction which moral evils are likely to take.

It seems to me that on the whole the moral influence of the new knowledge has been beneficial. The air that blows round Science is like the air of a mountain-top, thin but pure and bracing. Heracleitus had already caught some of its inspiration when he said, "Wisdom is to speak the truth and consciously to act according to nature." And Lucretius recognised with thankfulness the great emancipation which *naturæ species ratioque* bring from superstitious terrors and the crimes which they instigate. I will enumerate some of the moral gains which we owe, at least in part, to the modern spirit.

Even in religion and politics, where passion and prejudice are most potent to obscure the intellect and distort the judgment, there is a higher standard of veracity and more respect for evidence. Rhetoric and advocacy are distrusted, and those who practise the art of persuasion try to disguise the craft which they once exercised openly. The scientific spirit has transformed history, and has infused a new conscientiousness into literature and public speaking. It is needless to add that very much remains to be done.

Curiosity, condemned as *turpis* by monkish morality, is now praised as it was by the Greeks. The search for truth, as Lessing and others have been found to assert, brings more benefit than the possession of it. In the highest quests the struggle is the prize, and we have recovered the conviction that one of the noblest of quests is to learn the laws by which the universe is governed. I will give two quotations to illustrate the strength with which this conviction is held. Carveth Read writes: "All that Aristotle says of the philosophic life is true, namely, that it is the exercise of that which is highest in our nature, and concerned with the highest things, the being and laws of the universe; that it is a more enduring activity than any other; that it gives the purest enjoyment to those who sufficiently practise it; that it is less dependent than any other pursuit upon external conditions. More than anything else it is its own end and reward; it is the noblest occupation of that leisure in which human life perfects itself. Such are Aristotle's sublime reflections upon his own occupation; for the most part as true now as ever they were." Huxley thus sets forth the aims of his own career: "To promote the increase of natural knowledge, and to forward the application of scientific methods of investigation to all the problems of life to the best of my ability, in the conviction, which has grown with my growth and strengthened with my strength, that there is no alleviation for the sufferings of mankind, except veracity of thought and action, and the resolute facing of the world as it is, when the garment of make-believe, by which pious hands have hidden its uglier features, is stripped off."

The centre of gravity in morals, as in theology, is changing from authority to rational motive and the conscience of the individual. We can hardly overestimate the importance of this emancipation of the conscience and reason. New ethical demands arise from the new knowledge, and from new circumstances. These demands are very easily silenced by authoritative tradition. Examples will be given below; the victory of moral autonomy is not yet secure. Nor shall I hide my conviction that much caution is necessary in setting aside moral tradition. What impatient innovators call taboos may be the fruit of long racial experience. The man who disregards the accepted standard of good taste and good manners is a barbarian, and the new convention that fiction is not bound by conventions of decency is, I think, unfortunate. Rash experiments in morals very often bring disaster. "Wise men," says Burke, "instead of exploding general prejudices, employ their sagacity to discover the latent wisdom which prevails in them."

Although Science is agnostic about the existence of a personal God, it is positive enough in rejecting indignantly much that has been believed about God. God, if there is a God, is not a capricious Oriental sultan, nor a magnified schoolmaster, nor the head of the clerical profession. Seeley was quite right in saying that science reveres a worthier God than the average churchgoer. The God of traditional Catholicism and Calvinism, though not lustful like Jupiter, was far more cruel and unjust. Nothing so revolting as the damnation of unbaptised children, of all Jews, Turks, infidels, and heretics, or of those who without fault of their own were predestined to reprobation, was ever taught by Paganism. Mill's well-known refusal to call any Being good who is not what we mean by good when we apply the word to our fellow-creatures is in accordance with the conscience of our time. "Shall not the Judge of all the earth do right?" Abraham's question is now asked confidently; and an affirmative answer sweeps away a mass of iniquity which ought never to have been attributed to the Father of our Lord Jesus Christ. False, not to say blasphemous, beliefs about the character of God and His dealings with men, have been responsible for a large proportion of the crimes and frauds which have stained the history of the Church, and for the rejection of the Christianity in which they were brought up by many high-minded men and women.

The abandonment of miracle is almost pure gain. It would have been well if medicine had not been so slow to accept the wise words of Hippocrates on the Sacred Disease (epilepsy). "Things are divine or not as you wish, for the distinction makes no difference, and there is no need to make the division anywhere in nature, for all things are alike divine, and all things are alike human." Europe is still plagued with priestly frauds, imaginary cures, and superstitions of every kind. But Science has laid the axe to the root of the tree, and we may hope that by degrees all such beliefs and half-beliefs will be either discredited or placed on a scientific basis.

The modern mind asks what a man is good for, not what he is bad for. This too is a salutary change, and thoroughly Christian. It is also in accordance with the method of Christ to attack diseases instead of their symptoms, and to hold that prevention is better than cure.

That man is a part of nature, not a wholly unique creation, the solitary "person" in a world of "things," is a far-reaching truth. It is the basis of our duties, not only to the lower animals, but to the earth whose beauties modern civilisation is defacing, and whose resources it is wantonly squandering. The fine, if difficult, poetry, of George Meredith is inspired throughout by his "love of earth," an emotion which belongs to our own time, and, we may hope, still more to the future.

Lastly, the fruitful conception of rational self-determination, the confidence that both we ourselves and our environment can be progressively modified for the better, is a modern acquisition. "The rapture of the forward view" is ours. The greatly extended horizon which Science has opened for the human race, in place of the "Come, O Lord," of the first-century Christians, has supplied an idealistic element even for modern secularism. When purged from its superstitions and apocalyptic accessories, it may restore for us some of the enthusiasm with which the early Christians awaited the second coming of Christ. It would not be fanciful to find some analogy between the joyous trust of Christ in the Father in heaven who makes His sun to rise on the evil and on the good, and without whom no sparrow falls to the ground, and the reverent spirit in which the man of science accepts whatever facts his studies reveal to him, confident that "the universe is friendly" to him who devotes himself without reserve to the discovery of truth.

THE AGE OF INDUSTRIALISM

The other determining factor in modern civilisation is industrialism, with the marvellous advance in applied science and technology which it has fostered. This is, of course, the direct result of that progress in Science of which I have been speaking; the two factors in modern life are closely interrelated.

One great change which this awakening of the West brought about was the decisive triumph of Europe over Asia in material power and prestige. We often forget that throughout the dark and the middle ages Europe was in a state of blockade, cut off from the Far East, and in terror of subjugation by Saracens, Tartars, and the Grand Turk. The tide of conquest has swung backwards and forwards from very early history; but never before have the European races so nearly mastered the whole world as in the period before the Great War. This expansion gave to the West a new and overweening confidence in its own intrinsic superiority. It seemed plain that God, or Nature, was on the side of the white man, and, some would add, of the Christian religion, since the Crescent could no longer contend on equal terms against the Cross. It even seemed that God was on the side, especially, of the Protestant nations, who showed themselves more inventive, more energetic, and (for a time) more prolific than the Mediterraneans. No attempt was made to trace the connexion of the Protestant religion with the possession of the best coalfields and of the geographical position most favourable for trade. A kind of Deuteronomic religion was popular in Britain; because we were a righteous and Christian nation, our trade increased, our debt diminished, and our children possessed the earth. The rivals of Christianity were no longer formidable; even the tribesmen of Jenghiz Khan, by adopting Buddhism, had become harmless and peaceful, unlike Mohammedans or Christians. But this complacent Christianity was a secularised religion. The modern man laboured religiously when he knew that evolution was on his side; he rested his faith on progress—that is, on that form of advance which can be measured by statistics. Christianity became what it had never been before, a rather vulgar this-world religion. The middle ages had made religion a business; the nineteenth century made business a religion. I need not go to America for an illustration; the *Times* obituary notice of Holloway (of the pills) will suffice. "Money-making is an art by itself; it demands for success the devotion of the whole man. Sleeping or waking, his thoughts must be devoted to it. It is not everyone who is capable of such single-hearted attention as this. Most men wish to be wealthy, but with a want of steadiness and singleness of purpose. Politics or love are great things to them; they are not willing to give them up as so many snares by which the path of money-making is beset." An older authority said, "Ye cannot serve God and Mammon." An American has said, "To mix religion and business is to spoil two good things," but he wished to have them both. Our journalist agreed with Christ, except that he admired those who choose Mammon and let the Other go.

Romanticism, which was essentially a revolt on behalf of the higher values, helped to undermine both the complacency of the age and the ruthless industrialism which that complacency tolerated. Carlyle held up a candle to the grim realities of "the condition of

England"; Ruskin saw that our total indifference to ugliness, whether in town-planning or in masculine dress or in painting, was an ethical blot on the national character. Humanitarianism helped by arousing pity for the poor; the poor themselves were becoming conscious of their power. The industrial system was indeed destroying the conditions of its own permanence. Science itself became uneasy about racial degeneration, and exposed the unwisdom of a reckless increase of population, which absorbed wealth as soon as it was created. Various reforms were introduced, in spite of the fears of the employers; and for a time industry was able to bear the new burdens. For various reasons, the competition of the cheaper countries was, for a considerable time, less severe than had been expected.

The fundamental question for publicists is whether the dense population of Great Britain, and the high standard of living to which our people are accustomed, can be maintained if the economic system which brought about those conditions is drastically changed. It is almost certain that under collective ownership, since the most powerful motives for hard work and improved technology would be removed, there would be a general decline in output and a great loss of foreign trade. Such a change might easily cause a very disastrous increase of unemployment, and a heavy fall in the aggregate income available for distribution. Experiments in collectivism, and still more in Communism, have not been at all encouraging to supporters of revolutionary schemes. Meanwhile, an alternative solution of the problem of poverty seems to be offered by standardised production on a large scale, and by the use of improved machinery. In the United States this system has diminished manual drudgery, increased real wages, and placed within the reach of the working man a number of comforts, luxuries, and especially amusements, such as was never thought possible at any earlier time. So far as it is possible to predict the economic future, it is in this direction, rather than by the confiscation of all private capital, that the nations of the West are likely to move.

The problems of production, distribution, and consumption are thus mainly intellectual, not ethical, though it is a moral duty for all who have a share in political power to form an intelligent judgment on the probable effects of the reforms which are put before them, and above all not to base their decisions on the narrow interests of the class to which they belong. But frequent attempts have been made to claim that the Church, as a corporate body, ought to take an active part in supporting political measures of social reform, and that in doing so it is only carrying out the precepts of the Gospel. Many persons would say that the establishment of "the Kingdom of God" on earth under a reign of social righteousness is the most important of "modern ethical problems." It will therefore be worth while to give a sketch of the attitude of Christianity in the past to economic questions. We shall then be in a position to judge whether what is now called Socialism is in the true line of development of Christian Ethics.

SOCIAL TEACHING OF THE EARLY CHURCH

The characteristics of Christ's social teaching have been stated in an earlier chapter. He proclaimed a "transvaluation of all values," according to which an avaricious man is stigmatised as "thou fool"; and there is no "profit" in gaining the whole world and losing one's own soul. God is just; but His justice is not dealt out in the world's currency. "Some of you they shall kill and crucify; and there shall not a hair of your head perish." The prerogative of service should alone distinguish the "great" among the disciples from the rank and file. The Gospel is quite original in affixing moral censure to worry and anxiety, which proceed from covetousness and want of trust in God.

This Gospel of spiritual redemption has often bifurcated into two principles, which may seem contrary to each other. One is the quietistic, resigned temper, the other is the radical. Christ and His disciples stood entirely outside all political and social agitation. The early Christians accepted the existing political and social conditions; even under persecution they were never provoked to advocate rebellion. On the other hand, it is easy to see how indifference to civilisation may pass into hostility to it. Sectarian Christianity has sometimes been revolutionary.

But if the Gospel cares little for outward liberty and equality, it cares a great deal for fraternity. The Christian is to combine detachment from the world with a warm attachment to the men and women who live in it. Nor does the Gospel draw any hard line between the spiritual and temporal needs of our neighbour. Christian Ethics are not ascetic where the wants of others are concerned. If there is here any inconsistency, the law of love takes the responsibility. Robert Louis Stevenson makes the profoundly true observation that it is the dealings of God with others, not with ourselves, which often shake our faith in divine justice.

The Acts of the Apostles describes a sort of communistic experiment, on purely voluntary lines. There has always been a slight tendency in Christianity to regard community of goods as the ideal; but the only serious attempt to carry it into effect was in the monasteries. I have already said that history seems to have proved that Communism is possible only under two conditions—a religious basis and celibacy.

The modern idea that the moral and spiritual order ought to be reflected in social and political institutions did not affect early Christian thought. When the clash became intolerable, the Church counselled only retirement from the world. It would be unreasonable to expect anything different from a sect which was politically powerless, in a society devoid of hope and drifting into decrepitude. The Carpocratian Gnostics preached that "property is theft," and advocated "poverty," like the Franciscans later; but there was no organised Communism even among these sectaries. Nor was there any expectation of great social changes. The Christians did not expect that the barbarians would destroy the Empire. For Barnabas, Irenæus, and Hippolytus the Empire is the fourth world-power predicted by Daniel, and destined to endure till the return of Christ. Lactantius, somewhat less confident, says that all Christians ought to pray that "the abominable tyrant who will conceive such a crime as the extinguishing of the light of Rome, which sustains all things, may not come sooner than we think."

Trade was disparaged by the early Christians, and interest on capital forbidden "as between brothers," but not on the Aristotelian theory that money is naturally barren. There was no glorification of work, as itself a service of God; for this we must, in the main, wait for the Reformation. Work was a duty, but also a punishment.

Nevertheless, Christian homiletics in the fourth century were increasingly socialistic. Ambrose, the Christian Stoic, follows Seneca in a rather rhetorical denunciation of riches, and many other similar passages, detached from their context, have been collected by modern Socialists. But I think that these are rather flowers of oratory than prophetic warnings uttered in deadly earnest. Gregory the Great and many others distinguished between the right to own property and the right to use it for personal enjoyment.

The Stoical Law of Nature had a great influence upon Christian thought, an influence which abides to this day in the Roman Church. But the Roman lawyers were not all of one mind about the contents of the Law of Nature, and this uncertainty was reflected in the teaching of the Church. Gaius (about 150 A.D.) makes no distinction between *ius naturæ* and *ius gentium;* Ulpian (about 190 A.D.) sharply distinguishes them. Gaius traces the authority of *ius gentium* to *naturalis ratio.* The distinction is between the primitive ideal and actual conventional practice. The Christians taught that the change is the result of man's fallen state. Florentinus makes private property primitive and natural; Ulpian is not explicit on this point. We cannot say that even the Stoical lawyers regarded private property as only part of the *ius gentium,* though they went further in this direction than Aristotle. The *ius civile* was a third category, the actual law of the State.

The Christian writers usually accept the doctrine or doctrines of the Stoical lawyers; Lactantius, Ambrose and Augustine make much use of Cicero, particularly the "De Officiis." The practical consequences which they drew from the theory, as regards private property, may be illustrated by the following passage from Lactantius: "Some one will say, Are there not among you some rich, some poor, some slaves, others masters? Are there not differences among individuals? There is no other reason why we call each other brothers, except that we believe ourselves to be all equal. But since we measure all human things not by the body but by the spirit, although bodily conditions are diverse, yet for us slaves are not slaves, but we regard them and speak of them as brothers in spirit, as fellow slaves in religion. Riches, too, confer no distinction except that they make it possible to be more conspicuous in good works. Since then we are equal in humility of mind, freemen with slaves and rich with poor, yet in the sight of God we are distinguished in point of virtue. In proportion as a man is just he is exalted. If he bears himself not merely as an equal but as an inferior, he will attain a much higher degree of dignity in the judgment of God. For in this earthly life all things are short-lived and fragile." This is very characteristic. Equality is justice, but equality is only equality before God; it carries with it no claim to economic equality, but only (a very important thing in a slave-State) to equality of consideration.

The Church doctrine was that the Law of Nature is adapted to the state of nature. Gregory the Great quotes the Stoical dogma, *"Omnes homines natura æquales sumus";* but adds that as a punishment for sin and as a remedy against it, God has sanctioned the civil power, with its hierarchy. This was the regular teaching of the middle ages. The belief in an unconditioned standard of justice was not forgotten, and in the monasteries the aim was to live according to this standard without any accommodation.

SOCIAL TEACHING OF THE MIDDLE AGES

There has been too great a tendency to judge the middle ages by the standard either of the original Gospel or of the modern period. It is a chapter of European civilisation to be judged by itself, conditioned as it was by the circumstances belonging to a stage in human evolution which it is the business of the historian to understand.

The policy of the Church was to prevent a repetition of the disruption which wrecked the secular Empire. I have dealt with the moral results of this theocratic imperialism in an earlier chapter, and have admitted that before the Renaissance the Church rendered valuable services to civilisation. The virtues inculcated by feudalism—the characteristic social structure of the middle ages—were loyalty and service on the one side, knightly courage and protection on the other. This ideal was not wholly alien to Christianity, and the Church made some attempt to moralise chivalry, emphasising the duty of helping the weak and redressing wrong. Romantic love was very different from the pictures of it in Tennyson's "Idylls," but at least the love of the sexes was, almost for the first time, idealised and given a mystical value. We can see by the example of Dante and Beatrice how one variety of chivalric love, the idealisation of a woman who could never be possessed, was brought into the service of religion. There was, in fact, a compromise between Christian sex-ethics and the secular morality of chivalry, which was developed especially in Provence. The Church also tried to draw militarism into its service by the Crusades and the fighting orders, half freebooters and half monks.

But the medieval town, squeezed in behind its walls, was a far better field for the development of Christian social morality than the feudalised country districts. The towns desired peace, freedom, mutual service, and industry. The towns built their noble churches, they had their trade guilds, all on a religious basis; they had their schools, colleges, and universities. The evils of capitalism were still in the future. The medieval town was on the whole more favourable to Christian life than the ancient city had ever been. It was a community of free workmen, still closely connected with country life. In Italy especially this type was well developed, though not without some outbreaks of class-warfare. Christianity had always been a town religion. St. Paul kept to the main roads, and founded his churches in the large cities. The name Pagan (if we accept the older explanation, which is now disputed) shows how comparatively slowly the Church won its victory in remote country districts. So it was in the medieval towns that a Christian culture first arose, and it was the towns that produced the authors of standard books, like St. Thomas Aquinas, who has held a unique position of authority in Western Catholicism. To his social teaching I must now turn.

Aquinas has much to say about the Law of Nature. It is the Law of God, residing in the mind of God Himself. Every created being shares in this eternal reason after its manner, but rational creatures share in it rationally, and this sharing in the eternal law by a rational creature is called *lex naturalis.* Human laws are the application of the Law of Nature to particular circumstances. In support of this doctrine Aquinas cites Aristotle, Cicero, Augustine, and Isidore.

But, as I have said already, the doctrine of the ancient philosophers about private property was not uniform. The Stoics taught that the original Law of Nature was Communism; this was not the view of Aristotle. So the Schoolmen admitted a *lex naturalis humana,* a relative Law of Nature which had the validity of the absolute Law of Nature for mankind in existing circumstances, or, as the Schoolmen put it, under the state of sin. But could the Law of Nature, which is the unchangeable Law of God, be changed by circumstances? The question was not easy to answer. Aquinas says that "utility" has made legitimate modifications of the Law of Nature, and that this utility, or expediency, has introduced the principle of private ownership. Communism belongs only to the state of innocence; it is impracticable, and therefore wrong, for man in his fallen state.

But the Decalogue was now added to Aristotle and the Stoa. It was not, I think, put into the catechism till after the Reformation, but it was declared to be authoritative. By interpretation its simple prohibitions were given a very wide extension—a method with which most of us were made familiar in our childhood. Aquinas can say that Christian morals are contained in the Decalogue *sicut conclusiones in principiis.*

Nevertheless, the distinction between an absolute and a relative Law of Nature was in process of being suspended by the newer dualism of natural and supernatural. The supernatural or divine Law, often identified with the "new law" of charity, transcends all natural law. From this point of view the Decalogue was only propædeutic, a preparation for the Gospel. The supernatural life, according to the developed Catholic theory, is normally mediated only through the sacraments, though mysticism was a standing refutation of this claim. The effect of this supernaturalistic dualism was necessarily to put all natural perfection on a lower plane. The whole of secular civilisation, with its Ethics, is determined by the state of sin, in which the world stands.

The Pauline doctrine of society as an organism dominated scholastic and post-scholastic thought. The organism, in accordance with the whole trend of the middle ages, was conceived on patriarchal lines. The hierarchy of Aristotle was based on the recognition of the natural *inequality* of mankind. The female sex, he thought, was naturally inferior to the male; and some persons, perhaps even some races, were only 'fit for servitude—φύσει δοῦλοι. When we remember the language often used to-day about "inferior races" we have no right to throw stones at Aristotle. But the Stoics and Cicero indignantly repudiated the theory of natural slaves; and I do not think the Church ever admitted it. Aquinas dwells rather on the idea of the human race as a *corpus mysticum,* and the grades of society are also *corpora mystica.* "The distinction of members," he says, "is the work of Nature, and Nature does this as the instrument of divine providence." It is, he says, right and natural (here he follows Aristotle) that those who are intellectually superior should rule, and that those who are only bodily robust should serve. The mischief is that this "natural" supremacy of the intellectual aristocracy is frequently violated in practice. Providence permits this to happen, without approving it. Aquinas therefore believes in aristocracy and a hierarchical order of society; he only wishes that his aristocracy should be actually a rule of the best. He even says that "distributive justice" gives more of the "common goods" to those who hold leading positions in the community, and in proportion to their positions of authority.

But Aquinas meant his proviso about *true* aristocracy to be taken seriously. It must not be supposed that the middle ages were at all submissive to bad laws and bad rulers. Feudalism, from top to bottom, was essentially a system of contractual relations, not of arbitrary power. We are astonished at the explicitness with which the right of revolt—even the right of assassination—is maintained by several medieval writers. Even Aquinas, who is conspicuous as a supporter of law and order, lays down the important principle that "in the court of conscience there is no obligation to obey an unjust law." There was an undercurrent of dislike of the State, as something conventional and unnatural, all through the middle ages, and afterwards till Rousseau. It is therefore possible for Catholic political theory to take a revolutionary turn, on the ground that the power is in the wrong hands. Catholicism has usually been and still is mainly a Conservative force; but it is always easy for a Catholic to find arguments for Socialism, if not for Communism, as we see in many Anglo-Catholics in England to-day.

Thomism certainly strengthens the traditional stability of social stratification; but this very Conservatism has made Catholicism, which is still based on Aquinas, unfriendly to the industrial revolution, towards which Calvinism has been on the whole sympathetic. And the mixture of organic and individualistic ideas which we find in him may be so interpreted as to favour Liberalism.

The idea of divine right, not in the absurd form in which it was preached by James I and the royalists of the Stuart monarchy, dates back to Gregory the Great. The secular power is a divine institution and derives its authority from God. The social contract is also a medieval conception, which limits the doctrine of divine right. It was this side of medieval theory which the Stuarts ignored, to their own undoing. The oath of allegiance is cancelled if the King is mad or bad, because an oath to do evil is null and void. A king who breaks his side of the contract may be deposed, or even put to death, as John of Salisbury and Marsilius of Padua affirm.

Lastly, Aquinas gives a new importance to "my station and its duties," a doctrine which implies that civil society has a positive value. In spite of his Aristotelian class-ethics, he is saved by his Christian individualism from the exaltation of the State and neglect of the rights of the individual, which we find in Plato and Aristotle, and which was revived in modern times by German political philosophy. But he did not fully solve the question—Is the ideal the actualisation of objective value in itself, or the sharing in it by individuals? This is one of the deepest problems of social Ethics. The idea of unity tends to be changed into the idea of authority; in the middle ages this refuge from difficulties was always near at hand. Distributive justice cannot be rendered in this life; natural inequality makes it impossible, and attempts to rectify this inequality by legislation would destroy the organic structure of the nation. After death distributive justice is dispensed fairly to all. But even in heaven there are grades of beatitude, as Beatrice informs Dante. Saints and virgins have something over, to help others.

So there was still no Christian idea of social reform. To the ancient Church this had been too difficult; to the medieval Church it was superfluous. The actual order was idealised and identified with the Law of Nature. To this day, Catholic social reform is theoretically a return towards the Law of Nature, under the direction of the Church. Enthusiastic patriotism was excluded by the whole point of view. For better and for worse, loyalty to the nation and glorification of the State were both repressed.

The town rather than the country was the norm for medieval thinkers, who in this respect were less influenced by feudalism than is often supposed. Modern Catholicism, on the other hand, is agrarian in its sympathies, and is comparatively weak in the large cities of our day. The traditional condemnation of usury, which goes back to Aristotle, has made Catholicism unsympathetic to "big business" of every kind.

The Catholic Church did nothing to abolish slavery, which subsisted in Spain till the eighteenth century. It was excused on the ground that the slaves were usually not Christians. This is one of the cases in which sectarian Protestantism gave a lead in a moral reform which had been delayed too long for the credit of Christendom. The backwardness of the United States and Brazil in the New World (one a Protestant, the other a Catholic country) in abolishing slavery is deplorable, though it may be palliated in view of difficult social conditions.

SOCIAL TEACHING OF THE REFORMERS

The forces which produced the Reformation were gathering strength from the close of the dark ages. Each movement claimed to be a return to the original Gospel, and the claims had some partial justification. But the Reformation was not only religious. It was part of a great upheaval which altered the whole structure of society.

The middle ages had been economically a system of city-States, with feudalism reigning outside the town walls. This system was now breaking up in Western Europe, and Western Europe was, at that time, Christendom. For Christendom had shrunk sadly since the seventh century. The Saracens and their successors had overrun many lands which were formerly Christian—Palestine, Syria, Asia Minor, North Africa, and the greater part of Spain. In the middle of the fourteenth century the Ottoman Turks seized Gallipoli and part of the Balkan peninsula, thus cutting off Constantinople from the rest of Christendom. A hundred years later the East Roman Empire ceased to exist, and the Turks threatened the German lands. They were before the walls of Vienna in 1527, and only the Adriatic separated Europe from the Ottoman Empire.

Five nations, England, France, Spain, Germany, and Italy, included almost the whole area of European culture, and a process of consolidation was going on in each of them. The half-independent nobility of England perished in the Wars of the Roses. A great economic revolution had taken place, expedited by the Black Death, which led to fifty years of prosperity for the surviving labourers. The great agricultural strike, as we should now call it, under Wat Tyler and the priest Ball helped to change the serfs into free people working for wages. A new middle class, recruited partly from the younger sons of the feudal magnates, sprang up; and England, first among the European peoples, became a compact nation. Trade flourished and money was abundant. Meanwhile Louis XI was consolidating his power in France by breaking the great feudal nobles, and by a revolt against the authority of the Pope almost as drastic as that of Henry VIII. But Francis I was obliged to make a compromise with Leo X in 1516. Spain was expelling the Moors, and uniting its independent provinces. Germany and Italy remained disintegrated, from causes which we need not now consider: but there was at any rate the *idea* of unity, in Germany under the Emperor, who called himself "Imperator Cæsar Divus Maximilianus Pius Felix Augustus," and in Italy under the Pope, who increased his territorial domains as well as his spiritual and temporal claims. In both countries the feudal system survived the blows which shattered it in England and France.

Of the Renaissance Symonds says: "It was the emancipation of the reason in a race of men intolerant of control, ready to criticise canons of conduct, enthusiastic of antique liberty, freshly awakened to the sense of beauty, and anxious above all things to secure for themselves free scope in matters outside the region of authority. Men so vigorous and independent felt the joy of exploration. There was no problem they feared to face, no formula they were not eager to recast according to the new conceptions."

The Popes, as is well known, were well disposed towards the new learning, and many have speculated whether, if Luther had not come forward to "distend his huge Wittenberg lungs" and "bring back theology like a flood over Europe," the Catholic Church might not have reformed itself in the manner that Erasmus desired, and found a congenial task in debarbarising Christianity, bridging the gulf between the old civilisation in which it took its rise, and the new which was deriving its inspiration from the newly-recovered literary and artistic treasures of civilised antiquity.

But the abuses of the Papal government made a Reformation on humanist lines impossible. The humanists were not fighters; the times called for rougher men and rougher measures. Indeed, on one side the Reformation was a medievalist reaction against the Renaissance, which was degenerating into Neo-Pagan æstheticism and licence. The moral conscience of Puritanism, which has always been strongest in the northern races, rose in revolt against the manners of Italy.

Another predisposing cause of the Reformation was the break-up of the unification of dogma and philosophy, of the Law of Nature and positive divine ordinances, which Thomas Aquinas and his school had attempted with so much apparent success. Nominalism is always a disintegrating philosophy; thinkers like Occam undermined the basis of the medieval synthesis. This decay of medieval ideas helped to set free the spirit of Protestantism, which had been moving restlessly in all Catholic lands for centuries.

We are to consider the effect of the Reformation on the preaching of the Kingdom of God—that is, on the relation of religion to the world-order.

Luther individualised piety. He released the religious interest from its entanglement with world-politics. The growing importance of national States, towns, and business interests made this release easier. The change may be summed up as a change from hierarchic sacramentalism to the religion of personal conviction. This change really involved the fall of the Catholic supernaturalistic dualism. There was no more supernature sharply distinguishable from the natural order; no more counsels of perfection to be realised only in the monastic life. The Christian is face to face with the world as he finds it, and must conquer it for Christ.

Nevertheless, Lutheranism was in part reactionary, not only in its attitude towards humanism and science, but in its negation of the idea of development. Catholicism even at this time had more notion of development than Luther, for whom the Fall, the Atonement, and the final restitution of all things were the only important facts in history.[1] And in spite of all changes, Lutheranism belongs to the Church-type, not to the Sect-type. It aimed not at a new Church, but at an *instauratio Catholica*. The word of grace, and preaching, to which it gave a new prominence, to some extent, but not entirely, took the place of the Sacraments. The invisible Church is not really a Lutheran idea. But Luther never succeeded in reconciling his emphasis on spiritual and personal religion with his doctrine of the Church. He did not incorporate in his system the best teaching of the Sect-type of Chris-

[1] There is, however, not much to choose between the staticism of Luther, Calvin, and the Catholics. Luther says: "If outside of Christ you wish by your own thoughts to know your relation to God, you will break your neck. Thunder strikes him who examines." Calvin: "Everything pertaining to the perfect rule of a good life the Lord has so comprehended in His law that there remains nothing for man to add to that summary." And the Council of Trent: "He who is gifted with the heavenly knowledge of faith is saved from an inquisitive curiosity."

tianity, which had chiefly kept alive or restored to life
the spirit of the original Gospel. In his appeal to
the Bible he neglected the Synoptic Gospels, and interpreted Christ through St. Paul, and through a St.
Paul whom he never thoroughly understood. The enthusiastic and mystical side of St. Paul's religion fell,
in his interpretation, far behind the dogmatic and ecclesiastical. Luther was essentially a Church reformer,
driven into rebellion by the hostility of the central government, and by forces which, when once liberated,
were far beyond his control.

He was not a clear thinker, but a courageous and
rough-handed man of action, by no means lacking in
political wisdom. At times he insists on taking the
Sermon on the Mount in the literal sense, as binding
on all Christians, and so approximates to the Sect-type,
of which we have said something already and shall have
to say more. But he also asserts the divine authority
of all earthly institutions, a Catholic doctrine, as we have
seen, but one which was commended to him by the absolute necessity of enlisting the support of the German
princelets on his side. He quite explicitly justifies war
as legitimate and necessary. I think this is important,
because it was evidently one source of the German
militarist Ethics, the consequences of which other nations have had cause to deplore. The doctrine, sometimes explicitly stated, sometimes merely assumed, is
that Christianity is, on the moral side, a system of individual Ethics, a principle of personal conduct, but that
it is not concerned with national and international
politics, in which the interests of the State are the
supreme law. It would not be fair to blame Luther
or Lutheranism only for this unhappy theory, which is
propounded in the notorious "Prince" of Machiavelli,
and hardly less plainly in our own Francis Bacon and
Thomas Hobbes. When the authority of the Pope

in international politics was repudiated, there was nothing to take its place. Grotius and others did their best to formulate principles of international law; but there was no clear doctrine of the supremacy of the Gospel over the relations of peoples. Luther and the Lutheran Church have been, I think, especially unfortunate in handling this problem, and their ready acceptance of war as a permanent necessity for human societies has been a weapon in the hands of militarist parties. Even before the war I have read strangely unethical utterances by responsible and representative Germans on this subject.

I must devote one paragraph to the teaching of Luther on the Law of Nature. "You have often heard from me," he says, "that political and economical ordinances are divine, because God Himself ordained them as He did the moon and other creatures." And yet: "There was no polity (*Politia*) before sin, for there was no need of it; for polity is the necessary remedy for corrupt nature. For cupidity must be restrained by the bonds and penalties of the laws, that it may not wander freely. So you may rightly call polity (political institutions) the Kingdom of sin. For it is the one, or the chief, work of political institutions, to keep out sin." But we may ask how he identifies the Law of Nature with the Christian Law of Love. He makes the Decalogue the mediator. The Law of Moses, according to him, consists partly of ceremonial and partly of moral precepts. The former were only of propædeutic and temporary validity; the latter, the moral precepts, summarised in the Decalogue, are a promulgation of the Law of Nature, and are interpreted on the positive side by the Law of Christ. Certainly the *relative* Law of Nature, conditioned by the state of sin, is far below the ideal Law of Christ. We are *all* under these two laws. "The world," he says, "is and remains unchristian; the evil are far more numerous than the good."

It is plain that this is a conception which gives but little practical guidance; it reflects a real contradiction in Luther's mind. The absurd overvaluing of the Decalogue has left its traces in numberless old-fashioned churches in England as well as in other countries, where the Two Tables of the Law, along with the Creed and the Lord's Prayer, and sometimes even alone, occupy the last wall of the chancel. They were ingeniously interpreted so as to contain all Christian Ethics. The Anglican Church Catechism contains a very favourable example of this method.

In his attitude to the secular power, the principle of obedience to authority prevailed in Luther's mind over the principle of the Law of Love. Non-resistance was defended as a part of the Law of Nature. Thus Luther was politically a Conservative. In his anxiety to have secular authority on his side—an anxiety which is to be explained rather than justified by the desperate position in which he found himself—he committed the worst error in his career. The attitude which he took up at the time of the Peasants' Revolt closely concerns our present subject.

The age was one of seething discontent and bitter class-hatred. The landlords had lost while the tenants were gaining in prosperity, and the landlords used their political power to introduce new and oppressive legislation, enclosing commons and steadily reducing the peasants once more to the condition of serfs. A series of bad harvests, and a sudden mysterious rise of prices, due not so much to American gold and silver, which had hardly yet begun to circulate, as to the opening of new mines in Europe, increased the distress. Agrarian revolts were endemic, especially in South Germany, for the peasants, who had tried their strength on the field of battle against the knight in armour and had often beaten him, were no longer submissive.

The oppressed classes looked to Luther as their champion. He had published an "Appeal to the German Nobles," in which he set forth the grievances of the common people and foretold trouble if they were not redressed. The Humanists also were sympathetic; these were the days of Sir Thomas More's "Utopia" in England, and books of the same kind, though of less note, in Germany.

The revolt broke out in 1524, suddenly and without preparation. It was not confined to the poorest class, and it was violently anti-Church. Forty monasteries were destroyed in Thuringia and the Harz Mountains. The less revolutionary among the insurgents drew up statements of their grievances. They complained of the enclosure of common land, of the *corvé* (forced labour for the landlords), and of arbitrary punishments. They claimed that each parish should choose its own pastor, with power of dismissal; that the lesser tithes (of eggs, lambs, foals, etc.) should be abolished; that serfdom should cease; that all should be allowed to fish and shoot wild game; that the enclosed commons should be restored; and that other illegal exactions should be stopped. The townspeople asked that there should be no class-barrier in appointing to municipal offices; that all citizens should have votes for civic appointments; and that better provision should be made for the poor. Other demands, made by the more advanced section, went much further.

The movement was ruthlessly suppressed by military force; it is said that from 100,000 to 150,000 insurgents lost their lives. The masses were left worse off than they were before.

Luther, whose unmeasured language had done something to encourage the rising, was divided between a genuine sympathy for the poor and an extreme respect for constituted authority. Unfortunately the latter prevailed. He hounded on the princes to exterminate the insurgents. This was not only an indelible blot on the character of Luther. It estranged the official Reformation in Germany from democratic sympathies and ideas. Henceforward, Lutheranism was in the main a middle-class movement; the artisans of the towns were the chief supporters of the Anabaptists.

Luther condemns speculation and monopolies, but he passionately defends inequality, without which, he says, no earthly State could subsist. He even tells the Christian slaves of the Turks that they must not rob their masters of their bodies, which their masters have bought. His social Ethics are patriarchal and medieval, not modern, and when the patriarchal system passed away, and an era of absolutism succeeded, Lutheranism had no more any valuable social message.

We now come to Calvinism, which has been one of the most potent religious forces in modern times. In England its influence is no longer powerful; but in Scotland and the United States the aftermath of Calvinism is still a living tradition.

Jean Cauvin or Calvin was born at Noyon in Picardy, in 1509, the son of a distinguished lawyer. No province in France had produced so many supporters of Wyclif and Hus as Picardy, and the supporters of those "heresies" were far from extinct at the beginning of the sixteenth century. He was trained for the Church, but his father, who had been excommunicated by the ecclesiastical authorities of Noyon, transferred him to the law school at Orleans. When his father died in 1531, Calvin determined to forsake law for literature, and made friends with some leading French humanists. His learned and excellent edition of Seneca on Clemency was probably meant as a protest against the persecution of the Protestants, for Calvin had already been converted. In 1533 he was driven from Paris, where he was studying and lecturing, and took refuge in Switzerland. The famous "Christianæ Religionis Institutio," by far the ablest statement of the Protestant position that had yet appeared, was published at Basle in 1536. In the following year, at the age of 27, he took up his residence at Geneva.

Geneva, like every other medieval town, had a variety of police regulations which interfered with private life at every turn. They were usually a dead letter, but from time to time a moral fit seized the city fathers, and maidservants were summoned for wearing silk aprons, or rich burghers for giving too good dinners. Calvin's regulations were quite in accordance with familiar practice in these matters. But his avowed object was to restore the discipline and practice of the primitive Church. The Holy Communion was to be administered much more frequently and evil livers were to be forbidden to communicate. The censures of the Church were to be enforced by the civil power. But there was great opposition to excommunication; and if we wish to see how Calvin's ideas were put into practice, we must look not so much at Geneva as at the French Huguenots and John Knox in Scotland.

Calvin made Geneva the citadel of the Reformation, and a city of refuge for persecuted Protestants from other lands. The native population of 13,000 was swelled by some 6000 refugees. He was a great organiser, and after his expulsion and recall he was able to set his stamp on the government of the town.

His great aim was to make the invisible sovereignty of God, revealed to man in Holy Scripture, as tangible and visible as the medieval Church had been. It was a great and necessary work to prove that to adopt the Protestant religion was not to surrender discipline or moral and social obligations.

Calvinism was more intellectual and more friendly to humanism than Lutheranism. It also laid more stress on law and discipline than on pure doctrine. It was far more active than the rival school, which has always led, on one side, to quietism and acquiescence. Calvin taught that we are fellow-workers with a transcendent God, not in the mystical sense, for Calvin was no mystic, but as an army on the side of God against the powers of evil. Energy rather than deep feeling was the proof of justification; the consciousness of being justified was a spur to action. Majesty, holiness, and grace, rather than love and mercy, are the attributes under which the Calvinist thinks of the Deity.

Calvin was fighting for the existence of Protestantism, and it is no wonder that he borrowed some weapons from the enemy's armoury. An "expiatory monument" was set up in Geneva some twenty years ago in honour of Servetus, the Unitarian whom Calvin helped to send to execution. And he proclaimed, like any curialist theologian, that *extra ecclesiæ gremium nulla est speranda peccatorum remissio*. The great Reformers after all were men of their age, the sixteenth century.

The Judaising tendency of Calvinism cannot be denied. Biblical infallibility was more trenchant and earlier formulated than the infallibility of the Roman pontiff. The letter of Scripture was regarded with superstitious reverence. The idea of a covenant between God and His people was revived. The Church was a new Israel, with a new Law. Lutheranism needed the Bible only to prove the work of Christ, and rested mainly on some of St. Paul's Epistles. Calvinism made the whole book a universal oracle, with some terrible consequences—*e.g.* the belief in witchcraft. Calvinism is combative, not passive and patient. While the Lutheran holds fast by God, the Calvinist is held fast by Him.

The consciousness of election to salvation, instead of producing a paralysing fatalism, inspired a vigorous and confident energy, rising to fanaticism. The creature is of no value except as a means; the elect is a chosen vessel in God's hands; his life is given him for a definite purpose. A strong and steady self-control, extending over the whole of life, is practised. Perfection is not a counsel for the few; it is the end which all the elect are bound to pursue. Calvinistic asceticism, as I have said in an earlier chapter, is something quite distinctive in Christian history. Self-denial has no merit in itself: it is merely a means to promote the victory of Christ's kingdom. In practice it means the reduction of all sensuous enjoyment to what is necessary or useful. This has given not only to Calvinistic morality but to the societies influenced by Calvinism a quite peculiar character, on which I shall have more to say presently.

Calvin laid great stress on a man's "calling." All work is taken up into the religious sphere; there is no distinction between sacred and profane. For the first time in the history of Christianity the dignity and value of work as work are fully insisted on. It is God's ordinance that men should work; without work there can be no holiness. Consequently, idleness is the worst of sins.

It is often brought against Calvinism that it is a brutal and prosaic creed, hostile to beauty and to art. This is really not true. Calvin himself was a humanist and a fine scholar. The Puritan was often a student, a connoisseur of art, an accomplished musician. A good example of a Puritan home is that of the Milton family. John Milton's father was a musician, and often regaled his household with madrigals of his own composing. The boy John sat up till midnight studying Greek, Latin, French, and Italian. Colonel Hutchison, the regicide, was a student of the arts, a collector of art treasures, and a lover of music. The Puritans dressed plainly, but well and carefully; they were very cleanly in their persons, more so than their opponents. Some of them endeavoured to act out Milton's fine words, that he who would speak well on noble subjects must make his own life a true poem.

In Calvinism the distinction which we have noticed more than once, between the absolute and the relative Law of Nature, is much weakened. Private property now becomes without qualification, a part of the divine law. Our division of the Decalogue is Calvin's, and is not without meaning. The First Table included the command to worship God without images, magic, and ritual, and the Fourth Commandment is treated as still binding. Spirituality in Calvinism gets a new meaning, being opposed not to "the Law" but to materialism in religion.

The teaching of Calvin with regard to obedience to authority is curious. The "private man" must obey, but the lower magistrates sometimes ought to resist the higher. We are bidden to obey them, but only in the Lord, he says. There is not the same patient submission which was inculcated by Luther.

Calvinistic peoples are still marked by a strong individuality and initiative, with power of combined action. Their natural tendency is towards a Conservative democracy. The idea of equality, so dear to the Latin races, has no place in Calvinism.

Was Calvinism in favour of Christian Socialism? Yes and No. It accepted the system of capitalism as it then existed, but severely condemned its abuses. Monopolies, usurious interest, shoddy manufactures, fraud of every kind, came under the lash of the Church. All luxurious and ostentatious expenditure was blamed. Industry and thrift, in the service of the people of God, were commended. The system tended to drastic reform in social matters, but not at all to revolution. Calvin himself was anti-democratic, but the logic of his system favoured democracy. John Knox was much more revolutionary in his ideas than Calvin; but he lived in Scotland, where kingly and feudal tyranny was a real and obvious danger. He proclaimed the rights of the people against "tyrants," and advocated democratic popular government. Yet even he was at bottom Conservative. The Levellers, the real revolutionary party in England, were not Calvinists.

Calvin was convinced that the Christian spirit is compatible with trade and industrialism even of the newer type. He preferred capitalism to feudalism, because the former, when regulated as he desired, gives encouragement to hard work and thrift. Thus, while Lutheranism was linked with the old agrarian and patriarchal type, Calvin reaches out a hand to modern industrialism. The atmosphere of Geneva—though Geneva was not a great business centre—was very different from that in which Luther moved. In most countries, Calvinists took to trade, partly no doubt because they had few opportunities of entering public life.

So we can understand how Calvinism created that curious product, the modern business man,[1] who works like a slave in accumulating money which his tastes

[1] Baxter in his "Christian Directory" even writes: "If God show you a way in which you may lawfully get more than in another way, without wrong to your soul or to any other, if you refuse this and choose the less gainful way, you cross one of the ends of your calling, and you refuse to be God's steward."

and principles forbid him to enjoy, and about the value of which to himself and others he asks no questions. No system was ever devised so effectual in promoting that kind of progress which is measured by statistics. If a nation can be convinced that steady industry in profitable enterprise is eminently pleasing to God, but that almost all unproductive ways of spending superfluous wealth are wrong, that nation will become very rich.

But the Calvinistic social system is rapidly breaking up. The asceticism which was an essential part of it has almost disappeared; for if the American millionaire still sometimes leads a very austere life, his wife squanders enough for two. And the leadership in what Aristotle called the chrematistic life has passed from the individual manufacturer, directing his own business, to the banker and financier. The religious basis of capitalism[1] and productive industry has been undermined, and the question "What is the value of these activities?" is being asked with more and more insistence. Bentham tried to answer the question by saying "The standard is the greatest happiness of the greatest number." This attempt to affix quantitative values to the higher interests went far to break Calvinism. Utilitarianism, just because it seems to have much in common with it, but has not, has proved its deadly enemy. The Manchester school was not Calvinistic.

The Modern Period

There is not much to say about the social teaching of the Church in the eighteenth century, which ends, for the

[1] What it has come to may be judged by the following quotation from Lippmann's "Preface to Morals," p. 88. "The sponsors of the Broadway Temple in New York City put the matter in a thoroughly modern way when they proclaimed a campaign to sell bonds as 'a five per cent. investment in your Fellow Man's salvation'—Broadway Temple is to be a combination of Church and Skyscraper, Religion and Revenue, Salvation and Five per cent.—and the five per cent. is based on ethical Christian grounds —and also, they hastened to add, 'on a gilt-edged real estate mortgage.'"

historian, not in 1800 but in 1789. The articulate portion of society at that time somewhat resembled the men of the Augustan age at Rome. It was cultivated, rational, and suspicious of enthusiasm. The sermons of the divines tended to be moral essays on the reasonable conduct of life. There seemed to be few political problems, for there was not much social discontent in England, and in France the condition of the common people, which had been very bad, was rapidly improving. What caused the catastrophe of 1789 was the incompetence and extravagance of the Court, which made the State bankrupt, the unscientific taxation, with exemptions for privileged classes, and the very narrow base on which political power was balanced. But the writings of Rousseau and others were a contributory cause. Perhaps the French Revolution has occupied too large a place in history. Revolutions are always a mistake; they lead to reactions and set back reform as much as they promote it. The so-called Industrial Revolution, which was not a revolution in the ordinary sense, was far more important than the destruction of the French monarchy. It began in England, about 1760, and since that time the economic problem has increasingly predominated over the political.

The social question, as we are accustomed to call it, has had a great effect on the teaching of Christianity. It has led to a profound secularising of the Gospel, such as the world had not seen before, and to a revolt against religion in general, which is also new. The revolutionary movement is bitterly anti-Christian, though in illogical England attempts are made to effect a compromise.

Western Europe, in the throes of the long and exhausting Napoleonic War, was quite unprepared to deal with the new problems raised by the progress of mass-production. England especially, where the new processes were mostly discovered, had no leisure to do anything except preserve its existence. Nor was economic science in a forward state. It is significant that Napoleon thought that the way to ruin England was to allow imports, especially of food, while closing all the ports of Europe against British exports. In this way, he hoped, he might drain England of money.

Then came the peace, and the recovery. When we condemn the abuses of trade at that time, and bring a heavy indictment, as (for example) Mr. and Mrs. Hammond have done, against the landlords and employers of labour, we have to remember that the country was staggering under gigantic losses, which it endeavoured very successfully to make good by increasing, through every possible means, the aggregate wealth of the nation. Hard work, low wages, and thrift were necessary to give England that predominance as a manufacturing country which it desired to obtain. In those days, instead of shutting our doors against cheaper and more efficient Asiatic labour, we went to war to compel China to trade with us. Lancashire was then in no fear of Oriental competition. There was immense material progress and an immense expansion of the rapidly increasing British race over all parts of the world. When politicians and ecclesiastics inveigh in unmeasured terms against the social system which produced these results, we may remind them that every great achievement involves self-denial and severe labour, and that the employers took their share in promoting what they believed to be the welfare of their country.

The revolt against modern social conditions had begun in the eighteenth century with Rousseau, before the effects of the Industrial Revolution had begun to be felt in France, or even in England. The influence of this sentimental rhetorician has perhaps been more pernicious than that of any other man who has ever lived. "The great muddy stream which is submerging us" (says M. de Vogüé) "flows from the writings and the life of Rousseau like the Rhine and the Po from the Alpine reservoirs which feed them perpetually." He is the founder of sentimental humanitarianism, that mawkish travesty of Christianity which transforms morality by basing it solely on pity, and transfers guilt from the individual to the State under which he lives. Man is always innocent, the government always guilty. The truth on this matter was spoken long ago by Aristotle. "Legislation against private property may have a specious appearance of benevolence; men readily listen to it, and are easily induced to believe that in some wonderful manner everybody will become everybody's friend, especially when someone is heard denouncing the evils now existing in States, which are said to arise out of the possession of private property. These evils, however, are due to a very different cause, the wickedness of human nature." The morality of Rousseau is the morality of Tolstoy, and perhaps no foreign influence to-day is more subtly mischievous than the writings of these prophets of unreflecting sentimentalism, who begin by assuming that authority is always wrong and all punishment immoral. Without Rousseau there might have been no Karl Marx and no Bolshevism. Rousseau's "virtue" is a glorification of the instinctive and subrational. His "love" is a parody of Christian charity. Man in a state of nature, according to him, is virtuous and communistic. With the invention of property "equality disappeared, and work became necessary, and the vast forests were changed to fields that had to be watered with the sweat of men, in which slavery and wretchedness soon grew with the crops." All evil is due to human institutions. The poor are to be taught that they are the only virtuous class, and that they are the victims of a conspiracy. Everywhere in Rousseau we hear the voice of the angry and envious plebeian, fomenting class hatred. He confesses to "a proud misanthropy, an acrimony against the rich and happy, as if they were so at my expense."

So Rousseau, who initiated nothing, threw the torch into the powder magazine, and the conflagration is not yet extinct. Unluckily, as Anatole France says, when one starts with the supposition that all men are naturally good and virtuous, one inevitably ends by wishing to kill most of them. Sentimentalism, as Russia has proved once more, ends in tyranny and homicidal mania. Rousseau himself declares: "If anyone, having publicly recognised these dogmas, conducts himself as if he did not believe them, let him be punished with death." "These priests and nobles are not guilty," said Danton, "but they must die because they are out of place, interfere with the movement of things, and stand in the way of the future." Here surely we have the genesis of Bolshevism, and of the two million executions by the Cheka.

Where this teaching is listened to, the spirit of restraint and discipline has almost disappeared. The wants of men are assumed to be identical with their needs, in direct contradiction to the teaching of Christianity. Every kind of self-denial is scouted as an impoverishment of experience. Repression, according to the newest psychology, is an evil, harmful to the constitution; as if the restraining power, which seeks to bring the whole of life under the control of our highest faculty, the Stoic *Hegemonikon,* were not itself part of our natural endowment, and a part which cannot without the greatest peril be allowed to rust unused or atrophy from want of exercise. And do we not also see the truth of one of Burke's wise political reflections? "Society cannot exist unless a controlling power upon will and appetite be placed somewhere, and the less of it there is within, the more there will be without. It is ordained in the eternal constitution of things, that men of intemperate minds cannot be free."

Carlyle was right in calling Rousseau's doctrine anti-Christian. "A Gospel of brotherhood not according to any of the four old Evangelists, calling on men to repent and amend each his own wicked existence, that they might be saved; but a Gospel rather according to a new fifth Evangelist, Jean Jacques, calling on men to amend each the whole world's wicked existence, and be saved by making the Constitution. A thing different and distant *toto cælo.*"

Of course there is another side to this. I have ventured to call it an omission in the original Gospel that it paid so little attention to social reform. Bad institutions are a fatal obstacle to progress, and make the practice of Christian Ethics intolerably difficult. The real indictment against modern agitators is that in the first place they greatly exaggerate the evils of our present system, and that in the second place they make but little appeal to loyalty, and the love of honest work, without which no social system can hold together.

Social discontent, says Charles Wagner, "comes of the consciousness of a contradiction between economic development and the social idea of liberty and equality which is being realised in political life." It is also the effect of the spreading downwards of the acquisitiveness long practised and extolled among the employers of labour. As Aristotle says, "Wherever the chiefs of the State deem anything honourable, the other citizens are sure to follow their example." I have myself compared the present situation to the internecine battle between two communities of bees, when a mass of unappropriated honey has been carelessly left between the two hives. The new machinery has called into existence a vast quantity of wealth, which was created neither by masters nor men, and which cannot be said to belong to anybody. Capital and Labour are fighting for this unearned increment.

The remedy is not to attack our institutions indiscriminately. Here I entirely agree with Dr. Jacks (in the *Hibbert Journal,* 1924 and 1925). "Preoccupation with social evils is not good for men in general. When the accepted method of reform is to attack the system which produces them, there comes into being a habit of mind which lowers the social vitality and causes a loss of social nerve at the very points where the need for both is greatest; while the temper of society, always the chief factor of its health, becomes sour, embittered, despondent, and quarrelsome. . . . The vast growth of the literature of discouragement and the general demand for the exposure of social culpability, might suggest the conclusion that a conspiracy exists to deprive society of its self-respect." "There was a time when theology waxed eloquent over the total depravity of human nature. As much harm is being done to-day by the doctrine of the total depravity of the social system." If it were not for our orators, many who are now cursing their fellow-men for the faults of our social system would be praising God that we have any social system at all.

I have spoken of the effect of the Industrial Revolution in England, and I wish to add what von Harnack says about its results in Germany; but I will first quote a few sentences from an acute critic of society with whom I seldom agree, Mr. Bertrand Russell. It exposes the brutal facts of the situation, which religious reformers are too apt to ignore.

"Industrialism increases the productivity of labour, and thus makes more luxuries possible. At first, in England, the chief luxury achieved was a larger population with an actual lowering of the standard of life. Then came a golden age when wages increased, hours of labour diminished, and simultaneously the middle class grew more prosperous. That was while Great Britain was still supreme. With the growth of foreign industrialism a new epoch began."

Theoretic Socialism reached, I think, its highest point about the end of the last century. Since then, though it remains as an ideal, and as such still evokes enthusiasm, it has declined as a programme. The radical divergence and incompatibility between State Socialism, in which the State is everything, and Syndicalism, in which the State is nothing, have become glaringly apparent. The ugly brat, Communism, seems likely to destroy its parents, and the attempt to carry out the theories of Marx in Russia has condemned the second largest empire in the world to a prolonged crucifixion. Communists have repudiated any alliance with democracy and liberalism, and trust only to propaganda, coercion, and terrorism. The olive-branch tendered by some earnest Christians to the revolution has been rejected with scorn and hatred.

But in England of forty years ago the idea of a secularised Kingdom of God, to be realised in the near future, took a strong hold of religious minds. The contrasts between wealth and poverty were more glaring then than they are now, and women's labour especially was cruelly sweated. It would not be possible to paint such a dark picture to-day as some of our eloquent preachers gave us, not without exaggeration but truly in the main, in Queen Victoria's reign. It is only fair to give some credit to religious leaders like Maurice, Kingsley, and Barnett for stirring the public conscience, and in the next generation to the members of the Christian Social Union, such as Westcott, Scott

Holland, and Bishop Gore, for carrying on their work.

What is to be our conclusion about the duty of the Church in trying to bring about a better social order? I have deprecated political action on the part of religious bodies. No Church ever goes into politics without coming out badly smirched. We have seen crafty priests building up temporal power and wealth for their own order. We have seen Luther interposing passionately on the wrong side in the Peasants' Revolt. We have seen the English Church in the eighteenth and part of the nineteenth centuries identifying itself too much with the landed interest, and showing small sympathy with the efforts of the landworkers to secure conditions of a civilised life. And now, when the power has definitely passed into the hands of the masses, we see large numbers of Churchmen repeating the same mistake under colour of rectifying it. And yet we have admitted that social abuses are also moral abuses, and spring largely from those vices against which Christ showed Himself most severe. Can we hope to steer between immersion in party politics and the curse of Meroz: "Curse ye, Meroz, said the angel of the Lord, curse ye bitterly the inhabitants thereof, because they came not to the help of the Lord, to the help of the Lord against the mighty"?

In all Protestant Churches, the Church means not the hierarchy but the laity, who are also citizens. It would be absurd to say that a man's deepest convictions ought to have no influence upon his civic conscience. We are nominally a Christian nation, and we wish that our institutions, and the spirit in which they are made to work, should reflect the ethical code and the standard of values which Christ revealed to us. In questions of right and wrong it is the duty of Christians to speak and to vote as Christians and it is natural for those who think in the same way to organise themselves to give effect of their convictions, and to persuade others to support them. Though, as we have seen, the early Church had no political or social programme, it was never silent about moral evils, among which the oppression of the weak had a prominent place. Christ Himself took no interest in formulas and dogmas and ceremonies; but He took a deep interest in the application of the law of love to our dealings with our fellow-men.

On the whole, I agree with Harnack that "the Church has nothing to do with such practical questions of social economics as the nationalisation of private property and enterprise, land-tenure reforms, restrictions of the legal hours of work, price-regulations, taxation and insurance; for in order to settle these matters, such technical knowledge is required as is altogether outside the province of the Church, and if it were to meddle with them at all it would be led into a secularisation of the worst description." But "it is its duty to interfere in public conditions whenever it finds that serious moral evils are being tolerated. Can it be right for the Church to shrug its shoulders, as it were, and pass prostitution by in silence, as the priest did the man who had fallen among thieves? Is it enough to collect money for penitentiaries? Does it keep silence when it sees a state of things destructive of the sanctity of marriage and of family life? Dare it look on calmly while the weak are trodden underfoot? Dare it hear without rebuking it language which in the name of Christianity destroys the peace of the land and sows scorn and hatred broadcast"?

"When warm-hearted Christians take up economic questions they tend to favour radical projects. They are wont to claim the support of the Gospel for a socialistic programme. Even Protestantism is not free from the danger that some day a second Arnold of

Brescia may arise, and that some clerical students of political economy may attempt to prescribe to others the attitude which, if they are to retain the name of Christians, they must assume towards social questions. There is a danger in thus coquetting with the Social-democratic movement. As long as the leaders of that movement inculcate a life devoid of religion, of duties, of sacrifice and of resignation, what can we have in common with their conception of life as a whole? It is again a more than questionable procedure to condemn 'the rich' and whole classes of the nation, and dream that beginning at the bottom a new Christian commonwealth may be constructed."

A mistake often made by religious social reformers in England is to confound the duty of every citizen to form a conscientious opinion on political and social questions, and to work, if he feels moved to do so, for the success of causes in which he believes, with the alleged duty of "the Church" in its corporate capacity to take a side in controversies on which good men notoriously differ. The real object of the latter policy is to make the Church a political power, to organise a Church vote which politicians will be obliged to take seriously, to be able on occasions to make a deal with political leaders or managers. In Roman Catholic countries there is, as we all know, a Catholic vote. The leaders of that Church have certain seats for the Chamber of Deputies, or the Reichstag, in their pockets, and they can bring pressure to bear on the government when their own interests are at stake. This conception of the province of the Church I believe to be wholly wrong. I do not think that the political power of any Church is often used for purely religious and moral ends. I do not think that it is at all to the advantage of the State that a party of "the Centre" should exist in it, and it is notorious that political

Christianity excites bitter hatred against the Church, such as is almost unknown in countries where there is no such organisation. Here, it seems to me, is a clear principle. If as a citizen I am in favour of imperialism or Socialism or free trade or what not, I am right to try to persuade others to agree with me; but I have no right to say, This is the programme of the Church, or the teaching of the Gospel. Churchmen are likely to differ in politics, like everybody else. If the hierarchy drills the flock to give united support to any party programme, two things are certain—it will not be in any true sense a Catholic Church, and it will injure the State by organising a body of voters who will not give their votes according to their free convictions. Popular government is imperilled whenever this latter state of things is allowed to exist, and is doomed to destruction whenever sections, organised for limited interests or intestine warfare, disown their primary duty to the nation of which they are a part. The choice for the Church is between political power and moral influence. We cannot doubt on which side a true follower of Christ should range himself.

Besides this, the crucial question is no longer about the remuneration of labour, but about its conditions. It has been proved by impartial and competent statisticians, such as Professor Bowley, that the artisan, while he is in work, receives quite his due share of the national income. For we must add to his wages the various doles, exemptions from taxation, and pensions which he receives. A few persons, as is well known, receive enormously more than their share; but their number is so small that if all their income were divided up (which could not be done) the product would increase very slightly indeed the wages of the working man. Many of the large fortunes are made entirely out of other capitalists. As for the professional class, if we deduct from their earnings the expense of their education, which usually costs from £2000 to £3000, the rank and file of the professions certainly need not excite the envy of the skilled workmen. The cost of "social services," which are often called socialistic, but which are really a substitute for Socialism, a ransom paid by the minority and a bribe to the electorate, is far larger in England than in any country which is under what is called the Socialist party. I quote from the chapter by Mr. Ian Colvin in the "Universal History," edited by J. A. Hammerton: "A Treasury return issued in November, 1927, showed that the expenditure on social services had increased from £22,-644,334 in 1891 to £355,515,957 in 1926." [1] But this is only part of the sum, since besides the contribution of the State, which is met by taxation, there is a direct cost to industry itself. A parliamentary Committee gave the following estimate of the cost per head of the five social services in the various industrial countries of Europe: "Great Britain £3 18s. 6d.; Germany £1 17s. 6d.; France thirteen shillings; Belgium five shillings and sixpence; Italy three shillings and sixpence. It is not surprising that industries thus overburdened are disabled in their power of employment." Perhaps the worst example of cynical wastefulness has been the lavish erection of houses at the public expense, when it is notorious that the country already contains far more families than it can find work for. The whole policy might seem to have been designed to increase unemployment; but in reality it was dictated by fear of revolutionary outbreaks, and by the hope of out-

[1] This year (1930) Lord Melchett gives the following figures: "During the past 30 years our outlay on social services had risen from 14s. per head of our population to £8 6s., while the actual cost of these services has gone up from £22,000,000 a year to £366,000,000. Out of the present total expenditure on social services the taxpayers provide about £177,-000,000 while £89,000,000 comes from the rates."

bidding political rivals in putting up to auction the worldly goods of the minority.

Apart from these evils, which are the direct result of universal suffrage and corrupt party politics, the question is hotly debated whether a machine-made civilisation is good for humanity or not. Those who admire American institutions point with justifiable pride to the enormous output of useful commodities, to the unheard-of wealth of the country, to the numbers of comforts, luxuries and amusements which large-scale production has placed within the reach of the working man, whose wages are high and the hours of labour few; to the comparative contentment of the whole population, as shown by the weakness of revolutionary propaganda; and to the great reduction in the amount of heavy muscular toil, which is a boon conferred by machinery. The critics of the system emphasise the vulgarity of a civilisation where all habits and desires are standardised; to the decay of the skilled craftsman; and above all to the degradation of human nature involved in setting a man to go through the same mechanical action, such as adjusting a screw, thousands of times a day. It is assumed that in the middle ages every workman had a craft in which he could take an interest and practise skilled workmanship.

This last assumption is certainly not true. "In the heyday of the medieval guild," wrote Mr. and Mrs. Sidney Webb, "there were always far more manual workers outside the favoured circle than within it. What a multitude of labourers quarried the stones, dragged and carried the stone, and lifted the stones of the cathedral walls on which half a dozen skilled and artistic masons carved gargoyles!" The decay of small industries has undoubtedly turned many skilled workmen, such as shoemakers, into minders of machines;

but machinery has greatly reduced, not increased the amount of heavy drudgery.

It is also stated that most of the beautiful hand-worked lace, and other fine work wrought by hand, is produced under shocking conditions, and in fact could not be produced under any other conditions. "Persian rugs are made by little children employed for twelve or fourteen hours a day."[1] On the whole, the friends of machinery have rather the best of the argument[2]; though it must not be forgotten that in abolishing ill-paid labour we are also eliminating the ill-paid labourer, for whom there will be no room in a thoroughly mechanised society.

It is often assumed that the one question which need be asked is whether the workers are contented with the conditions of their labour. But here the ethical side of the problem comes to the forefront. It is a commonplace that greed is never satisfied; even a millionaire envies the half-dozen plutocrats who are richer than himself. Many Americans are far from agreeing that discontent is unusual in their country; some of them say that much of it arises from sheer boredom. Political agitators have much to answer for, with their silly talk about "wage-slaves," as if a slave were not by definition a worker who gets no wages, and as if the essence of the wage system were not that under it a man may sell his labour without selling himself.

Dr. Jacks[3] insists that the only contented class in society consists of those who enjoy the labour by which they live. Those who have no work to do, and those who dislike their work, are bound to be discontented. The work may be monotonous, or the man may be

---

[1] *Hibbert Journal*, Oct. 1929.

[2] On the other side, see a trenchant indictment of mass-production in the *Hibbert Journal* for July 1924, and April 1925, by Dr. Jacks.

[3] *Hibbert Journal*, Jan. 1925.

monotonous. The most monotonous man is he whose whole existence is a demand for *more* (the Germans have borrowed the Greek word *pleonexia*), and who notices nothing except the persons and things which help or thwart his cupidity. The Labour party on the whole assumes that labour is an evil, and that the valuable part of life is leisure. It follows that whatever shortens labour and lengthens leisure is desirable. Its leaders champion the worker at the expense of his work. American "consumptionism" tends in this direction, though the American worker is too intelligent to wish to diminish the output on which his own comforts depend. The remedy, Dr. Jacks thinks, is to dismiss the idea that work is an evil, and to find in work well done the chief blessing of life, and the best training of character. Some who know mechanised labour at first hand do not think that the work of a factory, subdivided as it is, is necessarily boring and soul-destroying.

My own opinion is that economic moralists have devoted too much attention to distribution, and not enough to consumption. Who is it that ordains that the whole labour of myriads of men shall be wasted—devoted to producing things that nobody ought to want? Not the capitalist, but the consumer. The demand creates the supply, and in all the richer countries a large portion of the demand is vulgar, senseless, and selfish. The amount of money wasted on champagne, women's dress, cosmetics, sweetmeats, betting, and other barbarous indulgences, would amply suffice to put an end to poverty and to restore the financial credit of the war-stricken nations. It seems to me that though the New Testament has very little to say about distribution, it has a great deal to say about consumption, and that the homely maxim, "Waste not, want not," may be what society most needs to-day. On the whole, this is an argument for indirect taxation, applied to the luxuries of rich and poor alike.

Dr. Rathenau, the German statesman and financier whose career, to the great loss of his country, was cut short by assassination, pleaded earnestly for greater simplicity and a reduction of waste. "If the restriction of useless consumption is made the primary thing, the riddle of efficiency is spontaneously solved." We should spend far less on such unnecessaries as pearls, champagne, silks, and alcohol. "How can society tolerate such squandering of the national wealth?" "A reflective person must be horrified when he studies the shop windows." The upper and middle class women, he thinks, are mainly responsible. "The decay of the handicrafts is the fault of women buyers." "All the worst customs of retail trade are the outcome of the qualities of women buyers." But it is the merchandising of life that has condemned so many bourgeois ladies to a life of futility. "Man has wrenched the key from her hand, and given her a purse instead."[1]

But the most startling figures on the growth of extravagant spending are to be found in Mr. Beard's "Whither Mankind?" (1928). The writer of the chapter on "Play," Mr. Stuart Chase, gives the following facts about the annual cost of amusement in the United States. The grand total is 21,000 million dollars, which exceeds the entire aggregate income of Great Britain. Two years of American play would pay off our national debt, not only what we owe to the United States, but the whole of our debt. The largest items are pleasure-motoring, travelling and holidays, moving pictures, newspapers, broadcasting, entertainments, night clubs, etc., "candy, chewing

[1] These quotations are from Rathenau's book, "The Days to Come," an essay full of earnest moral exhortations, but too utopian about the future, and rather too severe towards innocent relaxations.

gum, hard and soft drinks," tobacco, theatres, concerts, and games, of which golf seems to be easily the most costly. "Over a billion" (he means a thousand million) "dollars change hands every year in poker playing." Betting is part of the ritual of golf in America. "Try to get into a foursome and refuse to bet, and see how often you will be asked to play again."

"In the eighteenth century," says Mr. Chase, "prize-fighting was a sport." In 1850 Tom Sayers fought forty-four rounds for five pounds a side. "In the first Dempsey-Tunney fight for the championship Mr. Dempsey received 750,000 dollars for thirty minutes' work, Mr. Tunney 450,000, while the profits of the promoter were 437,000." No wonder that we read, "The boxing *industry* is reaching gigantic proportions, and the time has arrived for big business methods." Baseball and football have also entered the ranks of big business, and a lady who swam the English Channel "received over a million dollars' worth of commercial offers."

All these weird facts are the result of "consumptionism." In any country less wealthy than the United States there would be a protest against pouring down a drain money which would be enough to abolish poverty, and to provide an ample endowment for all the higher activities of a civilised community.

In order that I may not be blamed for taking my examples from a foreign country, and for choosing feminine extravagance for special reprobation, I will give the shameful figures of our national Drink Bill for 1929. The total is £288,800,000, with which may be compared—Bread, £80,000,000; Hospitals, £14,000,000; and contribution to the League of Nations, £115,500.

Further, it must be remembered that we have no right to employ labour to make useless commodities.

Resentment against the futility of the work which many of them have to do is a perfectly justifiable source of unrest and discontent among the workers.

My conclusion, after this lengthy discussion of the social question, is that Christian Ethics cannot be said to favour any political party, since economic questions are not primarily ethical but intellectual. Christianity gives us no economic programme; it gives us a standard of values, which demonetises much of the world's currency, and takes most of the bitterness out of economic rivalry. Christianity condemns avarice; it condemns selfish luxury; it condemns discontent and the anxious temperament. The law of love forbids the exploitation of our neighbours, envy, hatred, and jealousy. It is a simple fact that the acceptance of the Christian standard of values by the majority, even in the imperfect form in which it is already accepted and acted upon by a minority in every class of life, would quite certainly produce a far happier social life than can be found in the best ordered community to-day. It is the business of the Church to inculcate this truth in season and out of season. *Nunquam nimis dicitur quod numquam satis discitur.* But the Christian teacher should remember that anything like violent partisanship on either side will deprive his exhortations of all influence upon those whom he considers to be most in need of moral guidance.

THE POPULATION QUESTION

One of the most ominous and discreditable symptoms of the want of candour in present-day sociology is the deliberate neglect of the population question. It is or should be transparently clear that if the State is resolved, on humanitarian grounds, to inhibit the operation of natural selection, some rational regulation of population, both as regards quantity and quality, is imperatively necessary. There is no self-acting adjustment, apart from starvation, of numbers to the means of subsistence. If all natural checks are removed, a population in advance of the optimum number will be produced, and maintained at the cost of a reduction in the standard of living. When this pressure begins to be felt, that section of the population which is capable of reflexion, and which has a standard of living which may be lost, will voluntarily restrict its numbers, even to the point of failing to replace deaths by an equivalent number of new births; while the underworld, which always exists in every civilised society—the failures and misfits and derelicts, moral and physical—will exercise no restraint, and will be a constantly increasing drain upon the national resources. The population will thus be recruited, in a very undue proportion, by those strata of society which do not possess the qualities of useful citizens.

The importance of the problem would seem to be sufficiently obvious. But politicians know that the subject is unpopular. The unborn have no votes. Employers like a surplus of labour, which can be drawn upon when trade is good. Militarists want as much food for powder as they can get. Revolutionists instinctively oppose any real remedy for social evils; they know that every unwanted child is a potential insurgent. All three can appeal to a quasi-religious prejudice, resting apparently on the ancient theory of natural rights, which were supposed to include the right of unlimited procreation. This objection is now chiefly urged by celibate or childless priests; but it is held with such fanatical vehemence that the fear of losing the votes which they control is a welcome excuse for the baser sort of politician to shelve the subject as inopportune. The Socialist calculation is probably erroneous; for experience has shown that it is aspiration, not desperation, that makes revolutions.

It is, however, only right to say that a few scientific men do not admit the urgency of the problem. Of these the most notable is Professor Raymond Pearl, of Baltimore, who from the study of the insect called *Drosophila* has evolved a theory that the growth of population follows what he calls a logistic curve, apparently independent of human volition. Although I have had the advantage of conversing with this eminent biologist, and seeing his laboratory, I remain unconvinced by his arguments. It seems to me clear that the birth-rate is chiefly determined by deliberate choice, and that it would be quite easy to influence this choice by legislation. I shall show reason for thinking that in this country the quantitative problem is in process of solving itself, but by no means in the best way. The problem of quality is not solving itself at all.

In dealing with a question in which ignorance is rampant and prejudice unusually strong, the first requisite is a plain and impartial statement of the relevant facts.

In all living species, the perpetuation of the type is secured by an immense prodigality, which if we were dealing with purposive agents we should call waste. An oyster may have sixty million eggs; a crab between half a million and three millions. The number of male germs liberated at one time is still greater—over two hundred millions in our species. "It has been calculated that a single cholera bacillus can give rise to sixteen hundred trillions of bacilli in a single day, forming a solid mass weighing a hundred tons." [1] "There is no exception," says Darwin, "to the rule that every organic being naturally increases at so high a rate that, if not destroyed, the earth would soon be covered

[1] Carr Saunders, "The Population Problem," p. 54.

by the progeny of a single pair. Even slow-breeding man has doubled in twenty years, and at this rate in less than a thousand years there would literally not be standing room for his progeny."

Nature's methods of clearing the ground are various. The young of most species supply food for some other species. Failure to find a suitable environment, whether organic or inorganic, necessarily prevents increase.

However we may explain what looks like a teleological provision, reproduction is throughout nature correlated with the dangers which the young incur. As Sutherland shows in his "Origin and Growth of the Moral Instinct," fecundity diminishes greatly when parental care of the young comes into play. It might be inferred that if this is so, fecundity would reach its minimum in the human race, and especially in highly civilised countries. But nature has not yet had time to make this adjustment. Savages, it is true, are not very fertile. Travellers are agreed that, if we take all the backward races together, the average family is not more than four. In exceptional cases, such as in some of the South Sea Islands, the population is rapidly diminishing from want of births. But in civilised man the change has been in the opposite direction. Some savages still have a rutting season; with us the only trace of such an arrangement, and that a doubtful one, is stated in Tennyson's line that "in the spring a young man's fancy lightly turns to thoughts of love." The desire on the part of the male is now constant, and is more easily stimulated in civilised races than among savages, who often need the most provocative songs and dances to call it into activity. According to some physicians, there are even the beginnings of a change in women towards a fortnightly instead of a monthly period. The effect of ample food and comfortable conditions is to hasten physical maturity in girls. In the upper classes girls begin to menstruate quite a year earlier than among the poor. [1] If we admit unconscious purpose in these developments, which I am not inclined to do, we may associate this increased tendency to fecundity with the mortality caused by disease. There is very little disease among savages till the coming of civilised races introduces among them devastating bacterial epidemics.

In speaking of the small families among savages, we ought to take into account the preventives which even the most primitive peoples everywhere adopt. One of the chief of these is prolonged lactation, sometimes coupled with abstention from intercourse during the whole time when the child is at the breast. This ensures a salutary spacing of births; it is plain that the wife of a nomad could hardly take care of more than one baby at the same time.

But more drastic methods are generally in use. There are few primitive races which do not practise abortion.[2] The same is true of infanticide, from which only a few savage tribes are free, except in Africa, where it seems to be comparatively rare. War is another steady cause of restriction, though in many savage communities the carnage is not great. Child-mortality, even apart from infanticide and wilful neglect, is generally high.

In ancient Greece and Rome abortion was freely practised; Plato makes Socrates mention it casually —"if midwives wish to procure a miscarriage, they do so." Ovid, however, says that the operation was "often" fatal to the mother. It was frequently resorted to, from selfish motives by rich Roman ladies, as the sati-

---

[1] Carr Saunders, p. 92.
[2] See the list in Carr Saunders, pp. 145, 146. Westermarck says that it is still very common in Turkey and Persia.

rists tell us. After the victory of the Christian Church the practice was much diminished. There was very little pressure by the dwindling population on the means of subsistence; surgery was rough and unskilled; and the Christian Church set itself very energetically against the practice, on the ground that children in the womb have souls, which are imperilled if they die unbaptized. In all European countries, except Bolshevik Russia, the act is, I believe, treated as a crime by the law. It is common in India and China, and is far more prevalent in the white man's countries than is commonly known. Wherever the law discourages the prevention of conception, abortion takes its place. Attempts to procure miscarriage by taking drugs, some of which have not much effect, while others, such as diachylon, a preparation containing lead, are real abortifacients, and by more violent measures, are exceedingly common among the poor. Leroy-Beaulieu gives a very high estimate of the number of abortions which occur annually in France. [1] In England, the investigations of Miss Elderton revealed a state of things in Lancashire and Yorkshire which few had suspected. Julius Wolf estimates the artificial abortions in Germany to-day at 600,000 a year. But the United States, where the law punishes with great severity any attempt to diffuse the knowledge of preventives, is the classic land of abortion. Hirsch, in his learned work on the subject, estimates that two million infants are so destroyed every year in the American Union; and though this number appears to me incredible, I have seen an even higher figure suggested. I do not know what methods are usually adopted in America. There are many surgeons and midwives in all countries who live by performing "illegal operations"; but in England if the woman dies of peritonitis from an accidental

[1] Carr Saunders, p. 268.

puncture, the doctor may have to stand a trial on a capital charge. In New South Wales, a recent statement assigns 13 per cent. of puerperal deaths to attempted abortions. Among the English poor, according to Miss Elderton, all known devices are tried, one after another. It is needless to say that the practice of abortion, however induced, is not only immoral, as involving the destruction of a life which has already begun, but is in some degree dangerous to the mother. That it should be so freely resorted to by married women shows how strong the motives must be to prevent an undesired increase in the family.

That female infanticide is still practised in China is the opinion of almost all who know the country, in spite of the vehement denial of the late Professor Giles. But I am disposed to think that the extent of the practice in China has sometimes been exaggerated, on the simple ground that where marriage is practically universal, there can be no desire for a great disparity in the number of the sexes. It is admitted that male infants are hardly ever destroyed, though the infant death-rate in both sexes, which is caused not only by ignorant treatment but by what looks like wilful neglect, is prodigious. There is probably no country where war takes a smaller toll of male lives, and the emigration of male labourers, though considerable, is not enough to produce a great superabundance of women in China. There is some reason to think that infanticide is resorted to chiefly in times of famine.

In India female children are either destroyed or allowed to die in very large numbers. "Wilful neglect," says one who knows India, Mr. W. Wilkins, "operates destructively in every town and village throughout the length and breadth of India."

Recent researches have revealed the extraordinary prevalence of infanticide in ancient Greece. The Greek father had a right to decide whether a new-born infant was to be admitted to the family. Too often the orders were those given by a husband in a letter found at Oxyrhynchus: "When—good luck to you—your child is born, if it is a boy, let it live, if a girl, expose it." In Ephesus alone of Greek cities, so far as we know, the father had to prove poverty before he was allowed to destroy a child. The condemned infant was often exposed in a jar; anyone who thought it worth while might rescue the baby and rear it as a slave. But this was seldom done. At Gela in Sicily, where a graveyard has been excavated there are 233 "potted" burials out of 570. Mr. Zimmern has pointed out how seldom any daughters of well-known Athenians are mentioned. I have myself pursued this inquiry on new lines. The orator Isæus, an Athenian of the fourth century before Christ, was employed by clients in cases of disputed inheritance. It is possible from these speeches to construct the family trees of eleven typical Athenian families, belonging to the middle class; in one case no less than five generations are involved. In these pedigrees the names of 97 males are mentioned, and of only 37 females. In 27 families, there are no daughters; in 19 one daughter; in 3 there are two daughters; in 2 there are four. These figures are confirmed by the researches of Mr. W. W. Tarn in his brilliant book on "Hellenistic Civilisation." "Of some thousand familes, who received Milesian citizenship from 228 to 200, details of 79, with their children, remain. These brought 118 sons and 28 daughters. Of these families, 32 had one child and 31 two. The inscriptions bear this out. . . . More than one daughter was practically never reared. Of 600 families from Delphic inscriptions, second century, just one per cent. reared two daughters. . . . Telos boasts a family of seven, the only known Hellenistic family over five except the eight children of

Cleopatra Thea by three marriages." Polybius says that the Greeks in the middle of the second century refused to rear more than one or two children.

In spite of the wholesale sacrifice of female infants which such figures indicate, it seems that nearly all Greek men were married. But after the loss of Greek independence the race dwindled rapidly, from causes which are not fully known, though infanticide must certainly be given a prominent place among them. The main cause why, in spite of this practice, there was little or no disparity between the numbers of the sexes was undoubtedly the constant warfare between the little Greek States, and the massacres of the entire male population which sometimes followed the capture of a city. Whether depopulation could have been avoided, when the old outlets for emigration both in the east and the west had been closed by foreign Powers, is not certain. There is much evidence that the soil of the Mediterranean lands was becoming less productive during the classical period. In some places the destruction of the woods for fuel, or by goats, caused the soil to be washed off the hillsides by rains. Nevertheless, after the conquests of Alexander, Western Asia was again open to Greek settlers. If they failed to take advantage of the opportunity, the blame may be laid at the door of this most shameful of Greek customs, the destruction of infant lives. But, as Mr. Tarn has shown conclusively, the Roman government sucked the life-blood out of its Eastern subjects, and diminished their will to live.

Infanticide was much less common in Italy and the western provinces of the Roman Empire, because, after the Punic wars, there was no pressure of population on the means of subsistence. This was the result of the very high death-rate both at Rome and in Spain, and of the unexplained fact that the expectation of life was considerably higher for males than for females. Macdonell, working on figures for the *"Corpus Inscriptionum Latinarum"* of the Berlin Academy, found that whereas in England the expectation of life for boys at the age of fifteen is 45 years,[1] and for girls 48 years, in Rome it was 20 and 15 years respectively; and again, whereas in England at the age of thirty the expectation of life for men is 33, and for women 36 years, in Rome it was 19 and 14 respectively. Though the death-rate was less high, the position was much the same in Spain as in Rome.[2] These figures, which have only recently become known, are enough to account for a decrease in the population, a tendency which was augmented in the richer classes by a distaste for marriage and parentage, often lamented by satirists and moralists at Rome, and by the institution of slavery, which is almost always unfavourable to growth in population. In consequence of these converging influences, we see in Italy under the Roman Empire the very rare phenomenon of actual depopulation. The evidence, as collected by Seeck, is quite conclusive.[3]

After the third century the influence of Christianity on the growth or decline in population becomes an important factor. In the chapter on Asceticism I have given instances of the wild denunciations of marriage and procreation which can be found in the Fathers of the Church. "Why should we wish to have children," asks Tertullian, "whom, when we have them, we desire to send before us out of this most wicked world, from which we ourselves long to be delivered?" Such language is symptomatic of a general pessimism quite sufficient to depress the birth-rate of the population.

[1] These figures are out of date: the expectation of life in England is now much higher at all ages below fifty.

[2] Carr Saunders, p. 246.

[3] I have summarised it in my "Outspoken Essays," First Series, pp. 61–64. Bury, however, argues against Seeck.

Against this must be set the feeling of the sacredness of human life, which operated in the opposite direction. The killing of an *unbaptized* child was a shocking crime, and till the end of the eighteenth century infanticide was a capital offence except in Russia. [1] But in the early period I do not think that the influence of the Church favoured growth in numbers.

Throughout the middle ages, and in the earlier modern period, the population of Western Europe was held in check mainly by two causes. One was the pestilential condition of the medieval walled town, where the deaths probably always exceeded the births. The other was the postponement of marriage among the country-dwellers, which was made necessary by the impossibility of finding cottages for young couples. Each rural area was almost self-contained, and there was no desire to find housing accommodation for a larger number than the parish could support. Statistics are scanty; but there is no doubt that the average age at marriage among the poor was much higher than it is now. Old pedigrees of the nobility and gentry show enormous families, of whom about half—sometimes much more than half—died in childhood, and a large number of adults after whose names appear *"ob.s.p."* (=*"obiit sine prole"*). To these causes must be added occasional famine, and devastating epidemics, of which the worst was the Black Death in the fourteenth century. Medieval battles were fought by very small armies, and were not as a rule very sanguinary; the recorded slaughter of 30,000 men at Towton is now discredited. But protracted wars, such as the Thirty Years' War in Central Europe, caused an enormous destruction of human life.

---

[1] I do not know the date of the last execution of an unmarried woman in England for the murder of her babe; but in real life Hardy's Tess would not have been hanged.

In countries where rice is the staple article of diet, we invariably find a dense population, living laboriously at a very low standard of comfort. These parts of the world are usually supersaturated with inhabitants, and when the maximum is reached which the land can support even with the most meagre nourishment, further increase necessarily ceases, the surplus being removed by famine, or by one or more of the methods mentioned above. This condition has been reached in many parts of India and China. In Japan the surplus of births is still very large, but that nation is becoming absolutely dependent on emigration and foreign trade. The introduction of the potato into Ireland produced similar conditions to those of the rice-eating countries; but in this case a famine, followed by wholesale emigration, reduced the population again by nearly one-half.

It ought to be universally recognised that the rapid increase of numbers in the nineteenth century was a wholly unparalleled phenomenon, and one which in the nature of things could not continue for ever. It was made possible by the new machinery, which vastly increased the output of commodities which could be exchanged for food, and simultaneously by the opening up of new food-producing areas beyond the seas. The new conditions of labour were favourable to rapid increase. The manufacturers built cottages to house all who worked for them. Until the factory legislation forbade the employment of young children for wages, each child, almost as soon as he could walk, became a pitiful asset to the family budget. There was no motive for postponing marriage, since a labourer might begin to earn his maximum wage at the age of twenty-one. In fact, instead of the prudential restraint of which Malthus spoke, there was a prudential stimulus to procreation.

In this abnormal state of affairs, the population of England and Wales, which had increased very slowly during and since the middle ages, was trebled in a hundred years. The census figures will show this better than any words.

Year.	Population (Thousands).	Decennial Increase (Thousands).	Rate of Increase (Per cent.).
1801 . .	8,893	—	—
1811 . .	10,164	1,272	14.0
1821 . .	12,000	1,836	18.1
1831 . .	13,897	1,897	15.8
1841 . .	15,914	2,017	14.3
1851 . .	17,928	2,013	12.6
1861 . .	20,066	2,139	11.9
1871 . .	22,712	2,646	13.2
1881 . .	25,974	3,262	14.4
1891 . .	29,002	3,028	11.6
1901 . .	32,528	3,525	12.2
1911 . .	36,070	3,543	10.9
1921 . .	37,885	1,815	4.9

The chief means by which this increase was effected, after the middle of the last century, was not a very high birthrate; for this, after fluctuating only between 30 and 36 per thousand, reached its maximum of 35.5 in the years 1871–1875 and then began to decline steadily, but a decline in the death-rate which in 1861–1865 was 22.6 and in 1911–1915 was 14.3. The decline has continued since the peace, and in a healthy year is now under 12 per thousand.[1] For a whole generation the downward slope of the birth-rate and death-rate was

[1] Dr. C. A. Winslow ("Whither Mankind?" p. 187) gives the following figures: "From 1838 we have full data for England and Wales, which may be cited in round figures. Expectation of life at birth, 1838–1854, 40 years; 1871–1880, 41 years; 1881–1890, 44 years; 1891–1900, 44 years; 1901–1910, 48 years; 1910–1912, 51 years; 1920–1922, 56 years." The statistics for the United States, so far as they are available, tell the same story. According to Dr. Winslow, the most striking improvement has been in the diminished mortality from tuberculosis, diphtheria, typhoid, scarlet fever and infant diarrhœa.

almost parallel, so that the survival-rate was only slightly less than before the birth-rate began to fall. The Great War naturally reduced the birth-rate, and though there was one year, after the soldiers came home, when the births went up to a high figure, this rise was not maintained, and the decline has since proceeded with accelerated rapidity, in a steeper slope than the deaths. The last recorded rate, 16.3 per thousand for 1929, is lower than the *real* (not the crude) death-rate; for actuarial tables show that the expectation of life at birth for both sexes is 57, which gives a true death-rate of about 17.6.

The causes of the rapid fall in the birth-rate are to be sought in the changed conditions, especially among the wage-earning class. The prohibition of child labour removed the chief prudential stimulus to large families. A rising standard of comfort in the home tended in the same direction. In the professional class it was becoming more difficult to find careers for the sons, and in addition there are two very important inducements to restrict the family—namely, the low salaries paid to this class before middle life, and the heavy expense of a "gentleman's education." A great advertisement was given to the use of preventives by the Knowlton trial in 1877, and it was at that very time that the birth-rate began to fall. But it would probably be a mistake to attribute a decisive importance to the Bradlaugh-Besant case, since the decline began almost simultaneously in several other European countries. Some attribute importance to the Compulsory Education Act, 1876, and to the Factory and Workshops Act, 1878, as diminishing the economic value of a child to its parents.

Urbanisation has hitherto diminished the birth-rate in continental countries more than in England. The following figures are instructive; they illustrate the world-wide diminution in the rate of natality, and also the fall in the death-rate.

		Births per 1000	Deaths per 1000
London	1860	33.7	22.5
	1928	16.1	11.2
Berlin	1860	33.6	22.7
	1927	9.9	11.4
Paris	1860	32.4	26.2
	1926	16.9	16.6
Vienna	1880	40.4	28.3
	1928	10.6	13.9[1]

In forming an opinion as to the desirability of a movement which in this country has reduced the birth-rate by more than one-half in less than fifty years, we must try to distinguish between the temporary and the permanent factors of the problem. Mr. J. M. Keynes says that "some of the catastrophes of past history, which have thrown back human progress for centuries, have been due to the reactions following on the sudden termination, whether in the course of nature or by the act of man, of temporary favorable conditions which have permitted the growth of population beyond what could be provided for when the favourable conditions were at an end." Such a change is probably coming over Great Britain. The former workshop of the world cannot hold this position any longer. Our industries had a long start, but our rivals are now catching us up, and we are handicapped by having the highest standard of living in any European country. The workpeople cling tenaciously to their high wages, which make it impossible to employ anything like all the labourers. These accordingly have to be supported in enforced idleness out of the profits of industry, which are thereby still further depressed. The doles drive out of employment those whom the tax-payers' money would have sup-

[1] Eugenics Review, April, 1930.

ported if it had not been taken from them; and vast sums are spent on building houses which in the interest of the country would be much better unbuilt. Thus political pressure aggravates the evil of unemployment, and makes it a permanent drain on the industry of the country. To this cause of unemployment must be added the progressive displacement of hand-labour by machinery, which needs a much smaller number of hands to work it. For instance, on the Boston and Maine railroad switchmen are eliminated. One man in a tower saves the labour of 400 workers. This displacement has led to unemployment in all the chief industrial countries. At the time of writing (February, 1930) there are three million unemployed in the United States, and two million in Germany. The increased employment of women as wage-earners—another permanent factor in the problem—has driven very large numbers of men out of work. Everything points to a much smaller optimum population in the future.

This state of things must continue until the population is reduced to what under the new conditions will be the optimum number, probably several millions less than the forty-eight millions who now inhabit the British Isles. This adjustment once made, the special problem created by the termination of a temporarily favourable condition will have been solved, as the congestion in Ireland was permanently removed by famine and emigration.

The proper method of dealing with a temporary congestion is by State-aided colonisation. Half the money which has been worse than wasted upon doles and housing would have sufficed to plant settlements of our countrymen in various parts of the British Empire. These settlements would have consisted of hard-working and contented people, who would have added strength to the loyal British element in the Dominions, like the small party of settlers which was planted long ago in Cape Colony. These are parts of the Dominions which remain undeveloped only because the initial cost of clearing, roadmaking and building is too great at the present price of white labour. Tasmania is a good example. That island, about the same size as Ireland, is covered with forests, which cannot be cut down without State subsidies; it is also exceptionally rich in electrical water power. Colonisation is only a palliative for a permanently excessive birth-rate, but it is a real remedy for such a temporary crisis as that with which we seem to be faced. Of course we must not forget that emigrants cannot be forced to go, nor the Dominions to receive them; nor could all our unemployed adapt themselves to the work which might be found for them overseas. But some pressure might with great advantage be exerted.

There is a real danger that since this remedy is not being adopted, the birth-rate may be further depressed beyond what the welfare of the British race demands. We have no reason to wish for fewer Englishmen and Scotchmen in the world[1]; there is still room in the Dominions; and it will be twenty or thirty years before a dearth of babies in 1930–1935 can begin to relieve the burden of unemployment.

I have summarised, at considerable length though very inadequately, the facts which constitute the problem of population. I do not think it is useful to discuss a moral question in the abstract without any reference to the circumstances with which we have to deal. Traditionalists do this in the problem before us. They take their stand on the command, "Be fruitful and multiply,"

[1] Dawson, arguing as a Catholic against birth-control, foresees a time when in England and Scotland the native population will be replaced by Irish immigrants, in France by Spaniards and Italians, in Germany by Slavs, and in the United States by Mexicans, Negroes, and immigrants from Eastern Europe. The remedy for which is to exclude immigrants by law.

which is said to have been given when the population of the world consisted of two persons, or on the alleged right of every man to have as many children as nature permits; and then brush aside all the arguments which prove that such precepts, and such rights, are wholly inapplicable to the conditions of modern civilisation. The result is that though their denunciations are listened to with courtesy, in practice they are treated with the neglect which they really deserve.

The main facts to bear in mind are, that restriction of numbers is inevitable; that our business is to find the least objectionable method of effecting it; that the world is filling up, and that the law of diminishing returns is asserting itself; and that (as regards this country) the abnormal expansion in the hundred years between the two Great Wars has definitely come to an end, since the advantage which we so long enjoyed of holding a privileged position in trade and commerce is ours no longer. We have to cut our coat out of a somewhat smaller piece of cloth.

I shall consult my own taste, and probably also that of my readers, by not entering upon any detailed discussion of the methods of "birth-control." Those who wish for medical opinions on the various devices now in use may be referred to a Symposium in *The Practitioner* for July, 1923, if that number is still procurable. Some of the writers seem to be a little prejudiced; but the impression left upon me is that some at least of the methods are more or less objectionable from the medical point of view, so that the problem, on this side, has not been fully solved.

I am far from wishing to dismiss with contempt the instinctive repugnance which many feel to the very idea of interfering with nature in this delicate matter. The change in public opinion since the time, well within my own recollection, when Bradlaugh, who was regarded as the protagonist of the movement, was called "the unsavoury member of Northampton," has certainly been enormous. I have not disguised my conviction that artificial restraint is necessary. But in my opinion, the revolt against all sexual taboos has gone much too far; I am not prepared to accept the verdict of the post-war years as final. Only I think that the conduct of husbands and wives in their most intimate relations must be left to individual taste and conscience; I cannot approve of the deliberate withholding of medical knowledge from adults who wish to obtain it. Judging from the very few cases that are known to me, I am inclined to think that total abstinence on the part of married couples who wish for no more children is less uncommon than is usually supposed; and that many others solve the difficulty by coming together only on those days of the month when conception is unlikely to occur. This, however, is not agreeable to the wife, and there are only about four "safe" days—many doctors say there are none—in each month.

But no one who knows anything of human nature could suggest that total abstinence is the solution of the problem. It is far more likely to wreck the happiness of married life, as St. Paul seems to recognise. And I cannot leave the subject without noticing the shocking teaching which is sometimes given by clerical opponents of birth-control. In a little book published in 1929 the author (whose name I suppress, since he is a personal friend) tells the story of a certain Mr. A., who was so constituted that he believed continence to be injurious to his health. His wife, on the other hand, had been warned that it would probably be fatal to her to have another child. The advice given to Mr. A. by his clerical counsellors was, "Come together again and leave the issue in God's hands." Mrs. A. duly died in child-bed, and "the way he bore it was a signal instance of the power of a true Christian." Whether the unspeakable Mr. A. still suffers from headaches, and if so what he does, is not recorded. Unhappily this is not an isolated instance. I know of a clergyman who caused the death of his wife in precisely the same way.

Cases of moral casuistry affecting personal conduct belong properly to my next chapter. But in this branch of the subject they cannot be separated from the population question, which is a matter of public morals; and I have thought it better to clear out of the way, in a single discussion, a topic which, however necessary and important, is unpleasant to author and readers alike.

The population question has two sides, quantitative and qualitative. I have given reasons for thinking that the quantitative problem will be ultimately solved through the general use of means to prevent conception. We may have great troubles in this country for the next twenty or thirty years, due to over-population; but a further reduction of the birth-rate is not the proper remedy, so long as the Dominions can find room for our emigrants, since on the basis of a stationary population the deaths already slightly outnumber the births, and a further reduction might lead to a relative weakening of the British stock among the peoples of the world.

I now come to the qualitative problem. The fall in the birth-rate has been due to prudential action on the part of those who are capable of prudence. It has hardly affected the dwellers in the slums, and still less the mentally deficient. How severe is the counter-selection to the detriment of those classes which society has hitherto agreed to regard as most worthy of encouragement, may be judged by the following figures, from Harold Cox ("The Problem of Population," p. 99).

England and Wales, 1911	Births per 1000 Married Males under 55
Upper and Middle Class .	119
Intermediate Class . .	132
Skilled Workmen . .	153
Intermediate Class . .	158
Unskilled Workmen . .	213

These are old figures; the conditions now are even worse. The following figures are based on the census of 1921. The relative fertility of marriage is shown thus: Teachers 95, Nonconformist ministers 96, Church of England ministers 101, Doctors 103, Authors and Editors 104, Policemen 153, Postmen 159, Carmen 207, Dock Labourers 231, Barmen 234, Miners 258, General Labourers 438. The learned professions have the smallest families; casual labour, which includes the wastrels, physical and moral wrecks, and those who for one reason or another have no regular place in the body politic, by far the largest. But there is one not very small class which is even more prolific than the slum-dwellers; I mean the feeble-minded. It is difficult to exaggerate the ominousness of these figures. The State may for one or two generations be able to mask the national degeneration by tapping the hitherto undeveloped abilities of the working-class. The level of ability in the professions may for a short time be maintained by recruiting them from the ablest sons of labourers; but the cumulative effect of such a drastic dysgenic selection as these figures indicate can only be the progressive deterioration of the British race.

This counter-selection is a comparatively new phenomenon; before the industrial revolution the birth-rate was probably higher among the richer classes, since the labourers, at least in the villages, usually married late.

The great diminution in infant mortality has also increased the survival-rate among the very poor more than among those who have been able to bestow greater care upon their children.

It is difficult to discuss this question without arousing political prejudice and provoking Labour politicians to rudeness. But there is really not the slightest doubt that although the inferiority of the casual labourer is partly nurtural, and capable of being reduced by better conditions, ability of the kind which leads to success in the intellectual professions is strongly inherited, and that a deficiency of births in that class, cumulative in its effect for two or more generations, must inevitably deplete the reserve of talent on which a nation has to rely in filling posts of responsibility. No unprejudiced person could regard the disappearance of our upper class and professional families as anything else than a calamity.

At the lower end of the scale a state of things exists which is a disgrace to a civilised nation in a scientific age. I will quote from a speech by Lord Buckmaster in the House of Lords. "Let me read to you some of these cases. Here is a woman who was married at the age of seventeen. At the age of thirty-four she had had eighteen pregnancies with eleven live children. Mrs. P., aged thirty, has eighteen children, is tuberculous, and has a uterine disease. Mrs. S. has six children, three of whom are mentally deficient and quite hopeless. Then there is a woman, married twenty-two years, with twelve children and five intentional miscarriages. Another pair had four children, all of whom had been born without eyes. The mother was suffering from *dementia præcox*. The children manifested not a single normal reaction to the tests that were given." Dr. Tredgold in 1924 estimated that we have 138,529 "aments" (persons born mentally defective) in addition to 125,827 insane. Carr Saunders estimates the real number of aments at 300,000 to 350,000. That these conditions are inherited there is not the slightest doubt.

Eugenists have a hard battle to fight against the indifference of politicians, the ignorance and prejudice of the public, and the determined hostility of the Roman Catholic Church. Sir Francis Galton used to say that eugenics ought to be a religion. It is a religion, and its name is Christianity. The Gospels contain the most uncompromising eugenic utterances. "Do men gather grapes of thorns, or figs of thistles?" "A good tree cannot bring forth evil fruit, neither can a corrupt tree bring forth good fruit." "Every tree that bringeth not forth good fruit is hewn down and cast into the fire." In this, as in several other matters, the new morality can appeal to the Founder of Christianity across long ages in which His followers have distorted His precepts or failed to understand them.

The new morality insists that if "everyone is to count for one," we must remember that the majority are not yet here to plead for themselves. Nietzsche urges in eloquent words the claims of posterity on the present generation. "Fatherland, say ye? Our helm is set thitherwards where is our children's land. Thither, stormier than the sea, storms our great longing." And I have quoted Meredith's "Keep the young generations in hail, and bequeath them no tumbled house."

An obvious objection will be raised that moral appeals will be entirely inoperative, except among those whose high character, even if combined with a delicate physical constitution, would make them desirable parents of the next generation. There is no answer to this, and the conclusion is that some kind of compulsion is necessary. Almost all eugenists advocate sterilisation of those who are unfit for parentage, a method which has been practised on many thousand persons in

America, chiefly in California. It is said that the results are good; but I cannot doubt that popular feeling against such legislation in our country would be extremely strong. The operation (which, it must be understood, does not interfere with the sexual life in any way except by preventing conception) is not a very slight one for women. On the other hand, the operation on the male is so slight and painless that it might become popular among men who for selfish reasons did not wish to have children, and in both sexes it might encourage promiscuity. For these reasons I should prefer penalising large families among those whose children are likely to be a charge to the community. For example, education might be free for three children of a marriage, contributory for any born over that number. Of course this suggestion assumes that instruction should be given in birth-control.[1] In any case, the evil is so menacing that something must be done to check it.

HUMANITARIANISM

Mr. Irving Babbitt[2] says: "A transformation in the very basis of Ethics has taken place in connexion with the great movement, partly utilitarian, partly senti-

---

[1] On this point the example of Holland is instructive. Dr. Darlington of New York writes:— "The necessary information for the limitation of families has been available to the mothers of Holland since 1880. Since that year the rate of increase in the population has grown. . . . The number of marriages has increased, and the age of marriage has been lowered. From my observation, having been in Holland a great deal, I know divorces are rare compared with other countries. Brothels are forbidden, and what is more they do not exist. Venereal diseases are infrequent and the number of illegitimates is very low." (The number is 19 per thousand, compared with 43 in England and 87.9 in France.) The death-rate of Holland (9.6 in 1928) is the lowest in Europe; the birth-rate (23.3) higher than that of any except Spain, Hungary, and the Slav countries.—(Eugenics Review, Oct. 1929.)

[2] "Democracy and Leadership," p. 47.

mental, that I have defined in its totality as humanitarianism. What is singular about the representatives of this movement is that they wish to live on the naturalistic level, and at the same time to enjoy the benefits that the past had hoped to achieve as a result of some humanistic or religious discipline." The thesis of this thoughtful and brilliant writer is that the humanitarian movement has no standards, not even the utilitarian calculus of Bentham. It is based neither on the will nor the intellect, but on sentiment; and history has proved that "the end of sentimentalism is homicidal mania."

The words humanity and humanitarianism ought to be kept distinct; but the essence of the humanitarian movement is that they are not kept distinct. Leonard Hobhouse has said that the conception of a self-directing humanity is the basis of scientific Ethics. Comte thought that now that the theological stage in the evolution of the race has outlived its usefulness, the welfare of humanity for its own sake may provide a satisfactory standard. In his hands and those of his followers, Humanity became a mystical concept—the development of the divine in man, so that the positivist Comte almost joins hands with absolutist Hegel. We may agree with Hobhouse that Ethics have now become the test to which religion must submit. The moralising of religion is in the true line of progress. But the question is whether humanitarianism, or even the idea of the welfare of humanity, gives us any standard of right and wrong which will serve as a safe guide to conduct. Scientific Ethics are hardly sufficient to show us in what the highest welfare of man consists; but they can show us how certain ideals, which we may have chosen to accept, may be realised. Emotion and sentiment may suggest to us what to aim at—for example, the diminution of human and animal pain;

but they are most treacherous guides as to how our aims may be realised. Sentimentalism is usually kind only to be cruel; and beyond the impulse of pity it has no standard at all.

Nevertheless, the movement has a long list of salutary reforms to its credit. We have almost forgotten the cruelties which disfigured European civilisation before humanitarianism gathered strength in the eighteenth century. In such matters, the eye affects the mind much more than the ear. I therefore suggest that those who wish to realise the vast change which has come over the conscience and feelings of the most civilised nations should pay a visit to some museum like the old dungeon at The Hague, where all the instruments of torture—racks, hot irons, hammers and crowbars for breaking on the wheel, whips of all kinds, and other engines for tormenting the human body— are kept in working order, with the frames and blocks to which the victims were fastened. Let them reflect that these machines were in use when the great Dutch masters were painting their pictures; the contrast between the glorious works of art in the Gallery of Amsterdam and this inferno seems almost incredible.

It would be unnecessary to enumerate all the cruelties which have been abolished within the last two hundred years. The moral advance has been prodigious, and there is no other field in which we may feel so confident that the change of heart has been spontaneous, genuine, and permanent. Cruelty now excites a degree of moral indignation which is not felt towards any other class of offenders. Many who in theory reject the retributive theory of punishment will be heard to advocate vindictive penalties for cruelty to children and even to animals. This has been the most important change in ethical sentiment during the modern period. We are amazed at the callousness which tolerated pub-

lic strangling for criminals, an extremely painful mode
of death which sometimes tortured the victim for five
minutes or even longer; savage floggings in the army
and navy and even in schools; the chaining and beating
of lunatics; and many other atrocities which it would
be easy to mention.

This change in moral sentiment has made once for
all incredible the pictures of torments in hell which
were taught without the slightest compunction, by Protestants and Catholics alike. It is almost universally
felt that a God who could administer justice in this
fashion would be a tyrant or a demon. But in the days
when graphic representations of these horrors were the
usual decoration of church walls, no objections of this
kind were expressed, and it is doubtful whether this
exaggeration of criminal justice, as it was then exercised on earth, even acted as a strong deterrent to
sinners.

It is disquieting for Christians to have to admit that
the growth of humanity, in the sense of humaneness,
does not owe much to the Churches, in spite of the
teaching of Christ, whose sympathy extended even to
the birds. We are sorry to find even St. Paul asking,
"Doth God take care for oxen?" The treatment of
Jews and heretics in the middle ages surpassed in
cruelty even the habitual brutality of the time. Nor
were churchmen very prominent in the modern humanitarian movement, which awoke the sympathies of unbelievers like Voltaire. It cannot be doubted that the
belief in eternal torture for the wicked had a disastrous
effect upon men's minds, though that belief was itself
possible only when humane feelings were very weak.

The humanitarian movement began in the eighteenth century, outside the range of clerical influences.
It was the age of "sensibility." That there was something maudlin and ridiculous about it is now plain to

everybody; but a revolt against the age of insensibility was badly needed, and long overdue. It has developed rather one-sidedly as a revulsion from the sight or thought of physical pain, and this has made it seem somewhat weak and unmanly; for instance, hysterical denunciations of the very moderate corporal punishment now inflicted in schools show a defective sense of proportion. On the other hand, the refined moral cruelty of a long-drawn *cause célèbre,* with the utterly unfeeling treatment by the newspapers of the criminal and his family, for the most part escape censure.

A peculiar phase of humanitarianism is an agitation against capital punishment. There are few subjects in which public opinion, and the law which reflects it, are in such confusion. The death-penalty was formerly inflicted not only for murder, but for various offences which were either specially obnoxious to the Government, or difficult to detect. To these were added certain offences against the moral law, such as sodomy, which were vaguely supposed to provoke the higher powers to visit with collective punishments the society in which they were allowed to occur. By degrees, in most civilised countries, all crimes ceased to be capital, except murder and high treason. It was often urged that although the State has no right to take life in other cases, a special exception in the case of wilful homicide has been made for all future time in the Book of Genesis. We therefore continue to execute murderers, using the minimum of physical cruelty and almost the maximum of moral cruelty.

The revolutionary movement usually declares against capital punishment altogether. As the leaders of revolutions have no scruple in shedding the blood of their political opponents like water, it is not easy to understand this squeamishness. In some European countries, convicted murderers are kept in solitary confinement for life, a punishment far more cruel than execution. In many places, and even in England, sympathy is shown for political assassins, though one might have thought that this detestable and socially most mischievous form of crime deserved a heavier sentence than private murders, which are sometimes committed under strong temptation.

In some countries, such as South Italy and South Ireland, the criminal is often made a popular hero. In others, such as the United States, which has the worst record for homicide of any country in the world, so small a percentage of murderers is brought to justice that to take the life of a fellow citizen is not considered very dangerous. It has been proved up to the hilt that the abolition of capital punishment, and still more the probability that a murderer will escape any kind of punishment, is invariably followed by a great increase in the number of homicides. A French professor of Law declared that if capital sentences were done away with it should be announced that "henceforth the law of France will guarantee the lives of none but murderers." On the other hand, to multiply capital offenses defeats its own object, for juries will refuse to convict. In England, before the reform of the criminal law, crimes nominally capital were very frequent, because it was known that the death-sentences were rarely carried out. The certainty of retribution is a greater deterrent than the severity of the punishment. It is unfortunately impossible to guess how many poisoners escape unconvicted and even suspected. An expert medical criminologist, in answer to a question from me, thought that a large majority escape.

The notion that the State has no right to take the life of an incorrigibly anti-social citizen will not bear examination. The placing of murder in a category by itself looks like a survival of the *lex talionis*. No appeal to the Old Testament can be made, for under the Mosaic Law even adulterers and sabbath-breakers were to be stoned. The Government has a right to protect itself against political assassins, and to protect private citizens from being murdered. Nor is there any reason why such hateful offences as arson and rape should not be capital. In parts of America the penalty for rape is burning alive, but only if the offender has a black skin.

The proper principle is surely that incorrigible offenders including habitual thieves, should be placed in a lethal chamber, without any unnecessary humiliation or publicity. They have been officially pronounced to be thoroughly bad citizens, and they may be removed by the same right which a gardener has to pull up weeds from his flower-beds. After the first offence the culprit should be sent to a reformatory, and discharged when he appears to be cured, with a clear warning of what his fate will be if he continues to make war upon society. Those who have seen a batch of prisoners discharged from jail—"fellows by the hand of nature marked, quoted and signed to do some deed of shame" —must admit the extreme folly of our present system. But at present there are no signs that any rational form of our criminal law is likely even to be considered; such changes as are suggested are sometimes for the worse.

So far, I have spoken of the humanitarian movement as it has affected the relations of men and women to each other. But it is also conducting a strenuous campaign in favour of the rights of animals. It is unhappily true that (in the words of A. Jameson in 1854) "the primitive Christians by laying so much stress upon a future life, and placing the lower creatures out of the pale of hope, placed them at the same time out of the pale of sympathy, and thus laid the foundation for an utter disregard of animals." The charming tales of St. Francis of Assisi, and of some hermits who made friends with wild animals, are not sufficient to absolve the Catholic Church from the heavy guilt of teaching that the animals have no souls and therefore no rights. To this day in the south of Europe if an Englishman protests against the brutal treatment of a horse or dog, he is met by the surprised answer, "He is not a Christian."

Catholics sometimes deny that their Church acknowledges no rights belonging to the lower animals. But Pius IX refused to allow the Society for the Prevention of Cruelty to Animals to work in Rome, on the ground that it is a theological error to teach that men have any duties towards animals. And it is the experience of those who have agitated for the protection of wild birds in the breeding season or for the prohibition of cruel sports, that it is generally useless to appeal to a Catholic for help or sympathy. As an example of the teaching officially given in the Roman Catholic Church, it is probably fair to quote from the "Moral Philosophy"[1] of Joseph Rickaby, S.J., a writer deservedly held in repute even outside his own communion. "Brute beasts, not having understanding and therefore not being persons, cannot have any rights. The conclusion is clear. They are of the number of *things,* which are another's; they are chattels, or cattle. We have no duties to them—not of justice, as is shown; not of religion, unless we are to worship them like the Egyptians of old; not of fidelity, for they are incapable of accepting a promise. The only question can be of charity. Have we duties of charity towards the lower animals? Charity is an extension of the love of ourselves to beings like ourselves, in view of our common nature and our common destiny to happiness in God. . . . We

[1] Pages 248–9.

have then no duties of charity, nor duties of any kind, to the lower animals, as neither to stocks and stones."

The horror which this passage will arouse in almost all readers is the measure of the gulf which separates the old Ethics from the new. We may thank God that the prediction of Jeremy Bentham has been partially, though not wholly, fulfilled. "The time will come when humanity will extend its mantle over everything which breathes. We have begun by attending to the condition of slaves; we shall finish by softening that of all the animals which assist our labours and supply our wants." Those who have seen the beautiful and absolutely unselfish affection which many animals, when they are decently treated, show to their masters, must feel the same kind of shame and bewilderment at the callous brutality often shown to them, that we feel when we read of the treatment of slaves in ancient Rome. *"O demens, ita servus homo est?"*

I have not space to discuss in detail the various ethical problems raised by our new recognition of the status of animals as the subjects of rights. The law protects them from wanton cruelty, thus recognising that they are not "even as stocks and stones." But have we a right to enslave them, to kill and eat them, to cut them open for purposes of medical research, and to hunt and shoot them for our amusement? These are not easy questions to answer, and I cannot argue for or against these practices in this book. My own attitude may be inconsistent; I cannot help that. We have, I think, a right to make the animals supply our needs, on condition of treating them kindly; we have a right to kill and eat them, for creatures which are not useful for food will not long be suffered to exist at all; we have a right to vivisect them under anæsthetics, but only if there is no other way of acquiring medical knowledge, and if no unnecessary pain is inflicted; but to take a pleasure in killing our helpless cousins in fur and feathers seems to me a disgusting relic of barbarism. Personally, I have never killed anything larger than a wasp, and that was in self-defence. It is not necessary or possible to draw hard and fast lines; what is necessary is that we should recognise that the animals have as good a right on the earth as we have; that "our heavenly Father feedeth them," and wishes them to have such happiness as they are capable of; and that they are, in fact and not in metaphor, our own kith and kin.

THE POSITION OF WOMEN

I pass to another modern movement which, like humanitarianism, has been on the whole discouraged and repressed in the Latin countries, where the Catholic Church is still strong enough to be a social and political force—I mean the changed position of women. I shall try, in dealing with so vast a subject, to bear in mind that the ethical side of the question is what concerns us in this book. I must also remind my readers that matters of personal morality, such as the obligation of sexual purity and the stability of marriage, are reserved for the next chapter. In this chapter I am dealing with changes in public opinion such as may be reflected in institutions, laws, and customs.

Lecky, in his interesting chapter on the position of women, rightly calls attention to the strange physiological blunder almost universal in antiquity and the middle ages, to the effect that the father alone is the active agent in procreation, the mother being, as Æschylus makes Apollo say, only "the nurse of the embryo." It is probable that no scientific error has ever had such a powerful social influence. From it comes the habit of tracing pedigrees through the male, the Salic law and the custom of entail, and the calling of children of both sexes by the family name of the father. St. Thomas Aquinas accepts the notion. It is hardly necessary to say that the contribution of the two parents to the physical and mental constitution of the child is now known to be equal, so that from the biological point of view female descent is as important as male.

Something has already been said about St. Paul's attitude towards women. The most important statement is that "in Christ there is neither male nor female." Christianity in principle abolished all man-made distinctions by ignoring them. The outward distinctions of rich and poor, learned and simple; the political distinctions of Greek, Roman, and Jew; the social distinctions of citizen, free man, and slave, all vanish when we think of human beings as children of God and brethren one of another. Lastly, the most radical difference, that implanted by nature herself in distinguishing the sexes, is seen to be irrelevant when our business is with immortal souls. St. Paul is obliged to make regulations for his churches with an eye to existing social conditions; that these regulations are sane and moderate will be admitted by those who know anything of the excesses which arise in periods of religious enthusiasm, as among the Montanist circles in the Churches of Asia.

In another chapter I touched lightly upon the thoroughly unhealthy feeling towards women fostered by the extravagant asceticism of the post-apostolic Church. It is unnecessary to dwell further on an aberration which, at least in Northern Europe, has completely passed away. Our chief concern in this chapter is with the feminist movement, which has swept over the world within the last half-century.

In most societies, whether civilised or barbarous, the employments of the sexes are sharply differentiated.

In primitive communities, the man is the hunter and fighter, the woman does nearly all the ordinary work. Where agriculture is practised, the two sexes usually work side by side; it is a peculiarity in the new communities across the seas that the women, at any rate of the Anglo-Saxon stock, do not work in the fields. Even in England, we do not often see women field-labourers —one of the most familiar sights in France. In the Proverbs of Solomon we have a picture of the model housewife, whose day is completely filled by her household duties.

But in the middle ages the economic competition of women was already felt by the men. At first attempts were made to force the women into the trade-guilds; then they were excluded from them. This was a masculine victory. After this, we do not hear many murmurs of revolt until the eighteenth century. There were some compensations for the restrictions imposed upon women. The influence of Mariolatry, whatever we may think of its theological propriety, went far to make up for the contumelious language of the monks against the female sex, and chivalry, though it by no means encouraged prudish morality, gave, at least to young and beautiful women, a measure of homage which they had never received before. Puritanism probably caused a certain reaction towards masculinism; for Calvinism is the most masculine type that Christianity has ever assumed, and it favoured a return to Jewish ideas, which emphasise the intrinsic inferiority of women to men.

At the time of the French Revolution, though that cataclysm was said to have "forgotten half the human race," since it did nothing for the emancipation of women, writers like Cordorcet in France, and Mary Wollstonecroft in England, began to plead the rights of women. George Sand, Robert Owen, William

Thompson and John Stuart Mill continued the agitation. But the real cause of the movement was the change in economic conditions which became apparent soon after the beginning of the industrial era.

The family, organised communistically, gave women a recognised position, with a right to maintenance, in return for various unpaid services. The industrial revolution took away the woman's household industries, and almost drove her into economic competition with men. This naturally aroused sex-antagonism on both sides. Mr. Havelock Ellis, writing in 1888, quotes a working man at Blackburn as saying: "A thing of beauty is a joy for ever; but when the thing of beauty takes to doing the work for sixteen shillings a week that you have been paid twenty-two shillings for, you do not feel as if you cannot live without possessing that thing of beauty all to yourself, or that you are willing to lay your life and your fortune (when you have one) at its feet." The thing of beauty no doubt felt equally resentful at being obliged to take six shillings less than the man. At the present time, this disparity of remuneration has been somewhat reduced; but female labour is still cheaper, and much of our unemployment is caused by taking hundreds of thousands of women into wage-earning work. This, of course, is not necessarily bad for the country. A new asset of great value has been discovered in female labour, which makes it possible to do all the work which the community needs by means of a smaller number of families.

Nevertheless, many women, formerly engaged in home industries, have lost their occupation. "In the patriarchal family," says Havelock Ellis, "the women still had a recognised sphere of work and a recognised right to subsistence. It was not till the development of the industrial system, and the purely individualistic economics with which it was associated, at the beginning of the nineteenth century, that women in England were forced to realise that their household industries were gone and that they must join in that game of competition in which the field and the rules had been chosen with reference to men alone." Olive Schreiner writes to the same effect: "The spinning-wheels are broken, and steam-driven looms produce the clothing of half the world. Steam shapes our bread, and the loaves are set down at our door. Factory-produced viands take a larger and larger place in the dietary of rich and poor. Even the working-man's wife places before her household little that is of her own preparation. Our carpets are beaten, our windows cleaned, our floors polished, by machinery, or by extra-domestic, often male labour. Looking round on the entire field of women's ancient and traditional labours, we find that fully three-fourths of it have shrunk away for ever, and that the remaining fourth still tends to shrink.

The wives and daughters of the rich, most numerous in America but well represented at home, are the largest and most irresponsible leisured class that the world has seen. Their insatiable thirst for pleasure, their vulgar ostentation and extravagance, make them a peculiarly pernicious influence in the society in which they live. In America their every whim is indulged, and often nearly the whole of the monstrous fortunes which the law allows Americans to accumulate is wasted year by year by their women on the senseless rivalry of profligate expenditure. As Havelock Ellis says, "It is impossible for anyone under these conditions to lead a reasonable and wholesome human life."

Too much importance has been attributed to the noisy hooligans and hysterical or sexually inverted women who under cover of legitimate political agitation brought disgrace upon their sex and country in the years before the Great War. The women of England much more than retrieved whatever disrepute was thus incurred by their noble work during the war, which silenced even those who had been most opposed to giving them votes. The cause of these outbreaks has probably been rightly stated by Professor Percy Gardner: "The insurgent class has an enormous field to draw upon. [1] . . . And without knowing much about physiology, everyone can understand what a vast reserve of energy lies waiting to be tapped. Every woman is descended from an endless chain of female ancestors, every one of whom was a mother, and devoted a great part of her strength and energy to the production and tending of children. To this purpose above all others nature has destined women, except a few who were defective. When the stream has gently flowed through thousands of generations, it cannot suddenly be stopped without the most noteworthy results." Many have doubted whether it is wise to entrust the training of children to unmarried or childless schoolmistresses. Northern Europe has decided against a celibate priesthood, for the same reason.

The chief moral problem which confronts the emancipated woman arises from the conflicting claims of self-realisation and of duty to society. Both fatherhood and motherhood involve many self-denials; but whereas the childless husband usually works almost as hard for his wife and himself as he would do if he had children, the wife is spared an immense amount of labour if she

---

[1] The Professor here falls into a very common mistake, in supposing that, even apart from war-losses, there is a large permanent surplus of women of marriageable age. This is not so. About four per cent. more boys are born than girls. But since women live on an average about four years longer than men, females of all ages largely outnumber males. This, however, does not apply to those between twenty and forty, the marrying ages. At these ages the numbers are almost exactly equal. There is therefore a lad for every lass—if the lad wants a wife.

has no family. It would be most unfair to attribute the greater part of the fall in the birthrate, which was absolutely necessary in this country, to culpable selfishness; but there are undoubtedly many women who evade their duties to the next generation merely in order to find time for self-regarding interests and pleasures. Others resent having to be helpmates or partners of their husbands, and do all that in them lies to spoil the careers of the men whom they have married. We shall see in the next chapter that they are increasingly ready to claim complete exemption from their marriage-vows. This abuse of their newly-won freedom threatens to bring about a disintegration of society, and an increasing aversion from marriage on the part of men. Already, as has been often pointed out, the married woman is the spoilt child of the law. Mr. Meyrick Booth sums up the situation thus ("Woman and Society," 1929): *"Wife's Rights.*—The right of maintenance. The right to work outside the home, even against the wish of her husband. The right to determine the place of her residence. The right to invite her friends to the home and entertain them at her husband's expense. The right to accept or refuse motherhood. The right to delegate the housework to servants, who must of course be paid by the husband. The right of complete self-possession, meaning presumably that the wife no longer recognises that sex union is part of marriage contracts. And in a general sense, the right to full personal freedom. *Husband's Rights.*—None." It is no wonder that Sir Edward Parry writes: "Now that woman is legally on her own, it is both degrading to her status as well as unjust that she should maintain the legal privileges which were necessary to her in her chattel days."

The whole trend of Christian Ethics is towards maintaining the solidarity of the family as a training school of unselfishness and pure affection. There will be many of both sexes who are called to serve their generation, perhaps more effectively than most married persons, in the single life. But few can have observed recent developments without being convinced that the emancipation of women has reached a stage when it is a danger to society, or would be if it were not, after all, confined to a comparatively small class. "No man liveth to himself, and no man dieth to himself." We have all to discharge many unpaid and voluntary offices in return for the immense and unpayable debt which we owe to society, past and present; and this kind of charity, for most people, "begins at home."

WAR

Human institutions arise when they are inevitable, and neither common sense nor moral indignation can destroy them while they are inevitable. There is reason to think that war has not always been inevitable; that during the greater part of human history it has been inevitable; and that a time is approaching when it will no longer be inevitable.

The duels of male animals, usually for the possession of the females, do not resemble war, and are seldom fought to the death. Organised attacks by a whole community on another community of the same species are almost confined to ants and bees, which resemble mankind in having established civilisation and ownership of property.[1] Man as a hunter usually has his own hunting grounds, and avoids trespass, though he indulges sometimes in a judicial man-hunt or a vendetta. War in the proper sense began with the discovery of metals, a discovery which resulted, as we ought to remember, in saving nascent civilisation from the constant menace

[1] Havelock Ellis, "The Philosophy of Conflict," p. 44.

of destruction by marauding barbarians. But this discovery was quite recent. It seems that war, which Bagehot called the most showy fact in human history, has been in existence for six or seven thousand years at most out of the million years or so during which men—*homo sapiens* and his immediate progenitors—have lived on the earth.

Some writers have found a hopeful analogy in cannibalism, which from being originally unknown among men, and very rare among animals, became a widespread custom, sometimes, as among the Aztecs, a part of religious ritual; but which at a certain grade of culture disappears rapidly and completely, not on utilitarian grounds, for human flesh is nutritious and easy to come by, but because among civilised races the idea of eating it arouses instinctive disgust. Why, it has been asked, should not the same feelings of repulsion come to be excited by war, in which far more revolting things are done than eating our dead enemies or relations?

War, says Havelock Ellis, is a phase of conflict, and without conflict there can be no life. "In yes and no all things consist"; or, as Heracleitus said, the harmony of life is like the equilibrium of a strong bow or a lyre, created by the tension of opposite forces. War, *certatio per vim,* as Grotius defines it, is a form of conflict, but an obsolescent form, since even in politics we now usually count heads instead of breaking them, and even in religion we have substituted malediction for the rack and the stake. To abolish competition would be to emasculate human nature; but it may pass into less destructive forms than it has assumed in the past.

"To fight," says Santayana,[1] "is a radical instinct; if men have nothing else to fight over, they will fight over words, fancies, or women, or because they dislike each other's looks, or because they have met walking

[1] "Reason in Society," p. 81.

in opposite directions. . . . To fight for a reason and in a calculating spirit is something your true warrior despises.[1] The joy and glory of fighting lie in its pure spontaneity." William James, writing in a country which is invulnerable, and where in consequence there is less feeling of responsibility than in Europe, gives expression to the pleasurable excitement which the idea of war still arouses among the citizens of the United States. "The plain truth is, people want war. They want it anyhow. It is the final bouquet of life's fireworks. The born soldier wants it hot and actual. The non-combatants want it in the background, and always as an open possibility to feed imagination on, and keep excitement going. Let the general possibility of war be left open, in heaven's name, for the imagination to dally with. Let the soldiers dream of killing as the old maids dream of marrying. But organise in every possible way the practical machinery for making each successive chance of war abortive." William James, it is plain, was no militarist; but writing before the Great War, and in America, he could say without fear of contradiction that "people want war." Roosevelt said the same about his countrymen, and specified Great Britain as the country with which Americans would enjoy picking a quarrel.

But this kind of pugnacity is a baser thing than chivalrous love of fighting; at bottom it is a wish to see the newspapers made more interesting, and politics more exciting. One cannot imagine these penmen emulating the valour of the hero at Chevy Chase who when both his legs were smitten off, still fought upon his stumps. Nor could they enter into the feelings of two Maori tribes, one of whom sent a message to the other

---

[1] So Ennius made Pyrrhus say:—

Non cauponantes bellum sed belligerantes
Ferro non auro litem cernamus utrique.

in the middle of a battle: "We have no more ammunition. Unless you will send us some, we shall have to stop fighting"—a request which was promptly granted. Fighting used to be a game, and even a religious exercise. Savages prepare for it by ascetic discipline, and put on a ceremonial costume for the occasion. The entire disappearance of the spectacular and sporting side of militarism in the Great War, except in the air service, was often noted. It was "a common-sense change"—war is war, and business is business. But if war is reduced to business and common sense, it will soon vote for its own abolition.

The primitive or typical war is a predatory raid, by nomads or other barbarians, upon settled provinces. The Assyrians were raiders, pure and simple; and the invasions of the nomads of the Asian steppes, under the different names of Huns, Mongols, Tartars, and Turks, destroyed civilisation in its most ancient seats. If Christians had been as pacific as Buddhists, or if Western Europe had been as well suited to hordes of cavalry as Russia and Hungary, there is scarcely any doubt that the "legacies" of Greece, Rome, and Palestine would have been finally and totally extinguished.

Out of the raid was developed the war of conquest, as the result of which the invaders quarter themselves permanently on the conquered country as a ruling class. Thus was created a very common type of nation; and since the invaders have, on our side of the equator, usually come from the hardier and less fertile regions of the North, the ruling caste has often been of nordic race. Sometimes the invaders, under a king or an emperor, have pillaged the inhabitants without mercy, taxing them for purposes of luxury and ostentation, or for wars in which the conquered peoples have no interest. At other times they have discovered that their advantage lies in establishing orderly government, forbidding any except themselves to practise extortion, protecting their dominions from foreign aggression, and encouraging the increase of wealth and culture. Some governments of this type have been better than the subject races could have had without them. That which began as mere tyranny becomes a symbiosis, profitable both to rulers and ruled; and therewith comes a fusion of races which may produce a stronger and more gifted type than that of the original inhabitants. Even a splendid Court, which can be supported only by placing unnecessary burdens on the taxpayer, is not always unpopular or useless; it symbolises the greatness of a country, and encourages the arts. Santayana may be going rather too far when he says that all great upheavals and regenerations have been brought about by successful invasion; but he is able to give an imposing list of examples. Yet we must not forget the numerous examples of nations being paralysed for centuries by foreign conquest. Asia, and the Turkish Empire in Eastern Europe, furnish the chief examples of this. Homer was not wrong when he said that Zeus takes away half a man's virtue when he makes him a slave.

The Roman Empire gives an admirable example on a large scale of a military domination. The early wars of Rome were wars of consolidation, like the Civil War in America. It was better for Italy, and better for the United States, that they should be united under one political system. We may hold that such wars were justified, since a beneficial unification could have been brought about by no other means. But when the Roman Republic launched upon overseas conquests in the East, the expansion was no longer beneficial. Recent researches like those of Tarn have shown that the Romans pillaged their "allies" more mercilessly than the contemporaries of Clive plundered the Indians. Rome soon became a parasitic city, to which the wealth of the civilised world was brought to be squandered. In return, the provincials received the "Roman peace" and free trade, boons which were not of much value while the empire was torn by civil wars. But the barbarians on the north and east were kept out for centuries, and this was the real reason why Roman rule was tolerated. In the West, though not in the East, Rome also appeared as a civilising Power. But in the end, the Roman Empire died of Rome. The central government exhausted the resources of the provinces, and spread paralysis over the whole organism.

For a thousand years after the fall of the Western Empire Europe was tormented by every known kind of war, and civilisation, after being almost destroyed in the incessant and brutal slaughter and rapine of the dark ages, as they are justly called, recovered but slowly. One prominent cause of the recovery is seldom noted. "By 1300, the defensive had obtained an almost complete mastery over the offensive, so that famine was the only certain weapon in siegecraft." [1] It may be said, by the way, that the impossibility of defending any fortified town, which was demonstrated by the Great War, is one of the most ominous symptoms in the condition of civilisation, unless indeed wars can be abolished. [2]

After the beginning of the fourteenth century the only kind of war which could be made to pay consisted of pillaging raids by small armies. The foreign wars of the Plantagenets in France were of this type. They were popular at home, and, from the point of view of the kings, useful in keeping turbulent gangs of armed retainers out of England—but when the French,

[1] Oman.

[2] No doubt we may set against this the unprofitable stalemate of trench warfare, predicted by Bloch, scoffed at by military specialists, and signally verified in the Great War.

goaded into unity by desperation, expelled the marauders, condign punishment, in the Wars of the Roses, soon fell upon the descendants of those who had organised the raids. The Black Prince and Henry V did not deserve to be made heroes.

During the modern period, the outstanding fact in the political history of Europe has been the attempt of one great Power after another to establish by force of arms supremacy over the continent. Wars became somewhat less frequent, but on a larger scale, and above all they became far more expensive. The application of science to warfare, and the possibility of financing it by loans instead of out of current expenditure, raised the costliness of war beyond all precedent. The ambitious attempts of Austria, Spain, France, and Germany to dominate the continent were foiled by coalitions, and the balance of power could not be finally upset as long as Britain remained mistress of the seas. This service rendered to Europe and the world by the British sea-power has been so great and so obvious that no coalition has been formed against us, and the other nations have acquiesced in our annexation of the best parts of the world outside Europe. The unwritten terms of the understanding were that Britain should keep her land army too small to be a menace to any great Power, and that no obstacles should be put in the way of the trade of other nations. No nation gained more by this British peace, between 1815 and 1914, than the United States; and it is possible that the main cause why America entered the Great War was one which it could never avow—namely, a sudden realisation that the British Empire was in danger, and that its fall, however agreeable to hyphenated Americans, would have highly inconvenient consequences to the United States.

In the earlier part of the modern period men massacred each other in the name of what they called religion; in the latter part the chief appeal has been to chauvinism or jingoism, miscalled patriotism. The Thirty Years' War, one of the most destructive conflicts ever known, depopulated large parts of Germany, and threw back the progress of Central Europe for centuries. It was also marked by hideous atrocities, such as the massacre of the whole population of Magdeburg. The spirit of nationality, which Napoleon, against his will, helped to quicken into extraordinary activity, promoted militarism in various ways. It claimed independence and "self-determination" for all populations which on racial or historical grounds could assert their right to these benefits, and thus tended to disunite those composite empires in which the bond of union had been loyalty or allegiance to the same monarch. To this apple of discord was added another—the claim that separated kinsfolk should be joined together in a single self-governing State. These two claims have been recognised on the one hand in the unification of Italy and Germany in the nineteenth century, and on the other, in the dissolution of Turkey in Europe, Austro-Hungary, and the United Kingdom in the twentieth. The time may come when the justification of such claims may seem less obvious than is now generally assumed.

Besides nationalism, quasi-religious fanaticism, in the strange form of anti-Christian Communism, has already caused civil wars in more than one country; and Syndicalists like Sorel shriek for civil war as the only way to destroy the capitalistic *régime*.

But we must go behind these temporary habits of thought, which evidently provide pretexts for the outbreak of more permanent passions. What are the psychological causes of this scourge, which is continually threatening, and often arresting, the progress of humanity?

Ruskin, following Aristotle and the Epistle of St. James, finds the source of war in the lusts that war in our members. "The first reason for all wars, and for the necessity of national defence, is that the majority of persons, high and low, in all European nations, are thieves, and in their hearts greedy of their neighbours' goods, land and fame. But besides being thieves they are also fools, and have never yet been able to understand that if Cornishmen want pippins cheap, they must not ravage Devonshire—that the prosperity of their neighbours is in the end their own also; and the poverty of their neighbours, by the communism of God, becomes also in the end their own." This is effective rhetoric, but a sweeping indictment of human nature is not helpful towards solving a problem in which we have to take human nature as it is, even when we hope to make it better; and since "Devonshire and Cornwall" have long ago ceased to raid each other's farms, some other explanation may be required of the fact that such obvious considerations do not always operate over larger areas than English counties.

Hobbes, in a well-known passage, finds, "in the nature of man, three principal causes of quarrel. First, competition; secondly, diffidence; thirdly, glory. The first maketh man invade for gain; the second for safety; and the third for reputation. The first use violence to make themselves masters of other men's persons, wives, children, and cattle; the second to defend them; the third for any sign of under-value, either direct in their persons, or by reflection in their kindred, their friends, their nation, their profession, or their name." This classification, too simple to cover the whole field, is nevertheless useful.

The ambition to "paint the map red," or to go down

to history as a "Mehrer des Reichs," is one of those childish aims which men have not yet outgrown. It is analogous to the desire to add house to house and field to field, which the Greeks called *pleonexia,* and modern writers acquisitiveness. We have perhaps forgotten that our nation had a sharp attack of this disease in the last three decades of Queen Victoria's reign, when the music halls became ecstatic over the spirit-stirring ditty, "We don't want to fight, but by Jingo if we do." Except in very barbarous societies, it is disguised as consciousness of a mission, a call to spread the blessings of our civilisation or culture over populations who would surely desire them if they understood them. At times when a nation is on the crest of the wave, rejoicing in a prosperity which "increases by leaps and bounds," it is natural that it should feel compassion for the "lesser breeds without the law," whose institutions and habits are so manifestly inferior to its own. The prosperous nation pictures itself as a "weary Titan," staggering under the too vast orb of its fate, sacrificially carrying the torch of enlightenment to the dark places of the earth. This was the mental condition of Germany in 1914, as it was in England a generation earlier. Such teaching is like a heady wine, intoxicating a nation with the fumes of arrogant patriotism. It provides a condition under which war may be gladly accepted by the majority of a people.

The desire for new markets, or new fields for emigration, has been the direct cause of many "little wars" against weak and backward races; but the gains from a new tropical colony are so small compared with the tremendous cost of a war between two great Powers that no nation would deliberately commit so great a folly. Nevertheless, colonial disputes may easily lead to a great war, since the diplomatists on both sides brandish the threat of war much as solicitors threaten a law-suit; war is the last instrument of diplomacy, a weapon held in reserve when other methods fail. The Power which is known to be the strongest may have its way by merely rattling the sabre in its scabbard; it may bully its neighbours and extort a series of concessions from them without ever striking a blow. But the time comes when this repeated pressure is felt to be intolerable. Alliances and coalitions will be formed, till at last the superior Power throws down the gage of battle once too often. The challenge is accepted, and the Power which has exploited the fear which it inspires in its neighbours is obliged either to fight or to lose its very profitable prestige by a humiliating retreat. This was in fact the origin of the Great War, which was not desired by any of the belligerents. Germany hoped till the last that the opposite group would shrink from the ordeal. Lord Haldane said to me not long after the war broke out, "The real war-guilt of the Germans consists in this, that their government drove Russia into a position from which, as they ought to have known, no retreat was possible." The impossibility, I suppose, was that of accepting a diplomatic humiliation which would have been tantamount to an abdication of influence in south-eastern Europe.

International hatreds seldom lead to war, but they may destroy the desire for peace, and make the nations ready to find a *casus belli,* in a small dispute. The letters of Sir Cecil Spring Rice show how much he feared the anti-English propaganda which he found in almost every country to which he was sent. But the threatened coalitions against Great Britain always miscarried. When I was in Berlin about four years before the war, the eminent German publicist, Professor Hans Delbrück, said to me: "International animosities matter very little; but where there is fear there is danger." The truth of these words was proved in the Great

War. Behind the disputes which were the immediate occasion of the outbreak, there was mutual fear, genuine and reasonable. The writings of diplomatists, like the letters of Spring Rice just mentioned, show how much afraid the Powers were of exposing a vulnerable flank to attack, even for a few days in profound peace. It was the deliberate opinion of this high-minded and pacific statesman that a Power known to be unwilling or unable to fight must expect to be insulted and robbed on every occasion. In the years before 1914 these mutual fears were chronic. Germany and Austria feared a sudden attack by Russia and France as soon as the Russian strategic railways were ready. France feared an unprovoked attack by Germany, like that which England and Russia helped to avert in 1875. England, who would have preferred to keep as clear of entangling alliances as the United States, feared, and probably with good reason, that a German victory would have been followed by an attack upon these islands, in which, as Asquith said, "we should have been left without a friend in the world." I have been informed by a Cabinet Minister that it was even suggested, during the fateful debate at the beginning of August 1914, which was to decide between intervention and neutrality, that if we left the French to fight Germany without us, the next war would be a Franco-German coalition to divide up the British Empire.

When the sword has once been drawn, hatred often blazes out with such fury that the idea of a reasonable compromise is rejected with scorn, and the conflict has to be continued till one or both combatants are completely exhausted. Atrocities occur in every war, and the exploitation and exaggeration of them in order to rouse popular anger into frenzy have now become a diabolical art practised with studied malignity by all belligerents. Hatred and revenge are more impracticable passions than calculating selfishness; they disregard even the most obvious considerations of self-interest. Shakespeare puts into the mouth of young Clifford, standing over his father's dead body, the vow of a vendetta of this kind:—

> "Even at this sight
> My heart is turned to stone, and while 'tis mine
> It shall be stony. York not our old men spares;
> No more will I their babes; tears virginal
> Shall be to me even as the dew to fire;
> And beauty that the tyrant oft reclaims
> Shall to my flaming wrath be oil and flax.
> Henceforth I will not have to do with pity."

Nietzsche speaks of "the deep impersonality born of hatred, the conscience born of murder and cold-bloodedness, the fervour born of effort in the annihilation of the enemy, the proud indifference to loss, to one's own existence and to that of one's fellows."[1] Here we seem to have reached sheer madness or devilry; and perhaps we may congratulate ourselves that the passion of revenge, as an abiding mood, is no longer felt in advanced races as it is in many half-civilised peoples. The English, on the whole, are bad haters, though hard fighters; our national character is happily free from the unforgetting vindictiveness which is the most unattractive feature of the Irish character.

The reproach has often been brought against Christianity that it has done so little effectively to deliver mankind from this monstrous evil. Buddhism, we are told, has really created as well as inculcated a peaceful disposition. We must try to consider this question impartially.

---

[1] Quoted by Canon Grane, "The Passing of War" (1913). I have borrowed other quotations from this excellent volume, which I think has not met with all the recognition which it deserves.

The Old Testament contains many records of revolting atrocities perpetrated by the Israelites in the invasions of Canaan. It is useless to palliate these crimes, as Newman did, by saying that the Canaanite children, who were butchered without distinction of sex, were suffering for the exceptionally odious vices of their fathers; and that their murderers were aware that after the general resurrection God would rectify any miscarriages of justice. This precious argument was used before at the massacre of the Albigenses. Nor does the alleged pacifism of the prophets come to much more than political advice not to fight against hopeless odds.

We are in a very different atmosphere when we come to the Gospels. The teaching of Christ seems at first sight to be decisive in favour of non-resistance to injury of any kind. To requite hatred with love is often the best way to overcome it; but if not, the disciple of Christ, it appears, must not stand up for his rights. So some Christians have always thought. Others have pointed out that Christ often used hyperbolical language; and that He was not legislating for national governments, but laying down principles for personal conduct.

The majority of the early Fathers of the Church, if they refer to the subject, condemn war absolutely as inconsistent with Christianity. Such is the opinion of Justin Martyr, Tertullian, Irenæus, Origen, Cyprian, Athanasius, and Lactantius. "It is not lawful," says Lactantius, "for a just man to engage in warfare, since his warfare is justice itself."[1] Basil (Epist. 188) says that soldiers after their discharge are excluded from communion for three years. This unqualified condemnation of war is one of the tenets of the Society of Friends and of the late Count Tolstoy.

But this extreme position was not adopted by the

[1] Hastings, "Encyclopædia of Religion and Ethics," "War."

official Church. In the Acts of the Apostles the centurion Cornelius is admitted to the society of believers without demur, and the writer to the Hebrews inscribes several warriors on his roll of honour. John the Baptist did not order the soldiers who came to him to leave the service. Before the end of the second century there were many Christians in the Roman army. Clement of Alexandria applies to the military profession the Pauline maxim that a Christian shall remain in his calling. Constantine saw the importance of having Christian soldiers on his side; they must therefore have been numerous in the early part of the fourth century.

The attitude of the Church towards war was settled, to a large extent, by Augustine. It is impossible, he says, for the government not to use force against murderers and robbers, and it is equally impossible for the State to acquiesce in an unprovoked foreign attack. The real interests even of the aggressor compel us to resist him in the only possible manner. At the same time, an empire founded on injustice is only a band of robbers on a large scale; and war should always be waged for the sake of peace. The uncompromising injunctions in the Gospels, he says, refer to inner states of the mind, which should always be directed to the good of others.

In 314 the Council of Arles condemned conscientious objectors who deserted their colours. But the Councils of the Church still forbade the clergy to fight, and ecclesiastical canons, made in the reign of William the Conqueror and confirmed by Norman prelates, ordained that a soldier must do a year's penance for every man he has killed in battle. It seems incredible that this regulation was carried out.

But the Church was early on the warpath against Arians and then against Moslems. Massacres of Jews, heretics, and Mohammedans were considered eminently meritorious, though Gratian is of the opinion that the slayer of a Jew or Pagan should do penance, *"quia spem futuræ conversionis exterminat."* This was not the view of the pious St. Louis of France, who in answer to a question said "the best answer which a layman can make to a contentious Jew is to run his sword into him as far as it will go." The Old Testament was often appealed to as sanctioning wars for the help of the Lord against the mighty. The Crusades against the infidel were officially encouraged, and Crusades might be ordered against any Power which opposed the papal policy.

Thomas Aquinas, by rather sophistical arguments, urges that the Gospels do not prohibit just wars, or fighting in self-defence. Luther and Calvin explicitly justify wars in a good cause. Calvin thinks that the Old Testament teaching is still valid for Christians; was not David, the man after God's own heart, a mighty man of valour? Luther argues that self-defence is a natural right, which the Gospel must be understood to presuppose. I do not think that there was much difference between the teaching of the reformed and the unreformed Churches in this matter. The Council of Trent mentions the massacres in the Old Testament as ordered by God. In this as in some other matters the sects, in their desire to apply the teaching of the Gospel universally and in the literal sense, were more uncompromising than the great Churches.

Chivalry, as a code of arms, flourished from the eleventh to the sixteeth century. It reached its zenith in the fourteenth, and ended by falling into ridicule. Originally a rule of conduct in war for cavaliers or feudal gentlemen, it allied itself with the Church in the attempt to rescue Jerusalem and the Holy Places from the infidel. The orders of soldier-monks, the Hospitallers and the Templars, were founded soon after 1100.

They were vowed to chastity, and some of their members, like Sir Galahad, no doubt observed the vow. These Orders acted as a sort of police to protect pilgrims on their road to the East, and fought with bravery against Saladin's Moslems. Chivalry has been called a curious bastard between war and Christianity; it exactly suited the pugnacious French knights, always eager *jouer le gros jeu*. When there was no fighting to be done, tournaments, which often ended in death or grievous wounds, were a welcome substitute; and these were preceded by masses and confessions. The laws of courtesy certainly introduced some mercy into the usages of war, and this was encouraged by the Church, which also ordained close seasons during which military operations must be suspended, under the name of *truga Dei*. This truce, however, was not always observed even by the Popes. The failure of the Crusades deprived the military monks of their excuse for existing; they became the Pope's militia, and the Templars met with the same fate at the hands of a King of France as the Janissaries of Turkey at the hands of a Sultan.

In the Anglican Articles of Religion it is said that Christian princes may wage "just wars," but the adjective has disappeared from the English version. Jeremy Taylor says that war is "the rod of God in the hands of princes"; and J. B. Mozley in a celebrated sermon has no doubt of the legitimacy of warfare between Christian peoples. On the other side, the Lollards and Anabaptists condemned the practice, as did Colet and his friend Erasmus. The protest of Erasmus is very forcible. "Nothing is more impious, more calamitous, more widely pernicious, more inveterate, more base, or in sum more unworthy of a man, not to say of a Christian, than war. . . . The man who engages in war by choice, whoever he is, is a wicked man; he sins against nature, against God, and against man, and is guilty of the most aggravated impiety." At the same time his friend Colet, with remarkable courage, sounded his protest from the pulpit of St. Paul's Cathedral, at the very time when Henry VIII was preparing an unnecessary war against France. "An unjust peace," he said, "is better than the justest war." "When men out of hatred and ambition fight with and destroy one another, they fight under the banner not of Christ but of the devil." It is pleasant to be able to add that Henry admired the preacher's courage, and forgave the inopportuneness of the sermon.

Voltaire and the Encyclopædists, Rousseau, Kant, and Bentham may be reckoned among those who have denounced war; Hegel, Ruskin, and Nietzsche among its defenders. Bacon is purely Machiavellian on the subject; his utterances deserve to be pilloried with those of Treitschke and Bernhardi.

Attempts have often been made to distinguish between the clergy and the laity. It has been held that it is the duty of the layman to fight for his country when called upon, but that the duty of the clergy is to pray, and to set an example of ideal Christian morals in their full integrity. David was not allowed to dedicate the Temple because he had been a man of war and had shed blood; and so a Christian priest who had shed blood, even accidentally, like Archbishop Abbot, who shot a beater while hunting, became *ipso facto* "irregular." It is said that the "shedding of blood" was taken so literally that martial prelates in the middle ages went into battle with heavy maces, with which they could pound their enemies into pulp without breaking the skin. Similarly, the Church, while committing a condemned heretic to the secular arm for punishment, expressed a pious hope that he might be dealt with "without effusion of blood," which in practice meant that he was to be burnt alive. Thomas Aquinas decides that since fighting "tends to the spilling of blood," clerics and spiritual persons must not be allowed to fight, *nisi in necessitatis articulo,* whatever that may mean.

Martensen, a Lutheran divine, strongly opposes permission being given to ministers of the Gospel to fight. In the late war, the Roman Catholic Church, though on political grounds it tried to impede recruiting in Canada, allowed French priests and abbés to serve in the trenches, and many of them did good service in battle. The Anglican Church, after much hesitation, discouraged parish priests from volunteering for active service, but did not forbid it. The Church of Scotland left it to the individual judgment of ministers whether they should join the army as fighting men or not.

It is needless to say that in the New Testament there is no trace of a double standard of Ethics, one for the clergy and the other for the laity. On the whole, the Quakers seem to me to be reasonable in saying that war, in any given case, must be either right or wrong for all alike, and that we must not hold that it is right for some men and wrong for others. On the other hand, in most wars it is not left to individual judgment to decide whether a war is just or unjust, and in the numerous cases where the question of right or wrong is not quite clear, it may be better for ministers of religion to abstain from actual fighting, if the State allows them the choice. The question, in fact, is by no means easy to settle.

Nor is it easy to judge the case of the "conscientious objector." In France, the authorities took the logical ground that it is not the business of the State to decide whether a man's dislike of fighting is due to conscience, want of patriotism, or personal cowardice; and in consequence the few who refused to serve were shot. In

England, even after compulsory service was instituted, men were allowed to plead conscientious scruples, but things were not made pleasant for them. A considerable number thus escaped the danger of being shot, including not a few high-minded men who were willing to face extreme obloquy for the sake of protesting against what they believed to be a transgression of the law of Christ. Others, no doubt, were cowards, or revolutionaries who acknowledged no duty towards their country, like the socialist regiments who allowed the enemy to penetrate the Italian line at Caporetto. Some of the conscientious pacifists volunteered to do dangerous war-work such as mine-sweeping; but the stricter objectors thought that to aid and abet fighting was almost as bad as fighting oneself.

The tendency in England is to respect the individual conscience; relief has even been granted to those who think themselves debarred, on conscientious grounds, from taking oaths in a law-court. But public opinion on the whole condemned the objectors in the Great War. It was felt that when the whole country was in imminent danger of a defeat from which it might not have recovered, it was not a time for private judgment to set itself against the will of the large majority, and thus to endanger the liberty of all. All citizens alike enjoy the protection of the law, with security of life and property, advantages which cannot be assured without the presence of armed force; it is not just that anyone should claim this protection and yet refuse to contribute to it. It was not denied that some wars have been so manifestly unjust that a Christian ought to be willing to suffer any punishment rather than take part in them; but no one, it was generally thought, could maintain that the action of Great Britain in taking part in the Great War fell under this condemnation. Mistakes might have been made in the diplomatic proceedings which led up to the war; but when once the sword had been drawn, it was manifestly a life and death struggle, failure in which would mean the permanent loss of our position among the great nations of the world. While admitting that any great war must present a difficult moral problem to Quakers and others who think like them, my own opinion is that those pacifists decided rightly who determined to throw in their lot with their fellow-citizens, and share their sacrifices for the common cause.

Those who approach the question from the philosophical side usually take the same view. To protect oneself against aggression is said to be a natural right, and if so, a nation has a claim upon the assistance of all its citizens in repelling an attack upon its corporate existence. Grotius, while arguing that the well-being of society requires that violence should be checked by violence, adds the curious reflection that the Creator would not have endowed His creatures with natural weapons if He had not intended that they should use them.

Philosophers have always attempted to find some criterion to distinguish just and unjust wars. Aristotle, who carried to an extreme the doctrine that some races are naturally inferior to others, and born for subjection, does not give much help. Augustine, who uses scathing language about predatory empires, allows wars which have for their object the punishment of evildoers, reparation for injury, or the direct command of God—the last being added to justify the wars of the Israelites. In the middle ages the right of rebellion was often discussed. Lutherans and Anglicans mostly maintained the duty of non-resistance to tyranny; Calvin, like many medieval casuists, admitted that when misgovernment becomes intolerable, it is justifiable for subjects to rebel. Grotius admits the right of rebellion if a sovereign invades the privileges of a free people. If these pleas in favour of "just wars" are admitted, the duty of a private citizen to support his country in such a war is indisputable.

For the most part the justifications of war as an institution do not commend themselves to the moral sense of the modern man. They are, however, of different degrees of value, and they cannot be rejected summarily.

The first is a problem which perhaps will not have much importance in the future, since the swarming period of the white races has plainly come to an end, but which cannot be neglected if we are to justify the manner in which the Europeans have spread over the earth's surface. Was it an injustice not to leave North and South America to the redskins, Australia to the blackfellows, New Zealand to the Maoris, and South Africa to the Kaffirs? It seems impossible to say that it was unjust, especially when we remember that many of the tribes whom the Europeans dispossessed were themselves invaders and conquerors. The Aztecs had been in Mexico only for a few centuries; the Maoris had come to New Zealand from overseas; the Bantus were migrants from more northerly parts of Africa. But can we draw any line and say in what circumstances a civilised race has a right to appropriate the hunting grounds of the savage or the mud villages of the barbarian, and to introduce what we consider a higher type of social life, perhaps at the cost of exterminating the aborigines? It is certain that without war and violence a large portion of the land surface of the globe, well suited to be the abode of the progressive nations, would have remained scantily peopled by very backward races. The conquest of the two Americas was stained by shocking acts of cruelty; but do we seriously urge that it cannot be justified at all? If we justify it, we are claiming that a superior race has the right to expropriate an inferior, for no other reason than because it is the superior race.

But there is another aspect of this question which may very closely concern the white races in the future. The superiority of the European is mainly a military superiority. Intellectually, we are not superior to the civilised Asiatic nations; physically we are less robust than some barbarians. It is in virtue of our vastly superior military and naval equipment that Europeans have annexed, colonised, or reduced to impotence nearly the whole of the habitable world, the only important exceptions being the two great nations of Eastern Asia, China and Japan. It is not likely that the white man will again attempt to annex territory already fully occupied by either of these two Powers. But if the advocates of disarmament were to get their way, and the white races were to beat their swords into plough-shares and their spears into pruning-hooks, what would be left of their superiority? The brown and yellow races are kept out of North America and Australasia solely by the threat of violence. The white men in those countries know well that in economic competition they could not hold their own against the cheaper races, who are content with a lower standard of living and longer hours of work. When we talk of disarmament, we usually think only of the crushing burden of militarism upon the nations of Europe. Are we prepared to surrender the weapons which outside Europe have made the European the lord and bully of the whole planet? The white man, as soon as he is threatened, thinks that he has the right to maintain by force of arms his high standard of living, even if he is obliged to keep his own country half empty and underdeveloped while the Asiatics are in urgent need of homes for their teeming population. Can we maintain both that we had a right to seize North America from the Red Indians in order to people it with our surplus population, and at the same time that the Japanese have no right to settle in California and Australia, or the Hindus in South Africa? We hold our position in the world solely by the right of the sword; in the arts of peace we have no such advantages. Are we sufficiently convinced of the iniquity of war to repeal our exclusion laws, and let the best man, in the economic sense, win? I have heard this point urged very forcibly by a Japanese gentleman. "If we are still to be kept out by force," he said to me, "from countries which we could colonise successfully, why should we feel any enthusiasm over the League of Nations?" I do not know why they should.

Apologists for war have sometimes argued that the strongest, most virile, and most intelligent races have always been warlike..Even in Borneo, it is said, the head-hunting tribes were more vigorous than the peaceable tribes.[1] All great peoples have been great fighters. "Eternal peace," wrote Moltke to Bluntschli in 1880, "is a dream, and not even a beautiful dream, and war is a part of God's world-order. In war are developed the noblest virtues of mankind, courage and self-sacrifice, fidelity and the willingness to surrender life itself. Without war the world would be swallowed up in materialism." This old soldier was only repeating a *cliché* which was too popular in Germany at that time. As a matter of fact, Germany was beginning to be "swallowed up in materialism"—though no nation is by nature less materialistic—as the direct result of combined militarism and commercialism. Boswell supplies

[1] The Swiss determined to establish a chamois reserve, since those animals were in danger of extermination. The flocks of chamois protected from all their enemies, began to deteriorate rapidly. The remedy, which soon restored their former agility, was to introduce a few wolves among them!

a good corrective. "Dr. Johnson laughed much over Lord Kaimes' opinion that war was a good thing occasionally, as so much valour and virtue were exhibited in it. A fire, said Johnson, might as well be thought a good thing; there is the bravery and address of the firemen in extinguishing it; there is much humanity excited in saving the lives and properties of the poor sufferers; yet after all who can say a fire is a good thing?" War may be a school of virtue in bringing out noble qualities which would otherwise be latent; it can hardly create those qualities, which may also find abundant outlets in time of peace.

It is only too easy to frame crushing answers to apologies for an almost unmitigated evil. To begin with, the animosities created and encouraged by war are factitious and unreal. Carlyle's paragraph about the thirty peasants from "Dumdrudge" is familiar to all. In the Great War the soldiers had to be stopped from fraternising by their officers. Tommy Atkins, unlike the journalists and (alas!) most of the women at home, spoke almost affectionately of "poor old Fritz," and all the belligerent governments had to manufacture or exaggerate tales of atrocities in order to work up their people to the desired frenzy of hatred. When we remember the state of our minds at the end of July 1914, when the nation was preparing for its summer holiday without a thought of enmity against anyone except the suffragettes and the Sinn Feiners, the artificial character of the war-spirit leaps to the eyes. It must be a very bad cause which does not fill the streets of a capital with a shouting crowd on the day after the declaration of war; but very few in any country would vote for a war in cold blood, unless it was a question of throwing off a foreign yoke.

The notion that war is good for the virility of a nation is absolutely untrue, at least under modern conditions. The courage which it evokes it did not implant; the injury which it does to the racial stock continues to impair the quality of the race for many generations. There is no difference of opinion among eugenists on this point. Thucydides tells how an Athenian ungenerously taunted a Spartan prisoner by asking him whether all their brave men had been killed. "The arrow would be a useful weapon," was the reply, "if it picked out the best men to hit." So would the bullet. An epigram in the Greek Anthology says bluntly that the war-god spares not the good but the bad. (Ἄρης οὐκ ἀγαθῶν φείδεται ἀλλὰ κακῶν.) This is more true of modern than of ancient war. "The effect of war," says Professor Starr Jordan, writing in the year before the Great War, "is to spoil the breed, by the simple process of the reversion of selection." "There is not a nation that is for to-day what it might have been if it had chosen its best survival instead of slaughter." Nations have always chosen for war the best men they could get, and they have always got better than those whom they left at home. This counter-selection was one cause of the decline of Greece and Rome, and in the same way at the beginning of the modern period the vigorous race of Spaniards was enfeebled by war and persecution. "Castile makes men and wastes them," says an old writer. Some persons naïvely expressed surprise that after a hundred years of peace in Europe Englishmen fought better than ever. And yet Japan, after two hundred years of peace, had astonished the world by the valour of her soldiers in her war with Russia. Napoleon "peopled Hades with the *élite* of Europe"; the evil which he did can never be measured. Starr Jordan thinks that the United States have never fully recovered from the dysgenic slaughter of the Civil War from 1861 to 1865, in which nearly one in thirty of the whole population lost their lives. The statement often repeated that the Napoleonic War lowered the average height of Frenchmen, some have said by three inches, seems to be untrue; but there is no doubt that the war increased defects and infirmities in the next generation. That "war children" tend to be inferior was known before the Great War. There is really no doubt whatever that war, next to wholesale class-bribery by taxation, is the most dysgenic factor in modern life. I cannot refrain from quoting the vigorous language in which Santayana (in 1905) emphasises this truth, preaching, alas! to deaf ears: "There are panegyrists of war who say that without a periodical bleeding a race decays and loses its manhood. Experience is directly opposed to this shameless assertion. It is war that wastes a nation's wealth, kills its flower, narrows its sympathies, condemns it to be governed by adventurers, and leaves the puny, deformed, and unmanly to breed the next generation. Internecine war, foreign and civil, brought about the greatest set-back which the life of reason has ever suffered; it exterminated the Greek and Italian aristocracies. Instead of being descended from heroes, modern nations are descended from slaves, and it is not their bodies only that show it. . . . It is the unmutilated race, fresh from the struggle with nature (in which the best survive, while in war it is often the best that perish), that descends victoriously into the arena of nations. . . . To call war the soil of courage and virtue is like calling debauchery the soil of love."[1]

The horrors of war are not minimised by soldiers who have taken part in it. The words of the American General Sherman have often been quoted: "I confess without shame that I am tired and sick of the war (the American Civil War). Its glory is all moonshine. It is only those who have neither heard a shot nor heard

[1] Santayana, "Reason in Society," p. 82.

the shrieks and groans of the wounded, who cry aloud for more blood, more vengeance, more desolation. War is hell." The soldiers who fought in the Great War were strangely silent when they came home. Not only was the traditional *miles gloriosus*, who loves to fight his battles o'er again, never met with, but the demobilised soldier seemed to wish to put the hideous memories of those terrible years clean out of his mind, so that those who were not at the front habitually forget that any middle-aged man whom they meet has probably been through what General Sherman calls hell. Nor was there very much in the numerous war-books which appeared in the first few years after the armistice to reveal the squalid and hideous side of modern trench-fighting. But since then the veil has been lifted. Especially in Germany books have been published which expose in deliberately obscene and revolting detail what the soldiers had to endure during those terrible four years. Those who have read "Sergeant Grischa" and "All Quiet on the Western Front" feel that no word except General Sherman's is adequate to the facts, and that to let loose upon the world a repetition of that tragedy would be an unspeakable crime.[1]

As for the economic ruin wrought by the war, there were prophets who foresaw and foretold the truth. It is believed that the Germans counted on a single campaign to be finished in a few months, though the Polish banker and economist, Jean de Bloch, who died in 1902, had given reasons for thinking that a war between Powers of nearly equal strength would be a suicidal deadlock, ruinous to both parties. Battle in the open, he foresaw, would mean annihilation, but entrenched

---

[1] I do not ignore the soldiers' protest against these books, which tell us little of the idealism which inspired the combatants. The armies cheerfully bore terrible things for their country; it does not follow that governments have a right to demand such sacrifices from them again.

positions can be carried only by a frontal attack. The attacker also would have to entrench himself. Two long lines of trenches would face each other, and there would be continuous battles without any decisive result. In almost every particular the predictions of this keen-sighted civilian were verified in the Great War.

Equally prescient were the arguments of Norman Angell as to the economic ruin which would be entailed on victor and vanquished alike. The old maxim *vae victis* might now be changed into *vae victoribus*. If your chief rival and your best customer own the same head, it is not good business to cut that head off. Large indemnities cannot be paid except in kind, and payments in kind merely create unemployment in the nation which receives them. To disarm an enemy while keeping up a large army and navy is to take a millstone from the neck of the beaten foe and to hang it round our own. All these and other equally cogent arguments against war were brought by Mr. Angell, and never answered except by rudeness; every one of them was verified in the Great War.

It is no doubt possible to exaggerate the importance of the destruction of property in war. As John Stuart Mill remarks, we are often astonished at the rapidity with which a city which is recorded to have been sacked and burnt seems to have been rebuilt and to have recovered its prosperity. It has been estimated that the greater part of the concrete instruments of wealth, such as machinery, is normally used up and replaced in ten years or less. But even ten years of poverty and misery are a great evil; and if material losses are so soon repaired, what is the use of inflicting them upon an enemy whom it is desired to destroy, at the cost of approximately equal losses to the victor? Sometimes, however, the wounds are too deep to heal, especially if the internal condition of the country is unhealthy. To provoke a foreign war as an alternative to revolution is a desperate expedient.

If ever the fatalism of Thomas Hardy were justified, it seemed to be so by the proceedings of the Great Powers in making the war, and the peace.

"Spirit of the Years.

Observe that all wide sight and self-command
Deserts these throngs now driven to demonry
By the Immanent Unrecking. Nought remains
But vindictiveness here amid the strong.
And there amid the weak an impotent rage.

Spirit of the Pities.

Why prompts the Will so senseless-shaped a doing?

Spirit of the Years.

I have told thee that it works unwittingly,
As one possessed not judging."

If war is inevitable, can it be humanised? This question has been constantly asked, and numerous attempts have been made to lay down laws of war, which shall mitigate its horrors, especially for non-combatants. The Laws of Manu forbade the use of barbed or poisoned arms, or those "the points of which are blazing with fire." "Let not the King smite a suppliant, or an unarmed man, or a fugitive, or a mere spectator of the battle; nor one whose weapons are broken, or who is wounded severely." (These no doubt are rules of chivalry, for single combats.) The prophet of Israel asks the king indignantly, "Wouldest thou smite the captives of thy spear and bow?" In spite of the ruthlessness of its early wars, Israel was probably more humane than Assyria. In early Greek history there are traces of the use of poisoned arrows, of which Homer and his *clientèle* seem to be already ashamed.

333

This may be one explanation of the contempt felt for archers in classical Greece. But throughout Greek history it was the right of the conqueror to massacre the men of a conquered city, and to sell the women and children as slaves. Thucydides gives instances of Athenian cruelty at Mytilene and Melos. Plato proposes very humane regulations for wars between Greek cities; there is to be no wanton destruction of property, though standing crops may be seized. The wars of the Diadochi, waged mainly by professional soldiers, were relatively humane; the Roman practice was much more cruel. And yet the Romans admired chivalry and magnanimity, and handed down stories of generous conduct shown even by their enemies, such as Pyrrhus of Epirus. The torture of prisoners was practised by the Assyrians, on at least one occasion by David, by some African and Asiatic tribes, and very generally by the American Indians. It is probable that in the original saga Achilles dragged Hector alive at the tail of his chariot. The custom of sacrificing prisoners has been common among barbarians, and we are surprised to find relics of it even in civilised Greece and Rome. The Aztecs ceremonially massacred all their prisoners at the altar of their war-god Huitzilopotchli.

In the early middle ages the horrors of war were increased. Mohammed in the Koran enjoins no mercy to unbelievers. "Fight strenuously against unbelievers and heretics, and be stern to them, for their fate is hell, and an evil journey shall it be. The reward of those who fight against God and his prophet is to be slaughtered or crucified, or to have their hands and feet cut off on alternate sides!" And yet the Arabs were more humane than the Turks. The Huns under Attila, the Mongols under Jenghiz Khan, and the Tartars under Timour exterminated the whole population of many large cities; Gibbon estimates that Timour slaughtered between four and five million human beings. The Franks, and the Teutonic invaders of Britain, spared neither age nor sex; the majority of the Romanised Britons probably perished during the invasions, though, as Gardiner says, "a considerable number of women were preserved." Charlemagne passed for a comparatively merciful warrior; yet he beheaded in one day 4500 Saxon prisoners. The Venetians slaughtered all their Genoese prisoners after the battle of Cagliari. The Black Prince, among other atrocities, put to death either the whole population of Limoges, or 3000 of them, and Edward III massacred his French prisoners after the battle of Sluys, hanging many of the captains on their own masts. A change for the better appears in the fifteenth century; Henry V was far less bloodthirsty than the Black Prince, and the Wars of the Roses produced no such savageries as the struggle between Stephen and Matilda. The Great Rebellion was on the whole a very mild war. From the fifteenth century doubts began to be expressed as to the right of an invading army to ravish women promiscuously. Grotius in the seventeenth century thinks the practice undesirable, though "many think it lawful." In the eighteenth century it was universally admitted that wars were far more humanely conducted than in former times, and the great conflicts at the beginning of the nineteenth, though they caused terrible misery, were not stained with much wanton cruelty, except when the French encountered the guerillas of Spain. Nevertheless, there were orgies of rape and plunder when Wellington's troops entered Badajoz and Ciudad Rodrigo.

Since the Napoleonic War, and before 1914, there were numerous wars in various parts of the world, but no general conflagration. Hideous cruelties were perpetrated in the Greek war of independence, including a general massacre of the inhabitants of Chios by the Turks. Since then, the Turks have lived up to their reputation by slaughtering, at different times, over a million—perhaps two millions—of Bulgarians, Armenians, and Greeks. In fact war in the east is still carried on savagely. A distinguished Polish lady, who had seen unspeakable things with her own eyes, said to me, "You in the west have no conception what war is like in the east of Europe." The struggles between highly civilised nations in the nineteenth century were conducted in a moderately humane manner; but the chief improvement was in greater care for the health of the troops. Until quite recently, the losses from disease in almost every campaign far exceeded those caused by the weapons of the enemy. The facts, collected by the researches of Samuel Dumas and K. O. Vedel Petersen (1923) are so little known and so interesting that a summary of them will be welcome to my readers.

In the British Navy, from 1793 to 1815, the losses were: Killed by the enemy, 6,663; drowned or killed in shipwrecks or fires, 13,621; died of disease or accident on board ship, 72,102. In the land forces the figures are: Killed and died of wounds, 25,569; died of disease, 193,851. The Russian campaign of 1812 almost completely destroyed the army of Napoleon, which had been swept together from several continental nations by methods resembling a slave-raid; the Russians lost nearly half a million killed or unfit for military service. In the Crimean War the French, out of 309,-268 effectives, lost 20,240 killed, 75,375 from disease. The British, out of 97,864 effectives, lost 4,602 killed, 17,580 from disease. In the American Civil War, the statistics of which are uncertain, Frölich gives the losses of the Federals as 110,038 killed, 224,586 died of disease, 24,872 died from other causes. The Confederates, according to Haan, lost 72,345 killed, 120,000 from disease, and (an amazing number) 384,381 "missing." In the prison camps of the North the mortality was 121 per thousand; in those of the South 291 per thousand. Prisoners on both sides were treated with great barbarity in the hope of inducing them to desert; this is recorded in Stanley's autobiography.

In the Franco-German War the deaths from disease are already noticeably less, though an outbreak of smallpox killed 25,000 French soldiers. In the Russo-Turkish War of 1877–8 about 35,000 Russians were killed and over 81,000 died of disease. The wastage in a Russian army is always excessive. In the Boer War our losses are given as 7,534 killed, 14,382 died of disease. These deaths were mainly from enteric fever. In the Russo-Japanese War of 1904–5, the deaths by disease were, almost for the first time, fewer than the fatal military casualties. Gaedke estimates the Russian losses at 52,623 killed and 18,830 died of disease; but these numbers are said to be too large. The Japanese lost about 59,000 killed and 27,200 from disease. In this war both sides showed a remarkable contempt of death.

In the Great War the military forces alone lost eleven million men, eight millions killed and three millions who died of disease. This does not include the pandemic of 1918, which it was agreed to call influenza. This killed over seven million people in India alone; and the mortality all over the world was probably about double this number. Whether this pestilence was caused by the war it is impossible to say.

Although the respective losses of the belligerents do not strictly belong to my present subject, the following table, taken from Vedel Petersen, will be of interest.

Military and Naval Losses (Killed), 1914–1918

British Empire	.	766,139	Other estimates give exactly
France .	.	1,095,221	800,000
Germany	.	1,600,000	
Austria-Hungary	.	905,299	
Italy	.	330,000	

These totals are all much too small, since they do not include the missing, nine-tenths of whom may be reckoned as dead. In the German statistics, 772,522 are numbered as missing. Nor do these tables include deaths from disease. The Russian casualties exceeded even the German, but they are not accurately known.

Attempts to found a League of Nations to prevent war have been made from time to time. Towards the end of the sixteenth century[1] Sully inspired Henri IV of France with the idea of a Council of European States. Fifteen nations were to send four members to the Council, which was to sit at Metz or Cologne. The Confederation was to keep on foot an armed force, to coerce recalcitrants and protect Europe from Asiatic invasion. Twelve of the fifteen Powers, including Queen Elizabeth for England, had promised to co-operate, when Henri IV was murdered, and the scheme broke down. It is fair to say that France has taken the pioneering part in this good work. The Abbé de Saint-Pierre (1658–1743) published his "Mémoires pour rendre la Paix perpetuelle à l'Europe" in 1722. He was no visionary, but an acute and clear-headed man of affairs, secretary to the French diplomatists who arranged the Treaty of Utrecht. The fundamental parts of his plan were as follows. 1. There shall exist between the signatory Powers a perpetual alliance. 2. Each shall contribute to the expenses of the Grand Alliance in proportion to its revenues and the charges on them. 3. The Allies renounce for ever the method

[1] Havelock Ellis, "The Task of Social Hygiene," p. 314.

of arms, and agree always to adopt the method of conciliation through the mediation of the rest of the Allies. If mediation is unsuccessful, they agree to submit to the judgment of the plenipotentiaries of the other Allies, a majority of votes to determine the matter provisionally, three-fourths definitely after five years. 4. The grand Alliance shall take offensive action against an Ally refusing to submit to this judgment, and shall oblige the recalcitrant Power to make good all the military expenses caused by its hostile actions. 5. New articles may be carried by a majority in the permanent Assembly, but the fundamental articles shall be unalterable except by the unanimous consent of the Allies. It is interesting to observe that number 4 of this scheme had been already suggested by William Penn the Quaker in 1673, in his "Essay Towards the Present and Future Peace of Europe." He fully recognised that armed intervention, or the threat of it, would be necessary to keep the peace. Kant took up his parable to the same effect. "The greatest problem set to the human race is the formation of a political organisation under which justice will be dispensed to all, and a branch of this is the subordination to law of the external relations of particular States."[1]

A cynic may notice that the arguments of pacifists seem most conclusive just before a great outbreak of hostilities. It was so before the Great War, when writers like Norman Angell and Canon Crane almost convinced us that so monstrous a crime and folly could not be committed again. But the desire to abolish war is far stronger now than ever before. Mr. Garvin has said: "Everywhere the revolt of human feeling and reason against war is a movement incomparably more powerful and systematic than civilisation has seen up to now. Already it has exercised a profound effect

[1] Quoted in Hastings, *l.c.*

upon human institutions and relations. For the first time in human affairs there is a practical possibility that lasting international peace may be established; and this gain is one of the greatest facts in history."

General Smuts, lecturing at Oxford in November 1929, said: "That the Covenant was largely the work of a small band of so-called idealists I freely admit; but that the scheme was visionary and out of relation to the actual world-situation I stoutly deny. . . . The time may come when the world will recognise that the authors of the Covenant were the only really practical people at the Peace Conference. So far from the Covenant being visionary, it sprang out of the actual situation at the end of the war, and the temper it had created in the minds of men. It was the child of the human race, and of no individual or set of individuals. The movement of history is often creative in the true sense; great events interacting with the human spirit on a vast scale become pregnant with new meaning. Out of the clashes, the sorrows and sufferings of the time arise vague anticipations of a new order, and finally, suddenly, unexpectedly, and as if by sheer accident, the embodiment of some great hope or thought, which once formulated acquires an independent existence and movement of its own, becomes a new force in the world."

Such professions of faith from leading publicists and statesmen may well encourage us. We may add that the secondary activities of the League on such matters as international conditions of labour and trade, public health, and the suppression of anti-social trades like the decoying of women are already very valuable, and may come to be generally regarded as indispensable aids to civilisation. There is room for almost unlimited expansion in these reforms.

The activities of the League during the ten years

of its existence are summed up in "Headway" for January 1930. The experimental phase covered the first three or four years. Foreign ministers stayed away, looking askance at the League. Nevertheless, the League got its machinery working. It straightened out the finances of struggling States. It adopted the statutes of the Permanent Court of International Justice. But the United States were "undisguisedly hostile." The Supreme Council of the Allies looked like a rival authority. In 1923, in the two questions of the Ruhr and of Corfu, France and Italy ignored the League and impaired its prestige. But from 1924 onwards the sky brightened. Foreign ministers began attending the Council meetings, Sir Austen Chamberlain setting the good example. The Locarno agreement brought Germany into the League in 1926. America became more amenable. The Conference of Ambassadors has disappeared from the public eye. Prime Ministers and Foreign Ministers attend the Assembly in increasing numbers. The survival of the League is assured. On the other side, Brazil has left the League, and the Argentine Republic is virtually outside it. Russia, Turkey, and Mexico still exclude themselves. Neither plans for disarmament nor the Economic Conference of 1927 have any successes to boast of, and at the time of writing the prospects of the Naval Conference in London are not bright.[1] "The League as a whole is still too much European"; and some European governments are not good Europeans.

The difficulties which confront the League of Nations are partly moral, and it is with the moral difficulties that we are concerned. The problem may be put very simply in this form. Are there two standards of

[1] This Conference, as is well known, ended in a Three Power Pact between Great Britain, the United States and Japan, France and Italy standing out. The general opinion is that something substantial was achieved, if not all that sanguine persons had hoped.

Ethics, one for the individual and the other for the nation, or was Burke right when he said that "the principles of true politics are but those of morals enlarged"? Most of us would agree with Burke, but it is possible even for a sociologist like McDougall[1] to take the opposite view. In Germany before the Great War Christian writers openly repudiated the notion that the Sermon on the Mount had anything to do with international relations. McDougall quotes from Naumann, an acknowledged leader of Christian thought in Germany: "I do not know how to help myself in the conflict between Christianity and other tasks of life, save by the attempt to recognise the limits of Christianity. . . . The State does not belong to the sphere where if a man takes away my coat I am to let him have my cloak also, nor to that where sins are forgiven as soon as they are repented of. The State forms part of the struggle for existence. This is, in all harshness, a prerequisite of culture; its pattern is in Rome, not Nazareth. We possess a knowledge of the world, which teaches us a God of power and strength, who sends out life and death, and a revelation, a faith as to salvation, which declares this God to be our Father. . . . Military power is the foundation of all order in the State and of all prosperity in the society of Europe. . . . All the evils of a military power are slight compared with the misery of a country in which no such rule exists. An armed peace is not beautiful, but it is better than all past conditions known in history. . . . Alongside of our religious creed, we must have a political creed as well."

Since McDougall on the whole agrees with Naumann, I will briefly summarise his arguments, which amount to a challenge to Christian Ethics on a side where it has been generally assumed that the teaching

[2] "Ethics and Modern World Problems."

of the Gospel is accepted by almost everybody, though circumstances may arise which make it difficult to practise.

There are, we are told, two systems of Ethics, national and universal; Judaism belongs to the former class, Christianity and Buddhism to the latter. National Ethics are political, universal Ethics are individual. The Ethics of Greece and Rome were national, but "the national system was in each case undermined and fatally weakened by the speculations of philosophers." In the case of Rome, Christianity, by substituting a universal and non-political system for the national system "destroyed the foundation of her power and the foundation of her greatness."

Now I cannot attribute so much importance to "the speculations of philosophers"; nor do I think that Christianity was responsible for the disintegration of the Roman Empire. It was Roman selfishness and greed that turned Rome into a parasitic city, which sucked the life-blood of the provinces. It was Rome, not Nazareth, that killed the Roman Empire. Nor can I agree with the author's opinion that Islam was ruined by becoming non-national. The Arabian civilisation was destroyed in the west by Spain, in the East by the Mongols. In Modern Europe he finds the two "incompatible" ethical systems held concurrently. "All the wars and bloody persecutions which have figured so largely in the history of Europe have been in the main the outcome of the rivalry between the two ethical systems." There is no doubt that the wars of religion were inspired on the one side by the idea of a universal theocracy, and on the other by the idea of national independence; but to say that the former idea alone was Christian is to beg a very large question.

In the Great War, McDougall sees a struggle between a nation which had completely subordinated universal Ethics to national and a group in which both systems were honoured. At present, he finds that France, not Germany, is the embodiment of national Ethics.

Some synthesis between the two must be found. Internationalism, strongly favoured by such writers as H. G. Wells, might abolish national loyalty, and enthrone in its place other associations, which for the most part are narrower and less unselfish. It might also destroy the special contributions which each nation ought to make to the comity of the civilised world. Patriotism is far too precious a thing to be surrendered. For this reason, we ought, he thinks (and I agree), not to discourage the new patriotism of India, which we have ourselves planted and watered, even though some of its manifestations may be inconvenient to us. As George Eliot says, "an individual man, to be harmoniously great, must belong to a nation. A common humanity is not yet enough to feed the rich blood of venous activity which makes a complete man. What is wanting is that we should recognise a corresponding attachment to nationality as legitimate in every other people, and understand that its absence is a privation of the greatest good."

National sentiments are so powerful that when they are strongly stirred all other considerations give way before them. The economic motive, which ordinarily sways men in their votes and general behaviour, is too weak to withstand the loud call of patriotism. Is this to be regretted or not?

McDougall thinks that an acceptance of universal or Christian Ethics would "tend to the general degradation of human nature and to the destruction of civilisation and of all the higher culture." This startling statement he proceeds to justify as follows. Universal Ethics would allow "the peoples of the lower cultures" to settle in the white man's countries, where they would squeeze out the whites, who would have either to reduce their standard of living or "deny themselves the luxury of children." This danger is not imaginary, and I have already argued that advocates of disarmament cannot afford to forget it; but I see no reason why a good Christian should wish to import Chinese labourers into England or America. Whether the expensive races can permanently hold their own against the cheap races is a very important problem for statesmen and economists; I cannot see that it is a religious question. He then refers to the dysgenic factors in modern civilisation, which are largely increased by humanitarian Ethics. This danger, a very serious one, has been dealt with already in this book. We have no right to assume that Christianity must always be on the side of the flabby sentimentalism which is kind only to be cruel. Christianity is a stern creed; it is ready to suffer pain, and does not always shrink from inflicting it. Nor do I understand why the strange state of affairs in the United States, where a mechanic is much better paid than a university professor, should be, put down to "universal" Ethics. Huxley's famous Romanes Lecture is referred to as admitting the indifference of the cosmic process to our moral ideals. But we are part of the cosmic process; it includes our ideals and all that we do to realise them.

Utilitarians have proposed to us two goals—the greatest happiness of the greatest number, and the highest development of the potential capacities of the human race. The former is free from objection, if we remember that the "greatest number" have not yet been born; but we must recognise that the greatest happiness may perhaps exist on a very low moral level. Professor McDougall next attacks democracy as a form of government, in which I also have no great faith; but

I do not see what democracy in this sense has to do with Christian Ethics. Equality of consideration does not necessarily imply "one man one vote." The book ends with a plea for an international air-force to compel peace.

As a defence of patriotism, the noblest emotion on which men are likely to act together, the book is excellent. As a contribution to Christian Ethics in relation to modern world-problems I find it disappointing. Patriotism is what we can make of it. It may be a half-way house between selfishness and sympathy with our fellow men, "whether they be Jews or Gentiles, bond or free." Or we may repeat the words of Marcus Aurelius, "The poet says: Dear city of Cecrops; shall I not say, Dear city of God?" The city of God in which he wished to live was still that city in which he was called to play his part "as a Roman and an Antonine." We ought to admit freely that patriotism in practice often consists of a vulgar and ignorant contempt for foreigners, of absurd pride, of sheer pugnacity and acquisitiveness. These false opinions and base qualities lead straight to war, and I do not find that the upholders of "national Ethics" are on their guard against them. Experience has proved that the "armed Peace" which Naumann admires is like playing with matches in a powder magazine. Other nations, with equal right, also wish to be secure, and there is no way to be secure except by being stronger than any possible enemy. Europe has tried this experiment, with disastrous results.

Our literature was formerly as bellicose and Machiavellian as that of any other country. Bacon tells us that a State "ought to have those laws and customs which may reach forth unto them just occasions of war." We do not find that men talked of the bankruptcy of Christianity during the wars with Napoleon.

Most people then accepted war as an institution among Christian nations as among any others. And yet patriotism was less intense a hundred and twenty years ago than it was in the Great War. To some extent, I think, the love of country, though increased, has been moralised. There has lately been a genuine consciousness of a mission in the world, blending with ignoble passions. England, France, and Germany have all been conscious of qualities which give them a right to a great position among the nations; unhappily, they are not always ready to recognise the contributions, perhaps equally valuable, which their neighbours have to offer. In wars of independence the claim for justice and opportunities of self-expression burns like a flame, and is not extinguished even by centuries of oppression. But it is not often that a belligerent nation can feel the absolute assurance which Abraham Lincoln professed in his famous declaration: "With malice towards none; with charity for all; with firmness in the right as God gives us to see the right—let us strive on to finish the work we are in."

Patriotism, when purged of its dross, is love of our country as we wish it to be, of the England "the type of which is laid up in heaven," as Socrates said. There may be an element of illusion in it, as there is in our love for individuals. But without this element of illusion, or rather of idealisation, our feelings are likely to be cold and our language insincere. "Our true country," says Lowell, "is that ideal realm which we represent to ourselves under the names of religion, duty, and the like. Our terrestrial organisations are but far-off approaches to so fair a model; and all they are verily traitors who resist not every attempt to divert them from this their original intendment. Our true country is bounded on the north and the south, on the east and west, by justice, and when she oversteps that invisible boundary-line by so much as a hair's breadth, she ceases to be our mother, and choses rather to be looked upon *quasi noverca."* How much these eloquent words gain in appeal if we can say, "Such is, or ought to be and shall be, the conviction, the aspiration, which binds Englishmen together"!

It is indeed unfortunate that appeals to patriotism so often made awake only suspicion in the working classes of Europe. But it is neither to be wondered at nor altogether deplored. The working man often feels more solidarity with his own class abroad than with the rich at home; he sees, more clearly than those who have had a different education, the absurdity of international animosities, and the obstacles which militarism places in the way of social improvement. Tolstoy says: "Patriotism to the peoples represents only a frightful future; the fraternity of nations seems an ideal more and more accessible to humanity, and one which humanity desires." This, however, could hardly be said of the armies of the Western nations, in which a noble courage and self-devotion were equally apparent in all classes. There is something in our national character which rebels against the flag-waving and lessons in patriotism by which the Americans quite legitimately teach the children of immigrants to love their new country; to the Englishman, to praise his country is too much like praising his wife. But more might reasonably be done to make our school-children interested in the past of their country as well as in its future. For patriotism requires a living tradition, as the Jews have always well understood.

The time is favourable, not for ending patriotism, but for mending it. Militarism has dug its own grave. We at any rate could not finance another war, and those who have anything to lose know that if there is another war they will certainly lose it. And so there is a chance of making patriotism what it should be, a strong sentiment like the loyalty which a man feels for his old school or his native town, a spirit of emulation purged of rancour and jealousy, a part of the poetry of life. Those who cannot feel this loyalty to such a country as ours are not to be envied; and they are not likely to be good Christians. The appeal to Buddhism leaves us cold. It is, as I have said,[1] the weakness of Buddhism that it has no room for a rich kingdom of values, a spiritual world, between the vain shadow of earthly existence and the empty heaven where nothing is desired. It is in this home of the aspiring soul, the "intelligible world" of the Platonist, that our ideals take concrete forms and become the objects of our love. In that world lives the fatherland whose imperfect copy we know on earth.

[1] Page 38.

CHAPTER VI

PROBLEMS OF PERSONAL ETHICS

I⊤ is not easy to separate social from personal Ethics, since we are everyone members one of another. What the Greeks called the life of the Cyclopes, who, according to Homer, ruled among their families and flocks and cared not for one another, is not possible for human beings living in society. And it may be questioned whether the duties of family life belong to social or to personal Ethics. But I have thought it convenient to divide this long discussion of modern ethical problems into two parts, and to consider in the second part which follows the effect of new conditions and new ideas on the ordering of the individual life and the ideals of personal character. This subject will bring us into closer contact with religion; for Christianity, though it finds its chief outward expression in our duty to our neighbour, begins with the individual, and teaches us that "from within, out of the heart of man," proceeds all that makes him a blessing or a curse to his fellows.

The question was often raised, while the Great War was still raging, whether the moral consequences of that upheaval were likely to be good or bad, and, in particular, whether there would be more or less religion when the struggle was over. Just at first there was a rush to the Churches, but we could not forget the cynical rhyme, "when the devil was sick." It was not easy to see how the wrath of man, and the hatred which was artificially stimulated, could "work the righteousness

350

of God." A very acute observer predicted, in conversation with me, that the effect of the war would be to injure the higher kind of religion, and to encourage the lower kind. To all appearance this has happened.

Liberal Protestantism had been trying to establish a working agreement with science and humanism, treating respectfully secular moral ideas and endeavouring to incorporate them in a progressive science or philosophy of conduct. When the war seemed to threaten civilisation with bankruptcy, and exposed the weakness of moral safeguards against international strife, the Christianity which was aiming at being a factor within that civilisation shared the discredit. The Churches, it seemed, had failed exactly where they ought to have made their influence felt. The disillusionment of the votaries of progress and democracy was terrible, and many persons took refuge in superstitions which promised them an anodyne, or in the support of a venerable tradition which had never made terms with the modern spirit. Several cultivated men and women made up their minds that there was no logical choice except between Roman Catholicism and scientific humanism on purely secularist lines; and they chose the former. They decided, as I believe, wrongly. Latin Catholicism is neither primitive nor modern but medieval, and whatever form the civilisation of the future may take, it is most unlikely to revert to a hierarchic theocracy claiming universal dominion. The social revolution through which we are passing has ploughed much more deeply into the soil of our civilisation than the theatrical disturbances in Paris a hundred and forty years ago. Modern Neocatholicism will be even more futile and barren than the attempts of Chateaubriand and de Maistre to rekindle the old loyalties out of the embers of revolutionary fires. The younger generation seems to be resolved to follow Nietzsche's advice to "live dangerously." The dangers, as I shall argue presently, are grave enough; but the temper which runs into any port during a storm will not be the prevailing temper of the twentieth century, unless indeed (as I do not expect) the Red International terrifies Europe into throwing itself into the arms of the Black. No religion can satisfy the needs of our time which does not both understand secular aspirations and transcend them. The Church of the Spirit must satisfy the conscience of the modern man, without making any compromise with his ingrained secularity.

We seem to be in the last phase of a long movement of *emancipation*, which divides the modern period from the medieval. The modern period has seen the emancipation of Northern Europe from the Latin theocracy, of subjects from their despots, of serfs from their feudal lords and of the town-labourer from the factory owner. It has emancipated parliamentary electors from their representatives, now turned into delegates, and finally it has given the rights of citizenship to women, and partially broken up the home by persuading young girls that they have the right to "live their own life."

There are undoubtedly signs of reaction. Liberty has been temporarily destroyed in Russia, Italy, and other countries. Where there is no freedom of speech or public meeting, where the press and literature are rigidly censored, and education is in fetters, the priest is only waiting his time. Besides this, the anonymous and squalid tyranny of public opinion is a serious nuisance in some democratic countries. Many think that Western civilisation is menaced by the tyranny of the average, the rule of the half-educated, with standardised religion, ethics, manners, and tastes. Nevertheless, what strikes everyone in the present situation is the complete emancipation of the individual, at least in the younger generation, from moral and social conventions.

The war is not the only cause of this revolt, though it enlarged the horizon of millions of soldiers, who saw foreign countries for the first time, and created in the minds of the young a deep distrust and indignation at the blundering of the older generation, which had landed the world in a ruinous internecine struggle, and had sent its sons to the shambles to expiate the follies of their parents. Meanwhile, the new inventions were breaking down barriers of space and local custom more effectually than even the geographical discoveries at the end of the fifteenth century. Air journeys have abolished frontiers; broadcasting has made us cease to smile at Aristotle's dictum that all the citizens of a State ought to be able to hear the voice of a herald. The wireless installation and the cinema are the poor man's university, theatre, lecture-hall, and opera-house. A panorama of the world is shown for a few pence. Newspapers and popular books purvey information on every subject; the illustrated weeklies contain admirable articles on astronomy, physics, and natural history. The education so given may be superficial, but the enlargement of interests has given millions of people an entirely new outlook on the world. The sudden influx of so much new knowledge is intoxicating to many eager young minds; but none can doubt that it has had a civilising influence, especially in the country districts.

It is no new thing that as soon as a great war is over, and even while it is still in progress, many young people should abandon themselves to amusement and to various forms of social excitement. Nervous tension sometimes demands relief of this kind; and there can be no doubt that many young men, thinking that they had a poor chance of being alive a year later, enjoyed themselves rather recklessly before leaving England for the Front. After the peace, thrift was discouraged by crushing taxation; men preferred to spend their earnings rather than keep them to satisfy the rapacity of the exchequer, or, on the Continent, to see them melt away under inflation of the currency. We must therefore discount something from the orgy of dissipation which broke out after the war. It is, in part at least, a transitory phenomenon, which has already begun to pass.

But the reaction against Puritanism had gone far before 1914, and must not be attributed primarily to any external event which might have happened otherwise. Calvinism cannot be acquitted of an absurd and unsympathetic attitude towards innocent amusement. In the nineteenth century, especially in the earlier half of it, the "gospel of work" was preached in season and out of season. As late as 1872, a Methodist school in America thought to make itself attractive by the following prospectus. "We prohibit play in the strongest terms. The students shall rise at 5 o'clock summer and winter. Their recreation shall be gardening, walking, riding, and bathing without doors, and the carpenter's, joiner's, cabinet-maker's or turner's business within doors. The students shall be indulged in nothing which the world calls play. Let this rule be observed with the strictest necessity; for those who play when they are young will play when they are old."[1] Even the kindly John Colet, in his statutes for St. Paul's School, ordered that the boys are to have no "remedies" (*i.e.* holidays).

It need hardly be said that psychologists are unanimous in condemning these monstrous ideas. Play is a valuable part of life, for young and old alike; for children it ought to be a large part of life. Good teachers introduce a great deal of play into their lessons.

But besides this, the modern man is no longer convinced of the necessity for long hours of hard work.

---

[1] Beard, "Whither Mankind?" pp. 334-353. The author, Mr. Chase, also quotes from another source: "A young girl should never play; she should weep much and meditate upon her sins."

At the beginning of the industrial age productivity and thrift were extolled as the indispensable conditions of national prosperity. The Gospel of Work was fulminated by Carlyle, and echoed from a thousand pulpits. We are now being told that machinery has made drudgery superfluous, and that in many trades there is over-production. Mankind has come into its fortune. As Aristotle said, not thinking of mechanical inventions, which the Greeks despised or neglected, "if the looms would go of themselves, we should have no more need of slaves." America, by perfecting labour-saving appliances, has created a prodigious surplus, which she spends as we have seen. Accumulation of capital may be carried further than the amount which expanding industries can absorb; in England before the war there was a competition of capital seeking investment, which drove down the rate of interest to a very low figure. The old ambition to "found a family" appeals to the modern man less than it did to his grandfather, and the new taxation has made it impossible. America has a leisured class; but a sensible American does not wish to tempt his children to join it. The kind of career which Samuel Smiles, the author of "Self-Help" and other works, held up to our admiration is no longer attractive enough to make men "scorn delights and live laborious days." The economic Ethics of Calvinism are under a cloud.

Whether the seductive gospel of "take thine ease, eat, drink, and be merry" is an improvement on the old Gospel of Work may be doubtful; but I am inclined to agree with those who think that under modern conditions unremitting drudgery is no longer a duty. We need rather to give our attention to a neglected problem, how to use our leisure to the best advantage.

Nevertheless, I have confessed that I am strongly opposed to the theory which Americans call "consumptionism." To multiply wants—wants of a highly stand-ardised type—in order to keep trade humming, is to bar-barise leisure and diminish happiness. The best type of man has few wants, and those which he has are individual and rational. An educated Oriental, who knows the value of solitude and meditation, watches without any admiration the bustling activity and tasteless diversions of the Western man. The old ideal of the philosophic life is too valuable to lose, and perhaps it may be re-covered as a result of the shortened day's work.

Is it possible to present a clear picture of an ethical type which is so far prevalent as to deserve to be called the characteristic type of the modern man? In order not to complicate my task beyond what I can hope to deal with, I will confine my observations to the English-speaking nations. There is a great degree of solidarity in European and American civilisation, but differences of religion, institutions, origin, and climate make it impossible to draw a generalised picture of the whole white race. The difficulty is great enough without at-tempting this, for the ethical ideals of the working-class are different from those of the bourgeoisie and from those of the aristocracy. And it may be that the war has deflected for a time the normal evolution of morals.

The strongest emotion in the modern man is un-questionably humanitarianism, with which I have dealt in a preceding chapter. In no other field can we assert with so much confidence that there has been real moral progress in the modern period. The cruelty of past ages is now simply unintelligible to us.

The next feature which we cannot miss is the ex-treme secularity of the typical citizen in our day. On the intellectual basis of this outlook I have said something already. It is plain that faith in any life beyond the grave now burns very dimly, and that millenarianism has had a rebirth in the dreams of Socialists. But the change is perhaps neither so great nor so regrettable as it appears at first sight in the eyes of Christians. Popular eschatology has always been a mass of contradictions, and it has been thoroughly discredited by the barbarous notions of future torment, which we now read with even greater amazement than the records of the Spanish Inquisition. The pictures of future bliss were often as gross and unworthy as those of future punishment were incredible and revolting. Whether belief in the reality of a spiritual world—a kingdom of eternal values—is fainter now than it used to be is a question not easy to answer. I am inclined to think that the prospect of an entirely secular civilisation, in which social morality shall be inculcated without any religious sanction, and in which mankind shall direct its own destinies without reference to any superhuman authority, has actually driven the Christian hope, and the morals which depend upon it, into the background. This is the usual opinion, and it would be hard to controvert it. I believe, however, that there is a great deal of lofty idealism among our contemporaries, and a deep interest in religious problems among the young, though they have, as a rule, but little confidence in those who teach traditional theology. I was not surprised to hear that a religious address by Professor Eddington, the astronomer, reached a sale of a hundred thousand copies. It was an interesting essay, but it owed its popularity to the knowledge that it was written by a famous man of science. I have hopes that the time may come when the spiritual may gain what the supernatural has lost, and when the greater part of moral and spiritual teaching will be given by laymen.

Much attention was aroused by an article in the *Hibbert Journal* for April 1905 by Mr. W. H. Garrod, afterwards Professor of Poetry at Oxford, entitled

"Christian, Greek, or Goth?" The author objects that
we assume too readily that the moral standard by which
we live is Hebraic, with a strong tinge of Hellenism.
(Matthew Arnold, it will be remembered, regarded
these two types as the only alternatives.) The moral
systems east of Suez are treated as interesting but of
no value for us; and the morality by which we live on
weekdays, which is that of Northern Europe, is ignored
by writers on Ethics. And yet a treatise on morals
which ignores "Gothic" Ethics is as defective as a
treatise on architecture which treated only of the Greek
and Byzantine styles.

The ideal Christian type, Mr. Garrod says, is the
saint, the ideal Hellenic type is the *phronimos*. The
Renaissance in Italy tried to combine the two, and
failed; "the fruits of the Renaissance in itself consist
of every kind of moral corruption." But when "fugitive and exile Greece found a refuge beyond the Alps,"
in the words of Argyropoulos, it allied itself fruitfully
with the Germanic spirit.

Now the "Goth" does not really like either the
saint or the *phronimos*. He is tolerant of several acts
which the Church regards as deadly sins; but there is
one sin which in his eyes has no forgiveness—the sin
of being a cad, failure in the ideal of chivalry and the
ideal of honour. Neither the Jew nor the Greek came
up to this standard. (Inspired by this article, I once
preached on the character of David, as exhibited by
his conduct to Saul, Michal, Abner, Uriah, Shimei, and
others. My parishioners were so little pleased that I
decided to avoid Old Testament characters for the
future.) The "Goth" finds that the man after God's
own heart was no gentleman. He also finds Achilles
a violent and sulky savage, and Ulysses, the jolly sailor,
who had a wife in every port and a lie for every emer-
gency, an amusing rascal. The Goth would not ask

any of the three to dinner. Mr. Garrod thinks that Aristotle's *megalopsychos,* who thinks himself worthy of great things and is worthy of them, is like a nobleman in Disraeli's novels, but not like any other kind of gentleman. We have, however, produced one favourable specimen of the *megalopsychos,* in the late Lord Curzon.

Chivalry and honour, Mr. Garrod thinks, are virtues of the natural man, and they are "an undefined and instinctive protest against Christianity," which preaches "an unnatural, pusillanimous and impossible" morality. This rejection of the code of honour as unchristian brings to our minds the eloquent passage in Cardinal Newman, referred to in my third chapter, on Asceticism.

Now here we have a real ethical conflict; two quite incompatible ideals stand face to face with each other. We may brush aside Mr. Garrod's strange accusation that Christianity is pusillanimous and cowardly. One of the real reasons why there are so few Christians is that Christianity is a very stern creed, a creed for heroes, while we are good-natured little people, who wish to have a good time, and to give others a good time. But the clash of opinion with Cardinal Newman is much more serious.

Mr. Garrod is obviously right when he says that the code of honour and chivalry is the real religion of most laymen. The idea of a gentleman is the fine flower of our national character. Stripped of its adventitious connexion with heraldry and property in land, and with the class morality which brought it into disrepute when England was under an oligarchy, it is the finest ideal which a nation has ever set before itself. To it we owe most of the things in our history of which we may be reasonably proud. To it we owe our incorruptible magistrates, our habitual fairness, our instinct to help the weak and to hurry to the post of danger, our

respect for speaking the truth, our dislike for tortuous
and underhand procedures. We do not always live
up to our convictions, and of course many Englishmen
do not even try to live up to them; but for all the world
the English gentleman stands for a recognisable type.
It is, beyond question, the national ideal, and Mr. Garrod is quite right in saying that there is no forgiveness
among us for those who conspicuously fail to approach
it.

Is this ideal Christian? That a great many English gentlemen are sincere Christians goes without saying, and it is often assumed by such men, in earnest
talks with the young, for example, that the two words
are almost interchangeable. This is the staple moral
teaching in our public schools. Nor do I see anything
amiss in this amalgamation of the two ideals. Democracy has purified the idea of gentlemanlike conduct by
insisting that every human being has a right, and an
equal right, to have his or her personality respected.
This was always implicit in the chivalrous code, though
in times of great social inequality it was forgotten.
The "pride" of a gentleman is merely *noblesse oblige;*
he would fall short of his own ideal if he did not show
himself true and just in all his dealings. I can find
no point at which the code of honour and chivalry comes
into conflict with the standard of the Gospels or the
Ethics of the New Testament.

But those who identify Christianity with Catholicism must make a very different answer. I have no wish
to use language offensive to any body of my fellow-
Christians; but it must be obvious to all who have had
dealings with Roman Catholics, who have read their
books, or studied their public actions, that the Northern
code of honour and chivalry means very little to them
when they are acting as Catholics, under the direction
of their spiritual advisers and mindful of their duties to

their Church. It would, of course, be monstrous to suggest that in the ordinary relations of life a Roman Catholic, especially if he was born and bred in that faith, is likely to fall short of the standards which the honourable Protestant observes. I should be sorry if it were supposed that I had suggested such a thing. But Newman was right in saying that the two types are generically different. Catholics may hold, as Newman did, that their principles are higher than those of the virtuous and honourable Protestant. They may even argue that since his virtues are partly based on self-respect, which they miscall pride, they are only "splendid vices." That is a matter of opinion. What is certain is that the two ideals are widely different, and that in practice they lead to widely different moral behaviour.

But there is one direction in which modern thought has lost a very valuable feature of Catholic teaching. Sir Oliver Lodge has said that "the modern man is not worrying about his sins at all," and William James, writing before the war, congratulated his contemporaries on being sometimes able to pass from the cradle to the grave without ever knowing the meaning of fear. This means that we do not admit the desperate seriousness of the moral choice, as determining our acceptance or rejection by God. And yet, if the fact of sin is ignored, Christianity becomes unintelligible. Even the hideous pictures of future punishment, and the vulgar pictures of future bliss, which are so repulsive when taken out of their context in the life of devotion, have a meaning when we regard them as crude attempts to express the infinite difference between right and wrong—the blessedness of living in the presence of God, and the horror of seeing His face turned away from us. These violent contrasts awaken no response in those who contemplate the grey and colourless world of secularism. Catholics have often said that Modernist

Protestantism has a defective sense of sin, and I think the charge is true, not only of Liberal Christianity, but of the modern world generally. It is true that Christ seldom mentions sin except in connexion with forgiveness. It is true that many Catholics have tormented themselves morbidly and unnecessarily. But Catholicism stands for a great fact—"the corruption of man's heart," and for repentance and contrition as the only way to win divine forgiveness for our past misdeeds. "Religion without tears" is not Christianity, and the fear of the Lord is still the beginning, though not the end, of wisdom.

This judgment is strongly confirmed by a study of modern fiction, the mirror in which our society sees itself. There are many exceptions, but the majority of the most distinguished novelists share certain characteristics. In spite of the psychological analysis on which some of them pride themselves, there is a superficiality about their whole view of life and a conspicuous lack of nobleness in their pictures of human nature. If the objects of the writers were merely to present witty or satirical sketches of modern society, we should have no right to complain of the omission of the serious underlying realities. But these novelists are writing seriously; and yet the deeper aspects or meanings of life, on which to the religious mind all its value depends, scarcely exist for them. This may be a passing fashion; but these popular new books are very saddening to a Christian, quite apart from the sex-appeal which is too prominent in many of them. In the classical British novelists there was a tradition of nobleness which is dismally lacking in most of the fiction of to-day.

PROBLEMS OF SEX

I must now deal with the most delicate, but also the most important, side of personal Ethics—the group of problems connected with sex. It is no longer necessary to observe the reticence and squeamishness which Victorian writers thought (no doubt rightly) to be imposed upon them by public opinion at the time when they wrote. But I shall endeavour to keep plain speaking within the limits which are still desirable in a book intended for the general reader.

From the first, Christianity forbade all sexual intercourse except in monogamous marriage, and treated homosexual practices with much greater severity than Pagan public opinion had done. This was in accordance with the strictest teaching of the time, outside of Christianity. The very unsatisfactory standard which we find in Genesis, as in the repulsive story of Judah and Tamar, was no longer characteristic of Jewish morality, which, as I have said already, was probably much higher, in the first century of our era, than that of the surrounding nations. Some of the Stoics were beginning to preach the sinfulness of extra-marital indulgences. We have seen that Musonius Rufus took this view, and that Dion Chrysostom tried to rouse the conscience of his fellow-citizens to the wickedness of organised prostitution. As regards the unnatural practices to which St. Paul refers with indignation in the first chapter of Romans, we find a change of feeling coming about in Pagan society, but it is not well marked till after the first century. Marcus Aurelius thanks the Gods that he "touched neither Benedicta nor Theodotus," as if the two temptations were on the same footing. But in the middle of the third century Plotinus expressed the most unqualified disgust when a paper excusing the practice was read in his presence. The change may have been partly due to an alteration in the racial composition of the empire; but the influence of Christianity may already have made itself felt. The Christian literature of the second century indicates that the moral standard in the Church was at this time very high. When Christianity became the religion of the State it was natural that the believers, no longer sifted by the danger of persecution, lapsed to some extent from their former strictness. And after the fall of the Western empire the sexual morality of the people, nominally Christian though they were, seems to have gone completely to pieces. Shocking scandals among the Popes and bishops were too common to excite much attention. "Pope John XXIII was condemned, among many other crimes, for incest and adultery. The abbot-elect of St. Augustine at Canterbury, in 1171, was found to have seventeen illegitimate children in a single village; an abbot of St. Pelayo, in Spain, in 1130, was found to have kept no less than seventy concubines; Henry III, bishop of Liége, was deposed in 1274 for having sixty-five illegitimate children."[1] "The writers of the middle ages," Lecky proceeds, "are full of accounts of nunneries that were like brothels, of the vast multitude of infanticides within their walls, and of that inveterate prevalence of incest among the clergy, which rendered it necessary again and again to issue the most stringent enactments that priests should not be permitted to live with their mothers or sisters." Complaints were loud and frequent of the abuse of the confessional for seduction. The concubinage of parish priests was welcomed by their parishioners as a protection to their own wives and daughters. Anselm (Ep. III. 62), speaking of the *peccatum sodomicum,* says that "hitherto it has been so public that hardly anyone blushes for it; many have fallen into it in ignorance of the magnitude of their guilt." Lecky, from motives of delicacy, suppresses the evidence of the re-

---

[1] Lecky, "History of European Morals," Vol. II. p. 331. Lea gives many other instances.

crudescence of this vice, which the early Church had combated with much success.

It seems impossible to doubt that both in the dark ages and in the medieval period the Christian standard of sexual morality was openly and almost universally disregarded, except by a few ascetics such as the pre-Reformation mystics, and by persecuted sectaries such as the Albigenses. The Renaissance made matters, if possible, worse, and pederasty again became almost as popular as in ancient Rome. But in the sixteenth century there was a real reform of manners. The Lutherans indeed were by no means above reproach on this score; some have even maintained that the change in the Lutheran countries was for the worse; but the Calvinists and Puritans were very severe against sexual irregularities, and the populace was dragooned into virtue. The Roman Church at the same time made a strenuous effort to remove moral scandals; and from that time to this the character of the priests has been very much better than before the Reformation.

The diminution of promiscuous licence in the sixteenth century was probably connected with the appearance of syphilis in Europe. This dread disease, previously unknown, broke out within two years after the return of Columbus and his crews, and was naturally supposed to have been imported from America. Medical opinion is divided on this question; but there is no doubt that the contagion, finding a virgin soil, spread rapidly over Europe and caused frightful mortality. An entirely new terror was thus added to the moral denunciations of the Church, and as a natural consequence men and women became more careful.

It is always difficult to say with any certainty whether one age is more licentious than another. Where public opinion is strict, there will be more concealment; but on the other hand, temptation is then less obtruded, and men are more ashamed to transgress. It would probably be safe to say that when Puritanism is in the ascendant there is actually less vice. Periods of strictness and of profligacy seem to alternate, the one provoking the other. The Restoration, with its loose morals, followed the Protectorate; the reign of Queen Victoria was a reaction from the Regency. A great war or a revolution is usually followed by several years of great laxity.

A strange phenomenon in modern times is the sympathetic condonation of adultery. This aberration of the moral sense seems to have come to this country from the Continent, and especially from France, where the combined influence of *mariages de convenance* and of the absolute prohibition of divorce, under the old *régime,* produced a tolerant attitude towards a sin which under healthy conditions should surely be most strongly condemned. Popular fiction, making adultery its favourite theme, has had a corrupting influence, even if, with many who know the Latin countries, we believe that the continental novel gives a very false impression of the extent of conjugal unfaithfulness among the population generally. In England, adultery is largely an aristocratic vice, though it is common also among literary and artistic Bohemians. In the middle class, and I believe also among the labourers, it is comparatively rare. More must be said on this subject under the head of divorce.

The origin of what it has become customary to call sexual taboos has been very fully discussed by anthropologists and others. It is not denied that a pure woman feels an intense repugnance to the idea of giving herself except to her husband, and that a deep-seated disgust is generally felt towards incest, sodomy, and bestiality. But most writers on the subject try to rationalise these antipathies by connecting them with some tribal custom or religious superstition. Such theories tend to explain away the consciousness of guilt as something which has no universal and inviolable sanction. But the revolt of the healthy mind against some at least of these practices is too strong to be easily accounted for in this way. When, for instance, Lotze, in dealing with incest, speaks of "the protest of the mind against blending two distinct attitudes towards the same person," his explanation of the disgust which the idea of this crime evokes seems ludicrously inadequate. Still, we must not forget that the idea of violating an irrational and non-moral taboo, such as that against eating food which has been reserved for a chief, may cause as much horror as any offence against nature, so that savages have been known to die of shock after having inadvertently transgressed a sacred rule of this kind. In the case of sexual offences which are contrary to the custom of the tribe, fear of supernatural vengeance is often present, and as it is believed that this punishment may fall on the whole tribe, blighting their crops or smiting their domestic animals with barrenness, the tribe feels great indignation against the offender, and often puts him to death. Westermarck thinks that the horror which is so widely felt against sodomy has this origin, and that even in the medieval mind it was somehow connected with heresy.

I am, however, convinced that it is a mistake to set aside as irrational all moral judgments which seem to have arisen first among the confused notions of the savage mind. When the moral consciousness is fully developed, the idea of chastity is no barbarous superstition, but a sense of the duty which we owe to our own bodies as the seat of a higher principle, or, as St. Paul says, as temples of the Holy Spirit. This is unquestionably the foundation of Christian sexual Ethics. There is nothing impure in the act itself; but in becoming the symbolic expression of love it has acquired a sacramental value, and is therefore capable of desecration. In an earlier chapter I have discussed the misapprehension of this truth by extreme ascetics; but the principle is clear enough, and should be stated fairly. It is an absurd error to suppose that it is of purely Christian origin, and that no respect was paid to chastity in earlier times. Celibate priests and priestesses have, of course, been common in many parts of the world. But it may be worth while to quote a remarkable passage from Plato, in which he anticipates almost verbally St. Paul's appeal to the spiritual athlete, to exercise as much self-denial to obtain an incorruptible crown as runners and boxers do to win the garland of victory in the games.

"There is another matter of great importance and difficulty, concerning which God should legislate, if there were any possibility of obtaining from him an ordinance about it. But seeing that divine aid is not to be had, there appears to be a need of some bold man who specially honours plainness of speech, and will say outright what he thinks best for the city and citizens. . . . How will our young men and maidens abstain from desires which thrust many a man and woman into perdition, and from which reason, assuming the functions of law, commands them to abstain? . . . Upon reflection, I see a way of imposing the law, which in one respect is easy, but in another most difficult. We all know that most men, in spite of their lawless natures, are sometimes very strictly restrained from intercourse with the fair, and entirely with their own will." "When do you mean?" asks the other. "When anyone has a brother or a sister who is fair·. . . nothing unseemly ever takes place between them; nor does the thought of such a thing ever enter the minds of most of them." "Very true." "Does not a little word extinguish all pleasures of that sort?" "What word?" "The declaration that they are unholy, hated of God, and most infamous, and is not the reason of this that everyone from his childhood has heard men speaking in the same manner about them always and everywhere?" . . . "You are very right in saying that tradition, if it is unassailed, has a marvellous power." "The legislator then will consecrate the tradition of their evil character among all, and that will be the surest foundation of the law which he can make. . . . If a law (against all barren lusts) could be made perpetual, and gain an authority such as already prevents incest, such a law, extending to other sensual desires and conquering them, would be the source of innumerable blessings. . . . I can imagine some lusty youth who is standing by, and who on hearing this enactment declares in scurrilous terms that we are making foolish and impossible laws, and fills the world with his outcry. . . . Shall I try to find some persuasive argument which will prove to you that such enactments are possible, and not beyond human nature?" "By all means." "Is a man more likely to abstain from the pleasures of love and do what he is bidden about them, when his body is in a good condition, or when it is in a bad condition and out of training?" "He will be far more temperate when he is in training." "And have we not heard of Iccus of Tarentum, who with a view to the Olympic and other contests, in his zeal for his art, and also because he was of a manly and temperate disposition, never had any connexion with a woman . . . during the whole time of his training? The same is said . . . of many others; and yet they were far worse educated in their minds than your and my citizens, and in their bodies far more lusty. . . . And had they the courage to abstain from what is deemed a pleasure for the sake of a victory in wrestling, running, and the like; and shall our young men be incapable of a similar endurance for the sake of a much nobler victory, which is the noblest of all, as from their youth we will tell them—the victory over pleasure, which if they win they will live happily; or if they are conquered the reverse of happily?"[1]

In the chapter about Asceticism we found that an exaggerated and unwholesome emphasis was laid upon the preservation of virginity. Attempts were made in that chapter to account for a feeling which the Roman Catholic Church still tries to maintain, but which is almost unintelligible to the modern mind. Mr. Lippmann, in his recently published "Preface to Morals," suggests that the Church "knew what it was doing." There is, he says, a very intimate connexion between the sexual and the religious life. Unless the passions are strongly repressed, they may "intoxicate the whole personality to the exclusion of religious interests." On the other hand, if they are denied their natural outlet, they may be sublimated into the transferred eroticism of the cloistered mystic. Modern psychologists have taken pleasure in tracing to this ignoble origin the raptures of some medieval saints. I am not concerned to defend a state of mind which is obviously unwholesome; but the Christian idea of the spiritual athlete, which, as we have seen, attracted Plato not less than St. Paul, is not to be rejected. The presence in any society of men and women who have conquered their appetites completely is a standing witness against the popular error that this conquest is impossible. The ascetic, however unpopular it may be to praise him, is a useful member of society.

But though we may accept the Pauline doctrine that our bodies, as temples of the Holy Spirit, should

[1] Plato, "Laws," Book VIII. Use has been made of Jowett's translation.

be kept "in sanctification and honour," we may yet feel some doubt how far this should take us. There is a valuable discussion of the subject in Henry Sidgwick's "Methods of Ethics." The writer's standpoint is that of a high-minded and independent moralist, with no tendency to extreme asceticism.

The duty of Prudence, says Sidgwick, is the duty of aiming at our own greatest happiness. Of the self-regarding virtues which come under this head, temperance seems the most important. All agree that the appetites need control, but all are not agreed within what limits, on what principle, and to what end they ought to be controlled. In the case of food, drink, and sleep no one doubts that health and vigour are the end, nor that gratification ought to be checked when it tends to defeat this end. Some, however, think, beyond this limit, that bodily pleasure ought never to be sought; others that bodily pleasure should be sought only when it serves cheerfulness, social affection, and the like. For instance, solitary gormandising or drinking is considered degrading. In the case of purity or chastity, moral duty seems to go beyond mere prudence. Our notion of purity implies a standard independent, not only of prudence, but of law; for a legal union does not preclude impurity, nor should we choose the adjective impure to stigmatise all illegal unions. We find also a stricter and a laxer notion of purity, just as we have found a stricter and a laxer notion about the pleasures of the table. Some even maintain that the propagation of the species is the only legitimate motive in sexual intercourse; others that in wedlock pleasure may be innocently enjoyed. Again we may ask whether polygamy is essentially impure, even in the countries where it is sanctioned by law, and whether, if it is not necessarily impure for a man to have several wives, the same judgment should be passed on a woman who has several husbands—an arrangement not unknown among savages. Does Plato's eugenic State outrage our sense of purity? Is all sexual commerce without love, even between husband and wife, impure? Should divorce by mutual consent be allowed, since love, it is said, is essential to a pure union?

Sidgwick can find only two grounds for sexual morality—the maintenance of a certain social order, believed to be desirable in the interest of the race; and the promotion of habits of feeling in individuals, believed to be the most important to their perfection and happiness. This does not seem to me to represent our real attitude in condemning sexual irregularities. In so far as we condemn them, it is because we think them wrong in themselves, apart from their consequences. Those acts which are generally considered either most infamous or most degrading do no particular harm to society, and in some phases of civilisation have not been thought incompatible with personal dignity and self-respect. To base sexual morals on utilitarian arguments seems like a surrender of the citadel. And yet, it may be objected, apart from the direct or indirect social consequences of immorality, which sanction can we find except either there is at present a strong tendency to set aside, or bar external authority, the weight of tradition, which subjective preference, moral or æsthetic, which some declare that they do not feel? The subject is very difficult, and now that speech is free we are not likely to find any uniformity of judgment as to what is right or wrong.

In order to present in clear outline the theories now advocated by some who have rejected the old traditional standards, I will summarise a little book called "Hymen," by Dr. Norman Haire, who is known as an advanced thinker on these subjects. The subject of the book is the future of marriage. Vehemently as I disagree with the standpoint of the author, I think it necessary to show clearly how far the revolt against Christian standards has gone. Another recent book, Mr. Bertrand Russell's "Marriage and Morals," which is even more provocative in tone, should also be consulted by those who wish to know what teaching is new being given to the young. In America, Judge Ben Lindsey's accounts of the habits of students at a coeducational State university has been much discussed. I confess that I read this book with consternation.

Dr. Haire thinks that only one marriage out of four may be judged as even tolerably successful, and in a footnote fears that he has given an unduly large proportion of successes. Later on he says that though lifelong monogamous marriage is the ideal, it is suitable to, and attainable by, only a very small minority. Most men, he says, "are polygamous, in their desires at least; a large number are polygamous in practice; and of those who remain physically faithful to one woman, the majority do so only because of the fear of consequences in this life, or punishment in that after-life which has been invented and exploited by theologians." Mr. Russell is equally emphatic about the unhappiness of the majority of marriages.

My own observation has been so totally different to this that I find it difficult to take such judgments seriously. I suppose I have known at least thirty couples intimately enough to form a correct opinion about their relations to each other; and I should estimate that about three-quarters of these marriages have been happy, in the sense that the pair have continued to feel warm affection for each other, and to enjoy each other's society. In the minority of cases which are left over there has been a want of common interests, and perhaps irritability on one side or both; but I doubt whether even in these cases there is a definite conviction that the marriage has been a mistake. Passionate love no doubt fades after a time; but, as Augustine says, "when the warmth of youth has passed away there yet lives in full vigour the order of charity between husband and wife." My acquaintance has naturally been chiefly among professional and other upper middle class people. I am well aware that the record of the House of Lords and the idle rich in the matter of fidelity to the marriage vow is a very bad one. As for the statement that men are naturally polygamous, it seems to be overlooked that the average man, when he has pledged himself in honour and conscience to keep a very solemn contract, does not feel at liberty to break it, and that when the promise has been made to the woman who has entrusted her life and happiness to his keeping, he does not, if he is a decent person, feel any inclination to break it.

The objection to incest, except when one of the parties is under age, he regards as based on the evil effects of inbreeding on the next generation, and where "no child results from the union, this objection does not come into consideration." Here we have in an extreme form the assumption that "a religious taboo" may be simply disregarded. The words of Plato, above quoted, are perhaps a sufficient answer. I prefer not to quote the writer's remarks about prostitution, which show the same insensitiveness to the real basis of sexual morality. Dr. Haire wishes to legalise polygamy, and to grant divorce if either party desires it.

Experimental transplantation of the sex organs of a woman into an ape has been performed, he tells us, by a foreign *savant,* and the ape impregnated with the human male element. It is not agreeable to mention such disgusting tricks; but the public should know what happens when "mere religious taboos" are spurned. After this, we are not surprised that he is in favour of abortion, when an unwanted child is conceived, and of infanticide if it is born defective.[1] It is not to be denied that the problems of sex are very difficult, and though one cannot be expected to refrain from signs of repugnance when such actions as those mentioned above are described without disapproval, we ought to give a fair reception to suggestions which are put forward seriously. The root of the problem is that we are dealing with one of what Metchnikoff calls the disharmonies of our bodily structure. This appetite is now much stronger than is necessary for the continuance of the race. Man has not had time to adapt himself to new conditions. Physical maturity comes long before marriage is socially possible or procreation desirable. It is also true that reason often suggests to the individual that in his private and personal interests are being sacrificed to the good of the race. This can hardly be denied. Wallace and Weismann even maintained that human life has been shortened by nature in order that the older generation might make way more quickly for the younger. The passion of love, as Lucretius and Schopenhauer bitterly declared, is the chief of the baits by which Nature gets her hook in our nose; it is violent and blind, and its shadow is everywhere pain and sorrow.[2] Then reason finds various ways of outwitting nature—ways of securing pleasure, while evading the objects for which the pleasure was designed, of swallowing the bait without the hook. This is, of course, the object of birth-control, which, when practised by married persons, I have been unable to censure, since it seems to be by far the least objectionable means of avoiding an undue excess of births over deaths.

It is quite possible and consistent to take this view

[1] See "Hymen," pp. 9, 27, 56, 59, 61, 63, 81, 91.
[2] Carveth Read, "Natural and Social Morals," p. 31.

without agreeing with those who have urged that continence among the unmarried is either impossible or injurious to health. Sweeping assertions on both sides are frequently made, without much care for truth, and statistics are hard to come by. There are, as we might expect, considerable differences among civilised nations, caused in part by climate, public opinion, religion, and opportunity; there are also considerable differences between social classes. Among the few statistical statements about the practice of continence before marriage which I have been able to find is a monograph called "A Research in Marriage," by Dr. C. V. Hamilton of New York. He obtained answers from a hundred men and a hundred women, mostly under forty in New York. His conclusion is that "our men are becoming more virtuous, our women less so." Fifty-nine men and forty-seven women had been unchaste with other persons before marriage. Seventy-four women and ninety-seven men out of the hundred "seem to admit" solitary indulgence. Ninety-two men and eighty-seven women use contraceptives, in spite of the American legislation against the practice. This last statement seems to indicate that there were not many strict Catholics among those questioned by Dr. Hamilton. It is likely that the results in a country village would have been far more favourable than in New York. The fact that forty-one per cent. of the men were virgins at the time of their marriage (apart from the schoolboy bad habit which doctors say is seldom entirely avoided by the young) will surprise some people, but not so much as that only fifty-three per cent. of the girls came innocent to the altar. I should expect to find that in Paris the number of clean-living men was much smaller, and of chaste girls much larger. I do not hear confessions, and only occasionally receive persons who want advice. But judging from a small number of cases,

I should say that in not a few normal youths, the sexual instinct is quiescent until they fall in love, and that complete pre-nuptial chastity in men is by no means rare. I also find it difficult to believe that anything like ninety-seven per cent. of English schoolboys indulge frequently in bad habits when they are alone, though it may be true that curiosity overcomes nearly all of them at one time or another.

On the other hand, it is certain that to many men and some women sex is a continual torment, and that the struggle to resist temptation not only affects their spirits but sometimes causes minor disturbances of the nervous system. The advocates of "freedom" inveigh indignantly against the Churches for causing all this unnecessary suffering, and some psycho-analysts encourage them in bringing these complaints. Now on this subject a plain answer is necessary. The Church has never maintained that chastity is easy or possible for persons who lead self-indulgent and undisciplined lives, and who perhaps make no attempt to control their thoughts. It is a great mistake to isolate this particular temptation, as if it could be combated without paying strict attention to the whole conduct of life. Even so, the Anglican Prayer Book charitably allows that some persons "have not the gift of continency," and recommends early marriage as the proper remedy.

In December, 1927, the *Journal of Social Hygiene* published a statement prepared by the British Social Hygiene Committee, and adopted by the Council of the Society on March 22, 1926. "The British Social Hygiene Council are of opinion that (1) in the interests of the race and of the individual it is essential that the stability of the family in marriage should be preserved and social habits and customs be adjusted to this end. (2) There is an overwhelming evidence that irregular sex relations, whether in married or unmarried, lead to physical, mental and social harm. (3) There is no evidence, either from physiology or from experience, that for the unmarried sexual intercourse is a necessity for the maintenance of physical health. (4) There is no evidence, either from psychology or from experience, that for the unmarried sexual intercourse is a necessity for the maintenance of mental health." This declaration has been ridiculed by some extremists as manifestly prejudiced. But my experience of Christian medical men, who are a large body in this country, is that they are strictly truthful in their scientific statements. The following opinion from Havelock Ellis, who is not a Christian believer, may be taken as going as far as any English or American doctor of repute would be willing to go in the direction of admitting that abstinence may be injurious to health: "The old notion that any strict attempt to adhere to sexual abstinence is beset by terrible risks, insanity, and so forth, has no foundation, at all events where we are concerned with reasonably sound and healthy people. But it is a very serious error to suppose that the effort to achieve complete and prolonged sexual abstinence is without any bad results at all, physical or psychic. . . . The bad effects are never of a gravely serious character."

We may remind ourselves that we are often willing to do things which are not very good for our health, if we are assured that the effects cannot be serious, in the pursuit of some object, such as success in our business, which seems to us worth this small sacrifice. The acquisition of self-control, or as Plato puts it "the victory over pleasure," may be an object well worth what it costs.

Honesty, however, compels me to add that while medical opinion, so far as I have been able to ascertain, is positive that abstinence never has any serious evil effects upon men, many doctors refuse to say the same about women. Some women, I am told, suffer seriously in health from not being married.

Before leaving this subject, I will summarise and comment on the chapter upon sex in Canon Streeter's book called "Adventure." The writer is a very candid disputant, and has the advantage of knowing something of psychoanalysis.[1] He begins by speaking of the psychology of rebellion, which is very apparent in such writers as Bertrand Russell and H. G. Wells, and says justly that this bias is not favourable for a cool consideration of a very difficult subject. "The notion that sex-morality is nothing more than taboo belongs to the same order of thought as Rousseau's idea that the golden age would dawn when the last king had been strangled in the entrails of the last priest. We have since learnt that kings and priests came into existence because they performed functions useful to society." These taboos have survived for two thousand five hundred years, not in some savage island, but in Europe, the stew-pot of the world's thought. "No theory of marriage can be sound which looks upon it as predominantly concerned with sex, whether in its physical aspect or from the standpoint of romantic love."

On the latter subject Streeter quotes from H. G. Wells: "It is the fundamental falsity of the romantic tradition that man should subordinate himself to the egotism of a woman. Let her not dream of it. It lures her on to the development of an enhanced exaggerated ego, pitifully painted, scented, and adorned for worship. In that she sinks her actual personality." This is well said, and it needed saying. But obviously Mr. Wells' criticism has no application to the wives of the working men, nor of the poor professional class.

The romantic movement has also done great harm by exaggerating the part which sex plays in a normal

[1] He is not so well informed on the population question.

wholesome life. Real social progress—based largely on advance in technology and routine work—has very little to do with sex. The evolution of social life in the Northern countries tends to reduce the importance of sex still further. Popular fiction misrepresents the real state of society, and depicts the normal facts of life quite out of due proportion. The evil was not so great when novelists gave us a clean and sublimated eroticism. The unclean fiction of the present day exaggerates the sex-element still further, and degrades instead of refining it.

To return to Canon Streeter. He thinks that the true line of advance is in the promotion of comradeship and co-operation between the sexes, and also that what remains of the old ascetic notion, that the sexual instinct has in itself the nature of sin, must be wholly repudiated. Here we should all agree, though I have shown that the growth of this idea can be easily explained. But I do not think that he is on safe ground when he says (in answering the psycho-analysts) that self-control is totally different from repression. It is easy to talk of "sublimation," but it seems to me that much unreality has gathered round this word. I am in more thorough agreement with Mr. Urwick, who in his excellent book, "The Social Good" (pp. 16, 17), says: "It is urged that no impulse need be actually repressed, but, that all may be and should be guided to forms of satisfaction which are compatible both with the consistent organisation of our own life-purpose, and with the equal good or satisfaction of others. This I believe to be a dangerous error. Take, for example, the impulses connected with sexual desire. . . . Grant that under certain conditions, and for a time, these may be side-tracked or sublimated, and so allowed to be active and yet only to lead to satisfactions compatible with the harmonious good life. Nevertheless it is, I believe,

incontrovertible that over a great part of every normal
life there is no alternative whatever but to repress,
thwart, and deny these impulses, with much effort and
pain, and much feeling (at first, at least) of dishar-
mony. I am aware that it is not easy to give the
grounds for this belief. Only the experience of really
good people is pertinent; I cannot therefore appeal to
my own. But a fairly intimate knowledge of some good
people has convinced me that in their case without exception the rule holds good. And it is further borne
out by the very plain teaching of the greatest moral
authorities, such as Plato, St. Paul, and Christ Himself.
Consequently we must go on to assert that such dis-
harmony does not at all matter. . . . It only matters
if we regard happiness as a harmony of feeling. It
does not interfere with that harmony of the whole consciousness with reality which is the essence of happiness."

Mr. Urwick proceeds to say that if the suppression of fundamental impulses, like those of sex, is always
dangerous "the moral teaching of all our masters has
been false, utterly and fundamentally." What may
be true of abnormal cases does not apply to the normal.
The fashionable tendency is to tone down duty and
discipline till we think we have a right to take whatever
we desire. "We begin to take as our goal a social
harmony which shall result from all-round satisfaction
of as many desires as possible, with the minimum of
discipline, negation, or repression. But the true harmony is not a harmony of satisfied impulses, but a
harmony of conscious purposes; . . . and this probably
dependent upon unending discipline of desire." The
question at issue could not be better put. We must
choose between all our old guides, including Christ
and Plato, and the school of Freud and Jung. Nor will
an appeal to more primitive conditions serve the rebels.

Among savages the life of the sexes is regulated by a complex system of restrictions. As Malinowski has shown, the repression which lies at the root of social life is not, as with Freud, the suppressed memory of an instinctive crime, but a constructive repression of anti-social impulses.[1] The beginning of culture implies the suppression of instincts.[2]

It is hardly necessary in this volume to speak of the insult and injury to womanhood which is inseparable from commercialised vice. Canon Streeter says (and I have heard the same from other sources) that both the number of prostitutes and the rate of their remuneration have declined considerably of recent years. Streeter refers to the official Report on Common Lodging Houses for 1927. Unfortunately, the reason which is curtly given is "the competition of the amateur"! It is doubtful whether this ought to be considered a matter for congratulation, especially as the "amateur" is said to be a greater danger to public health than the professional. The pages of Lecky which deal with this subject are celebrated. In spite of a striking quotation from Augustine to the same effect, he shocked his public by pointing out that the fallen woman, "the eternal priestess of humanity, blasted for the sins of the people," is a protection of the virtue of her innocent sisters. Many sociologists think that "the oldest profession in the world" is too useful to be abolished, and that the members of it are at present treated with unnecessary social cruelty. But the democratic movement, which holds with Kant, and with Christ, that humanity should always be treated as an end, not as a means, revolts against the sacrifice of many members of the weaker sex. The institution, in fact, cannot be

[1] Dawson, "Christianity and Sex," p. 19.
[2] Malinowski, "Sex and Repression in Savage Society," p. 182.

justified; and we may hope that it will continue to decline, until it ceases to be a public disgrace.

But we cannot dismiss the question whether, granting that permanent marriage is and should be the normal arrangement, any other should be recognised as permissible. The opinion is often expressed, and is growing, that it is not the business of society to interfere with any arrangements that a pair of adults like to make for themselves, provided that no children are born and that public decency is not outraged. But we are here concerned not so much with social recognition as with moral condonation. The fallacy which seems to me to underlie many of the arguments of the rebels is the assumption that men and women cannot be close friends without carnal connexion. One great advantage of a high moral standard in these matters is to make innocent friendships between men and women possible and common. Every irregular union helps to undermine this freedom, which is one of the best things in our civilisation. Canon Streeter says very well that "the only guarantee is the bond of honour between husband and wife, which makes physical relationships with other persons unthinkable." Many honourable men and women, who have not found all the sympathy which they hoped for in their marriages, have gained great happiness from their innocent friendships with persons of the other sex. Streeter refers to Dante, who never seems to have wished to possess Beatrice. As the ideal of the *Ewig-weibliche* she was best worshipped at a respectful distance, while Gemma Donati did well enough as a *Hausfrau!* As for the practice of "keeping a mistress," it belongs to a state of society where social differences are more marked than they should be in a Christian community.

To grant any exceptions is dangerous. The passions grant dispensations more easily than the most accommodating father-confessor. The strongest case for relaxation of the rule is not that most commonly urged—the torment for a young man at having to live alone for several years before he can afford to marry. I have more sympathy with the position of women who feel that they are called to motherhood, but have had no opportunity of marriage. I agree with Streeter that the sacrifice should be accepted, but that the Victorian social ostracism of all women who have borne illegitimate children was too severe.

Perhaps it would be cowardly to shirk the unpleasant subject of homosexual proclivities, which has now begun to find its way even into fiction. Modern writers on the subject have maintained that there is a large number of "inverts" of both sexes, whose natural instincts are to form attachments with persons of the same sex. The claim is made that these cases should not be the subjects of moral censure, since this condition is a kind of disease. In Germany there is, or was till lately, a sort of cult of abnormal vice, and notorious scandals were the result. The French have always prided themselves on their comparative freedom from a practice which they like to regard as a sign of the moral depravity of the Teutons. I am afraid there can be no doubt that these practices are increasing in this country, now that the exaggerated horror with which they used to be regarded has been much abated. There was a time, not so very distant, when one method of practising this vice was a capital offence in England. In most continental countries the law does not interfere when both parties are adults, and is content to protect the young. Those who have studied classical literature written at a time when persons were allowed to indulge their propensities without let or hindrance, will doubt very seriously whether the theory of "inversion" is true, except for a few obviously pathological cases. The large majority of pederasts, I believe, are psychically quite normal; their offence is a sin, not a disease. I suspect that the rebellion against sexual taboos will be extended to this vice, and that increasing vigilance will be needed to protect the young, who will be in most danger from it.

DIVORCE

The kindred subject of divorce bristles with difficulties. It brings into strong opposition the Christian teaching on marriage and the new morality of emancipation. For Christians, the problem is complicated by the uncertainty about the intention of Christ when He spoke on the subject, about the meaning of His words, and even about the text in the Gospels. It is admitted that He came before His countrymen as a prophet, not as a legislator, and that He left us general principles, not anything like a code. But, say Bishop Gore and those who think with him, He who on other subjects refused to legislate, did legislate here. On marriage and divorce He gave not general principles but definite rules. The Catholic Church bases its prohibition of divorce on His teaching.

In what follows I shall make use of the evidence which I gave twenty years ago before the Royal Commission on Divorce and Matrimonial Causes. More recent discussions have not, I think, added much to what we may gather from the New Testament.

The passages in the New Testament which bear upon the question are Matthew v. 21–32; Matthew xix. 3–10; Mark x. 2–12; Luke xvi. 18; i Cor. vii. 10–16 and 39.

The chief problem raised by the passages in the Gospels arises from the fact that in Mark x. 11 and Luke xvi. 18 Jesus forbids divorce absolutely, while in the two passages from Matthew He makes an exception. But before discussing the discrepancy, as it may be well to consider the meaning of the exception, as it stands in our documents. Two questions are here important: (1) What is the offence for which divorce is here allowed? (2) Is the remedy divorce with freedom to remarry, or only separation?

The exception named is the case of "fornication" (*Porneia*). This word, in its proper signification, denotes intercourse with a prostitute, πόρνη being the ordinary plain-spoken name for harlot. A few critics have argued that the ground for divorce here sanctioned is the discovery by the husband that the wife has been unchaste before marriage. This, however, is impossible, and was never even suggested in the early Church.

Roman Catholic commentators have maintained that Christ sanctions separation in cases of adultery, but not divorce with liberty to remarry. This, however, is impossible for the following reasons. (*a*) The passage in Deut. xxiv. 1–4 with which Christ is dealing expressly permits remarriage. It must therefore be assumed that this permission remains in force, if not expressly rescinded. (*b*) The words "causeth her to commit adultery" assume that the divorced woman will remarry. The exception therefore implies that remarriage after divorce for adultery is not adultery. (*c*) Divorce without liberty of remarriage was unknown both to Jewish and Roman law.

But it has been urged in favour of the view here rejected that if the husband of the guilty wife may remarry without incurring the guilt of adultery, it is inconsistent to say that "he that marrieth a divorced woman committeth adultery." For adultery is a crime incidental to the married state, and if it be possible in either party, it must be because the bond of marriage still continues; and if the bond exists, both are bound. To this objection two answers are possible. (a) In the clause "he that marrieth a divorced woman" we must understand, as if it were repeated, the clause about *Porneia*. He who marries a woman divorced *for any other reason* committeth adultery. (b) The clause in question indicates that the prohibition of divorce was intended to be absolute, and that the "exception" is an interpolation. Taking the two passages in Matthew as they stand, we must admit that Christ allowed divorce, with liberty to both parties to remarry, in the case of adultery. That is to say, the passages in Matthew, which contain the exception, contradict the passages in Mark and Luke, which do not contain the exception. The question now arises whether the exception is interpolated.

No saying of Christ is better attested than the saying about divorce. It must have appeared both in the lost document generally called Q, the main source of the non-Marcan part of Matthew's Gospel, and in the other primitive document which is, in substance, our Mark. Secondly, it is easier to account for the discrepancy by supposing that there has been an unwarranted addition in Matthew, than by supposing that an important qualification has been suppressed in Mark and Luke. A motive for the alteration may have been the desire to bring the legislation of Christ into nearer agreement with Jewish custom, or with what may have seemed a practical necessity to the Christian Church. The hypothesis of interpolation is also supported by the exclamation of the disciples: "If the case of a man be so with his wife, it is better not to marry." Their surprise would be difficult to account for if Christ had merely reaffirmed the stricter Rabbinic interpretation of the Law, with which they must have been familiar already. On the other hand, if the prohibition of divorce had for the first time been made absolute, their astonishment was natural. Lastly, the expression "the cause of fornication" seems to be a translation of the Hebrew words (Deut. xxiv. 1) the ambiguity of which gave rise to the controversy. I believe that in Matthew v. 32 the words, which come in awkwardly, were inserted by the evangelist himself, or found by him in an interpolated copy of Q; for there is no variation in the manuscripts. In Matthew xix. 9 there are numerous variations; in fact the text is in confusion. The whole verse is probably a later interpolation.

The result of this examination has been to invalidate the supposed exception. But we cannot close the inquiry without asking whether it was not our Lord's method to make statements in an unguarded form leaving it to the common sense of His hearers to make the necessary qualifications. The Sermon on the Mount contains several startling injunctions of this kind. It is a tenable view, that the case of adultery was not in the speaker's mind at the time; it is even possible that to a Jew the right of divorce for adultery was too obvious to need reaffirmation. In all our Lord's words about marriage, it is not the occasional wreckage of a union which is in His mind, but the institution as God means it to be—the sacrament of love, which must be kept "in sanctification and honour."

In my evidence before the Commission I added a few facts bearing on the opinion and practice of the early Church before 250. Hermas (about 140) says that a husband who continues to live with an unfaithful wife is a partaker of her adultery. Tertullian (about 200) says that a husband ought to put away his wife for adultery, and that a wife may put away her husband for the same cause. Connivance is one thing; readiness to forgive after repentance is another. The early writers seem to be agreed in discountenancing remarriage after separation; "for the guilty party may repent." Lactantius, however (died 325), regards remarriage as allowable for a husband who has divorced his wife for adultery. There was, we remember, a prejudice against second marriage in all cases. Tertullian ("Ad Uxorem," II. 1) and Origen (on Matthew XIX. 9) seem to imply that the rule of the Church was not very strictly enforced. The "exception" in Matthew in quoted by Theophilus (about 180), by Clement of Alexandria, Tertullian, and Origen. There was no doubt that *Porneia* meant adultery; but some Christians thought that "worshipping other gods," which is called fornication in the Old Testament, and other crimes such as black magic, might be included as equivalent in guilt. Lastly, Justin mentions a Christian woman who served a notice of divorce on a heathen husband who wished her to submit to unnatural usage. She would probably not think herself at liberty to marry again.

St. Paul, in I Cor. VII, is discussing mixed marriages. He quotes "the Lord" as having forbidden a wife to leave her husband, and mentions no exception. But he proceeds, on his own authority, to allow an exception. If a Pagan husband puts away his Christian wife, she is "not under bondage," *i.e.,* as I understand it, she may marry again. But in such cases the first marriage was not a Christian marriage, and was contracted without a covenant that it was to be indissoluble. Some scholars think that no permission to remarry is implied; but I hold that it would be meaningless to say to a divorced and deserted wife, "You are no longer in bondage," if she were not free to marry again.

I have no space to discuss the Rabbinical interpretations of Deuteronomy, some of which gave the husband a right to divorce his wife because she was a bad cook, or because he found someone who pleased him better. The disciples probably meant Christ to decide between the stricter school of Shammai and the laxer school of Hillel. Instead of a direct answer, He replied, as His manner was, that by the will of God marriage is a life-long contract. I do not think that the death-penalty assigned to adultery in the Old Testament comes into the question. It had probably been a dead letter for a long time, in spite of John VIII. There was no serious intention of stoning the adulteress.

My conclusion is that Christ meant to inculcate a higher view of the sacredness of marriage than had been held by the Rabbis of either school. I do not think that He meant to lay down hard and fast rules. If a very hard case had been brought before Him, He might possibly have said, as He said about another commandment, "Marriage was made for man, not man for marriage." He does not say that Moses was wrong in allowing for the hardness of the human heart. Moses was a legislator; He was not.

Hard cases make bad law; but it is a bad law which multiplies hard cases.

The doctrine that marriage is absolutely indissoluble cannot be proved from the New Testament. St. Paul cannot have held it, or he would not have allowed even mixed marriages to be dissolved. By admitting the Matthæan exception into the Canon, the Church accepted an interpretation of Christ's words which is incompatible with the view that marriage is *per se* indissoluble. I meant that when the words were accepted as Christ's, they must have been understood to sanction divorce, not merely separation, for they are given distinctly as an exception to an absolute rule. Fifty years later than Matthew, the feeling against remarriage, which might have kept the exception out if it had prevailed earlier, was dominant. Some of the Fathers, as we have seen, were willing to discuss the question whether some non-sexual offenses might be morally equivalent to *Porneia.* The Christian emperors, apparently without much protest from the Church, allowed divorce with leave to remarry in certain cases. The Greek Church allows the innocent party to remarry, and has even made other concessions. The Roman Church is strict in theory, but decrees of nullity are granted to those who can pay for them. The Reformed Churches have allowed divorce with leave to remarry, for adultery and some other offences. In our own country Bills have (previously to 1857) taken the place of Papal decrees of nullity, and divorce was within the reach of those who could pay for it.

It follows that those Anglicans who maintain that since by Christian law marriage is *per se* indissoluble, no divorce should be granted in any circumstances, are making a claim which is historically untenable, and which the practice of the Christian Churches in all ages has proved to be unworkable. They are "laying a yoke on the neck of the disciples which neither our fathers nor we are able to bear."

The duty of a Christian State is to legislate with due regard for the imperfections of human nature, while at the same time recognising the duty to maintain the unique sanctity of the marriage contract, which Christ unquestionably intended to emphasise. It has a right to stigmatise adultery as a disgraceful offence, as well as a breach of the most solemn obligation which a man and woman contract in the whole course of their lives. I should be glad to see the marriage of an adulterer with his or her paramour absolutely forbidden. With regard to the innocent party, I think that the more merciful rule, that of the Greek Church might be accepted, though I believe the nobler part is for the injured person to remain unmarried. "He that is able to receive it, let him receive it."

If the law were thus tightened in the interests of

Christian morality, by forbidding marriage to white-wash an adulterous pair, I do not see why a Christian State should not grant divorce, with liberty to remarry, in a few other cases besides adultery. Such possible grounds are desertion, brutal cruelty, habitual drunkenness, venereal disease, conviction for felony, and concealment of bodily or mental defects. It is hard that a man should be tied for life to an imbecile whose condition has been carefully hidden from him.

But since such extensions go beyond what Christ is recorded to have sanctioned, we must accept the fact that the law of the State and the law of the Church would not be identical. The Church would have no right to brand as notorious evil livers those who had taken advantage of such concessions; but a period of discipline, with temporary exclusion from the Holy Communion, might perhaps be imposed, since we cannot be confident that Christ would have approved the liberties which the State allows.

The question, however, goes deeper than this. Very many citizens are not nominally Christian, and recognise no obligation to take life-long vows of fidelity in marriage. If, as seems probable, the State will be obliged to recognise this state of things, the only solution seems to be for the civil power to allow two kinds of marriage. Those who invoke the blessing of the Church on their union would be understood to have pledged themselves absolutely to life-long fidelity. They will have taken vows, to break which would be a scandalous and most dishonourable offence. But if two persons wish to enter into a much more limited contract, the terms of which are clearly understood on both sides, they have, I think, the right to claim that the State shall recognise their position better than mere concubinage. Whether such persons should be allowed to be members of the Church is a rather difficult question of discipline.

A few facts may be added to illustrate the existing laws in foreign countries. In France, the husband's adultery is considered unimportant unless he casts some indignity upon his wife. In Germany "grave breaches of marital duty" are included as grounds for divorce. In Japan, sterility, jealousy, and loquacity (!) are recognised as grounds. In Austria "invincible mutual aversion" may be pleaded; in the Scandinavian countries separation for a time by mutual consent is sufficient. In the United States the law differs in different parts of the country; but the facility with which marriages are dissolved in many of the States is rightly regarded by high-minded Americans as a disgrace to their country.

Suicide

Another question which presents serious ethical difficulties is that of suicide with which is closely connected the question of so-called euthanasia, the right to hasten death in order to shorten grievous suffering. Lecky goes too far when he speaks of the striking contrast between the teaching of antiquity on the one hand, and that of almost all modern moralists on the other. Suicide was often blamed in antiquity, and has often been justified by modern writers. But Christianity has condemned the act with peculiar severity, while the independent thought of our time refuses to endorse any indiscriminate censure upon it.

Some savage tribes laugh at the idea of a man taking his own life; others chiefly on a somewhat higher level of civilisation, practise it freely. The widespread custom of wives immolating themselves on the graves of their husbands, and slaves (sometimes voluntarily) on the graves of their masters, shows how lightly, in some circumstances, the thought of death is regarded.

But in some primitive religions suicides are threatened with torments in the next world, or are denied the rites of burial. In the Far East suicide has always been common, and the curious custom of avenging an insult to personal honour, not by challenging the aggressor to a duel but by committing suicide as a protest, has prevailed both in China and Japan. Till quite lately, those who died by voluntary hara-kiri were greatly honoured. In India self-immolation, often by burning, has been thought an acceptable service to the gods.

The Semitic religions discountenance suicide. The Rabbis forbid it to the Jews in all circumstances, and Mohammedans often say that to kill oneself is the worst kind of murder.[1]

In ancient Greece, tragic legend is full of suicides, and the sentiment that "the noble man must either live honourably or die honourably" was often interpreted in this sense. But the moralists, such as Pythagoras, Plato, and Aristotle, generally condemn it, either as an injury to the State, which has a right to every man's services, or on the religious ground that God has given us a station to guard, and that we must not desert it.

The Romans were divided on the subject. But their chief guides in philosophy and morals were the Stoics, who extol suicide as the appointed means of escape from all kinds of misery. Hegesias of Alexandria, who was accused of starting an epidemic of suicide among his pupils, and who was in consequence forbidden to lecture, was a Cyrenaic. Virgil places suicides in an uncomfortable place in Hades, and Cicero follows Pythagoras. The most passionate advocate of the right to die is Seneca, who nevertheless admits that some disagreed with him about the lawfulness of voluntary death. "As I would choose a ship to sail in, or a house to live in,

[1] Westermarck, "Origin and Development of Moral Ideas," Vol. I. p. 247.

I would choose the most tolerable death when I come to die. Do you like to be miserable? Then live. Do you dislike it? Then you may return whence you came." "Wherever you look, there is the end of evils. You see that precipice? There you may descend to liberty. You see that sea, that river, that well? Liberty sits at the bottom. You may find the way to liberty in every vein of your body." Valerius Maximus says that at Marseillès the magistrates kept a stock of poison, which they gave to those who convinced them that they had sufficient reasons for wishing to end their lives. Epictetus condemned indiscriminate suicide; but if life becomes intolerable, "the door of escape is open."

The Christian writers would allow no such excuses. The only cases which they viewed with leniency were those when Christian women put an end to their lives to save their chastity, and even this exception was disallowed by Augustine, on the ground that forcible rape does not destroy the crown of virginity. The main reason for this severity is given by Thomas Aquinas. "Suicide is the most fatal of sins, because it cannot be repented of." The laws of Christian nations endeavoured to punish the suicide in the only ways possible, by declaring him a felon, by outraging his dead body, and by confiscating his property. This was the law of England till 1870, when forfeitures for felony were abolished. In practice this injustice was usually avoided by a verdict of the jury that the deceased was temporarily insane. This procedure is still habitually followed, to spare the feelings of the relatives, and because it is rightly believed that since the subjects of severe mental depression will often destroy themselves under the delusion that their sufferings have some objective cause, this delusion may fairly be called a temporary aberration of the mind.

At the time of the Renaissance, the reverence felt

for the Greeks and Romans led to a modification of the severity with which suicide had been condemned. Sir Thomas More, in his "Utopia," wishes to institute a law like that which is said to have existed at Marseilles. The poet Donne, Dean of St. Paul's, wrote, in early life, "a declaration of that paradox or thesis that self-homicide is not so naturally sin that it can never be otherwise." Montaigne even says, *"la plus volontaire mort c'est la plus belle."* During the French Revolution, the classical example of *Catonis nobile letum* impelled several enthusiasts to seek a voluntary death.

Madame de Staël wrote against suicide in a temperate and reasonable manner, no longer condemning it as murder, but showing how in almost every case a man of high character would choose to live rather than renounce the providence of God by escaping from pain and sorrow.

Hume, on the other hand, recommended it in certain circumstances. "Suppose that it is no longer in my power to promote the interest of society; suppose that I am a burden to it; suppose that my life hinders some person from being much more useful to society. In such cases my resignation of life must not only be innocent but laudable." He argues, perhaps rather sophistically, that "any death, however voluntary, does not happen without the consent of Providence; when I fall upon my own sword I receive my death equally from the hands of the Deity as if it had proceeded from a lion, a precipice, or a fever."

At present, suicide is very prevalent in countries where the citizens have already access to lethal weapons; among soldiers, and also among financial speculators; it is somewhat more common in Protestant than in Catholic societies; among men than women; among the unmarried and especially among the childless than among those who have children; among the young and middle-aged than among the old. It seems sometimes to run in families, and is certainly contagious, in the sense that history records several epidemics of suicide. So much are those naturally prone to it influenced by the words and actions of others that some who share the views of Hume are afraid to express them, lest by evil chance they should encourage some person of unstable mind to commit the irrevocable act. Medical men say that dementia præcox, dementia paralytica, and especially melancholia, predispose to suicide.

Some of the arguments against suicide are losing their force. We are no longer convinced that a man's eternal destiny depends on the state of mind in which he quits this life, still less that the impossibility of repenting and receiving absolution for this particular sin stamps it as supremely dangerous. The argument that we have no right to deprive the State of our services does not touch Hume's plea; nor does the accusation of cowardice meet every case. It seems anomalous that a man may be punished for cruelty if he does not put a horse or a dog "out of its misery," but is liable to be hanged for murder if he helps a cancer patient to take an overdose of morphia. The "right to kill" has recently been partially vindicated in a trial in France, where a man shot his mother in order to end her sufferings. It is known that many doctors would be glad to shorten the agonies of some of their dying patients; sometimes, it is believed, this is actually done.

I confess that in this instance I cannot resist the arguments for a modification of the traditional Christian law, which absolutely prohibits suicide in all circumstances. I do not think we can assume that God willed the prolongation of torture for the benefit of the soul of the sufferer. Nor do I judge other suicides so severely as is the custom of Christian moralists. At the same time I hope, inconsistently perhaps, that if I were attacked by a painful illness I should have patience to wait for the end, and I do not think I should wish anyone near and dear to me to act otherwise.

THE TESTAMENT OF BEAUTY

Goodness, Truth, and Beauty are the three attributes under which God has revealed His nature to man. Though they are distinct, they are not separate; they are "a three-fold cord, not quickly broken." There are, as I have said elsewhere,[1] three marks or tests which give some of our experiences a much higher value than others, and make us feel that there is something divine about them. In the first place, they bring with them their own satisfaction; they are not means to something else. Secondly, they have a universal quality; they take us out of ourselves, and make us breathe a larger air. Thirdly, they delight and uplift us in such a way that when they are past we feel that we are permanently the better for having had them. These are the marks of what St. Paul calls the things of the Spirit—the higher and better world which is about us and among us and within us, though we often forget it or cannot see it. When we are brought into contact with Goodness, Truth, and Beauty we stand on holy ground. These experiences are to be reverenced and guarded from contamination with special care. The world, the flesh, and the devil are always trying to corrupt and spoil these revelations, in which God is giving us a vision of Himself. It is selfishness that most often spoils disinterested affection; it is pride which most often prevents us from keeping our minds open for the reception of new truths; and it is sensuality which most often poisons our appreciation of the beautiful.

It follows that the æsthetic side of life cannot be ex-

---

[1] "All Saints' Sermons," 1907.

cluded from a book on Ethics, and assuredly the prevailing ugliness of Western civilisation is one of the modern problems on which Christians may inquire whether the Gospels and the history of the Church have any light to throw.

I have already called attention to the parallel between our Lord's love of nature and that of Wordsworth. There is the same readiness to find moral lessons in rustic scenes; though Wordsworth's mind led him to a semi-pantheism which we do not find in the Gospels. There is no explicit philosophy behind our Lord's simple affection for all things bright and beautiful—fields, mountains, lakes, and the one thing in nature which is perhaps more beautiful than all these—little children.

The Greek Fathers laid great stress on the glories of nature as a revelation of God. But they tended to disparage art; it does not seem that they had any appreciation of the glorious works of the Greek sculptors and painters, which their contemporaries were destroying or allowing to perish. The arts were decaying, quite independently of Christianity; but though it was not till centuries later that Christian faith began to inspire great painting, we must not forget the splendid Byzantine Church architecture, the beauty of which has perhaps never been surpassed. Other styles of building succeeded in the early Middle Ages; Catholic art, both in architecture and painting, is one of the glories of the human race. But it was not till the Renaissance that Christians ceased to be ashamed of their bodies. The perfect beauty of Greek sculpture made no appeal to them, and Christian art took other forms.

Protestantism, like Judaism, found expression in poetry rather than in visible symbolism. But the works of men all over Europe remained beautiful till the Industrial Revolution, which brought in an era not only of indifference to the æsthetic side of life, but of such bad taste in the arts as the world had not seen before. From that time onwards we have become accustomed to expect a new town to be a blot on a landscape. About the same time, all attempts to make masculine dress picturesque and becoming were given up. A European or American crowd presents a drab uniformity, as if every man was afraid of being anything more than an indistinguishable member of the mob.

The instinct of beautiful production has not been recovered. In painting, indeed, there are now signs of a lower degradation than has ever been known. Anyone who has paid several visits to the unique collection of Italian paintings exhibited in London in the early part of this year (1930), and who has gone away almost intoxicated with the splendour of Italian genius in the time of the Renaissance, must feel a kind of horror and stupefaction at the revolting productions of the modernist school, which resemble now the work of a very unpleasant child, now the first efforts of an African savage, and now the delirious hallucinations of an incurable lunatic. In architecture, however, there are the beginnings of a genuine revival, most marked, I think, in the United States and in Sweden. And everywhere there is a genuine and pathetic desire to bring the reign of ugliness to an end.

The modern spirit is also returning to the Greek cult of physical beauty, though this movement is at present more prominent on the Continent, and especially in Germany, than in our own country. Bodily training is now practised with enthusiasm by the young of both sexes, who form associations for the purpose. On this branch of Ethics, for so I regard it, I will quote from an excellent chapter by Professor Percy Gardner, in his "Evolution in Christian Ethics."

The Greeks regarded the human body as the most beautiful of all gifts of the gods. They tried, by constant training and exercise to make their bodies perfect in every part. But for early Christianity beauty was a snare of the devil. The early medieval sculptor "has not the faintest conception of what is meant by physical beauty." The later cultus of the human form has been inspired by Pagan antiquity, and "never brought into close relation to the Christian life." "In all modern countries the sense of human beauty is in a terribly depressed condition." "Compare the fashion plates of our newspapers with Venus of Melos." Even in the pictures of Rossetti and Burne Jones "there is a painful lack of robustness and manliness." "Many a man is not ashamed to show his own body defects which he would not tolerate in his horse, and which by a little vigorous self-discipline he could remove."

The right view is that since our bodies are "temples of the Holy Spirit," we ought to keep them as fair and healthy as possible. The old notion that "the corruptible body presseth down the soul" is bad science and doubtful philosophy. Here then is another branch of Ethics in which we can be true to the spirit of Christianity while rejecting a time-honoured tradition.

The service of Beauty is the service of God, if we know what Beauty means. We must prepare hopefully for the next flowering-time of the arts, and make up our minds that when the radiance of the divine loveliness once more shines upon the minds of men, we will not leave this precious gift to be snatched by the world, the flesh, or the devil.

CONCLUSION

In reading through the manuscript of my book, I have become painfully conscious that it may be taken, in some quarters, as a sustained polemic against the most august and powerful of the Christian Churches. Nothing can be further from my intention than to show discourtesy to any Christian body; but though I have removed several passages which might be considered needlessly offensive, enough remains to make such a misrepresentation of my purpose almost inevitable. And yet it would be an entire misrepresentation. I have written with a very definite object before me— to advocate a return to the fundamental principles of the original Gospel as I understand them. I am convinced that historical causes, which are no longer operative, have led to developments of Christianity which are quite alien to the intentions of the Founder, and that a complete breach with militant ecclesiasticism is necessary if Christianity is to take its proper place as a factor in the civilisation of the future.

That our religion no longer attracts those who are shaping the thought of our time is notorious. I am not thinking of the alienation of "the masses"—Christ never thought of men in the mass, and had no expectation of finding the *vox populi* on His side; nor of the spirit of revolt against all conventions and traditions, which is probably a temporary phenomenon, an aspect of the general unrest caused by the break-up of a phase of civilisation. It is the best thought of our time which is partially estranged from the religion which ought to be its deepest inspiration, and the revolt is partly ethical.

This is the situation which has moved me to write this book.

Can we find, within the covers of the New Testament, any encouragement in our aspirations for a better world, for a happier state of society to be gradually realised through human effort? I have argued that we can, if we dig deep enough. But I hold that the whole history of Catholic imperialism has been an aberration which has lamentably retarded the spiritual influence of the Gospel. And wherever the secular progress of humanity has brought new hopes and new duties in sight, it seems to me that the institutional Churches have shown themselves unsympathetic or even hostile. To plead for a more friendly attitude towards the new Ethics has been a main object of my book; I have not been able to avoid remonstrances against the traditionalism which often places Christians on the side of the obscurantists. If my subject had been the life of devotion, I should have been glad to acknowledge my deep obligations to the writings of Roman Catholic saints and thinkers, some of whom are my frequent companions in my library.

I have been taught much by such modern thinkers as Eucken, Otto, and especially Troeltsch. These men see clearly that we need a new type of Christianity, more ethical, more mystical, and less dogmatic than the traditional forms. Troeltsch thinks that the new forms will owe more to what he calls the sect-type than to the great Churches, whether Catholic or Protestant. These "step-children of the Reformation" must be allowed to make their contribution; and with them the Church of the future must find room for the humanism of Erasmus, Colet, and More, which was, for the time, destroyed by the violence of the Reformation, the Counter-Reformation, and the Wars of Religion. To knit up these broken threads is part of the task laid upon us.

The remarks which follow are a *résumé* of the main arguments in the preceding chapters. It will be seen that I am somewhat alarmed by what the Germans call *Politismus* in religion, especially when this takes the natural form of backing the winning side in politics. But I hope it will be realised that I have no sympathy with the self-indulgent habits of the "idle rich." Bernard Shaw's definition of a gentleman as one who tries, in one form or another, to put into social life at least as much as he takes out of it, is a very sound application of the principles of the Sermon on the Mount.

Religion and Ethics are, for a Christian, inseparable. There are unethical religions, and there are irreligious ethical schools or societies; but these are not Christian. Ethical societies, in spite of their moral earnestness, seem dry and ineffective; and an unethical religion may sometimes be worse than no religion at all. Cicero's definition of *religiosi*, as *"qui omnia quae ad cultum deorum pertinent diligenter retractant,"* expresses precisely that idea of religion with which Christianity has nothing to do.

The moving force in ethical religion is the natural attraction which goodness, truth, and beauty exercise upon a healthy mind led, as we believe, by the Holy Spirit. This has never been expressed better than by Origen (*De Princ.* 2.11.4): *"Quod desiderium, quem amorem sine dubio a Deo nobis insitum credimus; et sicut oculus naturaliter lucem requirit et visum, et corpus nostrum escas et potum desiderat per naturam, ita mens nostra sciendae veritatis Dei et rerum causas noscendi proprium ac naturale desiderium gerit."* Man longs to transcend his empirical self and its surroundings; he stretches forward towards the eternal values, and he finds them in morality, in science, and in art.

It is through the divine life in men, the Christ in us, that Ethics belong to the eternal or spiritual world, and that moral conduct becomes as it were the sacrament, the outward and visible sign, of faith, hope, and love directed to a Being who in His nature sits above the conflict between right and wrong. What is relative and subjective in morality is thus anchored to absolute truth and goodness.

Christianity, as Benjamin Whichcote said, is a divine life, not a divine science; or, as Professor Peabody puts it, when St. Paul says that we walk by faith, he implies that faith is a way of walking, not of talking.

During nearly the whole history of Christianity, since the bold pioneers of the first century, the tendency to rely on authority and to appeal to the past has been too strong. The Church began its career in an age of stagnation or decadence; it kept its light fitfully burning during centuries of almost unrelieved barbarism. I repeat, what I have said before, that humanity owes a great debt to the Catholic Church for this service. At the Renaissance, Western Europe had to go to school with the ancients; in the wars of religion both sides were eager to claim a supernatural warrant for their doctrines. Thus the temptation to look back rather than forward for inspiration was overwhelming. Even in the modern period the natural conversation both of religion and of morality has made theology and Ethics timid and conventional. A bolder spirit is now needed, since civilisation is entering upon a new phase, as sharply distinguished from that which proceeded it as the Renaissance period was from the middle ages. As Professor W. Wallace writes ("Lectures and Essays," p. 65), "To us, looking at the facts in the light of history, it is hardly possible to say otherwise than that though it [the work of the Church] was well done, it was far from being thoroughly well done, or so done that it can be considered satisfactorily done for ever. But we need cherish no illusions as to what we can learn from the

past. The cry is again and again raised. Back to—
it may be only to Kant; it may be to Greece, or to
medieval Christendom, or to primitive Christianity, or
to Nature. . . . But the Nature, the Greece, the Christianity we go back to is not in the past; it is, seen through
the arch of experience, the gleam of that untrodden
world to which we move. To seek them in the past is
to seek the living among the dead. The gates of one
Paradise are closed . . . the gates of another Paradise
are eternally open."

Wallace adds that the modern ethical movement is
no solution, but a step towards a solution. Men speak
rashly of the fall of religious belief. "What has fallen
or is falling is not that central spirit of religion which
we found described as conscientiousness, devotion, reverence, loyalty, fidelity, enthusiasm, and heroism. It
is not that trust in the world-order, that faithfulness
unto death, that joy in well-doing, that cheerfulness of
good conscience, which made obedience no burden and
service a delight." What has "become suspect" is certain "metaphysical and historical dogmas which have
been knit up with religion." These dogmas do not
enter into our present subject.

Bishop Gore also ("Christ and Society," p. 27)
speaks of the "independence of history" shown by great
reformers. The one safe way of *not* resembling a
pioneer is to accept him as an infallible oracle. But this
has been the characteristic attitude of the Church towards authority. We may therefore agree with Dr.
McGiffert, that though "the rediscovery of Jesus has
always been the rebirth of Christianity," our motto
must not be "back to Christ," but "forward with Christ."

If this is true, we are sent back to the Gospels as the
fountain-head of modern Christianity, but not as a stag-
nant reservoir of unchangeable wisdom. For in them
we find a pure revelation of love and duty, not yet

overlaid with accretions which belong to this or that phase of human development. It is to be expected that the religious and ethical convictions of the new age will gradually construct a new framework in accordance with the prevailing philosophical and scientific theories of the time. But this will not be done in our lifetime, because modern science and modern philosophy are still in the melting-pot. We are in an age of transition, and we must put up with the inconveniences and uncertainties which always attend these times of rapid change.

Troeltsch thinks that there are at present two main types of social religion, Catholic medievalism and ascetic (*i.e.* Calvinist) Protestantism. "Both," he says, "are exhausted." We must have faith in the power of society to take free forms of its own choosing. In his opinion, there can be no stable alliance with the ecclesiastical reaction. I have in this book given my views on the prospects of these "exhausted" types.

In the little book called "Christianity and the Present Moral Unrest," which reflects the standpoint of "Copec," Dr. G. F. Barbour thinks that we can distinguish four divergent types of Ethics at work in the world, those of self-assertion, of legal observance, of renunciation, and of active love. Although we must choose by which of them we will chiefly direct our lives, all of them have their roots deep in the common ground of human nature. The first, independent individualism, he thinks, is disintegrating and anarchic at the best, though it may have some value as a protest against conventionality and sentimentalism. Dr. Barbour is evidently thinking of Nietzsche as a representative of this type. But if we wish to do justice to this scheme of self-training we ought to substitute "self-realisation" for "self-assertion," and to consider such a life as that of Goethe. To perfect one's own character as a work of art is not an ignoble or useless quest. But in practice it usually fails to produce a perfect character, from its want of sympathy, which cannot be forced. Goethe, for example, has been accused of sacrificing men, or at least women, to his plan of "building up the pyramid of his existence." It is for this reason that Christ rejects this type.

Since, however, many writers who belong to the school of thought represented in Dr. Barbour's essay, which I have selected as typical of ideas which are prominent just now in the Church of England, are fond of inveighing against "individualism," it is necessary to point out that their "socialism" is, on one side, intensely and dangerously individualistic, in contrast with the much more organic social theory of the industrial revolution, which brought great wealth and power to the British nation, at the cost, no doubt, of considerable privations for the labouring population. Those who were then the governing class were fully conscious of this organic ideal, and rejoiced in the success with which, as they thought, it was being realised. Macaulay looked out upon his world, and behold it was very good; he certainly did not rejoice because he was making his own fortune in it. Bishop Gore ("Christ and Society," p. 147) says: "The idea that all men have a divine right to a fair opportunity to make the best of themselves for their own good first, as also further for the future good of the world, has got hold of the conscience of almost all men; and it would seem as if we must either set ourselves in serious earnest to correspond with its demands or fall under the divine judgment." This is surely not socialism, but individualism carried to its logical extremity. By "divine right," it appears, no real sacrifice is to be demanded from anybody, except, I suppose, from the rich. The fullest self-realisation may be claimed by all, and God will punish us if it is not conceded. We may have great sympathy with the generous aspirations of the Bishop for the welfare of the poor, and yet feel that his theory is liable to the condemnation of being "disintegrating and anarchic," even more than the declarations of Nietzsche. I have said in an earlier chapter that all who live in society must abandon the idea of complete and harmonious self-realisation, and assuredly such sacrifices are clearly indicated in the New Testament. We cannot do anything well without surrendering our right to do or to be half a dozen other things. The fierce determination not to be "exploited" is radically unchristian; it has already brought the prosperity of our country to an end, and is endangering the stability of our whole social structure. The ideal of "joy in widest communalty spread" is a fine one, and we are committed to it in this country; but if we do not take care it will degenerate into *panem et circenses* for the masses, who are now indignant at the suggestion that they should attribute anything to the ever-increasing public burdens. So the pendulum swings; it is impossible to say that one class is by nature more or less selfish than another. But the Church, with its finger on the popular pulse, usually begins to show sympathy with a group as soon as it becomes unjust and predatory.

The second type is that of legal observance. There will always be a large class of good men and women who are religiously ungifted, but who "live ever in their great Task-master's eye." It is not for the mystic to disparage such. Christ never disparaged them; if I am not mistaken, the Twelve Apostles were chosen from this class. But the Law, as St. Paul said, should be a schoolmaster to bring us to Christ. A thing is not right because it is commanded by God—if we think that, we shall do many things which are neither right nor commanded by God; a thing is commanded by God because it is right. Christ gives us the right to appeal from the

God of authority to the God of the Spirit. As Emerson says:—

> "Not mine to look where cherubim
> And seraphs may not see,
> But nothing can be good in Him
> Which evil is in me."

Christianity is not antinomian, but it is nearer to Augustine's *ama et fac quod vis* than to Pharisaic legalism.

The Ethics of renunciation have been discussed at some length in my book. Dr. Barbour thinks that so far as this type aims at "deliverance," the social element in religion either disappears or remains as a mere obligation, not essentially related to the release of the soul. We have seen, however, that there are other motives in asceticism, and other ways of benefiting mankind than by combating social abuses.

The Christian Ethics of love are, he says, a venture of faith, in which the claims of the other types just enumerated have a recognition, though they are subordinate. Christians look back to renew their inspiration from the one perfect Pattern, but forward to meet the tasks which life lays before them.

George Tyrrell, in a document which he did not mean to make public, asks the startling question whether Catholicism, like Judaism, may not have to die to live. The same question may be asked about other forms of Christianity. Like other great movements it had its aggressive, conquering period, which seems to have come to an end long ago. Its attractiveness for those outside its pale seems to have almost disappeared, and among the white races who have nominally adopted it, it has rather the appearance of a hot-house plant, which must be carefully tended and protected. These misgivings, however, are much more disquieting when we consider the prospects of the Churches than when we take Christianity either as a moral revelation or as individual piety. These could perhaps continue to live without the support of an institution; though Troeltsch is probably right in thinking that the Church-type of Christianity has a greater survival-value than the Sect-type, and that we cannot afford to dispense with the strength and stability which come from corporate action, nor with the loyalty which the idea of the Church is able to evoke. But for a long time to come, the organised Churches, at least in Protestant countries, are likely to show signs of weakness. So far as this means that Christian Ethics are now autonomous, we need not greatly regret the decline of institutionalism. But I agree with Troeltsch that Christianity cannot live on moral aphorisms, or on a "galvanisation" of Platonism or Stoicism in Christian dress but only on the "Christus-mystik" which was the heart of St. Paul's religion, and which led him to lay increasing emphasis on the brotherhood of believers as "the body of Christ."

The concluding paragraphs of Troeltsch's essay on the future of Christianity, in the second volume of his collected works, are so striking that a summary of them may be useful, especially as the essay cannot be read in English.

Christian Ethics are "overwhelmingly religious." The Christian finds his full personality only in God, and his social morality is based on the communion of all the children of God with their heavenly Father. Christian morality contradicts the instincts of modern secularity, and refuses to exalt or deify the mere natural man. "Such an ethos has a heroic hardness and a noble gentleness"; but it encounters great difficulties in face of life in the world. We are brought up against the problem of absolute values, the conquest of relativism. Belief in absolute values carries with it belief in a higher sphere of being, in a metaphysical sense. But the two worlds must not be kept quite apart. The sensible world must be spiritualised; so only can "a synthesis of the inner-worldly and the overworldly" be accomplished. The problems cannot be finally solved; they continually break out afresh; but in principle they are settled by Christianity. We need not think of any separate new organisations in Europe; the existing Churches are enough, and the Protestant bodies will only be carrying the work of the Reformation further by establishing a free Christianity. Troeltsch ends by reminding us of the Logos-theology in the early Church. "The Christianity of to-day," he says, "is, in spite of all differences, bound to that of antiquity, in that in both the belief that God is in Christ is mingled with the belief in the Logos in the world. This is not only juggling with words." I agree that the Logos-theology of the Fourth Gospel and of the Greek Fathers has a great and permanent value. For it is dynamic, not static; it gives ample room for progress and development; it is spiritual, and rests on an absolute background; and lastly it brings the Person of Christ into essential connexion with the world-process itself, and so with the inner meaning of history and natural science. When Dr. Jacks says that Christian Ethics must be "cosmical," he probably means the same thing.

It is most difficult for a modern writer to resist the temptation to throw his interpretation of the "ought to be" into a vision of the "will be." The belief in progress as a predestined vindication of our ideals is so ingrained in the modern mind that if a man expresses doubt in the approaching victory of his cause he is supposed to be doubtful whether after all his cause is right. In vain has Bosanquet protested that to throw our ideals into the future is the death of all sane idealism. Every politician talks about the flowing tide which will carry him and his friends into the haven where they would be. Every controversialist stigmatises his opponents as reactionaries. The deadly sin of being in a minority today can be expiated only by the certainty of being in a majority to-morrow. Now this way of thinking is absolutely deadly for a student of Christian Ethics. Christ never appealed to men in masses; He never suggested that the voice of the people (which was soon to say "crucify him") was or ever could be the voice of God. "Strait is the gate and narrow is the way that leadeth unto life, and few there be that find it." "The world hath not known thee," He says to His Father. It cannot be asserted too often or too strongly, that there is no promise and no expectation that true Christians will ever be more than a small minority. The only way for a Church to become powerful and popular is to make unholy alliances, and to cajole or terrify the irreligious. When this is once recognised, the discouragement of Churchmen at their numerical weakness in the modern world is seen to be faithless and unreasonable. "If they have called the master of the house Beelzebub, how much more them of his household? If they have persecuted me, they will also persecute you; if they have kept my saying, they will keep yours also." Such was the clear-eyed and nobly honest promise of Christ to His disciples. They knew what to expect when they gave their lives to His service. And we babble about "the democratic Christ and His democratic creed."

Professor Peabody, as an American, shows courage in· speaking of the disciples of Christ as a "spiritual aristocracy." They were not a social or an intellectual aristocracy, but a spiritual aristocracy. And the prospects of aristocracies, of whatever kind, are not alluring. Let no one suppose that liberty of speech, or of thought, is secure in Europe. The word "intellectual" is almost a term of contempt. Let the intellectuals beware, for they are very few. Our politics are so corrupt that many would welcome a dictatorship. The barbarians overthrew the first great civilisation of Europe. There are quite enough barbarians in modern Europe and its colonies to overthrow our own.

These facts must be recognised; but they should only stimulate us to fight the good fight.

> "He's a slave who would not be
> In the right with two or three."

The Church of the Spirit will not be powerless. It may have much more influence than its numbers would suggest. We remember the parable of the leaven which leavens the whole lump. There will be no spectacular triumph; the prince of this world is no master of ours; but the Church may be again what the Church was in the days of the persecutions, before the fatal alliance with the decaying empire—a city set on a hill, the salt of the earth.

Only let the Church of the Spirit look for allies where they may be found, among all those who love the Lord Jesus Christ in uncorruptness. "If any man have not the Spirit of Christ, he is none of his." "Wherever Jesus Christ is," says Ignatius, "there is the Catholic Church." Let those who feel solitary and friendless, suspected, it may be, by their brother churchmen, remember this, and they will find friends where they did not expect to see them. The Catholic Church of the Spirit (I wish I dared say the Church of the future, but that no one can tell), resting on ethical not on institutional unity, excommunicates none but those who exclude themselves. As Phillips Brooks said: "The Holy Catholic Church, the Communion of Saints, is wherever men are praying, loving, trusting, seeking and finding God. In that body runs the true chain of sainthood, linking the ages together and making the eternal unity of the Church." Any narrower definition of the Church would exclude the Quakers, and this is surely a *reductio ad absurdum* of the theory which calls itself Catholic, for there are no truer Christians than the Society of Friends.

I have written at considerable length on what is sometimes called the Social Question, knowing how much space it fills in the minds of our contemporaries. It is natural that political parties should desire the support of organised religion, and equally natural that the clergy should wish to speak and preach about topics in which their people are interested. But I have already made it clear that the original Gospel was not, except indirectly, a message of social reform, and that the Church has its own message to deliver, a message which it cannot deliver if it mingles in political agitation. I shall not satisfy the ardent spirits who wish to preach the doctrines of Rousseau in the name of Christ. The plain truth is that power is always abused, and that the masses, who now have the power, and are morally neither better nor worse than the upper and middle classes whom they have supplanted, intend to pillage the minority for their own benefit. Christians may think that the rich, who have used their privileges none too well, may be spiritually benefited by losing them; but it would be difficult to argue that the forcible expropriation of the minority is a cause which ought to enlist the enthusiasm of the Christian moralist. We may be sure that in the future as in the past, sincere Christians will be found in all political parties, and that they will be everywhere in a minority.

I think however that the revolutionary party must be excepted, since its aims and beliefs are radically anti-Christian. Where the whole population is educated, and transitions from one class to another are easy, the old social distinctions become blurred, and economic distinctions come to appear either unreasonable or much too steeply graduated. This is a view which may be held by those who have no sympathy with revolution. But society is permanently threatened by the underworld of the slums, the refuse of the social machine, who have no organic part in civilised society, which would be much better without them, but who form the material form revolutionary movements. They always find leaders among educated persons who for some reason, whether moral or physical defect, or mere ill-luck, have failed to make good, and who in consequence are filled with a consuming hatred of the established order. Normally these subversive elements are easily held in check, but when the government of a country has been shaken by some crisis, they emerge from their hiding-places and sometimes set up a reign of terror, which is only brought to an end by a military despotism. This revolutionary movement aims at destroying at once religion, private property, and the family, discerning quite truely that these institutions stand or fall together. Christianity can make no terms with these *enragés,* who boast that they mean to uproot every variety of theistic belief, since, as Marx declared, "the idea of God must be destroyed; it is the keystone of a perverted civilisation." It is hardly worth while to prove in detail how the revolutionary creed flatly contradicts Christianity at every point.

In this country, however, and in Germany also, groups calling themselves Christian Socialists are fairly strong. There is nothing contrary to the Gospel or to Christian principles in collectivist experiments which do not involve confiscation. It is even possible that in the future some form of State Socialism may establish itself as a stronger and more intelligent type of government than democracy. These are the questions with which

Christianity as a religion has nothing to do. It can exist under almost any form of government. Under whatever rule, it must continue to insist that life develops from within, and that whenever there is a conflict between the wider and the narrower loyalty, the presumption is in favour of the wider, of loyalty to country rather than to class, and to the good of humanity rather than to that of one's own country.

The real function of the Church is to hold up steadily before both the conflicting forces the Christian standard of values. It is a task which is absolutely necessary in social conflicts, just as in international rivalries it must intervene with "Sirs, ye are brethren; why do ye wrong one to another?" The case is equally strong against foreign war and against civil war. Both are manifestly foolish and ruinous.

But have modern Christian Ethics any special warning for the rich? We must not water down the stern language of Christ to the rich of His day. Nor do I think that we shall wish to water it down. Luxurious living, absence of regular work, perhaps even the blessed absence of anxiety which in a society like ours is the reward of prudent saving and investment, are dangerous to the health of the soul. How often we see a kind of fatty degeneration of the conscience setting in when men and women have reached middle life! This is the *daemonium meridianum* from which (in the Vulgate translation) he who dwelleth under the defence of the Most High hopes to be delivered. Christ unmistakably recommends the simple life—not abject poverty—as the safest and most desirable, and the general moral feeling of our time, quite apart from politics, condemns the habits of the idle rich, even when it regards them with a slightly envious curiosity. A rather drastic simplification of life will certainly be forced upon the luxurious families, and it ought to be accepted, as I think it is being accepted, without great bitterness. They must reorganise their way of living on a simpler basis; it is by no means certain that they will be less happy than they were when conditions were more favourable to them.

Christians have the double duty of co-operating with the *Zeitgeist* wherever its tendencies seem to be favourable to true moral progress, and of resisting it wherever it seems to be incompatible with Christian principles. We must recognise that the special revelation which has been made to our age comes through natural science. The mere progress in knowledge of natural laws—especially about the conditions of health, and the young but obviously very important study of psychology, impose upon us now moral duties, or at least indicate new methods of discharging duties which have been long recognised. The science of heredity and eugenics is beginning to be important, and will become more so. The Church must eschew jealousy; it must not refuse to accept coins which are not stamped with its own superscription. It must gladly accept the diffusion of popular education, and help in what is really a new and most interesting experiment—that of imparting the best culture available to the whole population. In these and other ways Christians should make the best of the existing social ideals, and try to moralise them in the Spirit of Christ.

On the other hand, there are ideals now popular which Christians must resist without compromise. What these are I have tried to indicate. Practical materialism, secularity, and the negation of discipline, are, as we believe, really contrary to the laws of life as ordained by God and revealed in Christ. We are meant to live in fairly hard training, and to take life in a far more serious spirit than would be reasonable if we believed that we have no "citizenship in heaven." It would be well if

Christians quite openly professed and acted upon a higher standard than that of the world around them. This is unquestionably the Christian method of leavening society. The Christian Church suffers from what it is the fashion to call the inferiority complex. We are ashamed of being in a minority; we are distressed because our churches are half empty. Many of them would be much emptier if the Gospel was preached in them. Bishop Gore has said that we want, not more Christians, but better Christians, a saying which ought not to be misunderstood. It does not mean that the influence of Christian ideals is confined to those who call themselves Christians. It is certain that this is not so. Christianity has for very many centuries been one of the integral factors of Western civilisation. The Ethics of the Western world have long been, in the main, Christian Ethics. Parts of the Christian revelation have entered the life of Europe as a permanent enrichment of its culture. These are no longer dependent on the Church and clergy. But the structure of society, and the conduct expected of its members, falls in many respects far short of the Christian standard, and a society of convinced disciples of Christ is needed both to bear witness to the faith that is in them, and to support each other in resisting that confederacy of co-operative guilt with limited liability which the New Testament calls the world.

I feel that this must be said before I lay down my pen. I have undertaken to deal with modern ethical problems, and there are cases where the traditional Christian Ethics are being called in question, and possibly need revision. But by far the greater part of the old religious morality stands where it did. It is a well-defined attitude towards life, an attitude which it is not very difficult to understand in theory, though it is infinitely hard to carry it out in practice. I have not thought it necessary to discuss, with Martineau and others, the types of ethical theory; for the pressing problems do not lie in the field of theory. Our main difficulty is to get the fundamental principles of Christian Ethics accepted in a rather vulgar and materialistic society, and, in the words of Dr. Jacks, to recover the lost radiance of the Christian religion. Our subordinate but still very important task is to apply these fundamental principles to the situation created by new knowledge and new conditions. I have pleaded for courage and independence in facing these problems, because it is plain to me that the experience of the past is not sufficient to solve them. Civilisation, as I have said, is actually passing into a new phase. The Church, like a wise householder, must bring out of her treasure things new and old—not so much some things that are new and others that are old, as new things that are the legitimate interpretation of the original Gospel for a state of society of which the first Christians never dreamed, and old things upon which the illuminating Spirit has passed with quickening breath and revealing light. It will be long before European civilisation reaches a state of stable equilibrium. We may see strange experiments in practical Ethics, and the authority of Christ may be more widely rejected than it is to-day. But I have no fear that the candle lighted in Palestine nearly two thousand years ago will ever be put out. "Lord, to whom shall we go? Thou hast the words of eternal life."

INDEX

INDEX

Cassian, 135

Catholic Church, the growth of hierarchy of, 157 f.; and the Roman Empire, parallel between, 160; tradition borrowed from the Jews, 161; claims of, supported by forgeries, 164; Coronation of Charles the Great a landmark in the history of, 165; income of, 171; the Renaissance and, 172 ff.; monopoly claim of, 177; nothing Christian on its political side, 195; a formidable corporation, 197; and the Northern code of chivalry, 360; and divorce, 380

Catholicism stands for "the corruption of man's heart," 362

Cauvin, Jean, *see* Calvin

Celsus, 151, 154

Chamberlain, Sir Austen, 341

Channing, 22

Charles the Great, 165

Chase, Stuart, 263, 264, 354 *n.*

Chillingworth, William, 192

Christ, "Life" of, a best-seller, 40; misleading impressions on, 41; hyperbolical language of, 54

Christian Church, infiltration of Jewish ideas into, 146

Christian Ethics, 4; basis of, 25

Christianity, beginning of, 5–6; antagonism between, and Marxian socialism, 59; influence of, on growth or decline of population, 274 f.

Chrysostom, Dion, 95, 363

Chrysostom, St. John, 114, 179

Church history, no decline or decay in, 90

Church and State in East and West, relation between, 157

Church of Scotland, the, and the Great War, 322

Cicero, 214, 394

Clemen, Carl, 37

Clement of Alexandria, 7, 36, 116, 122, 318, 389

Colet, John, 321, 354

Collectivism, 221

Colvin, Ian, 254

Commercialised vice, 382 f.

Communism, 221, 228, 254

Comte, 289

Conciliar movement, the, 170

Conditions in the West of Europe after the barbarian invasions, 105 f.

Condorcer, Marquis de, 299

Constantine, 152

Consumption, problem of, 222

"Consumptionism," 264, 355–6

Cotter, Morison, 64

Coulton, Dr., 186, 199 *n.*

Council of Arles, A.D. 314, condemns conscientious objectors, 318

Council of Trent and massacres in the Old Testament, 319

Creighton, Bishop, 140

Cromwell, Oliver, 57, 180

Crusades, the, 319–20

Curzon, Lord, 359

Cynics, the ascetics of classical antiquity, 92

Cyprian of Carthage, 164, 177

Damascus, Pope, 164

Darlington, Dr., 288

Darwin, Charles, 203, 211, 267

Dawson, Christopher, 29 *n.*; on modern science, 201, 281 *n.*

Decalogue, the, 229 f.; overvaluing of, 239, 245

Decius, Emperor, 164

Deissman, 76

Delbrück, Prof. Hans, 314

Diaspora, Judaism of the, 34

Dietrich, 74

Dill, Sir Samuel, 105

Dirt, a repulsive form of asceticism, 119, 120

Divine right, doctrine of, 231

Divorce, St. Paul's advice on, 81; 385 ff.; the Catholic Church and, 385 ff.

Dobschutz, 94

Dominicans, and the Inquisition, 181 f.

Donne, John, 396

Dostoiesky, 188

Dreyfus, Capt., 189

Drink bill, our national, 264

Dublin Review, the, defends persecution, 186

Du Boise, 69

Dumas, Samuel, 336

Early Church, social teaching of the, 222 ff.

Eastern Church and fasting, the, 117

Eating and drinking, attitude of St. Paul on, 97

Ebionitism, Keim accuses St. Luke of, 60

Economic questions, attitude of Christianity in the past to, 222

Economics of the New Testament, 63 ff.

Eddington, Prof., 357

Edwards, Jonathan, 192

Elderton, Miss, 270, 271

Eliot, George, 344

Ellis, Havelock, sex antagonism, 300, 301, 305, 378

"Encratite" life, precepts of the, 100

INDEX

INDEX

Roman Catholics and Northern code of chivalry, 360; and divorce, 391
Roman Curia, Luther's description of, 167
Roman Empire and military domination, 308; killed by Rome, 343
Romanticism, 220
Roosevelt, Theodore, 306
Rousseau, Jean Jaques, 249 ff.; his "virtue" and "love," 250, 321
Royce, Prof. Josiah, 143
Ruskin, John, 67, 221, 312, 321
Russell, Bertrand, 26, 37, 205, 253
Russo-Japanese War, losses in, 337
Russo-Turkish War, losses in, 337

Sabbatarianism, 130
Sacramentalism, 156 f.
Saint Paul, Epistles of, 70 ff.; injunctions of, about sexual morality, 96
Saint-Pierre, Abbé de, and the Treaty of Utrecht (1658–1743), 338
Salimbene on "Procession of Flagellants," 120
Salisbury, John of, 231
Sand, George, 299
Santayana, 305, 330
Sarpi, Paul, 184
Saunders, Carr, 267 n.
Scandinavia, divorce in, 393
Schiller, 205
Schleiermacher on the Christian doctrine of morals, 20
Schopenhauer, 375
Schreiner, Olive, 301
Schweitzer, 14, 15, 74
Science, the age of, 201 ff.; agnostic about existence of a personal God, 217
Scott, Sir Walter, 130
Scott Holland, Canon, 254
Secular religion, decay of, 204
Seeck, 57, 274
Self-flagellation and asceticism, 120 ff.
Seneca, 123, 394
Sequence, uniformity of, 202
Servetus, 243
Sex, problem of, 362 ff.
Sexual taboos, 367
Sham fasts, 118
Shelley, P. B., 114
Sherman, General, 330
Sidgwick, Henry, 371 f.
Silence, a method of mortification, 113
Sin, 47 ff.
Sin, attitude of Christ towards, 47 ff.

Siricius, 125
Smuts, General, 340
Social teaching of the middle ages, 226 ff.; of the reformers, 233 ff.
Socialism and Christianity, antagonism between, Peabody on, 59
Socialists who claim Christ as one of themselves, 60; and think possession of capital inconsistent with Christianity, 64
Sorel, 311
Spain, recent persecution by Church, in, 187
Spanish Inquisition, the, 183; abolished by Napoleon and restored, 186
Spencer, Herbert, 62, 203, 211
Spiritual redemption, gospel of, 223
Staël, Mme. de, 396
Starr, Jordan, Prof., 329
State Church, beginnings of, 152
Stephen of Rome, 164
Stephen, Sir Fitzjames, 36
Stephen, Leslie, 193
Sterilisation of the unfit, 287
Stevenson, Robert Louis, 223
Streeter, Canon, 379–383
Suicide, 393 ff.; more common in Protestant than in Catholic countries, 396
Sutherland, 268
Swinburne, Algernon, 143
Symonds, John Addington, on the Renaissance, 234
Syphilis supposed to be imported from America, 365

Tarn, Mr., 273
Taylor, Jeremy, 192, 320
Temperance fanatics, 131
Tennyson's "Idylls" and romantic love, 227
Tertullian, 79, 151, 153, 155, 161, 163, 274, 388, 389
Theocratic imperialism, 140 ff.; socialism, 254
Theodosius, 152, 180
Theophilus, 389
Thirty Years' War, the, 311
Thomas à Kempis, 124
Thomism, 231
Thompson, William, 299
Thring, Edward, 139
Thucydides, 329, 334
Timour, 334
Tolstoy, 348
Torah, the, 30 ff.
Torquemada, atrocities of, 183
Tortures, a form of asceticism, 120; ordered by Papal Bulls, 182
Trade disparaged by early Christians, 224
Trade unionism, 151

426

INDEX

Tredgold, Dr., 286
Treitschke, 321
Trent, Council of, 162, 236 *n.*
Troeltsch, 62, and *n.,* 66, 125, 126, 407, 411, 412
Tyler, Wat, 234
Tyrell, George, 410

Ulpian, 225
Unemployment (1930) in United States and Germany, 280
Urwick, Mr., 68, 135, 380, 381

Valentinian III, 180
Vasari, 185
Vindictiveness of the Irish character, English free from, 316
Virgil, 394
Virginity, Methodius on, 100
Vogué, M. de, 250
Voltaire, 185, 321
Voronoff, 212

Wagner, Charles, 252
Wallace, Alfred Russell, 375
Wallace, Prof. W., 27, 137, 405
Wallas, Graham, 121
War, 304 ff.; condemned by the Early Fathers, 317; attitude of

the Church towards, 318; losses in, 332 ff.
Watkins, Mr. O. D., 124
Webb, Mr. and Mrs. Sidney, 260, 261
Weismann, 375
Wellington, Duke of, orgies of rape and plunder under, 335
Wells, H. G., 133, 344, 379
Westcott, Bishop, 63, 254
Westermarck, Dr., 118
Whichcote, Benjamin, 405
Whitehead, Prof., 22, 45, 207
Whittaker, Mr., 153, 154
Wilberforce, William, 129
Wilkins, W., 271
William the Silent, 185
Winslow, Dr. C. A. 277 *n.*
Witchcraft, trials for, terminated by rationalists, 189, 190
Wolf, Julius, 270
Wollstonecroft, Mary, 299
Women, St. Paul on the inferior status of, 81; the changed position of, 297 ff.
Wordsworth, William, 53, 54, 399

Zeno, 87
Zimmern, Mr., 272
Zöckler, Otto, 120
Zola, Emil, 188

427